THE TECHNOLOGY OF TEXT

PRINCIPLES FOR STRUCTURING, DESIGNING, AND DISPLAYING TEXT

THE TECHNOLOGY OF TEXT

PRINCIPLES FOR STRUCTURING, DESIGNING, AND DISPLAYING TEXT

DAVID H. JONASSEN
Editor
University of North Carolina at Greensboro

EDUCATIONAL TECHNOLOGY PUBLICATIONS
ENGLEWOOD CLIFFS, NEW JERSEY 07632

Library of Congress Cataloging in Publication Data
Main entry under title:

The Technology of text.

    Bibliography: p.
    Includes index.
    1. Information display systems. I. Jonassen,
David H., 1947-
TK7882.I6T4   621.3819'5832   81-22167
ISBN 0-87778-182-6   AACR2

Printed in the United States of America.

Library of Congress Catalog Card Number:
81-22167.

International Standard Book Number:
0-87778-182-6.

First Printing: June, 1982.

To Cristen,
whose education may hopefully benefit
from much of this work.

Acknowledgments

I would like to express sincere gratitude to all of the authors, all of whom are noted authorities in their specialties, for their contributions. The level of expertise represented in the papers would be impossible for one individual to duplicate, given the diversity of topics explored. Each of you are to be commended for your excellent papers. A special note of thanks is extended to Ann Jaffe Pace for her editorial review of parts of the book and for the lively discussion of its content. The feedback was essential. Special appreciation is extended to Polly Rich for typing and retyping my hieroglyphic notes and manuscripts. Thanks also to Theodore C. Hines, indexer/information scientist *extraordinaire*, for the use of BOOK-DEX and the flogging of his S-100 bus to produce the Index. As always, my wife Laurette deserves thanks for her tolerance and understanding, in addition to proofreading. Every writer should be married to an English teacher.

Preface

If you are asking yourself "How can there be a technology of text?" you are among those educators, philosophers, administrators, and others who still equate "technologies" with machines. To your potential dismay, I must proclaim from the very beginning that this is not a book about lithography, reprography, holography, printing presses, computers, or any other "machine" used to generate or reproduce text. Nor is this book about teaching or instruction *per se*. Rather it is about *the technology of sequencing, structuring, designing, and laying-out of the printed page, whether that text is reproduced on paper or in electronic signals on a cathode ray tube*. Text simply refers to written discourse (aggregates of words) in printed form. So, as the title avers, this book offers guidelines for displaying written discourse. That is sufficient. *The technology of text focuses on how written discourse can be most effectively presented*.

The theoretical foundation for the technology of text resides in the more contemporary paradigm (in the Kuhnian sense) of instructional technology (see Heinich, 1970, and Kuhn, 1962, for a detailed explanation). Such a conceptualization transcends the technology-machine equation. James Finn (1960) tried to rectify that misconception over two decades ago, during the paradigm shift from AV to instructional technology (a subtler shift now seems directed toward instructional/cognitive science). Technology, according to Finn, includes processes, systems, management, and control mechanisms (human and non-human). It is now generally accepted, at least by those practicing in the field, that the technology of instruction is a "process used to design a specific type of reliable and validated instructional product" (AECT, 1977). No mention is made of machines for delivering that product. Technology, in this modern sense, is synonymous with science (Ellul, 1964). So, *the technology of text is the application of a scientific approach to text design.* It exists as a counterpoint to the artistic and unsystematic approach to text design and layout that has prevailed since petroglyphs were first inscribed on walls. The technology of text design is a process based upon theories and research in learning and communication for designing textual instructional products—not novels, but instructional text, that is, discourse that informs and teaches. It is often referred to as "expository prose." This is an important distinction, for to attempt to apply these *techniques* (to use Ellul's term) in designing non-instructional text would be a mistake. While some of the principles can be effectively generalized to reference materials, their broad application to all discourse cannot be justified.

In this age of electronic information transmission, why should the design of print-oriented media be of concern to instructional technologists, educators, administrators, researchers, and others? Haven't the mediaphiles delivered enough impassioned eulogies to print media to obviate further consideration? Two major reasons argue against print's untimely demise. First, as suggested earlier, many or even most of the messages transmitted by electronic media are print-oriented. For instance, two of the primary instructional applications of computers are word processing and text presentation in the tutorial mode. Discourse will not disappear, as suggested by some visual *literati*. Text will prevail as a major form of recorded communication for the foreseeable future. The assumption of this book is that text can be more effectively designed, regardless of the medium through which it is transmitted.

Second, there is a current resurgence of interest in print materials, based upon the increasing importance of cost-effectiveness as a selection criterion for instructional materials. Perusal of current education and training journals will confirm this. Audiovisual materials (non-print) have failed to produce the panaceas predicted by their proponents and developers. Therefore, instructional technology is refocusing its concerns on the internal structure and design of instructional materials, rather than the medium of transmission. We are now examining how learners interact with and encode various structural properties of instructional materials into memory and how these properties facilitate retrieval, transfer, and so on. Recent advances in cognitive psychology, reading research, and information processing have suggested heuristics for the design of text. These are the content of this book (a hard copy, printed text). As elaborated in the introductions to Sections 1 and 2, this book focuses on two broad categories of techniques for structuring textual materials (see Table 1).

Table 1

Techniques for Structuring Text

	Implicit	Explicit
Method	Discourse Analysis Component Display Theory Elaboration Theory Pattern Notes Brain Functions	Labeling/Block/Space Numbering Algorithms Advance Organizers Tables (Tabular Material) Diagrams Information Mapping Illustrations Programmed Instruction Flowcharts
Characteristics	Implicit in Prose Enhance Organization Internal Components Structural Sequential Preparational	Discourse Punctuation Explicit Facilitate Access External to Discourse Adjunct Presentational Display Techniques

Implicit techniques for text design are concerned with the structure of the content and sequencing of the message. Research in learning and memory has clearly explicated the role of organization in the storage and retrieval of information. Knowing how much information to present and how to sequence it in text is the focus of the first section of the book. In Section 2, several authors explore the role, function, and technique (technology) of several explicit means of organizing and displaying text. In Section 1, the organization of text is implicit in the discourse, but in Section 2, the organization is overtly part of the textual design. Explicit techniques display the structure of discourse, that is, they *punctuate* the discourse. The results include an increased number of retrieval cues representing the overall structure of discourse as well as enhanced access to information embedded in the text. Serving as advance organizers for Sections 1 and 2, the introductions explore these issues further. While the techniques explored in the first two sections are not media-specific, some media, especially the electronic textual media, do present some specific design problems. These are sampled in Section 3. Finally, a consideration of how individuals differentially interact with text is considered in Section 4.

The methods for structuring, designing, and displaying text that are presented in this book are technologies. They represent the scientific applications of theories and principles of neuropsychology, perception, learning, memory, reading, and typography. They offer processes for systematically designing text. Completion of the book should convince you that there really is *a technology of text*.

D.J.
December, 1981

References

Association for Educational Communications and Technology. *Educational technology: Definition and glossary of terms*, Vol. 1. Washington, D.C.: AECT, 1977.

Ellul, J. *The Technological Society.* New York: Alfred Knopf, 1964.

Finn, J.D. Automation and education: III. Technology and the instructional process. *A V Communication Review*, 1960, *8*, 5-26.

Heinich, R. *Technology and the management of instruction*, Monograph No. 4. Washington, D.C.: Association for Educational Communications and Technology, 1970.

Kuhn, T.S. *The structure of scientific revolutions.* Chicago: University of Chicago Press, 1962.

About the Authors

Philip J. Brody is Assistant Professor of Curriculum and Instruction and Director of the Instructional Technology Center in the School of Education, University of Kansas. With an M.S. from SUNY-Albany and a Ph.D. from the University of Washington in Educational Communications, he has also served as an Instructional Design Specialist at the University of Southern Colorado. His primary research focuses on determining how pictures and their attributes function in various settings and the development of practitioner-oriented research techniques.

Esther U. Coke is a member of the Technical Staff in the Learning and Instruction Research Department of Bell Laboratories at Murray Hill, New Jersey. She received her Ph.D. in experimental psychology from New York University in 1968. Her main areas of professional interest are in scientific studies of stylistic factors that influence the effectiveness of technical writing, and in computer techniques for analyzing text.

Philippe C. Duchastel is an instructional researcher who is particularly interested in how students learn from text and in how principles derived from learning research can be applied to textbook design. He has conducted research on instructional objectives, illustrations in text, adjunct questions, and the use of quizzes in text learning situations. He has worked in instructional development and evaluation in Canada, Great Britain, and the United States. Dr. Duchastel is an Associate Professor of Psychology at The American College, Bryn Mawr, Pennsylvania.

Alan Fields is a lecturer at the Cranfield School of Management,

Bedford, England, with research interests in information mapping, critical path networks, patterning, and other aspects of educational technology.

James D. Hand is an Instructional Development Specialist in the Office of Educational Development, University of Arkansas for Medical Sciences. With a Ph.D. in Instructional Development from Michigan State University, he has worked at the Charles Drew Post-Graduate Medical School in Los Angeles and at the University of Southern Mississippi. In 1980, he was awarded the Outstanding Instructional Development Award by NSPI for the Neonatal Educational Project cited in his chapter.

James Hartley is currently Senior Lecturer in the Department of Psychology at the University of Keele, Staffordshire, England, where he has been since 1964. He received his undergraduate degree in Psychology and his doctorate in programmed learning from the University of Sheffield. Dr. Hartley has published widely in the fields of programmed learning, educational technology, university teaching methods, and designing instructional text. His major publications include *Strategies for Programmed Instruction* (1972), *Contributions to an Educational Technology* (with Ivor Davies, 1978), *Designing Instructional Text* (1978), and *The Psychology of Written Communication* (1980).

William Holliday is Professor of Science Education and Director of the Centre for Research in the Faculty of Education at the University of Calgary. He is also Executive Secretary of the National Association for Research in Science Teaching. He has a Ph.D. in Science Education from the University of Texas at Austin and a B.S. and M.S. in Biological Sciences from Purdue University. In addition to his professorship, Holliday has also taught junior high school science. His main research interests are the effectiveness of diagrams and adjunct questions in teaching science.

Robert E. Horn is president of Information Resources, Inc., of Lexington, Massachusetts, a consulting firm dedicated to improving communication and training. He is the originator of Structured Writing, for which he received the Outstanding Research Award by NSPI. He has taught on the graduate level at Harvard and Columbia Universities.

Paul A. Kirschner is an educational psychologist with Wolters-Noorhof Educational Publishers, where he is responsible for assuring the pedagogical and psychological qualities of their textbooks as well as editing a series of manuals for text editors. With a B.S. in psychology from SUNY-Stony Brook and a Ph.D. in educational psychology and educational sciences from the City University of Amsterdam, he has researched text characteristics and learning processes. He has also worked in the Department of General and Comparative Education at CU-Amsterdam.

Paul F. Merrill is Professor of Instructional Science at Brigham Young University, Provo, Utah. He teaches graduate and undergraduate classes in Instructional Design and Computer Applications in Education. He received his Ph.D. in educational psychology from the University of Texas at Austin. He previously served as Director of Course Development at the University of Mid-America and as Associate Professor at Florida State University. He has published extensively in the areas of instructional design and computer applications.

Ann Jaffe Pace received her doctorate in Learning and Cognition from the University of Delaware. She has taught at the University of North Carolina at Greensboro and at the University of Delaware, in both educational psychology and reading. Her major research focus has been on the development of reading comprehension abilities in school-aged children. She is currently involved in studying children's strategies for comprehending texts.

Charles M. Reigeluth is Associate Professor in the Instructional Design, Development, and Evaluation program at Syracuse University. His major interest is in improving public education, and his current work focuses on developing better instructional methods.

He holds a B.A. in Economics from Harvard and a Ph.D. in Instructional Psychology from Brigham Young University.

Linda Reynolds holds a B.S. in psychology and zoology and a M.S. in information science. After working as an information scientist in a research association and in publishing, she joined the Graphic Information Research Unit at the Royal College of Art in London. In recent years, she has worked on a wide range of projects, including studies of printed information, microforms, teletext, and directional signing systems.

I. Fulya Sari is a doctoral student in the Instructional Design, Development, and Evaluation program at Syracuse University. She holds a teacher training certificate, and a B.A. and M.A. in linguistics from Bogazici University, Istanbul, Turkey. Her major research interest is in motivation and learning strategies within instructional design.

Richard Showstack is a graduate of the University of California at Berkeley. He holds a master's degree in the teaching of English as a foreign language from San Francisco State University, where he also studied educational technology. He is interested in using technology to make learning more efficient. At present, he is an instructor at the International Christian University in Tokyo.

Robert Waller is currently Lecturer in Textual Communication Research with the Institute of Educational Technology at the Open University, Milton Keynes, England. A typographer by training, he works in a multi-disciplinary research group investigating text design and comprehension. He is also editor of the *Information Design Journal*.

William Winn is Associate Professor and Academic Coordinator of the Learning Technology Unit in the Faculty of Education, University of Calgary. He received his Ph.D. in Instructional Systems Technology from Indiana University. Before moving to Calgary, he taught at the University of Sherbrooke in Quebec. In addition to his research in diagrams, Winn has published widely in the general area of visual information processing and is currently studying relationships between visual presentations and learners' simultaneous and successive processing abilities.

Patricia Wright, Ph.D., is a cognitive psychologist with the Medical Research Council and lectures in experimental psychology at Churchill College, Cambridge, England. Her research concerns many aspects of written communication, such as the completion of forms, as well as the cognitive problems faced by those writing or designing documents of various kinds. In 1979, she was awarded the Sir Frederic Bartlett medal from the Ergonomics Society.

Table of Contents

THE TECHNOLOGY OF TEXT

PRINCIPLES FOR STRUCTURING, DESIGNING, AND DISPLAYING TEXT

Section One:

Implicit Structures in Text

1.

Introduction to Section One:
Implicit Structures in Text

David H. Jonassen

Two assumptions dominate the thoughts and writing in this section and in theories of discourse in general:

1. Knowledge is organized in memory as networks of interrelated representations of objects, events, and concepts that form the structural foundation of meaning. Without these knowledge structures, life would consist of a meaningless array of perceptions. Past events would not likely be accessible for explaining new events or for comprehending discourse.

2. The structure of text, like the structure of memory, plays a primary role in the comprehension of all meaningful, informative prose (Winter, 1977). Such structure is implicit in meaningful prose.

A review of these two precepts comprises the first two parts of this Introduction.

1. The most prominent model used to describe knowledge in memory is *schema theory* (Rummelhart & Ortony, 1977). The basic unit for representing knowledge, according to this theory, is the schema. Individual objects, events, actions, settings, or abstract ideas (e.g., hope, truth) are represented in memory as schemata (plural of schema). We develop schemata for different aspects of our experiences. These schemata are mental constructs which represent our knowledge of those experiences. For instance, the word automobile evokes a schema for an object, consisting of

several sub-schemata (schemata have variables that can be embedded within other schemata hierarchically), such as engine, body, wheels, etc. Each of these schemata possesses sub-schemata related to its existence—size, appearance, location. The car schema also possesses sub-schemata related to function—transportation, self-image, or action (driving). These other schemata may not represent super- or subordinate relationships to the activated schema. Rather, they may be heterarchically (different structures) related to it. Just as a car is an interdependent, interrelated collection of components, your schema for a car represents it as an interrelated, interdependent collection of embedded variables. Your schema for car is also related to numerous other schemata, such as highways, traffic signals, insurance, taxes, etc. Schemata, according to Rummelhart and Ortony, are stereotypes of concepts. These stereotypic mental representations are interrelated with other concepts in a network of interacting knowledge structures, which constitute our memory for the accumulated knowledge we have acquired.

One of the characteristics of schemata is that they are composed of variables or slots. For example, a diagrammatic representation for the SPEAK schema is presented in Figure 1.1 in the form of an active structural network (Norman, Rummelhart, & LNR, 1975), the normal method for diagramming schemata. The SPEAK schema has four variables (A, B, C, and D)—a speaker, a recipient, a message, and the words or sounds composing the message. Each variable or slot can be filled by any number of objects or other schemata. Any given speaking event represents an instance of this schemata, that is, it possesses these variables in that relationship to each other.

Another characteristic, as mentioned before, is that schemata are embedded hierarchically. Schemata may be related to each other in a hierarchical or a heterarchical network. The relationships between concepts are accounted for by filling slots in one schema with schemata from other parts of a person's semantic network (Pearson & Spiro, 1980). Relationships between schemata vary. Relationships within schemata are more consistent. Sub-schemata allow us to represent the variables of all schemata in

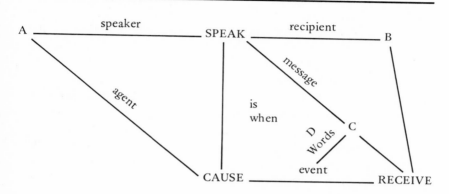

Figure 1.1. Diagrammatic representation of SPEAK.

a few ways, such as action, cause, and function. So schema formation is efficient. Schemata also vary in their level of abstraction. Just as we possess schemata for concrete objects or events, we also possess schemata for abstract concepts, such as irony, freedom, or for situations (otherwise referred to as scripts), all of which are necessary for understanding connected discourse. Finally, schemata represent knowledge of concepts—not definitions. That is, they are non-linguistic forms of abstract representation. We use language to describe schemata, but they are not the same.

The primary function of schemata is that they allow us to comprehend or make predictions about new information on the basis of our existing schemata. Hearing or seeing a word or word combination activates one's schema for that word or combination. We explain situations in terms of existing schemata. When information gaps exist in any message, we use schemata to infer the missing information. When no schema for an object exists, we can predict or infer some aspects of it using our existing schemata. So, we use schemata for remembering (representing knowledge) and for understanding (interpreting incoming information, based upon existing knowledge) in an interactive process. Schemata are essential for the comprehension of discourse. Words or word combinations trigger a continuous flow of schemata. The meaningfulness of discourse, it should be obvious, is a function of the availability of schemata in the reader. Also, the consistency between the knowledge or schematic structure of the author (speaker) and the reader (listener) is an important predictor of the meaningfulness of discourse. The greater the dissonance between these structures, the less meaningful any message is likely to be.

Summary. The network of concepts or schemata that combine to form our knowledge structure is one theory for representing the organization of memory. Without some sort of structure, knowledge relevant to new situations would be difficult to retrieve. New information could not be related meaningfully to past experience. Without an appropriate knowledge framework, an individual event could not be interpreted readily. Just as events do not exist in isolation, their representations in memory are not unrelated to other representations. The individual's network of interrelated schemata affects how text will be interpreted by him or her.

2. Just as knowledge structures are implicitly organized, discourse too depends upon organization to make it meaningful. While substantive and informational content is the basic ingredient of discourse, written or oral, the organizational structure is equally important. Both structure and content play an important role in memory for connected discourse (Thorndyke, 1977).

The most prominent methods for analyzing discourse (Crothers, 1972; Fredericksen, 1975; Kintsch, 1974; Meyer, 1975) represent the structure of text in schematic ways. These theories will be treated more thoroughly by Pace in her chapter on discourse analysis, but a few general remarks related to the two assumptions presented at the beginning of this introduction are in order. Knowledge is represented in memory as schemata; it is represented in text as propositions. The information conveyed in text evokes schemata which are needed for comprehension. For instance, the statement "John said 'good morning' to Sally" would evoke a schema like that in Figure 1.1. The individual variables would be instantiated (instances provided) by the author: A, John; B, Sally; C, greetings; and D, good morning. Our understanding of the statement is facilitated by the availability in our knowledge structure of a SPEAK schema. Rules exist that govern the arrangement of information in sentences. These individual meaning units are referred to as the micro-structure. Our sentence represents a situational unit made more meaningful by the order of words in the sentence. Sentences such as this are combined in a coherent manner to form meaningful connected discourse. The overall informational structure of text is represented by its macro-structure (Kintsch & van Dijk, 1978). This macro-structure represents the "gist" of text. For complete comprehension of text, comprehension of the gist as well as of the individual ideas (micro-structure) is required. Kintsch and van Dijk have suggested that micro-propositions (the individual ideas) are controlled by individual schemata and are used to construct macro-propositions, which designate the meaning of macro-structures.

Summary. Text bases, like schemata, contain idea units (propositions) that are hierarchical and can be embedded. However, the exact relationship between the two is not clear. Just as schemata represent individual knowledge structures, propositions combine to form the content structure of prose. This content structure is the focus of the chapters in this section of the book.

3. Which is more important to comprehension—the text-base structure or the reader's knowledge structure? Discourse theory usually predicts that the organization or content structure gets encoded into memory along with the specific content. This encoding hypothesis is based on the work of Melton (1967), who found that items of information are encoded along with information about the context in which the item was presented. Meyer (1975) found that the text-base structure was encoded along with the content, and that structure controlled the way in which the information was recalled. Shavelson (1972) concluded that a reader's knowledge structures were altered by the content structure of a passage. The role of organization of text is obviously very strong, if the reader's conceptual organization of knowledge can be altered or supplanted by the author's.

On the other hand, recent research by Anderson and others (1977, 1978) argues that comprehension is controlled by existing schemata in the reader. They found that groups with significantly different world knowledge interpreted the same text very differently, regardless of the structure of the passage. High-level schemata cause people to "see" messages in certain ways. In the second study, they concluded that the existence of schemata, or slots for fitting textual information, was the most significant contributor to comprehension. The importance of world knowledge, expectations, and goals for reading has been explored by others. Waller (later in this book) suggests that the purpose for encountering text is probably the most critical determinant.

Summary. The most effective transfer of knowledge would doubtless result when an author and a reader possess isomorphic, or identical, knowledge structures. Such an occurrence is practically and conceptually impossible (nothing could be *learned* from the other person). So, is comprehension of text data-driven (text structure controls the activation of schema in reader) or conceptually-driven (input from text controlled by motives, goals, or schemata of reader) (Bobrow & Norman, 1975)? The answer is not clear. It depends upon many factors, not the least of which is the cohesiveness of the text base vs. an individual's knowledge structure. The stronger the organization of text, the more likely it will be assimilated by the reader. The implications of organization for text writing will be explored throughout this book. *The importance of organization to text cannot be denied.*

4. The first section of the book explores the implicit or internal organization of text. The organization of text is manifested in the content structure of discourse. This structure is implicit to meaningful expository prose. The content structure, or macrostructure, controls to some degree the comprehension of the content contained in a passage. Studying the internal structure of the text base defines the domain of discourse analysis, which Ann Jaffe Pace reviews in her chapter, "Analyzing and Describing the Structure of Text." Analysis of the structure of propositions in text focuses on the nature of the relationships between them. An important technique that Pace reviews is the idea of *signaling*, where the author uses phrases embedded in text to point out the content structure of text. The second section of this book

describes explicit, or external, means for accomplishing the same result.

While considering such explicit topics as algorithms, the focus of Alan Fields' chapter is on the internal organization of material presented in discourse (he deals with text and talks, both forms of discourse). Pattern notes are excellent methods for "Getting Started," that is, organizing the ideas to be included in any discourse. A glance at a pattern note is enough to indicate that it graphically structures or maps the content of any passage. The degree to which these maps reflect an author's or a reader's cognitive structure is an issue currently being investigated. If employed properly, there is a direct relationship between a person's pattern notes and the content structure of any passage he or she writes. For that reason, pattern notes are also valuable for summarizing (taking notes) a speech or text, as noted by Fields. This technique is included in this section of the book because notes are not usually meant to be displayed in text. They only help the writer or reader determine the implicit organization of discourse. If getting the first paragraph on paper or the CRT is a source of frustration for you, this may be the most valuable chapter in the book.

The overall structure of a text can be controlled systematically by employing the *elaboration theory of instruction*. Based on the progressive differentiation of instructional units, elaboration theory organizes instruction in a top-down, general-to-specific sequence. It is theoretically grounded in schema theory (Merrill, Wilson, & Kelety, 1979). Elaboration theory determines the macro-structure of instruction; the micro-structure involves component display theory. Component display theory is a heuristic for determining the consistency and adequacy of instructional procedures. In this book, I. Fulya Sari and Charles M. Reigeluth apply both theories to the design and evaluation of instructional text. "Writing and Evaluating Textbooks: Contributions from Instructional Theory" elaborates a series of specific procedures for structuring text, based upon these increasingly popular systems of instructional design.

5. Reading comprehension is normally explained in terms of

hypothetical knowledge structures, as we have seen. Ultimately, text comprehension as all intellectual functions depends upon neurological processes. Generalizing our knowledge of these processes to the design of text might seem a speculative venture, until you read James Hand's paper, "Brain Functions During Learning: Implications for Text Design." Different forms of learning are traceable to a variety of brain functions. I think that you will find the implications and solutions proposed by Hand to be fascinating. They represent an area of research receiving increased attention.

While it *appears* that much is known about text comprehension, most researchers admit that, really, we know very little. The fact that theories of comprehension are predicated on hypothetical constructs suggests how little we know. As research and development in all of the areas represented in this book continues, more of the questions will have firm answers. These answers will no doubt engender more questions.

References

Anderson, R.C., Reynolds, R.E., Schallert, D.C., & Goetz, E.T. Frameworks for comprehending discourse. *American Educational Research Journal*, 1977, *14*, 367-381.

Anderson, R.C., Spiro, R., & Anderson, M.C. Schemata as scaffolding for the representation of information in connected discourse. *American Educational Research Journal*, 1978, *15*, 433-440.

Bobrow, D.G., & Norman, D.A. Some principles of memory schemata. In D.G. Bobrow & A.M. Collins (Eds.), *Representation and understanding: Studies in cognitive science.* New York: Academic Press, 1975.

Crothers, E. Memory structure and the recall of discourse. In J. Carroll & R. Freedle (Eds.), *Language comprehension and the acquisition of knowledge.* Washington, D.C.: V.H. Winston, 1972.

Fredericksen, C. Representing logical and semantic structure of knowledge acquired from discourse. *Cognitive Psychology*, 1975, 7, 371-458.

Kintsch, W. *The representation of meaning in memory.* Hillsdale, NJ: Lawrence Erlbaum Associates, 1974.

Kintsch, W., & van Dijk, T.A. Toward a model of text comprehension and production. *Psychological Review*, 1978, *85*, 363-394.

Melton, A.W. Repetition and retrieval from memory. *Science*, 1967, *158*, p. 532.

Merrill, M.D., Wilson, B., & Kelety, J.G. Elaboration theory and cognitive psychology. Working Paper No. 127. San Diego, CA: Courseware, Inc., 1979.

Meyer, B.J.F. *Organization of prose and the effects on memory*. Amsterdam: North Holland, 1975.

Norman, D.A., Rummelhart, D.E., & the LNR Research Group. *Explorations in Cognition*. San Francisco: W.H. Freeman, 1975.

Pearson, P.D., & Spiro, R.G. Toward a theory of reading comprehension instruction. In *Topics in language disorders*. Aspen, CO: Aspen Systems Corp., 1980.

Rummelhart, D.E., & Ortony, A. The representation of knowledge in memory. In R.C. Anderson, R.J. Spiro, & W.E. Montague (Eds.), *Schooling and the acquisition of knowledge*. Hillsdale, NJ: Lawrence Erlbaum Associates, 1977.

Shavelson, R. Some aspects of the correspondence between content structure and cognitive structure in physics instruction. *Journal of Educational Psychology*, 1972, *63*, 225-234.

Thorndyke, P.W. Cognitive structures in comprehension and memory of narrative discourse. *Cognitive Psychology*, 1977, *9*, 77-110.

Winter, E.O. A clause relational approach to English texts: A study of some predictive lexical items in written discourse. *Instructional Science*, 1977, *6*, 1-92.

2.

Analyzing and Describing the Structure of Text

Ann Jaffe Pace

Two areas of theoretical and empirical investigation related to the understanding and production of text have been receiving increasing attention during the past several years. One of these concerns the important role of a person's existing conceptual knowledge in text processing. This focus is most widely represented by what has come to be called "schema theory" and is discussed by Jonassen in the introduction to this section and in his chapter on individual differences. The other trend, developing from a number of different directions, is the attempt to analyze and describe the nature and structure of written discourse or text itself—that is, of coherent units of prose beyond the level of the individual sentence. That the term "text" already has some shared meaning is evident in the title and focus of this very volume. However, a major thrust of this latter line of inquiry is to make more explicit general features of texts and specific characteristics of different kinds of texts.

This interest in text structure and description has been motivated variously by theoretical, empirical, or pragmatic concerns, with the motivation generally reflecting the differing academic orientations of the several disciplines engaged in studying discourse. Thus, linguists have been concerned primarily with theoretical analysis and description of text, psychologists with studying the effects of different kinds and aspects of text structure on the recall and comprehension of prose, and educators with the possible implications of such investigations for practice.

Despite the sizeable body of literature which already exists in this area, a number of important questions remain, and few clear and unequivocal recommendations for educational practice or text design can yet be made. To present a picture of the current status of text analysis and its potential utility for the production of instructional materials, this chapter will review the major systems of discourse analysis now in use, summarize research findings that have been obtained, and make some tentative suggestions concerning the implications of these efforts for the design of instructional texts.

Before beginning this overview and in keeping with a central emphasis of this volume, some discussion of the relationship between prior knowledge and text structure may be appropriate. Quite obviously, a reader brings many kinds of knowledge to any act of reading or studying text. These include vocabulary knowledge and the ability to decode written representations of the lexical items used, knowledge of syntax, and some kind of implicit knowledge of text structure itself, probably acquired through repeated encounters with different forms of prose. Readers' expectations concerning relationships among ideas in a text enable them to identify and utilize the structure which an author has employed (Meyer, 1980). Additionally and importantly, of course, is the reader's (or listener's) background of conceptual knowledge about the topic or topics addressed in a passage. Not only does a person's knowledge provide a framework within which new information can be integrated, but also it permits predictions about the relative importance of ideas expressed in a text. Familiarity with the topic apparently enhances a reader's sensitivity to text structure (see the discussion of Neilsen, 1978, below). Clearly, then, the issues of prior knowledge and text analysis, while separable, are significantly interrelated, though the nature of this relationship has not yet been fully explored.

Systems for Text Analysis

Recent work in discourse analysis basically has proceeded in two distinct, but related, directions. One primarily involves the structural analysis of the content or informational base of a passage; the other focuses on the phenomenon of discourse itself, on describing what gives a text its textlike quality and makes it a recognizable whole rather than a collection of unrelated sentences. Several characteristics of prose are implicitly acknowledged in our culture and especially in educational practice. For example, pedagogic emphasis on the "main idea" is inherent recognition that well-organized texts typically have a central focus or theme which gets expanded through supportive detail, information, or argument. A related idea is that different parts of a text or passage vary in their degree of importance to this central theme. This notion has received empirical support with a method devised by Johnson (1970), which has been utilized by several investigators (e.g., Brown & Smiley, 1977, 1978) in studies of prose processing. This is a rather simple procedure in which a passage is first divided into pausal or idea units; these are then ranked empirically according to their perceived importance to the passage. An equivalent number of idea units are placed at each of four levels of importance. While this method is easy to use and thus has considerable merit as a tool for empirical investigations, it remains *ad hoc* and atheoretical. It offers no explanation for why one level is rated as more important than another, and it has no provision for analyzing the structure of ideas either within or between levels. For closer analysis, more complex and theoretically sophisticated procedures are needed, such as any of the methods of propositional analysis discussed below.

Propositional Analysis

Programs for analyzing the informational content of prose passages typically have employed some kind of propositional analysis. Methods utilizing such an approach have been proposed by Frederiksen (1975, 1977b), Kintsch (1974), and Meyer (1975, 1977). Although there are some differences among these systems, propositional analyses in general use principles derived from propositional logic to represent schematically and abstractly the ideas contained in a passage, as well as relationships which may hold among these ideas. Most simply, a proposition is composed of a predicate, or relation, and zero or more arguments of that predicate. For example, in the proposition which represents the sentence, "Bill hit the ball," "hit" would be the predicate and "Bill" and "ball" the arguments of that predicate. Most systems of propositional analysis have utilized semantic roles or case relations (as in Fillmore, 1968) to define the relationship between a predicate and each of its arguments. Thus, in the example above, "Bill" fills the role of agent (of the action "hit") and "ball," the role of object.

Analyzing the individual propositions in a text in this way can reveal the relationships between elements in a single proposition, as well as connections among ideas across propositions, since one proposition may serve as an argument of another one and arguments can be repeated across several propositions. Repetition of arguments in a text provides one indication of the importance to the overall theme of that passage of the ideas or concepts which those arguments represent. For example, if the sentence used above were in an article about the relative merits of different kinds of baseballs, we would expect that the argument "ball" (or its equivalent "baseball") would be repeated several times, or more frequently, in all likelihood, than if that sentence appeared in a narrative about the things Bill did while on vacation.

The principal use of propositional analyses in the research literature on memory for prose and text comprehension has been to compare the semantic content of the written recalls produced by subjects in experimental situations with that of the original passages they heard or read. The number and kind of ideas or propositions recalled can thereby be assessed independently of the exact words used to express them in the text.

A great many similarities exist among the various methods used for propositional analysis; however, there are also some important differences among them. Kintsch's procedure (1974; Turner & Greene, 1977) produces propositions both for those ideas which are stated explicitly in a text and for those which are implied by it. He also utilizes a special class of "connective propositions" to relate ideas across separate sentences by coordinating the other propositions in a text and providing textual coherence. Connectives illustrate several kinds of relations, such as conjunction, often with the use of "and," and purpose, expressed by such terms as "in order to," "so that," etc. (Turner & Greene, 1977). Thus, while this system focuses on the substantive ideas or content of a passage, it also has a way to indicate how these ideas hold together through connectives, either expressed or implied.

Frederiksen's system (1975, 1977b) also attempts to account for both the content of a text and the relationships which exist across propositions. Toward this end, he utilizes a semantic network to express the content and a logical network to connect the propositions produced by the former. Frederiksen's logical network functions very much like Kintsch's connective propositions in explicating the logical relations which give structure to the text as a whole. Unlike Kintsch, however, Frederiksen does not include inferred meanings in his propositional analysis. Instead, he has devised a taxonomy of inferences (Frederiksen, 1977a) to indicate the kinds of inferences which may be required for full comprehension of a given text.

Meyer (1975, 1977) has used a comparable system to analyze the content of a passage. However, her procedure includes a means for representing the overall structure of a text which goes beyond indicating the relationship between propositions. Following Grimes' (1975) semantic grammar of propositions, Meyer (1975, 1977) distinguishes between lexical and rhetorical predicates. Lexical predicates are similar to those described above and are used for relating the arguments of within-sentence propositions. Rhetorical predicates, on the other hand, describe the organization or structure of a prose passage. In effect, they are labels for classifying whole segments of text and the relationships among them (e.g., "response," "explanation," "collection," etc.). They indicate how some ideas are subordinate to or subsumed by superordinate concepts. This organization can be reflected on different levels. Thus, rhetorical predicates or relations, ". . . often relate together the information in a number of sentences or even paragraphs and chapters" (Meyer, 1975). Meyer's system, then, is clearly hierarchical, and thereby has utility for characterizing the structure of a whole text. Tierney & Mosenthal (1980) suggest, however, and with reason, that it is primarily useful for expository prose, the genre most likely to have such a hierarchical structure. Recently, Meyer (in press) has simplified her system of rhetorical predicates and identified five basic relationships for classifying the top-level structure of a text—collection, causal, response, comparison, and description. The schematic text organization outlined through identification of these relationships corresponds to what has been termed the "gist" or macro-structure (van Dijk, 1977) of a text.

Studies which have utilized propositional analyses have produced some consistent findings. In general, results have shown that the subjects' recalls tend to reflect the overall structure of a passage, in that ideas which might be judged more important are better remembered. Kintsch (1974) has demonstrated, for example, that when arguments are repeated across several propositions—a probable indication of their thematic importance—passage recall increases. Meyer's work (1975) showed that paragraphs which were high in the content structure of a passage, as determined by her system of rhetorical relations, were recalled better than highly similar paragraphs which were hierarchically lower in the structure of different passages. Similarly, Frederiksen has found (1975, 1977a, 1977b) that the recall of a superordinate proposition will increase the probability that a proposition subordinate to it will also be remembered. Together, these findings lend additional support to the general conclusion of a long history of research on memory for prose which has shown that people tend to remember the semantic "gist" or central meaning of a passage rather than supporting details or specific syntactic forms, results which are also consistent with the proposals of elaboration theory (see Chapter 4). Propositional analyses of text, however, go further, in that they are able to illustrate why certain ideas are more central or important in a passage than others. Further discussion of the differences among various systems for propositional analysis can be found in Meyer (in press) and Tierney & Mosenthal (1980).

Toward Understanding the Nature of Text

In contrast to the emphasis on content in propositional analyses, the other major focus of discourse analysis has been on the nature of text itself. In various ways, this effort has been directed at identifying those features of prose which make it textlike, which serve to create the impression that it is a coordinated whole. While van Dijk (1977) has aimed at establishing a formal discourse grammar, much of the work in this area has been less ambitious and more descriptive, attempting instead to characterize specific discourse phenomena. Several concepts refer to the flow or structure of the information in a passage and how this pattern gets expressed lexically and syntactically. A recurring proposal is that well-constructed prose has a central theme or focus which gets amplified or elaborated by supporting ideas in a passage. A paragraph which begins with a clear statement of the theme sets the context for the discourse and should be easier to comprehend (Halliday, 1980).

Another distinction is that between "given" and "new" information in discourse (Chafe, 1976; Clark, 1977; Clark & Haviland, 1977). Although different descriptions of "givenness" vary somewhat, basically they all refer to the idea that some information in a sentence can be considered given in that it has been mentioned in a preceding portion of the discourse or can be inferred from the situational context, while other ideas in a sentence are new since they are being introduced without immediate prior mention. Generally, though not always, the subject of a sentence reflects given information. When it does, it serves the function of tying together the ideas in a passage across sentence boundaries, since what was introduced as new in one sentence can then be presupposed as known in the next. For example, in the sequence: "Carol bought a novel yesterday. The book is an historical romance," the novel (book) is *new* information in the first sentence, but *given* in the second. The more new information in a single sentence, the more difficult it may be to process (Halliday, 1980).

Several of the phenomena which serve to connect the ideas in a text have been described under the concept of "cohesion," principally by Halliday & Hasan (1976). One of the clearest examples of cohesive elements is reference, which includes both personal pronouns and demonstratives like "this," "that," and "here." In general, there are two kinds of reference—anaphoric, in which a word refers back to a word or phrase in the preceding discourse, and less commonly, cataphoric, in which a word refers to an idea which occurs subsequently in the text. Two other cohesive devices are substitution—when a word or phrase is substituted for one mentioned previously—and ellipsis—the omission of an idea that can be assumed from the prior discourse or context. In the following example of verbal ellipsis, the words "read this book before" are omitted from the second sentence.

> "Have you read this book before?
> I have."

An important set of cohesive elements are connectives, which include not only common conjunctions like "and" or "but," but other linking words and phrases, such as "thus," "however," "on the other hand," etc. Use of such connectives significantly serves to bind together the ideas in one sentence or part of a text with those in another, thereby creating the distinctive feel of a text in contrast to a set of unconnected sentences.

Halliday (1980) has suggested that the use of cohesive elements helps to reduce the density of text, thereby making it easier to understand. Written discourse tends to be quite dense, containing a high proportion of lexical or content items. He has also indicated that the kind of cohesion which occurs in a text will vary according to the intent, seriousness, and spontaneity of the discourse and whether it is written or oral.

Thus far, empirical investigation of the effect of various cohesive elements on overall comprehension or recall of prose passages has been limited. Meyer, however (1975, 1977, 1980), has studied many of these aspects of discourse under the concept of "signaling." For her, signaling, ". . . is a non-content aspect of prose which gives emphasis to certain aspects of the semantic content or points out aspects of the structure of the content" (1975). Meyer has identified several types of signaling. These include ". . . explicit statement of the relations in the text structure, preview statements, summary statements, and pointer words or evaluative signaling" (1980). Relationships signaled at the top-most level in the text structure are Meyer's rhetorical relationships (1975, 1980, in press). When these relationships are explicitly stated by an author, they are said to be signaled. When these relationships are not made explicit, they must be inferred by the reader. This is the kind of signaling Meyer has investigated primarily. She acknowledges (1980) the relationship between this kind of discourse device and cohesive elements discussed by Halliday & Hasan (1976). However, she stresses that she is examining relations among elements—groups of sentences and paragraphs—within the macro-structure of a text's representation, rather than between clauses or individual sentences.

To assess the effect of signaling, investigators have generally employed two versions of the same passage, one version containing signaling devices, the other omitting them. Since overall results of such investigations have been inconclusive and even contradictory, Meyer (1980) has proposed a model to try to account for this inconsistency in the literature. In this model, she suggests several factors which could influence whether or not explicit signaling of rhetorical relations will affect text comprehension or recall. These include whether a reader can employ what Meyer (1980) terms a "structure strategy"—or an implicit attempt to detect the overall structure of a passage, the difficulty level of a particular text, the reader's decoding ability, and the text organization skills of the reader. Meyer (1980) proposes that when the difficulty level of a text matches the competencies of a reader and if that reader can effectively employ a "structure strategy," no effect for signaling may occur. Explicit signaling may be of use for comparatively difficult texts or for readers with limited sensitivity to the inherent organization of texts. Proficient readers, apparently, can infer important relationships in texts, even when they are not marked. Some support for this suggestion comes from a study by Neilsen (1978), who used fifth-grade, ninth-grade, and college students reading at or above grade level. Neilsen found no effect on comprehension of the explicit marking of logical relationships in texts, but did find that a hierarchical macro-structure facilitated comprehension, when the passage content concerned a topic familiar to the readers. The relative familiarity of a topic is one aspect of text difficulty.

While attention to the ideational structure of discourse and text characteristics is certainly important, Halliday's (1980) work suggests that pragmatic and contextual aspects of text production, comprehension, and processing are also highly relevant. Such concerns include the purpose for reading or writing, the audience for which a particular text is intended, the inherent interest someone has in a passage, and the situation in which a text is read. Hirsch (1977), in particular, has emphasized the importance of tailoring writing to the requirements of a particular audience. In doing so, an assessment should be made about how much or little the intended reader already knows about the subject of the discourse so that the writer can judge what needs to be said. Hirsch contends that, "A shrewd decision about the knowledge that the writer can tacitly assume in his audience may be the most important decision the writer makes." Harste & Carey (1979) maintain that all language acts, including reading and writing, are social events and occur in specific contexts. Thus, ". . . in order to understand the cognitive and linguistic processes involved in reading and writing, one must do so in light of both the linguistic and situational contexts in which that processing occurred" (1979). The context, and a person's past history with similar contexts, influence how a reader or writer will interpret the demands of a particular act of text production or comprehension.

Implications for the Design of Texts

These different perspectives on the nature of written discourse may not yet be able to provide precise prescriptions for structuring instructional text, but they do identify several factors which should be considered in producing them. As a general principle, the writer should do whatever is possible to facilitate the acquisition of new information by highlighting important ideas and limiting demands on the reader.

First of all, a writer should try to develop a clear conception of the audience for which the text is intended. This effort should provide a picture of that audience's prior experience with similar texts and thus what their expectations for such texts may be. Additionally, it will offer insight into the degree of knowledge readers already possess about the topic of the text and thereby guide decisions about what to include and omit and how to structure the introduction of new information so that excessive processing demands are not made. Second, the theme of each paragraph or section should be clearly stated at the beginning in order to focus the reader's attention on the main point or points being developed. To increase the probability that important information will be remembered, the overall organization of paragraphs within longer stretches of text should reflect judgments about the relative importance of the ideas being presented. Major concepts should not be buried in a mass of detail.

Within sentences, attention should be paid to the given-new distinction by, in most cases, treating sentence subjects as given, thus pointing toward new information, and by limiting the amount of new information included in any one clause or sentence. Making given information the subject of sentences also adds to the coherent flow of ideas across sentences. Additionally, the use of appropriate cohesive devices not only helps to create a sense of the overall structure of a text, but also reduces the density of the information load and alerts the reader to the relationships the author sees among the ideas in the text. Explicit signaling of these relationships can help ensure that readers of different levels of ability will be able to detect and use them. Further analysis and study of text structure, it is hoped, will be able to better our understanding of the importance of these various textual elements and offer additional recommendations for the effective design of instructional texts.

References

Brown, A.L., & Smiley, S.S. Rating the importance of structural units of prose passages: A problem of metacognitive development. *Child Development*, 1977, *48*, 1-8.

Brown, A.L., & Smiley, S.S. The development of strategies for studying texts. *Child Development*, 1978, *49*, 1076-1088.

Chafe, W.L. Givenness, contrastiveness, definiteness, subjects, topics, and point of view. In C.N. Li (Ed.), *Subject and topic.* New York: Academic Press, 1976.

Clark, H.H. Inferences in comprehension. In D. LaBerge & S.J. Samuels (Eds.), *Basic processes in reading: Perception and comprehension.* Hillsdale, NJ: Lawrence Erlbaum Associates, 1977.

Clark, H.H., & Haviland, S.E. Comprehension and the given-new contract. In R.O. Freedle (Ed.), *Discourse production and comprehension.* Norwood, NJ: Ablex Publishing Corp., 1977.

Fillmore, C.J. The case for case. In E. Bach & R.T. Harms (Eds.), *Universals in linguistic theory.* New York: Holt, Rinehart, & Winston, 1968.

Frederiksen, C.H. Representing logical and semantic structures of knowledge acquired from discourse. *Cognitive Psychology,* 1975, *7,* 371-458.

Frederiksen, C.H. *Inference and the structure of children's discourse.* Paper presented at the biennial meeting of the Society for Research in Child Development, New Orleans, 1977a.

Frederiksen, C.H. Semantic processing units in understanding text. In R.O. Freedle (Ed.), *Discourse production and comprehension.* Norwood, NJ: Ablex Publishing Corp., 1977b.

Grimes, J.E. *The thread of discourse.* The Hague: Mouton & Co., N.V., 1975.

Halliday, M.A.K. *Cohesion and register.* Paper presented before the conference of the National Council for Research in English at the annual meeting of the American Educational Research Association, Boston, 1980.

Halliday, M.A.K., & Hasan, R. *Cohesion in English.* London: Longman Group, Ltd., 1976.

Harste, J.C., & Carey, R.F. *Classrooms, constraints, and the language process.* Unpublished manuscript, 1979.

Hirsch, E.D., Jr. *The philosophy of composition.* Chicago: The University of Chicago Press, 1977.

Johnson, R.E. Recall of prose as a function of the structural importance of the linguistic units. *Journal of Verbal Learning and Verbal Behavior,* 1970, *9,* 12-20.

Kintsch, W. *The representation of meaning in memory.* Hillsdale, NJ: Lawrence Erlbaum Associates, 1974.

Meyer, B.J.F. *The organization of prose and its effects on memory.* Amsterdam: North Holland Publishing Company, 1975.

Meyer, B.J.F. What is remembered from prose: A function of passage structure. In R.O. Freedle (Ed.), *Discourse production and comprehension.* Norwood, NJ: Ablex Publishing Corp., 1977.

Meyer, B.J.F. *Signaling in text.* Paper presented at the annual meeting of the American Psychological Association, Montreal, 1980.

Meyer, B.J.F. Prose analysis: Procedures, purposes, and problems. In B.K. Britton & J. Black (Eds.), *Analyzing and understanding expository text.* Hillsdale, NJ: Lawrence Erlbaum Associates, in press.

Neilsen, A.R. *The role of text structure on the comprehension of familiar and unfamiliar written discourse.* Paper presented at the annual meeting of the National Reading Conference, St. Petersburg, FL, 1978.

Tierney, R.J., & Mosenthal, J. *Discourse comprehension and production: Analyzing text structure and cohesion* (Tech. Rep. No. 152). Champaign, IL: Center for the Study of Reading, University of Illinois, 1980.

Turner, A., & Greene, E. *The construction and use of a propositional text base* (Tech. Rep. No. 63). Boulder, CO: Institute for the Study of Intellectual Behavior, University of Colorado, 1977.

van Dijk, T.A. *Text and context: Explorations in the semantics and pragmatics of discourse.* London: Longman Group, Ltd., 1977.

3.

Getting Started:
Pattern Notes and Perspectives

Alan Fields

What's the Problem?
Have you been faced with requests like these?

"Just give me a written report about your project."
"Will you talk to our youth club about your work?"

Have you had ideas like this?

"I think I'll write up my work on pattern notes as an article for a journal."
"Can I prepare a structured text about Critical Path Method?"

Faced with these situations, we know that what is expected of us is to produce a linear account of our work in a form that our reader or listener can understand. Therefore, we would probably first take a sheet of paper and scribble down a list of points in a linear order, as in Figure 3.1. As you can see, this is rough and has been crossed out and altered, but eventually it gave a sensible ordering of points which are capable of being expanded into a written article or a talk.

It is very possible that Figure 3.1 is actually the end-result of several lists that were scrapped en route as our ideas about the presentation changed. Why can't we produce Figure 3.1 at a first attempt?

I assume here that we are dealing with a subject that is familiar to us, so that lack of subject knowledge is not the problem (indeed the converse, knowing too much, and therefore not knowing what to leave out is a much more likely difficulty). I would suggest that we cannot produce Figure 3.1 at a first attempt because, to do so, we are trying to solve simultaneously three interrelated problems:

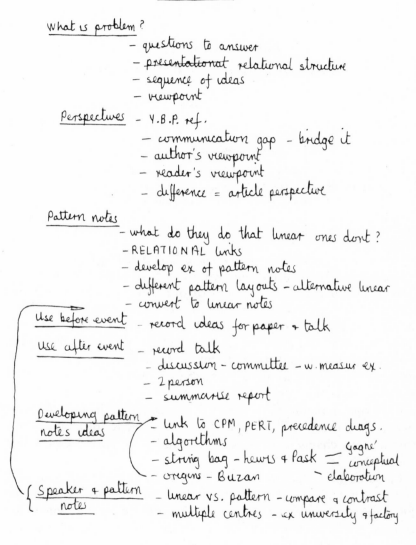

Figure 3.1. Linear notes of an article.

(1) to decide the presentational viewpoint;

(2) to name the key issues; and

(3) to order the issues in a relational framework based on (1).

Most of us are not very good at solving this type of simultaneous problem—hence all the crossing-out and alterations and scrapped versions of Figure 3.1 before we arrive at a workable version of the outline of our article.

The purpose of this chapter is twofold, first, to comment on the matter of the presentational viewpoint; and, second, having decided the viewpoint, to introduce the concept of pattern notes, which represent a way around the three-problem issue involved in providing a framework for the article. We shall see that the arguments presented are applicable both to the preparation of a written article and for a spoken presentation.

Getting the Ideas Together

Let us return to the situation where we have decided to write the article or give the talk. We are facing a blank sheet of paper and hoping for inspiration to guide our choice of items for the article. What sort of decisions ought we to be making now?

We are trying to bridge a communication gap. We know (perhaps because someone has told us) or assume that our potential readers and ourselves share some points of view in common about the subject under discussion, but that there are other points which we do not share, because of a difference of opinion, or because the potential reader is unaware of the extra information which we possess. Therefore, our objective in communicating with our reader could be one or more of the following: to produce a change in the reader's viewpoint that alters his or her image of the topic; to expand our reader's knowledge of the topic, or to make clearer or more certain to him or her some particular part of the view of the topic that he or she holds. We need to decide which of these objectives are the ones we will address, so that we arrive eventually at a wider shared understanding between reader and writer (or speaker and hearer) about the topic.

This chapter provides an example of the decisions involved in the last paragraph. As the writer, I need first to establish a common starting point with you, the reader, about the problem we are going to discuss. This is provided by the discussion on linear notes above, which method I assume we are all familiar with. I am also making the assumption that you agree with my criticism of the method, and would be interested in an alternative approach to organizing a talk. I also assume that you know nothing about pattern notes, because the editor tells me that this method of note-taking is not well-known, at least in the United States. As a reader of this book, you will be a professional man or woman interested in instruction and communication methods (and this also has implications about the vocabulary that I can use). In contrast, I have had experience in using pattern notes for a range of situations. I believe that they represent an advance over linear notes for many situations, and I want to try to convince you about that advantage, and to persuade you to use pattern notes to organize your initial thoughts about the next paper that you write, or the next talk you give.

Thus, I have established my image of you, my claims to write about pattern notes, the communication gap in your (assumed) lack of knowledge about the subject, and the eventual objective of widening your understanding through a shared knowledge of the topic. All of these decisions about the relationships between you, me, and the topic need to be decided in order to have a clear picture in my mind of the items that will be relevant and worth noting on the piece of paper with which we started this section. I have established the assumed perspectives of our two viewpoints and the communication gap between them, preparatory to developing the pattern notes for the article.

For a more detailed account of this matter of the reader's and writer's perspectives, see Young, Becker, & Pike (1970). The article by Ann Jaffe Pace in this book also deals in part with perspectives.

What Do Pattern Notes Do?

The problems of viewpoint, key issues, and sequence of the material need to be solved before the final linear notes are prepared, but in trying to prepare these we often try to decide our approach to our audience before we know what we want to say. Pattern notes are a means of reviewing alternatives as we think of other ideas to be included. Only when we have written down all the key issues will we need to decide their order and the viewpoint. We shall also be able to decide alternative sequences of the material and to choose the most appropriate for our audience. Pattern notes exploit the fact that our mind jumps from point to point in a non-linear manner as we think about ideas for a topic. The notes organize the material in a *relational*, as opposed to a linear manner, that is, they show the relational linkages between the topics (as when we say that mathematics has sub-topics of algebra, geometry, calculus, etc., and that algebra can be divided into linear equations, quadratic equations, simultaneous equations, etc.). From these relational orderings, a number of linear presentations can be considered, and the most appropriate one chosen.

How Do We Prepare Pattern Notes About a Subject?

We return to the blank sheet of paper that we were facing two sections back. First, we think about the issues of perspective that were described there and clarify in our minds our general aim for the topic and our perceptions of our readers and the knowledge gap between them and us. Nothing need be noted on paper about these matters, unless we anticipate that work on the article may be interrupted and we wish to note the perspectives to aid future recall.

It is useful if the sheet of paper is about 8½ x 11 inches in size. To start the pattern notes, we write our subject in block capitals, in the center of the page and box it in, thus:

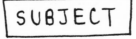

Next, we think about key issues of the subject. Suppose that we can remember two. We put these alongside the subject box in any

position we fancy, with a line under each issue joining them to the
box, as below:

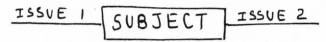

Further thought gives us two sub-issues of the first issue and
another key issue. The sub-issues form branches from the key issue,
and the third key issue is a new direction from the subject box, as
below:

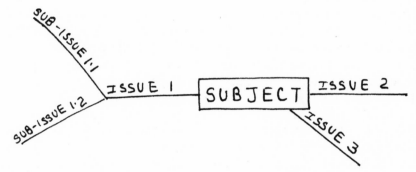

We continue in this manner until we consider that we have recorded
all the issues that are likely to be important. As we do so, we may
realize that some topics interlink with each other, as well as radiating
from the subject like the spokes of a wheel. This will give a diagram
like the one below:

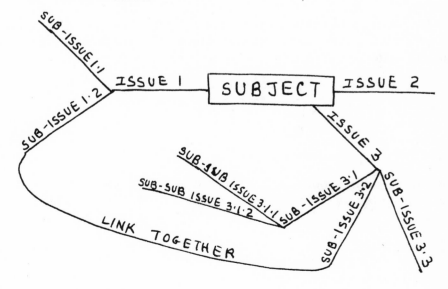

This ability to show the inter-linkages of complex issues in a relational manner is a major advantage of this system over other note-preparing systems. The general principle of the layout of a set of pattern notes is that the key theme is at the center of the page, with major issues radiating out from it, and minor issues radiating out from these, with interdependent links as required by the subject. The topics at the outer edges of the diagram are those of least importance (or they are least central to the issue under consideration).

The pattern notes for this chapter are shown in Figure 3.2.

Having prepared the pattern notes, what have we achieved?

We have identified the key issues and their relational interdependencies. Each of the spokes radiating from the central box, together with the subsidiary spokes joined to it, form one issue, together with the detail we wish to present about it. We can now visualize all the material that we have collected as a series of relational presentations (the spokes and subsidiary spokes). We have not yet put the issues in linear order. This is the next stage. Note how pattern notes have separated the problem of choosing the issues from that of listing them in a linear sequence, while summarizing the subject, including its interdependencies, in a pictorial form on one page. It would be very difficult to achieve all these with linear notes.

We can turn one set of pattern notes into several alternative linear sets of notes. Each presents the subject in a different manner, suitable for different audiences. We need to choose the most appropriate one to link with our audience's previous knowledge, so that they can rapidly follow the discussion. This choice relates to our perceived image of our readers that we considered two sections ago, and to what we hope is a practical way of bridging the communication gap between us. Below is the sequence of linear notes developed from the pattern notes of this chapter, guided by my assumed image of you that I presented earlier.

- What is the problem?
- Perspectives of author and reader
- Aim of pattern notes

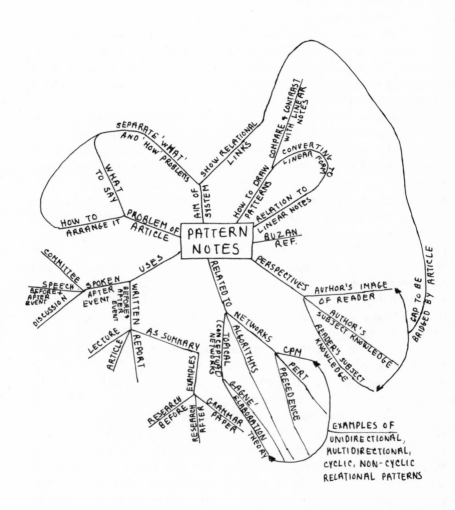

Figure 3.2. Pattern notes for this chapter.

- How to prepare pattern notes
- Use of pattern notes—preparing written and spoken topics
- Pattern notes and a speaker
- Beyond pattern notes—networks, algorithms, Gagné
- Other applications—summaries

My argument for making this particular choice is that I assume that you know nothing about pattern notes. Therefore, it is necessary to start from the organizational problem inherent in preparing an article or speech, showing the unique contribution of pattern notes, then through the method of preparation and use, and application to reporting a speech, to their relationship with other relational networks and other applications. This is an argument proceeding from the familiar to the unknown for a newcomer to the topic.

It is also possible to develop alternatively sequenced linear patterns from the same set of pattern notes, although these would presuppose different author-reader perspectives to the one above. Below are two alternative sets of linear notes developed from the pattern notes of this article, together with the potential audiences for which they are intended.

- Buzan reference
- Beyond pattern notes—networks, algorithms, Gagné
- Other applications—summaries
- Use of pattern notes—preparing written and spoken topics
- Pattern notes and a speaker
- Aim of pattern notes
- Problem of perspectives
- How to prepare pattern notes
- What is the problem?

Here we assume that, from the initial reference, the reader is familiar with the system and that we can discuss immediately some related system and further applications which are not stated in the Buzan reference. Mention of the aim of the method and its preparation, and the problem which it solves would probably be brief. This is a discussion among experts and could be difficult for a layman to follow.

- Use of pattern notes—for written and spoken topic preparation

- Use of pattern notes—for summaries
- Use of pattern notes—for reporting speeches
- Aim of pattern notes
- Problem of perspectives
- What is the problem?
- How to prepare pattern notes
- Relation to linear notes

Here we aim to use a range of applications at the start of the article to make the reader consider pattern notes as a solution to the general problem. We would then describe pattern notes as an answer.

Having arrived at these linear notes, the objective of the pattern notes is achieved, since what remains is to convert the linear notes into an article or talk. If we are developing a textbook, it is at this point that elaboration theory and component display theory, described by Charles M. Reigeluth and I. Fulya Sari elsewhere in this book, can be used to provide a more and more detailed linear structure around which the textbook can be written. Pattern notes provide the means of recording on paper and sequencing the topics for the first step of the development procedure, "select and sequence the organizing content."

For What Sort of Situations Can I Use Pattern Notes?

Like linear notes, there are two different circumstances where pattern notes can be of value. These are in organizing our thoughts before the event and in recording the event while it is in progress. The account so far has described the situation where we are organizing our thoughts before the event. Pattern notes can be used for the initial preparation of any spoken or written presentation that we wish to give. They can be used to organize our thoughts for lectures, speeches, debates and discussions, for essays, reports, reviews, theses, and examinations, and even for programmed instruction. We now consider the use of pattern notes to record an event.

Can Pattern Notes Help in Recording the Spoken Word?

We need to start by defining the circumstances in which we can hear the spoken word. I suggest that there are three situations where pattern notes could be helpful: first, in reporting a formal address, such as a talk, lecture, or sermon, second, in recording the decisions of a group such as a committee, and third, in a two-person discussion of an issue.

In the case of a formal address, we can expect the topic to be presented in a reasonably structured manner. It is possible for the address to contain more than one major issue; as, for example, if one were to compare the systems of financing a university and a small private company. Here there would be three areas of discussion; first, the methods available to finance a university; second, the methods available to finance a small company; and, third, a comparison of the two.

Linear notes of such an address would present the points in the temporal sequence that the speaker used, and may or may not show the interlinks of the sections, or suggest alternative sequences of presentation. There would be no difficulty in showing the start of the talk, since this would be the note at the top of the paper.

In contrast, pattern note writers may have difficulty initially in identifying the key issue if the speaker does not define his or her topic at the start of the talk, and there may be one or two false guesses before one identifies the true key issue. The notes will then build up the relational pattern between issues as the address continues. Pattern notes of the university-company example above would follow the basic structure in Figure 3.3, with three centers of interest.

Pattern notes do not show the temporal relationships of the points of an address, unless one specifically identifies the points in number sequence. They are not designed to capture this feature. If the address is one of a series, as in a set of lectures, the pattern notes for each lecture can be linked to their starting point in the earlier lecture, and a relational structure of the entire sequence of lectures will be built up as the course proceeds. This structure will also aid revision for examinations.

It is possible that the speaker will not give a well-ordered presentation of his or her material. Pattern notes have an

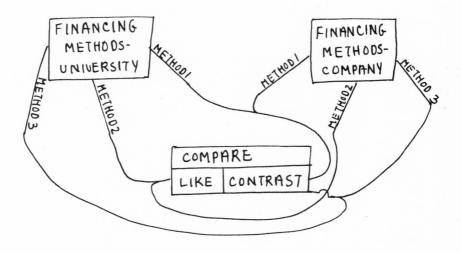

Figure 3.3. Pattern notes with multiple centers of interest.

advantage over linear ones in these circumstances, since they will show such relational structures as the speaker presents. Linear note-taking would have difficulty in presenting such material coherently.

Pattern notes can help a committee or group of people who are discussing a topic to record their differing viewpoints on one reference framework. The method is to develop pattern notes of the discussion on a chalkboard as the meeting proceeds. One person acts as the recorder, preparing the pattern notes from each speaker's contribution as he or she finishes speaking. It has the advantage that everyone's viewpoint is recorded, and all can see the issues developing. Conventional minutes can be prepared from the pattern notes, or they may be acceptable in pattern form.

Figure 3.4 is an example of pattern notes developed from different student contributions to the question, "What factors

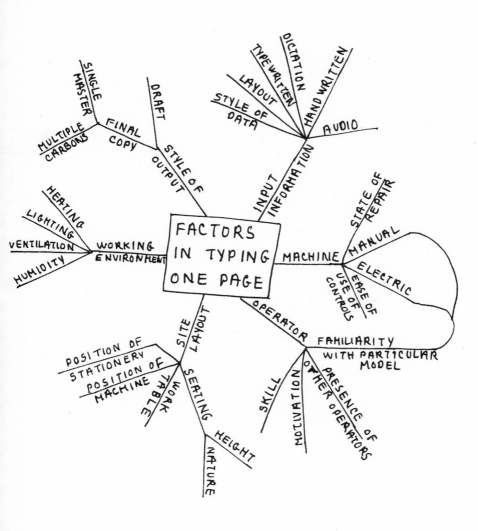

Figure 3.4. Pattern notes of a work measurement theme.

influence how long it takes to type a page of text?" (This discussion was intended as a lead-in to a study of work measurement.) Notice that the example looks identical in type to Figure 3.2. It is not obvious to the reader that it represents the views of a group, rather than an individual. The important difference for the group members is that everyone could see his or her comments on record, and each was given equal prominence in the presentation, with stress placed on the relational aspects of the information, not on the most voluminous statements.

The two-person discussion is a special case of the committee or group situation that was described earlier. Here the group is two persons, and as in the case of the formal address, the end-product will be a relational presentation of the points discussed. The key advantage of pattern notes over linear ones in a situation where the conversation may follow an unstructured route is that it is capable of organizing the points in a relational manner as they are presented. This is what we are doing when we write pattern notes for a talk, as I explained earlier, and the same process is occurring in the two-person discussion.

Using Pattern Notes to Summarize Reports

Pattern notes summarize information in a relational sequence. They can summarize proposals in a report. Figure 3.5 shows a summary for a research proposal, and Figure 3.6 shows the corresponding summary at the conclusion of the research. Such summaries answer that classic managerial comment about large reports, "Fine, now give it to me on one sheet of paper," since the pattern notes cover only one sheet.

The research proposals above are for private consumption, and therefore they may not be clear to a third party. They are shown here only as illustrations. A more private form still of pattern notes is Figure 3.7. This is a summary for my own use of a research paper on English grammar. The original paper is 123 pages of 7 x 5 inch typeset text. The purpose of the pattern note summary is to identify the major issues, their interrelationships, and their place in the text. Since the notes were written for my own use, they can be more cryptic than the other patterns quoted above.

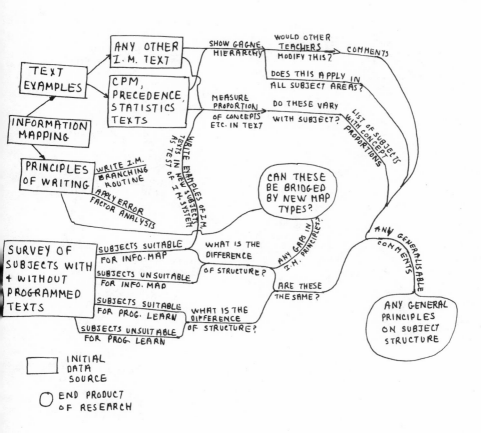

Figure 3.5. Summary of research proposal.

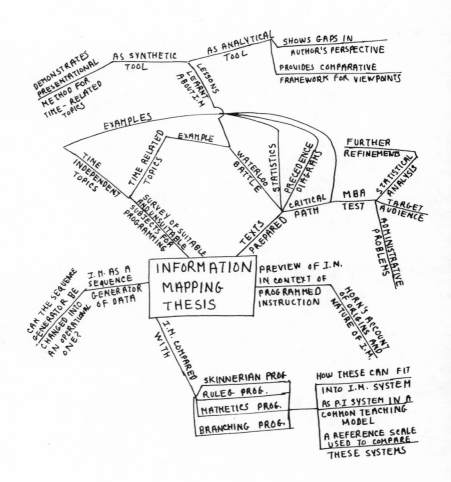

Figure 3.6. Summary of completed research project.

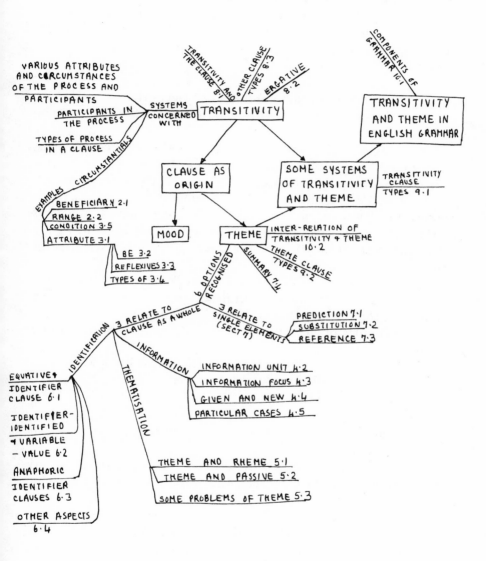

Figure 3.7. Summary of research paper.

What do we gain by using pattern notes to summarize information? We can show the relational links between items of information. This is difficult to achieve with linear summaries. The benefit becomes more obvious when the subject contains many cross-linkages between the topics, as in the research proposals examples.

Pattern Notes and Related Networks

What are the origins of pattern notes, and what else are they related to?

Diagrams of this type have existed for a number of years, sometimes being called topic networks. I have developed this account of the preparation of pattern notes from Tony Buzan's book, *Use Your Head*, where he introduces the term "pattern notes" for diagrams, such as Figure 3.2. The examples in Buzan's book only contain one center of interest, so that ones like Figure 3.3, with more than one center of interest, are an extension of his argument.

We can extend this point about networks which contain more than one center of interest until we reach those where each activity in the network is of equal relational importance. There are several examples of these types of network, such as the ones listed below:

- network analysis (critical path networks, PERT, and precedence diagrams),
- topical networks,
- algorithms,
- conceptual networks (related to the Gagné hierarchy and elaboration theory).

Each of these represent a slightly different relational situation and deal with slightly different problems. We will consider each in turn.

Critical path networks, PERT, and precedence diagrams are relational patterns which contain a single direction for the activities as they proceed from the start point (or points) of the work to its conclusion. They do not contain any cyclic events, since this would imply that the task covered by the network could never finish. Here a time dimension is superimposed on the relational picture. In relational terms, these networks are unidirectional, non-cyclic processes with one terminal event.

Topical networks resemble precedence diagrams. Figure 3.8, on the oxygen-carbon dioxide cycle, and Figure 3.9, on the tree ring formation, are examples. The stages of the networks are linked by chemical reactions in Figure 3.8 and by relational arrows in Figure 3.9. They are complete cycles, as in Figure 3.8, or contain cyclic sequences, as in Figure 3.9. This is in contrast to the network analysis techniques. In relational terms, topical networks are uni- or multidirectional processes containing cyclic sequences.

Algorithms are relational patterns which handle problem solving routines dealing with procedural (this-is-how-you-should-do-it) knowledge. Usually they resemble the precedence diagram without the time scale, but with the inclusion of decision steps. They are unidirectional and start from one entry point, but they can proceed to a number of exit points, depending on the needs of the user of the algorithm. They do not contain cyclic sequences. They are therefore relational patterns describing unidirectional, non-cyclic processes with several terminal events.

Conceptual networks are a way of visualizing the body of knowledge about a particular subject. Lewis and Pask (Lewis, 1974) propose that the concepts which make up the subject matter of a topic join together in what they describe as a "string-bag" of relationships, where the concepts are represented by knots in the bag and the relational linkages between concepts are represented by the string between pairs of knots.

This image implies that the total conceptual network can be viewed from a number of different positions where each observer will give differing emphasis on differing facets of the topic and where each observer will have differing initial knowledge about the topic. If we consider work measurement, then the industrial engineer sees this as a means of calculating times for industrial operations, the production controller as a basis for production scheduling, the industrial relations officer as a basis for manning levels and job descriptions, and the trade union officer as a factor in wage negotiation. Each person sees a different facet of work

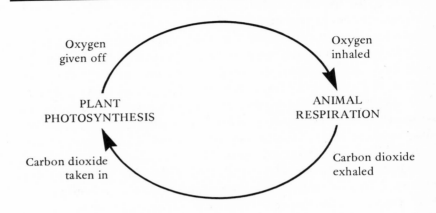

Figure 3.8. The oxygen-carbon dioxide cycle.

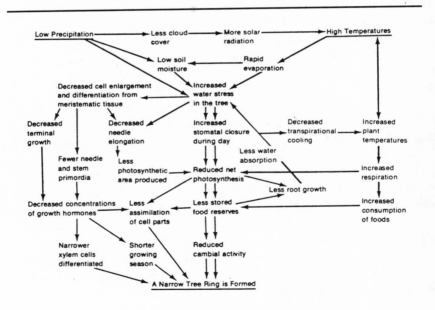

Figure 3.9. Tree ring formation.

measurement as the one most central to his or her interests, and relates it to a different environment.

One way of converting the conceptual network to a teaching sequence would be through a Gagné hierarchy. A particular hierarchy starts from a certain viewpoint and therefore a certain assumed initial knowledge. To obtain a Gagné hierarchy from the conceptual network above, we cut the string-bag at particular points corresponding to the initial knowledge of the hierarchy and suspend the resultant meshwork by the terminal issue in which we are interested, thus forming a particular Gagné hierarchy. Since four different viewpoints were suggested above, four different Gagné hierarchies would be obtained from the same conceptual network. All of these hierarchies interconnect to some degree, and each makes it own linkages to separate peripheral concepts. Thus, Lewis and Pask's work suggests that a Gagné hierarchy is a development of a multicyclic relational process that lies behind the hierarchy. It is a half-way house between the conceptual network that describes a topic and the teaching sequence that we require. A Gagné hierarchy is a relational diagram which builds up to the key issue from multiple entry points. It does not contain cyclic situations, and could be described relationally as a unidirectional, non-cyclic process with multiple entry points and one exit point.

Another way of dividing the material in a conceptual network into a teaching sequence is Reigeluth's elaboration theory, described elsewhere in this book. Reigeluth does not specifically link his work to the conceptual network model, but builds his method from the epitome of the topic, proceeding from this into greater and greater levels of detail as his method proceeds. In terms of Lewis and Pask's conceptual model, he is starting from one particular node, the epitome, and moving away to other nodes that represent elaborations of the concept of the epitome, until he has presented a sufficiently detailed understanding of the topic for the student's current learning needs. Structurally, one could conceive of the elaboration theory, as it proceeds from one point along many paths to its termination as the converse of the Gagné hierarchy structure.

Table 3.1 compares the various forms of network described in this section.

What can we therefore conclude about pattern notes and the other networks to which they are related?

It is easier to begin by stating what particular variation of a larger class pattern notes form. We have identified several relational patterns which show the interrelationships between stages of processes. These can be cyclic, as in the "string-bag" or some topical networks, or multidirectional, or unidirectional as in the network analysis, elaboration theory, and Gagné hierarchy examples, with multiple or single start and end points, and can contain several important issues along with minor ones, or, as in Buzan's pattern notes, only one central issue. Hence, we conclude that pattern notes are a specific relational network developed to handle the organization of initial information on a subject prior to presenting it as a linear sequence in a paper or a talk. They have moved relational patterns into the realm of organizing general spoken or written information as well as the technical and scientific areas.

Summary

We have been looking at pattern notes, an alternative method to linear notes for presenting the structure of a body of information.

We saw that we could use pattern notes in two types of situations, first to organize our thoughts in advance of a written or spoken presentation, and, second, to record the points of a spoken presentation as it took place, or to summarize a written one.

We saw that before we could start our thoughts on a topic, it was necessary to consider what our perspective and that of our potential hearer or reader on the topic were likely to be, and hence what was the communication gap between us. This study enabled us to aim our presentation more precisely at our reader's perceived needs and to communicate more accurately with him or her.

Having resolved this matter, pattern notes were used to develop our thoughts. We saw that the method showed how the relationships of the subject were organized and that this led us to observe readily the possible alternative linear orders in which the material could be presented.

Relational Pattern	Number of Centers	Contains Cycles	Multi/ Unidirectional	Time Scale	Single/Multiple Start Point	Single/Multiple End Point
Pattern (Buzan)	1	No	Multi	No	Not relevant	
Pattern (from talk)	> 1	No	Multi	No	Not relevant	
Network analysis	Many	No	Uni	Yes	Either, depending on type	
Algorithms	Many	No	Uni	No	Single	Multiple
Topical networks	Many	Yes	Either	No	Not relevant	
Conceptual	Many	Yes	Multi	No	Not relevant	
Gagné	Many	No	Uni	No	Multi	Single
Elaboration theory	Many	No	Uni	No	Single	Multi

Table 3.1. A comparison of types of relational patterns.

Moving from organizing our own thoughts, we showed pattern notes as a means of recording lectures, and saw how our original notion of a pattern with only one central theme had to be widened to include several major themes. We considered its use for committee situations and two-person discussions.

We showed that pattern notes could sum up a report on one page.

Finally, we looked at the origin of pattern notes and the links to other relational patterns such as critical path networks, PERT, precedence diagrams, topical networks, algorithms, Gagné hierarchies, and elaboration theory.

In all these cases, the major advantage of pattern notes was their ability to organize information relationally, showing complex interdependencies more readily than linear notes. The more complex the subject, the greater the advantage pattern notes have over traditional linear notes.

References

Buzan, T. *Use your head.* London: British Broadcasting Publications, 1974.

Lewis, B.N. *New methods of assessment and stronger methods of curriculum design.* Milton Keynes, England: Institute of Educational Technology, Open University, 1974.

Young, R.E., Becker, A.L., & Pike, K.P. *Rhetoric: Discover and change.* New York: Harcourt, Brace, & World, 1970.

4.

Writing and Evaluating Textbooks: Contributions from Instructional Theory

I. Fulya Sari
Charles M. Reigeluth

The purposes of this chapter are (1) to indicate that instructional theory can do much to improve the quality of textbooks, (2) to briefly discuss two theories of instruction which are attempting to integrate a broad range of our knowledge about instruction into a form that is most useful to textbook writers, and (3) to overview some procedures for writing textbooks, for evaluating textbooks, and for revising textbooks. Hence, this chapter serves mainly a motivational and introductory function. It is *not* intended to teach you how to use the procedures that are overviewed. Nor is it intended to teach you a proficient understanding of the two theories that are discussed. To truly teach a proficient understanding of the theories and to teach a proficient use of the procedures would require far more than the allotted space for this chapter.

It is important to realize that different purposes of writing require different styles and formats of writing. Newspaper articles have one kind of format, argumentative essays have another, short stories have another, and instruction has yet another (in fact, it has several). Given the purposes of this chapter, a cross between a newspaper article and an argumentative essay would perhaps be the most appropriate format (although we cannot claim much expertise at either). Hence, the ideas that are discussed in this chapter would be inappropriate to use for the design of the chapter. Rather, references are included as to where you can learn more about the ideas discussed herein.

53

The following is an indication of what this chapter contains and how it is organized:

I. *The Importance of Instructional Theory in Writing and Evaluating Textbooks.*

Instructional theory indicates how to improve the instructional quality of textbooks, which will be of special benefit to disadvantaged students, since they are hurt most by poor quality textbooks.

II. *Advances in Instructional Design: Component Display Theory and Elaboration Theory.*

Component display theory and elaboration theory are intended to integrate existing knowledge about instructional design into optimal models of instruction. They prescribe different models for different conditions (goals, content, learners, etc.). Each theory is analyzed in terms of the basic propositions on which the theories are based.

III. *A Procedure for Designing and Developing Textbooks Using Elaboration Theory.*

The seven-step design and development procedure is intended for use in a team approach to textbook writing. It describes the content analysis, methods selection, and development phases of instructional development models. The use of this procedure results in the determination of what ideas to teach, how to sequence those ideas, and how to present each idea.

IV. *A Procedure for Evaluating Textbooks Using Elaboration Theory.*

Evaluation (and revision) of existing textbooks is a very important activity for improving the instructional quality of textbooks. A procedure is outlined for performing an "intrinsic" evaluation of an existing textbook on the basis of the elaboration theory and its subset: component display theory.

V. *A Procedure for Revising Textbooks Using Elaboration Theory.*

Revision of existing textbooks (after evaluating them and finding problems with them) is another important activity for improving the instructional quality of textbooks. The revision procedure determines ways to correct each instructional problem identified as a result of the evaluation procedure.

VI. *Conclusion.*

More work is needed to integrate the proven principles of instructional design into theory. A major conscious effort in building better models now will enhance our ability to realize the potential of instructional design theory to improve the quality of textbooks.

The Importance of Instructional Theory in Writing and Evaluating Textbooks

Part of the importance of instructional theory for textbook writing and evaluation lies in the importance of textbooks. Current practice testifies that teachers tend to adopt—or even become "slaves" to—the content and organization of the textbooks they use (Rosecky, 1978; Yarger & Mintz, 1979). Also, Phase Two of the Beginning Teacher Evaluation Study (by McDonnald) found that the great majority of a student's productive learning time was spent in interacting with *materials* (usually textbooks), while only about five percent of their productive learning time was spent in interacting with the teacher. Hence, anything that improves textbooks is likely to have a major impact on learning. And this is where instructional theory comes in.

Instructional theory is a body of knowledge about instruction. Unlike curriculum theory, which focuses more on *what* to teach, instructional theory focuses more on *how* to teach (Snelbecker, 1974). Its major purpose is to improve the quality of instruction. It can do so by making it more *effective*—that is, by increasing the amount of learning and reducing the amount of forgetting. And it can do so by making instruction more *efficient*—that is, by decreasing the amount of time and effort required to learn the same amount of knowledge. And it can do so by making instruction more *appealing*—that is, by making learning more enjoyable and increasing the learner's desire to learn more. Of course, improving the quality of instruction in one of these three dimensions often has a positive effect on the other two also.

As a discipline, instructional theory is very young and far from being able to achieve its potential for improving the quality of textbooks, teacher behaviors, and other forms of instruction. But tremendous progress has been made during the past ten years. Ways of presenting knowledge are being identified, analyzed, and improved. And the kinds of situations in which each of those ways is better than all other known ways are being identified. Research and field testing have been major parts of both of these kinds of activities, so that instructional "theory" is now comprised of a substantial body of validated knowledge about instruction. And unlike learning theory—which is usually difficult to apply to the improvement of instruction—instructional theory is easily and directly applied by practitioners: it is a sorely-needed link between learning theory and educational practice (Dewey, 1900; Snelbecker, 1974).

Perhaps the greatest need for using instructional theory in textbook writing is reflected in the plight of slower and disadvantaged students in our classrooms. Most current textbooks are far from being stand-alone learning resources—in other words, only the brightest students (if any at all) can learn what needs to be learned without the teacher's help. Since, as was mentioned above, the great majority of learning results from interacting with materials, this practically guarantees that slower and disadvantaged students will not receive the instruction that they need in order to learn. Instructional theory can help to make textbooks an effective stand-alone resource for such students, while at the same time—through formatting techniques—not burden the brighter students with unnecessary material. In fact, such use of instructional theory for textbook preparation will also make learning faster and more enjoyable for average and gifted students. Through special formatting techniques, it is also possible that a single text can provide truly individualized instruction that meets the needs of students with different cognitive styles, abilities, and prior content knowledge (see section on "learner control" below).

Improved textbook quality would not at all eliminate the need for the teacher; rather, it would change the teacher's role a bit. First, more individual and small-group contact would become possible. Second, the teacher would be able to focus more on motivating students and on individual remediation where necessary. Third, since the basic content skills and knowledge will have been acquired prior to the class period, class time could be spent on more enjoyable and equally important activities intended to promote transfer, long-term retention, and even the development (through the content under study) of higher-level cognitive strategies, learning strategies, and generic skills (see, e.g., O'Neil, 1978). In fact, instructional theory can help to organize textbooks such that they help students to acquire these higher levels of knowledge.

Although instructional theory has a long way to go before it reaches its full potential for improving textbooks, we believe that we currently have the capability to make significant improvements over the textbooks that are currently produced. However, we would like to emphasize that, because instructional theory is in its adolescence, textbook writers and other instructional designers must not rely on instructional theory (however "proven" it may be) to the exclusion of intuition and trial-and-revision. In fact, it is likely that good instructional designers will always rely to some extent on these two additional sources of knowledge. However, to the extent that a validated knowledge base about instruction can reduce one's reliance on intuition and trial-and-revision, the textbook writing process is likely to become less expensive and more reliably effective.

A fundamental argument of this chapter is that textbooks should be written by a *team* comprised of at least one experienced teacher and one instructional designer. This need not make the cost of textbook writing much more expensive, because designer time usually runs between one-eighth and one-fourth the amount of teacher time required. And the benefits in terms of improved effectiveness should be substantial.

Advances in Instructional Design:
Component Display Theory and Elaboration Theory

During its infancy, the field of instructional design was focused on very general and vague method variables, such as discovery vs.

expository, lecture vs. discussion, and inductive vs. deductive methods. But it was soon discovered that there was more variation within each of these types of methods than between them.

This led instructional theorists and researchers to devote most of their efforts to analyzing methods of instruction into more elementary *components* and studying the effects of each such "strategy component" under fairly controlled conditions. This emphasis produced a substantial amount of knowledge about instruction in the form of better strategies and principles for making instruction more effective, efficient, and appealing. However, this knowledge has been either too piecemeal or too vague to be optimally useful to textbook writers and other instructional designers. Even though this emphasis on investigating very precise, elementary, strategy components has been an important phase in the development of the field, the resulting knowledge does not help designers and textbook writers to combine strategy components into optimal configurations for the design of their instruction.

Consequently, emphasis within the field of instructional design is beginning to turn to the *integration* of these highly reliable and validated principles into complete, prescriptive *models* for the design of instruction. For a description of some of the most important attempts at such integration, see Reigeluth (in press). The following is a brief summary of some recent work that has been done along these lines.

There are at least two major types of design considerations in writing textbooks: (1) *micro* considerations, which apply to teaching a *single* idea (such as the use of examples and practice); and (2) *macro* considerations, which apply to the teaching of *many* related ideas (such as sequencing and systematic review). About eight years ago, M. David Merrill and his associates began to integrate much of the existing knowledge about micro design considerations (for single ideas) into five major models of instruction. Those models, along with prescriptions for their optimal use, are referred to as Component Display Theory. About six years ago, C.M. Reigeluth and M.D. Merrill began to integrate much of the existing knowledge about macro design considerations (for many related ideas) into three models of instruction. Those models, along with prescriptions for their optimal use, are referred to as the Elaboration Theory. These two sets of models (which were designed to fit together) are primarily concerned with the effectiveness and efficiency of instruction within the *cognitive domain*. In addition, the Elaboration Theory devotes a moderate amount of attention to motivational considerations for instruction in the cognitive domain. These two sets of instructional models are briefly described below.

Component Display Theory

Merrill's Component Display Theory (Merrill, in press; Merrill, Reigeluth, & Faust, 1979; Merrill, Richards, Schmidt, & Wood, 1977) is based on the assumption that a given presentation can be segmented into a series of discrete displays, most of which are called "presentation forms." Component Display Theory is based on the following eight propositions: ·

1. *Primary Presentation Forms.* A segment of instruction should include all three of the primary presentation forms: generality, example, and practice. A segment is defined as that instruction designed to teach a single generality or coordinate set of such generalities.

2. *Primary Presentation Form Sequence.* The primary presentation forms for a given segment of instruction should be sequenced in some variation of generality-example-practice. Acceptable variations include the use of a reference example simultaneous with or previous to the presentation of the generality.

3. *Primary Presentation Form Isolation.* The primary presentation forms for a given segment of instruction should be identified and isolated in such a way that a student can easily locate, skip, or review any given form.

4. *Learner Control.* The student should be encouraged to alter his or her primary presentation form sequence by returning at will to previously presented forms after having studied subsequent displays. The student might return to the generality after studying an example or practice display, skip to a practice display before studying the generality, etc.

5. *Generality Representation.* The generality should be restated, represented in other than verbal form, and/or elaborated via a mnemonic or an algorithm.

6. *Mathemagenic Information.* Example displays should be elaborated via mathemagenic information prompting (such as underlining, bold print, color, exploded diagrams, or other kinds of attention-focusing devices) and more than one form of representation (e.g., a verbal description and a visual representation). Practice displays should include mathemagenic information on feedback, in addition to correct answer or right/wrong knowledge of results.

7. *Attribute Matching.* Example displays should include matched non-examples (i.e., non-examples that are as similar as possible to, and are presented simultaneously with, the examples that are provided). Practice displays should be randomly sequenced and unmatched to non-examples.

8. *Instance Sampling.* Instances in both example and practice displays should be divergent, range in difficulty, be presented in an easy-to-difficult sequence, and/or include a variety of representation forms.

Elaboration Theory

Elaboration Theory (Reigeluth, 1979; Reigeluth, Merrill, Wilson, & Spiller, 1980; Reigeluth & Stein, in press) was developed to integrate knowledge about instruction on the macro level (aspects of instruction that relate to more than one idea). This includes such considerations as the *selection* of the content to be taught, the *sequencing* of that content, the delineation of important *relationships* among the content ideas, and the systematic *review* of the ideas (Reigeluth & Stein, in press).

Elaboration Theory argues that: (1) structural relationships in content should be explicitly taught and tested, resulting in more meaningful, stable learning, and (2) the instructional sequence should be organized around these relationships, following an "elaboration approach" (Merrill, Kowallis, & Wilson, 1981).

Elaboration Theory prescribes one of three models based on the goals of the instruction. Each model is made up of the same seven major *strategy components* (Reigeluth & Stein, in press): (1) a special type of general-to-detailed sequence for the main structure of the course, (2) a learning-prerequisite sequence within individual lessons of the course, (3) a summarizer at the end of each lesson, (4) a synthesizer at the end of each lesson, (5) analogies where appropriate, (6) cognitive strategy activators where appropriate, and (7) a learner control format. Although these seven strategy components are present in all three models, some of their characteristics vary from one model to another. Each model provides a "blueprint" or description of what the instruction should be like for any piece of instruction.

The most fundamental aspect of Elaboration Theory is its prescription of an *elaborative sequence* for instruction. The instruction should start with the most general or simple ideas that are to be taught and should gradually elaborate on those fundamental ideas by adding layers of detail or complexity, one layer at a time. However, it is important to note that the simple or general ideas do not summarize the course content—rather, they *epitomize* the course content; that is, they are but a *few* ideas which are taught at the *application* level rather than many ideas that are lightly touched on at the remember level.

Another important aspect of an elaborative sequence is that it entails elaborating on a *single type of content relationship* (either conceptual, procedural, or theoretical—hence the three models, one for each type of relationship). The rationale is that elaborating on a *single* type of relationship will result in the student's development of more stable cognitive structures, which in turn should cause better long-term retention and transfer.

The elaborative sequence based on a single type of content relationship provides the "skeleton" or basic structure of the textbook, and the other two types of content are nested within relevant parts of the skeleton. For more information, see Reigeluth (1979, 1980), Reigeluth, Merrill, Wilson, & Spiller (1980), Reigeluth & Rodgers (1980), and Reigeluth & Stein (in press).

A Procedure for Designing and Developing
Textbooks Using Elaboration Theory

The procedure to design and develop effective, efficient, and appealing instructional materials according to Elaboration Theory (including its subset, Component Display Theory) varies in important ways, depending on which of the three organizations is chosen: conceptual, procedural, or theoretical. Nevertheless, all three procedures can still be characterized by seven general steps. More detailed variations are described elsewhere (as referenced below).

Using the seven-step procedure which is presented in this section will result in the determination of (1) what ideas should be taught in order to achieve the course goals, (2) how those ideas should be sequenced, synthesized, and systematically reviewed, and (3) what micro strategy components should be used to optimize learning for each idea. The third aspect reflects the Component Display Theory knowledge base that has been incorporated into Elaboration Theory's design and development procedure.

This seven-step procedure is intended for use in a team approach to textbook writing. The major members of the team are (1) a *teacher* who has several years of experience in teaching the subject matter of the textbook, and (2) an instructional *designer* who is experienced in using the seven-step procedure. Additionally, the team might include (3) a practicing expert in the subject matter to be taught, (4) an art/graphics expert, (5) a subject matter assistant, and (6) an editor. Naturally, these people will not all work the same amount of time on the project. Designer time seldom runs much more than a quarter of teacher (or SME) time; and the subject matter assistant (who is less expensive than the experienced teacher) can cost-effectively work up to two or three times as long as the experienced teacher during the writing of the textbook. Hence, a typical project might hire a full-time designer, a full-time experienced teacher, two or three subject matter assistants (development phase only), a half-time practicing expert in the subject matter (design phase only), and part-time art/graphics and editing people (early production phase only).

The seven-step procedure described below fits neatly into typical instructional development models. It describes the content analysis, methods selection, and development phases of such models. Assuming that the experienced teacher has indeed taught the desired subject matter to a representative sample of the target student population, then the data that would need to be collected during the learner analysis phase of most ID models will already be available in the experienced teacher's head and can be accessed by the designer as they are needed. Similar data for needs/goals would also be available. However, if such an experienced person is not available, then standard needs/goals analysis (see, e.g., Kaufman, 1972) and learner analysis (see, e.g., Davis, Alexander, & Yelon, 1974) should be performed prior to this seven-step procedure. Finally, it is always wise to conduct a formative evaluation and revision upon completion of this procedure, even though the firm foundation of the procedure in validated principles of instruction should greatly reduce the need for revision.

The seven-step procedure for designing and developing a textbook according to Elaboration Theory is summarized in Figure 4.1. Each of these steps is described in detail below.

1. Select and Sequence the Organizing Content Ideas.

There are three parts to this step:

1.1 Select the Kinds of Organizing Content Ideas.

This step requires the designer to help the experienced teacher to pick, based on the goals of the instruction, one of the three major ways of organizing the subject matter that is to be taught: a conceptual organization, a procedural organization, or a theoretical organization. This simply entails checking to see whether, on the basis of the general purpose of instruction, the emphasis should be on learning (a) concepts, which represent the "what" of any subject matter, (b) procedures, which describe the "how to" of any subject matter, and (c) principles, which represent the "why" (e.g., causes and effects) of any subject matter.

A concept is a set of objects, events, or ideas that share certain characteristics. A principle is a change relationship, usually a

---

Design and Development Procedure

1. *Select and sequence the organizing content ideas.*
    1.1 Select the kinds of organizing content ideas.
    1.2 List all of the important organizing content ideas.
    1.3 Arrange the organizing content ideas into an elaborative sequence and group into chapters.
    1.4 Allocate organizing content to chapters.

2. *Select the supporting content for each chapter, and sequence all content within each chapter.*
    2.1 List all of the important supporting content ideas for each chapter.
    2.2 Sequence both the organizing and supporting content within each chapter.

3. *Select strategies for relating new knowledge to prior student knowledge.*
    3.1 Decide what within-chapter synthesizers to include and where.
    3.2 Decide what cumulative synthesizers to include and where.
    3.3 Decide what student experiences can be used as instances.
    3.4 Decide what analogies to include and where.
    3.5 Decide what motivational components to include and where.

4. *Select the review strategies.*
    4.1 Decide which content ideas should be included in the within-chapter reviews.
    4.2 Decide where to put cumulative reviews and what to put in them.

5. *Select micro strategies for each idea.*
    5.1 Select the appropriate micro model for each idea or fact.
    5.2 Decide on the appropriate level of richness for that model.
    5.3 Write the test items and the primary and secondary strategy components for each idea.

6. *Write the remaining strategy components.*
    6.1 Write the integrative test items.
    6.2 Write the synthesizers.
    6.3 Write the reviews.
    6.4 Write the analogies.
    6.5 Write any remaining motivational components.

7. *Decide how to format all of the instruction.*
    7.1 Separate and label all ideas and strategy components.
    7.2 Format other aspects of the instruction.

Figure 4.1. A procedure for developing a textbook so as to implement the elaboration theory and the component display theory.

cause-and-effect relationship. And a procedure (or technique, method, skill) is an ordered set of actions for achieving a predetermined goal. So, in this step, to make the decision as to which type of organizing content ideas to use, the purpose of the course must be classified as to whether its emphasis is primarily on understanding the "whats" (i.e., the concepts), the "whys" (i.e., the principles), or the "hows" (i.e., the procedures) of the subject matter area.

To the best of our knowledge, *all* subjects include all three types of content, and therefore *all* subjects can have an elaborative sequence that is based on *any* of these three content types. For instance, the goals of a course in English Composition might emphasize knowing concepts: different kinds of compositions and the various parts of compositions (important elements which make up a good composition). Or, they might emphasize knowing procedures: how to write good composition. Or, they might emphasize knowing principles: ways in which certain factors influence the effects or quality of a composition. It is difficult to conceive of a course that is concerned with only one of these three types of knowledge. However, even when all three types of content are important, the goals of the course usually provide sufficient basis for identifying one type of content which should receive primary emphasis. Once one of the three types of content has been selected as most important, then that type (concepts, principles, or procedures) becomes the "organizing content" whose elaborative sequencing provides the "skeleton" of the textbook. The other two types of content are then added in to "embellish" the skeleton wherever they are necessary and appropriate. Due to their supporting role, they are referred to as "supporting content."

This step is an extension of, and is based on, goal analysis.

1.2 List All of the Important Organizing Content Ideas.

This step requires a teacher (possibly with a subject matter expert's help) to identify and list all of the organizing content (either concepts, procedures, or principles) that the student needs to learn. To be able to get effective outcomes from this step, the teacher should be made explicitly aware that the particular type of organizing content that was selected in Step 1.1 has structure (i.e., interrelationships). For the *conceptual organization,* the teacher should be aware of the notion of super/co/subordinate relationships among concepts and the notions of "parts" and "kinds" varieties of those relationships. The teacher should develop those structures to make sure that no important concepts have been overlooked. Also, those structures will be considered in a later step for possible use in teaching those relationships. For the *procedural organization,* the teacher should be aware of the notions of procedural prerequisite relationships and procedural decision relationships. The teacher should make sure that no important steps or branches (in those structures) have been overlooked. For the *theoretical organization,* the teacher should make sure that no important causal relationships have been overlooked. These kinds of relationships are described in more detail in Reigeluth, Merrill, & Bunderson (1978); Reigeluth, Merrill, Wilson, & Spiller (1980); and Reigeluth & Stein (in press).

For a general illustration of the results of this step, see Figure 4.2. This step is a form of task or content analysis and description.

Ideas: A, B, C, D, E, F, G, H, I, J, K, L, M, N, O, P, Q, R, S, T, U, V, W, X, Y, Z.

Figure 4.2. Results of step 1.2. Each letter represents a different organizing content idea, such that for a theoretical organization each letter represents a specific principle which should be taught in order to achieve the course goals.

1.3 Arrange the Organizing Content Ideas into an Elaborative Sequence and Group into Chapters.

This step prescribes that the organizing content be systematically analyzed to determine which aspect(s) of it will be presented in the first chapter and which aspects will be presented in subsequent levels of detail. The first chapter should *epitomize* all the organizing content—that is, it should represent the most general, simple, and/or fundamental aspects of all the organizing content.

For example, for a theoretical organization, this step requires identifying the most important, fundamental principle (or two) from the theoretical content that is to be taught. To identify this principle, there are two rules of thumb. One is to ask the teacher to decide which principle he or she would teach if *only one* could be taught. The other is to have the teacher arrange the principles in the chronological order in which they were discovered, historically. If this one principle is as much as a student can learn at the application level in one chapter (including all supporting content for that principle—which has not been identified yet), then all other principles should be presented in later chapters (i.e., elaborations).

In order to allocate the remaining organizing content to later chapters, the teacher should decide (with the help of the subject matter expert), what is the next most general, simple, and/or fundamental aspects of all the organizing content. For example, for a theoretical organization, the teacher (with the help of the subject matter expert) would identify the next most important principle (or two). Again, the two rules of thumb are helpful: ask the teacher which of the remaining principles he or she would teach if only one more could be included, or identify which principle was discovered next, historically.

This sequencing procedure is continued until all the organizing content has been allocated to chapters. The sequencing procedure is a bit different for the other two organizations: procedural and conceptual. For detailed descriptions of each, see Reigeluth & Rodgers (1980) and Reigeluth & Darwazeh (1981), respectively.

The result of this step is the design of the "skeleton" of the instruction, which was developed on the basis of epitomizing and elaborating on a single type of content (see Figure 4.3 for a pseudo-example). Carefully following this process arranges the organizing content ideas into an elaborative sequence.

1.4 Allocate Organizing Content to Chapters.

This step helps the teacher and the instructional designer to allocate material to chapters. To do this, there are three considerations: (a) sequence considerations, (b) grouping considerations, and (c) size considerations.

Level	Organizing Content Ideas	
0	G, M	(most general/simple)
1	C, D, F, . . . X, Z	
2	A, B, . . . S, U	
3	E, H, K, . . . W, Y	(most detailed, complex)

Figure 4.3. Results of step 1.3. For a theoretical organization, G and M would represent such fundamental/simple principles as the law of supply and demand in economics and Ohm's law in electronics.

Sequence considerations prescribe that instructional material should be organized in levels that elaborate on each other. General or simple material should always be presented before detailed or complex materials. Sequencing within each level is based on how *facilitative* and *familiar* the material is: ideas which contribute most to understanding the organizing content should be presented first, and ideas which are more familiar should precede not-so-familiar material.

Relatedness is an important factor for *grouping considerations,* which prescribe that those ideas which are most closely related to each other should be presented together.

Size considerations depend mostly on the optimal frequency of synthesis and review. For example, if a chapter is too large, then it will be difficult for the students to remember the material in the end-of-chapter review, and it will be difficult for them to interrelate the material in the end-of-chapter synthesizer. The optimal size is likely to vary depending on the difficulty level of the content and the ability level and related experiences of the

Chapter	1	2	3	. . . .	19	20
Organizing Content Ideas	G, M	F, T, X	C, N		E, W	H, K, Y

Figure 4.4. Results of step 1.4.

students. The number of organizing content ideas and the amount of supporting content per organizing content idea can both be varied to adjust the size of the chapter. Chapter size can always be adjusted up or down later, if necessary, but such will increase the length and expense of the development effort. Hence, estimation of optimal size should be as accurate as possible at this point. Figure 4.4 illustrates the nature of the results of this step. This step is a part of the design process, and more specifically is a part of sequence design.

2. Select the Supporting Content for Each Chapter, and Sequence All Content Within Each Chapter.

2.1 List All of the Important Supporting Content Ideas for Each Chapter.

This step embellishes the "skeleton" by adding other types of content which are important for achieving the course's goals. *Supporting content* is material that is highly related to the organizing content. It includes: (1) the other three kinds of content (e.g., concepts, procedures, and facts when principles are the organizing content) and (2) the learning prerequisites for all other content selected.

Conceptual supporting content specifies useful super/co/subordinate contextual knowledge that relates to the organizing content; *procedural supporting content* specifies useful procedural knowledge that relates to the organizing content; and *theoretical supporting content* specifies explanatory underlying processes or useful change relationships that are related to the organizing content (Reigeluth & Merrill, 1979; Reigeluth, Merrill, Wilson, & Spiller, 1980).

Conceptual organizations are often supported by (additional) conceptual supporting content; procedural organizations are often supported by conceptual supporting content (concept classification is an important part of most procedures—hence the usefulness of showing coordinate relationships and sometimes even super/ subordinate relationships); and theoretical organizations are often supported both by procedural supporting content (to teach an efficient way to implement a principle) and by conceptual supporting content. Therefore, except for conceptual structures, an organization structure will usually not have the same kind of supporting structure.

For each chapter, you should identify all the important supporting content for its organizing content, including all unmastered learning prerequisites for both organizing and supporting content. Do not include any supporting content unless it is necessary for, or otherwise highly related to, that chapter's organizing content, because supporting content should be added onto the "skeleton" at the *latest* appropriate point in the instruction. The process of embedding the supporting content (including learning prerequisites) into appropriate parts of the skeleton is called "nesting." For more details, see Reigeluth, Merrill, Wilson, & Spiller (1980) and Reigeluth & Stein (in press).

Typical results of this step are indicated in Figure 4.5. This step contains elements of both content analysis and instructional sequencing.

2.2 Sequence Both the Organizing and Supporting Content Within Each Chapter.

After *all* (both organizing and supporting) content has been allocated to the different chapters, this step requires establishing the best sequence of that content within each chapter. Specific guidelines for this include: (1) present a learning prerequisite immediately before the idea for which it is a prerequisite, unless several prerequisites are highly related, in which case they should

Chapter	1	2	3	. . .	19	20
Organizing Content Ideas	G, M	F, T, X	C, N	. . .	E, W	H, K, Y
Supporting Content Ideas	B_G...R_G D_M...Y_M	H_F...P_F A_T...N_T H_X...R_X	C_C...J_C F_N...M_N	. . .	B_E...Q_E D_W...T_W	A_H...Z_H C_K...Y_K E_Y...U_Y

Figure 4.5. Results of step 2.1. For a theoretical organization, each supporting content idea (e.g., B_G) could be a concept, a procedure, or a fact (such as the concept "supply" for the law of supply and demand).

all be presented together before their organizing ideas; (2) present non-prerequisite supporting content immediately after its organizing content, unless it is highly related to supporting content of other organizing content ideas, in which case those supporting content ideas should be presented together after all of their organizing content ideas; (3) present meaningful knowledge (e.g., a principle) before related procedural knowledge (Mayer, 1975); (4) present coordinate concepts together (in a group); and (5) rely on the teacher's intuition and experience. This is basically a sequence design step, and typical results are indicated by Figure 4.6.

3. Select Strategies for Relating New Knowledge to Prior Student Knowledge.

This step identifies ways of making new knowledge meaningful by relating new knowledge to related ideas that the student has

Chapter	Sequence of organizing and supporting content
1	B_G, F_G, H_G, G, R_G, D_M, J_M, K_M, L_M, M, T_M, Y_M
2	H_F, J_F, K_F, N_F, F, P_F, A_T, D_T, G_T, T, N_T, H_X, I_X, L_X, X, R_X
3	C_C, E_C, C, H_C, J_C, F_N, I_N, L_N, N
. . .	
19	B_E, E_E, G_E, E, K_E, Q_E, D_W, E_W, W, T_W
20	A_H, C_H, H, Z_H, C_K, D_K, E_K, K, M_K, Y_K, E_Y, F_Y, J_Y, Y, U_Y

Figure 4.6. Results of step 2.2.

already learned. Selecting the most appropriate anchorage for each kind of new knowledge (concepts, principles, or procedures) to facilitate meaningful learning is a crucial part of this step. See Reigeluth (1980) for details.

3.1 Decide What Within-Chapter Synthesizers to Include and Where.

This substep requires an instructional design expert and a teacher to decide what relationships among ideas should be taught and when. Relationships among organizing content ideas are almost always taught. For conceptual content, they take the form of kinds and parts relationships (superordinate, coordinate, and subordinate). For procedural content, they take the form of order relationships (i.e., the order in which steps should be performed) and decision criteria (i.e., the bases for deciding which steps to use). And for theoretical relationships, they take the form of branching (multivariate) chains of causes and effects. Relationships among these three kinds of content should also usually be explicitly taught (in addition to the within-kind relationships mentioned above). For more information about these kinds of relationships and how they can be explicitly taught, see Reigeluth, Merrill, & Bunderson (1978) and Reigeluth & Stein (in press).

3.2 Decide What Cumulative Synthesizers to Include and Where.
The execution of this step is quite similar to that for the within-chapter synthesizers (Step 3.1), except that cumulative synthesizers should relate chapter specific information to ideas from other chapters. The purpose of this step is to facilitate more meaningful learning by showing context and other relationships for new ideas. This step satisfies the condition for making new knowledge meaningful by relating it to other knowledge still within the immediate content area.

3.3 Decide What Student Experiences Can Be Used as Instances.
This step requires an experienced teacher to decide what familiar instances should be presented for each idea. *Familiar instances* are defined as instances (of new content ideas) that relate to students' previous experiences. Thus, this step requires enough knowledge about the backgrounds and previous experiences of the target population of learners for the teacher to be able to identify such instances for the content being taught. Familiar instances make it easier for the learners to learn how a generality applies to instances, and they also increase retention because they provide strong, meaningful anchorage for the new knowledge (Reigeluth, 1980). Typical results of this step are illustrated in Figure 4.7.

3.4 Decide What Analogies to Include and Where.
This step requires an instructional design expert and a teacher to (1) determine when it is useful to relate new knowledge to closely-related prior knowledge that is *outside* of the subject matter content of the course, and (2) find useful analogies,

Chapter	1	2	3	...	19	20
Organizing Content Ideas	G, M	F, T, X	C, N	...	E, W	H, K, Y
Supporting Content Ideas	$B_G, \ldots R_G$ $D_M, \ldots T_M$	$H_F, \ldots P_F$ $A_T, \ldots N_T$ $H_X, \ldots R_X$	$C_C, \ldots J_C$ $F_N, \ldots M_N$	...	$B_E, \ldots Q_E$ $D_W, \ldots T_W$	$A_H, \ldots Z_H$ $C_K, \ldots Y_K$ $E_Y, \ldots U_Y$
Within-Chapter Synthesizers	S_{1GM} S_{2GM}	S_{1FT}, S_{1XT} S_{2FTX}	S_{1CN}, S_{1NC} S_{2CN}	...	S_{1EW} S_{2EW}	S_{1HK} S_{2HK}, S_{2HKY} S_{3HKY}
Cumulative Synthesizers	S_{1GM}	S_{1FMG} S_{2FTGM} S_{3FTXM} S_{4FTXGM}	S_{1NX} S_{2CNX}	...	S_{1ENX} S_{2EN} S_{3WN}	S_{1YN} S_{2YKC} S_{3YWM}
Student Experiences	E_{1G}, E_{1M} E_{2M}	E_{1F}, E_{1T}, E_{1X} E_{2T}, E_{2X}	E_{1C}, E_{1N} E_{2N}	...	E_{1E}, E_{1W} E_{2E}	E_{1H}, E_{1K}, E_{1Y} $E_{,2Y}$
Analogies	A_{1G}		A_{1N}		A_{1E} A_{2E}	

Figure 4.7. Results of steps 3.1, 3.2, 3.3, and 3.4.

identify optimum ways to present or activate them, and sequence them well within each chapter. A good familiarity with the learners' backgrounds helps the attainment of this step greatly, because it facilitates selection of the most appropriate analogies for the learners, based on their previous experiences. For more about the use of analogies in the design of instruction, see Reigeluth (1980) and Reigeluth & Stein (in press).

3.5 Decide What Motivational Components to Include and Where.

This step requires the teacher to (a) identify likely motivational problems for the target student population and (b) select appropriate strategies for solving each of those problems. Keller (in press) has identified four major categories of motivational problems: (1) *interest,* which refers to whether the learner's curiosity is aroused and whether this arousal is sustained appropriately over time; (2) *relevance,* which refers to whether the learner perceives the instruction to satisfy personal needs or to help achieve personal goals; (3) *expectancy,* which refers to the learner's perceived likelihood of success and the extent to which he or she perceives success as being under his or her control, and (4) *satisfaction,* which refers to the learner's intrinsic motivations and his or her reactions to extrinsic rewards. Keller (in press) has also described a number of strategies that can be used to overcome each of these four types of motivational problems. The instructional designer should help the teacher to select the most appropriate of these or other alternative strategies.

4. Select the Review Strategies.

Elaboration Theory prescribes that instruction should have two types of systematic review: a *within-chapter review,* which summarizes all the ideas and facts presented within a single chapter, and a *cumulative review,* which summarizes the most important ideas and facts that have been presented in all chapters studied so far. Both kinds of summarizers are comprised of a concise statement of the generality, a reference example (i.e., a typical, easy-to-remember example), and diagnostic self-test practice (which is never used for assessment purposes and is always accompanied by immediate feedback) for each idea presented in the chapter.

4.1 Decide Which Content Ideas Should Be Included in the Within-Chapter Reviews.

This step requires that an instructional design expert, with the help of an experienced teacher, identify which supporting content ideas should be included with the organizing content ideas in the within-chapter review section. All organizing content should be included, but usually it is not necessary to include all supporting content. Learning prerequisites are the kind of supporting content that is usually omitted, because the behavior associated with them is incorporated into that of the ideas for which they are prerequisite. Within-chapter reviews precede within-chapter synthesizers in order to make them maximally beneficial.

4.2 Decide Where to Put Cumulative Reviews and What to Put in Them.
This step is to ensure that the organizing content and the most important supporting content are periodically and systematically reviewed throughout the course. The frequency of such reviews depends on the difficulty and novelty of the content in relation to the ability level of the students. Cumulative reviews also precede cumulative synthesizers in order to make such synthesizers maximally beneficial.

5. Select Micro Strategies for Each Idea.
After the "macro" design steps have all been followed (selection, sequencing, synthesizing, and summarizing), it is time to design and develop the equally important instructional components that actually *teach* each idea—the "micro" strategies. Micro strategies are strategies that relate to a single idea (e.g., a single concept, principle, or procedure) or fact. Micro strategies are the domain of Merrill's Component Display Theory (Merrill, in press). The Component Display Theory's procedure for evaluating textbooks is summarized in Merrill, Reigeluth, & Faust (1979) and is described in detail in the Instructional Strategy Diagnostic Profile Training Manual (Merrill, Richards, Schmidt, & Wood, 1977).

5.1 Select the Appropriate Micro Model for Each Idea or Fact.
This step first requires the design expert and a teacher to classify the desired level of performance for the idea or fact as one of the following: (1) *remember an instance,* at which the student is required to remember a specific case—either recall or recognition

and either verbatim or paraphrased—(2) *remember a generality*, at which the student is required to remember the statement of an idea—again either recall or recognition and either verbatim or paraphrased—and (3) *use a generality*, at which the student is required to apply a generality to "new" instances—either to identify new instances or to produce new instances.

The desired level of performance for the fact or idea determines which of the Component Display Theory's three instructional models is appropriate. (An instructional model is an integrated set of strategy components for a given type of learning outcome.) For example, the most common kind of objective—"applying a generality to new instances"—is at the use-a-generality level. For this level, the Component Display Theory prescribes a model that is comprised of three major strategy components: (1) a *generality*, such as the statement of a principle or the definition of a concept; (2) *instances* of the application of that generality, such as demonstrations of the principle or examples of the concept; and (3) *practice* in applying that generality to new instances, such as solving a new problem or classifying a new example of the concept. For an objective at a different level, other strategy components are required to optimize learning.

5.2 Decide on the Appropriate Level of Richness for that Model.

This step requires an experienced teacher to decide on the appropriate level of richness for that model. This depends on the difficulty of learning the fact or idea (at the desired level of performance), given the students' general ability level and prior knowledge. In order to increase the richness for each model, the number of instances and practice items can be increased. Also, each of the major strategy components (e.g., the generality or the instances) can be embellished with secondary strategy components. The richest version of any of these models would be appropriate either for a very complex idea or very slow (or low ability) learners, or both. But for an easy idea/objective in relation to student ability, the generality alone might be enough. In this case, the student will be able to relate the generality to instances already in his or her mind by himself or herself.

It is important to keep in mind that the "use-a-generality" model may actually be richer than the "remember-a-generality" or "remember-an-instance" model, but what we are concerned with is the level of richness for a model at a single performance level. The output of this step is illustrated in Figure 4.8.

5.3   Write   the   Test   Items   and   the   Primary   and   Secondary Strategy Components for Each Idea.

This step requires the experienced teacher to write the test items and the "primary" and "secondary" strategy components that have been prescribed (by the model and its richness as selected in Step 5.2) for each idea and fact in each chapter. The *primary strategy components* are generality, instance, generality practice, and instance practice. Practice offers learners the opportunity to solve a problem and then to find out how they did on it. It is identical to an instance except that the student is now shown how it is done until he or she has tried to do it. *Secondary strategy components* include feedback, isolation, mnemonic aids, attention-focusing devices, algorithms, progression of difficulty, alternative representation forms, and more. For example, for a "remember-a-generality" level objective, the generality (a primary strategy component) can be presented along with a mnemonic device and an alternative representation form (both are secondary strategy components). Also, asking the generality in different ways (another secondary strategy component) will facilitate generality remembering (as long as verbatim recall is not required). Mnemonic devices should also be present whenever the memory load is heavy and are often included in examples and practice feedback, as well as in generalities. See Merrill (in press) and Merrill, Richards, Schmidt, & Wood (1977) for further information. See Figure 4.9 for a sample output from this step.

6. Write the Remaining Strategy Components.

This step is designed to help write the remaining instructional components. They are: integrative test items, synthesizers, reviews, analogies, and motivational components.

Chapter	1
Organizing Content Ideas	G, M
Supporting Content Ideas	$B_G, \ldots R_G$ $D_M, \ldots Y_M$
Appropriate Micro Model	Generality_G, Generality_M Instance_G, Instance_M Practice_G, Practice_M
Richness	Gen_G Generality_M I_{1G}, I_{2G}, I_{3G} I_{1M}, I_{2M}, I_{3M} P_{1G}, P_{2G}, P_{3G} P_{1M}, P_{2M}, P_{3M}

Figure 4.8. Results of steps 5.1 and 5.2. G, M organizing content ideas are supposed to be taught at use-a-generality level.

Chapter	1
Organizing Content	G, M
Primary Strategy Components	Generality_G Instance_G Practice_G
Secondary Strategy Components	$\text{Gen}_{G1}, \text{Gen}_{G2}$ $\text{Ins}_{1G}, \text{Ins}_{2G}, \text{Ins}_{3G}, \text{Ins}_{4G}, \text{(easy)}, I_{5G}, \text{(difficult)}$ $\text{Practice}_{1G}, \text{Practice}_{2G}, \text{Practice}_{3G}, \text{Practice}_{4G}, \text{Practice}_{5G}$ $\text{Feedback}_{1G}, \text{Feedback}_{2G}, \text{Feedback}_{3G}, \text{Feedback}_{4G}, \text{Feedback}_{5G}$ $\text{Practice}_{1I}, \text{Practice}_{2I}, \text{Practice}_{3I}, \ldots$ $\text{Feedback}_{1I}, \text{Feedback}_{2I}, \text{Feedback}_{3I}, \ldots$

Figure 4.9. Results of step 5.3.

6.1 Write the Integrative Test Items.

Testing should occur at the level of relationships among ideas as well as at the level of individual ideas. The relationships among specific organizing content ideas are particularly important to test.

6.2 Write the Synthesizers.

The synthesizers are written according to the specifications from Steps 3.1 and 3.2. The generality is one or more subject matter structures (Reigeluth, Merrill, & Bunderson, 1978; Reigeluth & Stein, in press) plus any explanation that facilitates understanding those structures. The instance is an integrative instance that illustrates the relationship among the ideas. And the practice is diagnostic, as self-test items which allow the student to find out whether he or she understands the relationship among the ideas.

6.3 Write the Reviews.

Have the teacher write a concise statement of the generality, a reference example for the generality, and a few self-test practice items for each idea in each chapter according to the specifications in Step 4.

6.4 Write the Analogies.

The teacher should write all analogies according to the specifications prepared in Step 3.4.

6.5 Write Any Remaining Motivational Components.

The teacher should write all motivational strategy components that have not yet been written as parts of other strategy components. In some cases, it may be necessary to modify or add to previously written components in order to implement a given motivational strategy component.

7. Decide How to Format All of the Instruction.

One purpose of formatting is to make a textbook more *attractive* and more *communicative.* Principles of message design are relevant here. Another purpose is to make explicit for the student what the *important content* is to be learned versus what is primarily elaborative, motivational, or simply "nice to know" material. A third purpose of formatting is to facilitate *learner control* (Merrill, 1979), which allows individualization of the instruction based on learner differences. Learner control is a strategy whereby learners skip over some strategy components, refer back to earlier strategy components, and/or simply study the various strategy components in a different order. For example, a brighter student might look at a generality, think "I understand that!," and go to a hard practice item to test himself or herself. On the other hand, a slower student might spend considerable time looking at examples after studying a generality. Then he or she might look at the generality again before any practice items.

7.1 Separate and Label All Ideas and Strategy Components.

In order for a student to be able to exercise learner control easily and efficiently, each strategy component must be: (1) separated from other strategy components and other kinds of displays and (2) labeled for the student so that there is no ambiguity as to what is the main idea and what is illustration, elaboration, or clarification. For example, generalities should be labeled as such and should be separated from say, examples; practice should be labeled as such and should be separated from generalities and examples; review and feedback components should be labeled and separated, synthesis components and analogies should be separated and labeled, etc. With such separation and labeling of strategy components, brighter students will be able to skip over examples and secondary strategy components more easily and without fear of having missed something important; and slower students will find it easier to refer back to generalities, reviews, and synthesizers to compensate for the extra time they find they need to spend on examples, practice, and secondary strategy components.

Proper student use of learner control formatting requires some brief student training in (1) the nature of each strategy component, and (2) the way in which each component helps the student to learn (i.e., to overcome a different kind of learning problem).

With such knowledge, the student is well equipped to pick and choose from the "menu" of strategy components to make his or her own optimal, individualized instructional design. Here, to accommodate individual differences, *learner control over the selection of different strategy components,* rather than having different "tracks" for different types of students, is being advocated. This can be supported by two reasons; even if research shows that a certain strategy is always best for a certain type of student, (1) if the student characteristics cannot be changed—such as certain kinds of aptitude—it is important for the student to learn which strategies are best for him or her, and (2) if the student characteristics can be changed—such as poor learning strategy—it is much more important to improve that shortcoming than to provide an instructional strategy (or method) that minimizes it. For example, rather than designing "visual" instruction for some students and "verbal" instruction for others, make both representations available to all students, along with some knowledge about how to pick and choose, rather than studying everything. It is also likely that the vast majority of students are not strictly verbal or strictly visual and can therefore benefit from having both available.

7.2 Format Other Aspects of the Instruction.

This is done primarily on the basis of principles of message design. Separation and labeling of all major strategy components should be implemented, and their sequence or arrangement with respect to each other should also be designed according to principles of message design. Finally, the internal formatting of each individual component should also be done.

Motivational, clear, and easy-to-produce layout is always essential for easy, meaningful learning and good retention. No matter how instructionally useful each idea is and no matter how well-organized those instructional ideas are, they might not serve their function if they are not presented to the learner in the best possible format.

A Procedure for Evaluating Textbooks
Using Elaboration Theory

1. Analyze the Organizing Content:
Its Selection and Its Chapter-Level Sequencing.

1.1 Select the Kind of Organizing Content.
This step prescribes evaluating the selection of an "organization" on the basis of the goals or purpose of the instruction. It is a means to check whether or not the requirements for design/development Step 1.1 have been satisfied.

1.2 Identify the Most Important Organizing Content Ideas.
This step entails listing all important organizing content ideas that are presently discussed in the textbook.

1.3 Is All Important Organizing Content Included?
This step requires a subject matter expert and an experienced teacher to decide whether or not *all* of the important organizing content ideas listed in Step 1.2 (either concepts, principles, or procedures) have been included in the text. A subject matter expert is needed to prioritize the important organizing content ideas, and an experienced teacher (for the target population of students) is needed to identify, in consideration of time limitations for the course, a reasonable cut-off point for that prioritized list. The cut-off point is based primarily on the ability level of the students (e.g., average high school juniors) and the length of the course (e.g., one-hour meetings three times a week for 32 weeks).

1.4 Elaborative Sequence of Organizing Content and Good Chapter Allocation?
This step requires the design expert, with the help of a subject matter expert or an experienced teacher, to decide whether or not the chapters are sequenced in an elaborative way with respect to the organizing content and whether the organizing content is appropriately allocated to chapters. The resulting content distribution should satisfy sequence, grouping, and size considerations as described in design/development Step 1.4.

2. Analyze Both the Organizing and Supporting Content:
Its Within-Chapter Selection and Sequencing.

2.1 No Inappropriate Organizing Content Included?
This step requires a subject matter expert or experienced teacher, by referring back to the prioritized list of organizing content ideas and its cut-off point, to decide whether or not any inappropriate organizing content has been included within each chapter.

2.2 All Important Supporting Content Included?
This step requires an experienced teacher to decide whether or not *all* of the important supporting content ideas have been included within the same chapter as the organizing content ideas which they support.

2.3 No Inappropriate Supporting Content Included?
This step requires an experienced teacher to decide whether or not any inappropriate or unimportant supporting content has been included in any chapters. This decision will depend primarily on the degree of importance and the degree of relevance of the supporting content to the organizing content.

2.4 Organizing and Supporting Content Sequenced Well?
This step requires an instructional design expert and an experienced teacher to decide whether or not the organizing content ideas and supporting content ideas are grouped appropriately, according to the guidelines in Step 2.2 of the design/development procedure.

3. Analyze the Strategies for Relating New Knowledge
to Prior Student Knowledge.

3.1 Sufficient Within-Chapter Synthesis?
This step requires a design expert and a subject matter expert to determine for each chapter whether or not there is sufficient synthesis of the within-chapter content. This tells whether or not

important relationships among ideas are explicitly taught and appropriately located.

3.2 Sufficient Cumulative Synthesis?

This step requires the design expert and a subject matter expert to determine whether or not there is sufficient explicit teaching of relationships between content in one chapter and content in earlier chapters. They should also determine whether the location of such synthesizers is appropriate. Such explicit synthesis is likely to come at the end of a chapter or at the end of a unit.

3.3 Sufficient Familiar Instances?

This step requires an experienced teacher to determine whether or not there are sufficient familiar instances within each chapter. Familiar instances are examples of a concept, applications of a principle, or performance of a procedure that are closely related to the previous experience of the learner. Using familiar instances facilitates learning and increases motivation.

3.4 Sufficient Analogies?

Analogies relate new knowledge to closely-related knowledge that the student has already acquired *outside* of the subject matter content of the course. This step requires the design expert and a subject matter expert or teacher to determine whether or not sufficient analogies have been presented within each chapter.

3.5 Sufficient Motivational Components?

This step requires the design expert and teacher to determine whether or not sufficient motivational components are built into each chapter, based on the types of motivational problems that the teacher anticipates for the chapter content and the target student population (see Step 3.5 of the design/development procedure). Also, you should determine whether or not their locations are appropriate.

4. Analyze the Review Strategies.

4.1 Sufficient Within-Chapter Review?
This step requires an experienced teacher to analyze the chapter summaries to determine whether or not sufficient within-chapter review is provided.

4.2 Sufficient Cumulative Review?
This step requires an experienced teacher to analyze the unit summaries to determine whether or not sufficient cumulative review is provided.

5. Analyze the Micro Strategies for Each Idea.

5.1 Select the Appropriate Micro Model for Each Idea or Fact.
This step entails determining the appropriate micro model for each idea that is to be taught.

5.2 Select the Appropriate Richness for Each Model.
This step prescribes deciding on the appropriate richness for each model, on the basis of the difficulty of the idea that is to be taught in relation to student ability and experience.

5.3 Test Items and Primary and Secondary Strategy Components Appropriate?
This step entails determining whether or not the test items are appropriate and whether or not the optimal primary and secondary strategy components are presented in the textbook for each idea to be taught.

6. Analyze Integrative Test Items, Synthesizers, Reviews, Analogies, and Motivational Components.
This step checks to see whether or not integrative test items, synthesizers, reviews, analogies, and motivational components are all well-designed and written. Clarity and conciseness are important considerations (see design/development Step 6 for details).

7. Analyze the Formatting of All Strategy Components Analyzed Above.

7.1 Are the Ideas and Strategy Components Separated and Labeled?

This step requires a design expert to decide how well the strategy components are separated and labeled so as to facilitate learner control.

7.2 Are Other Aspects of the Formatting Appropriate?

This step requires a design expert to decide how attractive and communicative the page layout is.

A Procedure for Revising Textbooks Using Elaboration Theory

In addition to originating new text and evaluating existing text for instructional quality, instructional design theory can also be used as a basis for modifying and correcting instructionally problematic text. The following revision procedure is only used after the Elaboration Theory's evaluation procedure has been used to diagnose design problems.

For instructional materials which are found to be highly problematic with regard to all or most of the evaluation criteria (of the evaluation procedure), the optimal revision procedure is to deal with those design problems in the order that they were identified by the evaluation procedure. The necessary revisions for each problem are made by using the corresponding step of the design/development procedure.

However, if the instructional materials need revision only with regard to a few criteria, then revision should be done by using isolated parts of the design/development procedure. In this case, it is still recommended to do the revisions in the order in which the evaluation steps are listed, because otherwise you may waste time revising something which ends up being deleted altogether. For each weakness revealed by the evaluation procedure, you should find the comparable design/development step and revise the material accordingly.

After the revision procedure has been completed, a final check is recommended. You should go through the evaluation profile (the results of the evaluation procedure) once more to make sure that you have not missed any important points to be revised. If you have missed any such points, go to the appropriate steps of the design/development procedure to make required revisions. When you are finished with this final check, the revision procedure is concluded.

Conclusion

Instructional theory is at best in its early adolescence at the present time. It is only very recently that investigators have begun to build individual strategy components into optimal models of instruction for different goals and different conditions (e.g., different kinds of students and different kinds of subject matter). Much work remains to be done before instructional theory will realize its potential contribution to improving textbooks. Using ideas such as those presented in this chapter is likely to yield as much useful information as formal research, but there is clearly a need for much of both. It is our hope that this chapter will contribute in some small way to encouraging both kinds of endeavors to improve our knowledge about how to write effective, efficient, and appealing textbooks.

References

Davis, R.H., Alexander, L.T., & Yelon, S.L. *Learning systems design.* New York: McGraw-Hill, 1974, 93-98, 184-191.

Dewey, J. Psychology and social practice. *The Psychological Review,* 1900, *7,* 105-124.

Kaufman, R.A. *Educational system planning.* Englewood Cliffs, NJ: Prentice-Hall, Inc., 1972.

Keller, J.M. Motivational design of instruction. In C.M. Reigeluth (Ed.), *Instructional design theories and models: An overview of their current status,* in press.

Mayer, R.E. Information processing variables in learning to solve problems. *Review of Educational Research,* 1975, *45,* 525-541.

Merrill, M.D. *Elaboration theory and cognitive theory.* Paper presented at the annual convention of the Association for Educational Communications and Technology, New Orleans, 1979.

Merrill, M.D. The component display theory. In C.M. Reigeluth (Ed.), *Instructional design theories and models: An overview of their current status,* in press.

Merrill, M.D., Kowallis, T., & Wilson, B.G. Instructional design in transition. In F. Farley (Ed.), *NSSE Yearbook,* Vol. 80. Chicago: University of Chicago Press, 1981.

Merrill, M.D., Reigeluth, C.M., & Faust, G.W. The instructional quality profile: A curriculum evaluation and design tool. In H.F. O'Neil, Jr., (Ed.), *Procedures for instructional systems development.* New York: Academic Press, 1979.

Merrill, M.D., Richards, R.E., Schmidt, R.V., & Wood, N.D. *The instructional strategy diagnostic profile training manual.* San Diego: Courseware, Inc., 1977.

O'Neil, H.F., Jr. (Ed.) *Learning strategies.* New York: Academic Press, 1978.

Reigeluth, C.M. (Ed.) In search of a better way to organize instruction: The elaboration theory. *Journal of Instructional Development,* 1979, *2*(3), 8-15.

Reigeluth, C.M. Meaningfulness and instruction: Relating what is being learned to what a student knows (Research Report No. 1). Syracuse: Instructional Design, Development, and Evaluation Program, Syracuse University, 1980.

Reigeluth, C.M. (Ed.) *Instructional design theories and models: An overview of their current status,* in press.

Reigeluth, C.M., & Darwazeh, A. The elaboration theory's procedure for designing instruction: A conceptual approach. *Journal of Instructional Development,* 1982, 5.

Reigeluth, C.M., & Merrill, M.D. Classes of instructional variables. *Educational Technology,* March 1979, 5-24.

Reigeluth, C.M., Merrill, M.D., & Bunderson, C.V. The structure of subject matter content and its instructional design implications. *Instructional Science,* 1978, 7, 107-126.

Reigeluth, C.M., Merrill, M.D., Wilson, B.G., & Spiller, R.T. The elaboration theory of instruction: A model for sequencing and synthesizing instruction. *Instructional Science,* 1980, *9,* 195-219.

Reigeluth, C.M., & Rodgers, C.A. The elaboration theory of instruction: Prescriptions for task analysis and design. *NSPI Journal,* 1980, 19(1), 16-26.

Reigeluth, C.M., & Stein, F.S. The elaboration theory of instruction. In C.M. Reigeluth (Ed.), *Instructional design theories and models: An overview of their current status,* in press.

Rosecky, M. Are teachers selective when using basal guidebooks? *The Reading Teacher,* 1978, *31*(4), 381-384.

Snelbecker, G.E. *Learning theory, instructional theory, and psychoeducational design.* New York: McGraw-Hill, 1974.

Yarger, G.P., & Mintz, S.L. A literature study related to the use of materials in the classroom. A project report prepared for USOE, National Diffusion Network, 1979.

5.

Brain Functions During Learning: Implications for Text Design

James D. Hand

During the past ten years much has been written about the brain as "the last frontier" for scientific investigation; and indeed the number of investigators in this area has, by some estimates, doubled within the past five years alone. The resultant reports of scientific studies have been summarized and popularized by educators and, at least in some instances, misinterpreted. This chapter will focus on reports from basic scientists in the areas of neurobiology, neurobiochemistry, and physiology. Implications are suggested for the use of this information in the design of textual materials. These implications are in many instances untested hypotheses; and the reader is free to draw separate, conflicting conclusions, with the only caveat being that the original research reports should be read prior to generating those hypotheses.

Applied research regarding brain function, learning, and memory in the classroom is just beginning in this country, although classroom results have been reported in European journals since the mid-1960's. While it is still too early to make hard and fast judgments, the *implications* of results of basic science studies seem clear enough. At the very least, research on textual design may be stimulated in new areas of investigation to confirm or deny the educational importance of the presented research.

This chapter is divided into seven sections: (1) short-term memory and its pitfalls; (2) long-term memory storage; (3) left-right brain functions and holographic memory; (4) the triune brain; (5) use of reward systems, novelty, and sensory experiences in text design; (6) outlining, spacing, and repetition; and (7) giving the reader the opportunity to be active in learning. The first four of these topics include the background research and suggestions. The final three provide suggestions and remind the reader of research substantiating those suggestions.

Short-Term Memory and Its Pitfalls

Short-term memory, as used in this discussion, refers to storage of information which lasts from one-quarter of a second at the minimum to an hour at the maximum without rehearsal. With rehearsal, short-term memories can be maintained almost indefinitely but usually do not last beyond eight hours. The short-term memory storage is also known as "the working memory." When a person actively thinks and contemplates what is happening or has happened (i.e., is consciously aware), the short-term memory is being employed.

Pribram (1979) states that the most recent research indicates that when a person pays attention to a particular set of stimuli, electrical wave patterns can be detected within several areas of the brain. The areas stimulated correspond to the number and types of elements included in the event. In other words, if a person is reading, reacting, and learning from a text, brain centers processing the following types of information might become activated:

- written verbal and/or numeric inputs;
- auditory inputs if the vocal cords are used during reading;
- visuals in graphic or photographic form;
- manual writing or drawing motor processing, if the reader is taking notes;
- attitudinal information from the text and from the reader's experiences;
- information from the setting in which the reading takes place ("environmental noise"); and
- gross or fine musculature processing, if the reader is asked to interact with a model or equipment while proceeding through the text.

Each of the above involves a separate area of the brain in

short-term memory activities. As the reader interacts with the text, proteins present in membranes of nerve cells, synapses, and glia apparently enable the activation of very large numbers of neurons simultaneously. The more channels used to process the text materials, the more storage sites are activated (Hydén, 1977).

When learning starts, there is an increased synthesis of messenger RNA in nerve cells, which induces production of certain proteins and molecular pattern changes in brain cells. Hydén (1977) states:

> "The working hypothesis is that protein differentiation, caused by experience and learning, will secure the concomitant activation of all the neurons which have undergone a similar differentiation and on the same stimulus. It does not matter in what part of the brain the neurons are located . . . at learning, neurons become highly active. The learning mechanism of the brain in the first hand is *active*, not *reactive* like a reflex in a conditioned system." (p. 215)

Pitfalls of Short-Term Storage

One most important caveat: unless short-term memories are committed to long-term storage, they are quickly lost. The short-lived proteins are destroyed, so that the short-term memory is cleared for new inputs. Herein lie the pitfalls of short-term storage: masking, limitations of capacity, short duration, item and order information loss, and recency effects (O'Keefe & Nadel, 1978).

Masking occurs when items being learned are similar in some respect. This might occur with a young reader encountering Martin Luther after learning about Martin Luther King, Jr. The first learned item is generally stronger, having been rehearsed, meaning that attributes of the black civil rights activist might become attributed to the religious reformer of the Renaissance. To avoid the masking effects so that each similar item is remembered separately and distinctly, the differences must be stressed so that the brain can store them in separate categories or subcategories. With Martin Luther and Martin Luther King, Jr., it would be of little help to point out that both were clergymen. To avoid masking in this case, a picture of each, in their appropriate period apparel, would do much to separate the two men in the reader's mind.

The capacity of the short-term memory is severely limited when compared with that of long-term memory. Duration and recency compound the problem of capacity. By active rehearsal, recent inputs which have strong order identification can be accessed by testing memory sites for recently used representations. Those employed most recently will have lower synaptic thresholds, making it easier for the learner to recall the information. This is known as "cramming" to most students. The major pitfall for learners, teachers, and those who write instructional materials is that the learner can juggle enough information to pass most weekly or biweekly tests on individual chapters, units, or modules. And this can be done *without* committing the information to long-term memory. This indictment of non-comprehensive, short-term, fact recall or simple translation tests is but half the bad news. O'Keefe & Nadel (1978) indicate that the results of two studies strongly indicate that verbal information in short-term memory is stored in a "discrete neural area (the posterior parietal region), and not a part of any causal short-term memory to long-term memory chain." In other words, if the learner is memorizing words only for temporary use, as for a quiz or a fact-oriented test, the chances for long-term retention are apparently minuscule.

Suggestions

Several options exist for the text author and teacher in overcoming the pitfalls of short-term memory.

- Ask the reader to use the information in solving problems, as in simulations or role playing, essay responses, term paper assignments, study questions, or even well-constructed practice multiple-choice items for which the reader must make several correct decisions before identifying the correct response.
- The "discovery method" can be used. In some passages, the reader could be asked to analyze and synthesize information to discover an underlying principle, or suggest a solution to a difficult situation.

- Inductive-deductive switching can be employed. The author could use one of these reasoning patterns to present the information, and then present situations, problems, or study questions which ask the reader to use the other thought process.
- Direct the reader to visual, non-verbal information (photographs, line drawings, charts, graphs, etc.), which assist the reader in assimilating the verbal with the non-verbal, thereby breaking the word chain pitfall of short-term memory.

Long-Term Memory Storage

Information processed into long-term storage (LTS) is multiply encoded. Various aspects of the input are stored in multiple locations in the brain, because the experience itself has multiple aspects (Gazzaniga & LeDoux, 1978). Much of the human brain has been mapped for functions controlled and type of information stored at given sites. Pribram (1979) and others have found a high degree of correlation between areas active during both intake and recall, both in terms of latency (delay of activity) and amplitude (voltage of the encephalogram). Those areas stimulated during intake match those activated during recall. The more types of stimuli used in learning, the more sites used to store the information. (Additional information on this phenomenon is found in the next major section, Left-Right Brain Functions and Holographic Memory.)

Types of LTS Memory: Taxon and Locale

Many neurobiologists, cited by O'Keefe & Nadel (1978), now believe that two basic LTS systems exist: the taxon system and the locale system. The mechanics of the taxon system are not as well-defined as those of the locale memory. Taxon LTS seems governed by the principle of "category inclusion." This LTS is not contextual, not time-referenced, and is rote in nature. Memorization of the "I before E" rule of spelling would use the taxon system.

If a student memorized the names of the Presidents in serial order, with no real concept of the American society or momentous events of the time each man served, the taxon system would be the one employed. Think of a student who has memorized a Whitman poem for recitation in class, and who is interrupted for some reason. If the taxon system were used to store the poem, the student will almost assuredly have to begin anew. Taxon memories are not intertwined with others to make a whole cloth. There is an absence of order, time, and place information. There is substantial decay over time. And, it is primarily verbal in nature.

Locale long-term storage, on the other hand, is based upon context. It employs time and space coordinates, multiple channels for storage and retrieval of any or all of the relationships in the specific memory. It is relatively permanent. Locale memory also stores single occurrences with almost amazing longevity. A particular passage from a book, when it strikes a particularly strong note (either positive or negative), may be remembered almost indefinitely. The time and space coordinates of locale memory allow for fixing of events in spatial and temporal relationships. There have been times in nearly everyone's lives when they have met a person for the second time yet failed to remember that person's name: an embarrassing failure of the taxon system. Yet, after some thought, you are able to reconstruct the situation in which you first met the person, who else was present, what the surroundings were like, the activities in which you engaged, or what topics were discussed. This context, fixed in time and place, has been preserved in the locale long-term memory.

Memories which rely primarily on one communication mode, the verbal, will be nearly context free and will be stored in the taxon memory, subject to decay unless used often. By adding verbal or graphic imagery to the text, the reader can imagine, that is, construct a time-space context around, the verbal information to store it in the locale memory system. As an example, a European history text might mention the "defenestration of Prague" in conjunction with a discussion of the Thirty Years War. If left at that, the reader might look up the word defenestration in a dictionary and come away with:

de—Latin: out from
fenestra—Latin: window
to throw a person or object out of a
window

A little imagery has been added to the mind of the reader. But what or who was thrown from the window? By whom? For what reason? What happened to the person or object thrown from the window? How high off the ground was the window? A verbal description incorporating these facets of the act would cement the "defenestration of Prague" in the locale system of the reader. A picture could add even more, if the reader has difficulty with imagining.

Suggestions

- If what is to be learned is rote, verbatim, categorical, or rule-oriented, the taxon system should be emphasized.

An example of this would be the first step in teaching the concept "reptile" by defining the critical attributes: cold blooded, air breathing vertebrate, completely ossified skeleton, body usually covered with scales or bony plates. If this set of abstractions is practiced by the reader until the definition is recitable verbatim, the taxon memory has been encoded for "reptile." Repetition of the definition lowers the neuronal threshold, making it easier to recall in the future. (See "hyper-trophy" in Figure 5.1, Excitory Synapses.)

- If that which is to be learned must be applied to new and different situations, the locale (contextual) LTS should be emphasized.

The former example was predominantly verbal, abstract to those learning of reptiles for the first time, and without context. If the author now wishes the reader to apply the definition of reptile by selecting examples and non-examples of reptiles from a list of animal names or pictures, then a context must be presented so that the memory of "reptile" is established in the locale system. Herein lies another strong implication. Clarity of a memory is enhanced by increasing the number of neurones and brain centers activated when it is recalled from long-term storage. (See

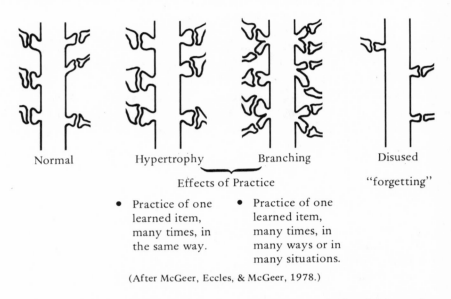

Normal	Hypertrophy	Branching	Disused

Effects of Practice   "forgetting"

- Practice of one learned item, many times, in the same way.
- Practice of one learned item, many times, in many ways or in many situations.

(After McGeer, Eccles, & McGeer, 1978.)

Figure 5.1. Excitory synapses: Plasticity of dendritic spine synapses.

"branching" in Figure 5.1, Excitory Synapses.) The number of neurones and centers activated during recall is limited to the number used to attend to and store the information initially. Maximizing the number of neurones and centers used during learning can be accomplished by using as many sensory communication channels as feasible, providing diverse examples, and asking analysis and synthesis questions for the reader to answer.

- Being careful to not detract from the clarity of the message, use as many types of sensory and theoretical inputs as feasible in setting the learning context.

Books are now being published with "scratch-and-sniff" plates, audiotape supplements, and guides for hands-on activities in which the reader can engage to add to verbal descriptions in the text, all of which at least theoretically add to the learning derived by the reader. All of these definitely increase the number of neurones and brain centers activated above those stimulated by reading alone. There are no rules regarding the characteristics of the setting in which a text can be used. Text authors would do well to keep this in mind, viewing the wide variety of settings in which a text can be used for study, and encouraging the reader to use that variety.

It is unreasonable to assume that instruction designed to reach and be stored in the taxon system will automatically become posited in the locale system as well.

- When teaching toward locale (contextual) memory, stress visual representations.

Haber (1970) and Franken & Rowland (1979) have found that human picture memory is remarkably efficient. There is a tremendously large storage capacity for pictorial information and, therefore, visual contexts through which to associate other items for recall. While most picture memory loses detail, the meaning or sense of the representation is retained, with enough of the pattern to reconstruct most of the main elements portrayed in the picture.

- Combine as much information as possible into a single impression for the reader.

If a series of items or steps must be mastered by the reader, it is best to present them as discrete elements at first. After allowing the reader to practice these, perhaps through study questions, the reader will be able to recall them more easily as a *set*. In teaching someone instructional design or to perform cardiopulmonary resuscitation, there are literally hundreds of separate steps to master. In the end, these steps should be logically grouped into sets such as "writing objectives" or "external cardiac massage." This becomes an effective, long-lasting form of mnemonic, the interactive mnemonic (Higbee, 1979).

- The more vivid and active the impression of what is being learned, the stronger the memory trace.

Imagine for a moment the level of neuronal excitement in a reader's brain when he or she sees the sentence, "The Earth is 93 million miles from the sun." He or she knows that this number will be used on a test somewhere along the line. But there is very little in the reader's referent system which will let him or her relate to the text's sentence in any kind of meaningful scale. If the author wishes to activate the neurones of the reader further, the reader could be instructed to take a b-b (representing the Earth) and a volleyball or soccer ball (representing the sun) to a basketball court. A full-sized court is 90 feet in length. Now he or she has a scale of approximately one foot per million miles. To understand the perspective, the author could direct the reader to place the volleyball three feet beyond the line at one end of the court, then walk to the other end and place the b-b on that endline. By looking at the sun from the Earth's end and then toward the Earth from the sun's end of the court, the meaning of 93 million miles becomes more clear. Pointing out to the reader that only Mercury (a speck of dust) and Venus (another b-b) orbit between Earth and the sun helps the reader understand the vast amount of empty space in the solar system we inhabit.

Higbee (1979) and Lozanov (1978) indicate that it apparently does matter whether this vivid, active imagery is developed internally or externally. Those who have a high ability for mental imagery find self-generated mediators more effective, drawing on their past experiences or constructing fantasies; while those with low ability (the very young, or mental retardates, for example) find images more effective when supplied by others.

• Practice is essential, but it has to be the right type.

Practice to enhance taxon memory should be rote: short, simple, and ordered in a logical sequence. It is also helpful if the passage has a lyrical cadence. Practice to enhance locale memory should incorporate several types of symbols: verbalizations and sensory channels.

Recall is more difficult than recognition, because recall involves reconstructing the memory first. Recognition involves analyzing a cue given the reader. Recall calls upon both the verbal and nonverbal. The verbal system can only report that which is stored there, or strongly networked with nonverbal storage sites. Therefore . . .

• Speaking or writing the information from one's own thoughts will enhance verbal recall.

The verbal portion of the brain has a limited storage capacity so only the most important, verbally practiced information is stored.

In recognition, as opposed to recall, nonverbal brain centers have an opportunity to express their memories by selecting or "pointing to" one of a series of objects or items. Most students would indicate that from time to time they are drawn to a particular answer on a test even though they cannot verbally express the reason for that attraction. The implication from recent brain research is that intuition is, at least in part, a recognition of the correct answer by a nonverbal part of the brain. To tie these nonverbal memories to a verbal recall system . . .

• Ask the learner to verbalize during the learning experience. By verbalizing, either in oral or in written responses to study questions, the learner develops a neural network for the memory which includes both words and other perceptual images. This allows the language system some access to memories stored primarily in the nonverbal systems.

Left-Right Brain Functions and Holographic Memory

The first scientific evidence that the two hemispheres of man's brain have differing functional capacities came from the work of Broca, who discovered the speech center, and Wernicke, who discovered the area which interprets speech. These discoveries occurred in the mid-nineteenth century. In the ensuing century, scientists have attempted to map the areas of the brain which house and control various human capabilities. Most brain structures in one hemisphere have a partner in the other hemisphere. However, that partnership is not always equal. That finding, first shown by Broca, spurred investigation of the lateralization of brain functions.

Among the myriad of scientists who have investigated the capacities of the left and right hemispheres of the human brain, Kimura (1973) seems to have made one of the most important discoveries: that both hemispheres *share* in mental activities. Scientists have yet to discover any one higher intellectual function controlled entirely by one hemisphere. When speaking of the brain, some scientists still refer to "the dominant hemisphere," meaning the side of the brain primarily responsible for language processing. While one hemisphere may contribute more than the other to certain tasks, the hemispheres do not function as entirely separate structures in the normal human. Therefore, it is not appropriate to state that verbal processing is entirely a left-brain function, nor that the right hemisphere is solely responsible for processing pictorial information. Kimura found a ratio of 1.88 to 1 for left-brain dominance of auditory word processing, indicating that approximately two-thirds of the brain activation during that test occurred in the left hemisphere. When stereoscopic depth perception was tested, the ratio was 1.28 to 1 in favor of the right brain. In both these cases, and all others reported by Kimura, both hemispheres shared the functions, although not equally.

Each hemisphere specializes in controlling and storing certain types of information, and each relies on the other to some extent for a complete view of the world (Gazzaniga & LeDoux, 1978). There are several structures in the brain which act as connectors through which pass impulses from one side to the other. These connecting pieces ensure the sharing of functions mentioned above. Still, certain inputs and outputs are controlled primarily by one hemisphere. Which hemisphere and the degree of control are partly functions of sex, age, handedness, and cultural upbringing (Debes, 1977; Gazzaniga & LeDoux, 1978; Geffen, 1976; Geschwind, 1979; Krashen, 1973; McGlone, 1978; Webster, 1977). Much of the research has been done with right-handed, Caucasian persons raised in Western culture. For these people, the hemispheres have predominant specialization as follows (Eccles, 1977):

Left Hemisphere	*Right Hemisphere*
verbal inputs	nonverbal inputs
linguistic outputs	musical and poetic processing
ideation (abstractions)	pictorial and pattern sense
conceptual similarities	visual similarities
analysis over time	synthesis over time
analysis of detail	holistic images
numerics, quantities, arithmetic	intonations, verbal emphasis
logic, sequence information	location in time and space

controls right side of body	controls left side of body
geometric configurations	intuition

This list holds true for over 90 percent of the tested adult right-handed males from Western cultures. There is variation when one looks at females, left-handed people, youngsters, and people raised in other cultures, a fact becoming more apparent in the past five to ten years. Looking primarily at the area of speech processing, investigators have found the following:

- Adult females from Western cultures show relatively more symmetry between the hemispheres for both verbal and performance tasks (McGlone, 1978).
- In the United States, left-handed adults with a family history of left-handedness display a right-hemisphere predominance for language in 65 percent of the cases (less so for females, as indicated above) (Kocel, 1977).
- Prepubescent children show no statistically significant differences between language lateralization in males and females.
- Adults brought up in Japanese culture who have learned both Kanji (a pictorial/ideographic language) and Katakana (which resembles English in its rules and orientation) show strong speech and writing skills in both hemispheres. In Kanji, the characters simultaneously represent both a sound and a meaning, and are represented bilaterally in the brain. Katakana is processed primarily in the left hemisphere. Left brain damage in such an individual disrupts the ability to perform in Katakana; yet damage to *either* hemisphere still leaves the person able to communicate in Kanji. As evidence that this phenomenon is cultural rather than genetic, Japanese raised in Western cultures do not show this trait (Debes, 1977; Geschwind, 1972).

Holographic Memory

Karl Pribram (1979) and other neurobiologists have developed a theory which states that memory works as a hologram does, on interference patterns established during sensory input. Brain cells with memory function apparently act as frequency analyzers and resonate to particular wave frequencies. Some cells resonate to specific auditory frequencies, others to specific light frequencies, and still others to other types of electrical wave frequencies within the brain itself. When recalling information stored in long-term memory, "what we call 'situational cues' for memory are no more than a set of wave forms that activate the appropriate hologram" (Pribram, 1979). This set of wave forms resonates the appropriate cells in numerous brain sites, causing many aspects of the memory to be reproduced. Thus, an entire memory, or at least the essential components, can be reconstructed by the learner.

As indicated earlier under the discussion of long-term memory, the greater the number of sensory inputs associated with the learning situation, the more are the sites in which the memory is processed and, as Pribram projects, the greater the number of wave forms associated with the memory. For partial recall to occur, only one of those sites and wave forms must be stimulated. These will, in turn, trigger other sites and activate additional wave forms to increase the amount of memory recalled.

If you cut a small corner from a hologram, and project lasers through that piece, the *entire* image will appear. This is part of the mystery associated with the technique. The wave forms in the piece will allow the entire visual "memory" to be reconstructed. Similarly, when humans are able to recall a portion of a memory, often much more of that memory can be reconstructed.

Implications for Text Design

The brain has tremendous capacity for storing nonverbal information in the locale memory system. Text writers can take advantage of this by either supplying nonverbal stimuli, or providing guides to the readers which encourage them to seek out or construct nonverbal stimuli to network with verbal text material.

In the German language text *Deutsch 2000*, conversational German is taught using a combination of words and pictures. An introductory picture is provided, with a one- or two-sentence introduction to the scene. Then each portion of the dialog is accompanied by a picture related to the discussion, as below.

```
┌─────────────────────────────────────┐
│                                      │
│   Picture: scene of the beginning    │
│   of the dialogue.                   │
│                                      │
│                                      │
└─────────────────────────────────────┘
```

Text: one or two sentences introducing the characters and situation.

```
┌──────────────┐     • Dialogue:   person #1
│              │     • Dialogue:   person #2
│   Picture    │
│              │
├──────────────┤
│              │     • Dialogue:   person #1
│   Picture    │     • Dialogue:   person #2
│              │
└──────────────┘
```

This pattern continues throughout the dialogue. The beauty of this text design, in terms of brain function, is that it provides all of the following:

- a semirealistic visual image of the persons and what they are doing, or a visual image of something they are discussing;
- a context which includes a place (the setting) and a concept of time portrayed by style of furniture, hair styles, clothing styles;
- pictorial cues for the meaning of words being learned; and
- use of the reader's left visual field to interpret the pictures each time the reader scans a line of verbal information.

The last comment may need some explanation. The human eye passes images to both the left and right hemispheres of the brain. Focus your attention on one of the dots next to the word "Dialogue" above. Everything to the left of that dot is being sent to the right brain. Information to the right of that dot is being sent to the left brain. For most persons, this means that picture information is being sent to the side of the brain which best processes that image. The same is true for the verbal information. Each time the eyes move from the end of one line to the beginning of the next, the right brain receives an image of the picture to the left of that line. While the reader may not be conscious of it, the right brain is tying the visual image to the words in the dialogue. If the instructor is also reading the dialogue aloud or if the reader is speaking the dialogue aloud, auditory word impressions are being stored with visual word and picture information. This means that at least four brain sites are being employed, including the one which interprets vocal intonations. Two of those impressions are primarily stored in the left brain and two in the right.

The next example incorporates several more stimuli. In the text *Endotracheal Intubation*, from the Neonatal Educational Project developed at the Charles R. Drew Postgraduate Medical School under DHEW-NIH contract #NO1-HR-52958, the first half of the book provides the reader with cognitive information. The second half of the text is a study guide. The reader is asked to view color slides, work with a model and a laryngoscope, as well as read directions and view black-and-white line drawings. Additional stimuli, beyond those found in the *Deutsch 2000* text, include tactile sensations, motor activity related to manipulating the model and laryngoscope, color representations from the slides and the intubation model, and a wide variety of views available when the reader manipulates the laryngoscope correctly and incorrectly. The readers are asked to intentionally make some incorrect moves so that they become familiar with the view of a trachea which has been improperly intubated. A videotaped sequence showing proper intubation techniques is also included in the program to allow the reader to relate motion images of the process to verbal and pictorial information in the text.

An example from the Neonatal Educational Project is shown in Figure 5.2. Note that the left column includes both pictures and a *time frame* for a series of actions. Also, in the bottom paragraph, note the use of italics to draw attention. Use of bold print can serve the same purpose. The small triangular shape at the bottom right indicates that the topic is continued on the next page, another nonverbal cue to the reader.

Texts in such subjects as English, social studies, or curriculum development, which are not intended to teach a procedure or a new language, can still be designed to incorporate auditory, tactile, and visual stimuli. Through the use of supplemental materials

CASE STUDY

INTRODUCTION

Here is a case study, taking an infant from the beginning of an apneic episode through external cardiac massage. The timing of the procedure is given at the left, so that you will see how quickly these actions take place.

TIME: 0:00

**POSITION
AND
SUCTION**

You note that an infant in the nursery has become apneic on room air, so you quickly position him and suction the mouth and nose. As you observe the chest, there is no respiratory effort.

TIME: 0:10

VENTILATE

The infant has not been recently fed, so you move immediately to ventilation with the bag and mask. After forming and checking the seal between the mask and the infant's face, you ventilate the infant 4-5 times in ten seconds.

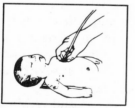

Next, you check the heart rate for five seconds, and note 3 beats. That means the rate is *below 40 per minute*. With a heart rate that slow, external cardiac massage must be considered.

▶

Figure 5.2. Example page from Neonatal Educational Project text.

provided with the text (usually an expensive alternative), study guides which direct the reader to commonly available materials, or such experiences as role playing and simulation, the reader can be exposed to stimuli other than the printed word and two-dimensional visuals.

The Triune Brain

One of the more exciting developments in brain research and theory in the past ten years is the evolution of a brain structure model termed the "triune brain" (Holden, 1979; MacLean, 1973). In MacLean's model (Figure 5.3), triune refers to three separate and distinct functional portions of the brain: the reticular formation (sometimes called the reptilian complex or R-complex), the limbic system, and the neocortex.

Each of these three portions has a separate mentality, according to MacLean; its own special abilities, its own view of the world, sense of time and space, memories, and its own motor functions (Sagan, 1977). The three are interconnected by neuronal pathways, but are anatomically, functionally, and neurochemically quite distinct from each other. Our behavior may be determined by any one of these portions at a given time, depending upon circumstances, past experiences, and genetically programmed survival mechanisms.

MacLean's experiments at the National Institute for Mental Health's Laboratory of Brain Evolution and Behavior indicate that the R-complex plays an important role in aggressive behavior, "territoriality, ritual, and the establishment of social hierarchies" (Sagan, 1977). Apparently, basic needs and sexual drive are programmed into this part of the triune brain.

The limbic system seems to control strong and vivid emotions, attitudes, prejudices, and motivations not tied to basic biological needs. This area contains the hippocampus, which triggers long-term memory storage, and the pituitary gland, which controls the endocrine system. Imbalance in the endocrine system alters moods, which provides an important clue to the relationship between the limbic system and our attitudes and mental states. MacLean (1973) states that malfunctions of the pituitary, amygda-

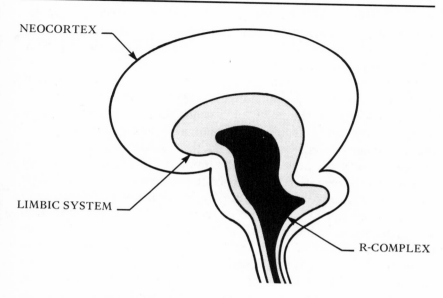

Figure 5.3. Highly schematic representation of the three portions of the triune brain, after MacLean (1973).

la, hippocampus, and other limbic organs can lead to rage, fear, or sentimentality that have no readily apparent external cause.

The relatively massive neocortex virtually surrounds the limbic system, which in turn surrounds the reticular formation (R-complex). The neocortex controls characteristically human intellectual functions such as logic, the quest for knowledge, anticipation of the future, anxiety, language processing, and other indicators of intellect.

Short-term memory and long-term memory triggering mechanisms are primary limbic system functions, yet long-term memories are stored in all three portions of the triune brain. Each portion is the site of specific types of information, related to the abilities and priorities of that portion: ritual in the R-complex, emotion in the limbic system, and reason in the neocortex. Similarly, selective attention to stimuli is controlled in the three areas by the abilities of each. For example, the R-complex will attend to the reader's hunger as lunch time approaches, the limbic system will concentrate on how the reader feels about the subject matter, while the neocortex is attempting to process the cognitive information being presented.

The R-complex apparently has preference in most situations. If a person is overly cold, emotions and the quest for knowledge will take a back seat to the need for warmth. Need for sleep will also overcome the limbic system and neocortex at some point. When the R-complex needs are satisfied, the limbic system then has preference over the neocortex. The hippocampus must be ready to accept new information and trigger the necessary proteins before long-term learning can occur. Finally, if both the R-complex and limbic system are satisfied, the neocortex can function optimally. The interconnectedness of these three allows the neocortex, at times, to dominate. Reason can prevail over emotional and basic needs for a time. However, it seems to be relatively uncommon for people to be able to set aside emotions, attitudes, and basic needs for long periods of time. Recall, if you will, the research on attention spans at various ages and levels of educational development which indicates that people with attention spans greater than 30 minutes are most unusual. Research also points out that adolescents and young adults are interrupted by "romantic thoughts" five to 20 times per hour. These findings show the high priority of R-complex and limbic system functions, to the detriment of neocortical functions.

Holden (1979), in an interview with MacLean, summarizes his beliefs as follows:

> MacLean believes that the people who are enamored of theorizing about the differences between the left (rational, verbal) and right (nonverbal, intuitive) cerebral hemispheres are missing the boat somewhat. 'I think they've got a lot of stuff maybe too high upstairs'—that is, many of the creative, emotional, and spiritual impulses ascribed to the right hemisphere are more properly attributable to the limbic system.

Kimura's research results, cited earlier, are in agreement that the hemispheres share in carrying out functions, albeit less equally than MacLean believes.

MacLean's model of a triune brain provides a few implications for text design, most of which are previously stated tenets but are nonetheless important to review.

- The setting in which the text is used is at least equally important to learning as the quality of content and design used to present the information.

Directions for use of self-study instructional materials should include suggestions for appropriate settings in which study may be most effective. If special equipment or other resources are to be used, this should be specified along with directions regarding where they are available, for how long they may be used, and other special circumstances which may impact on the use of these resources. If the material can be used by pairs of students or small groups for interactive study, directions should include suggestions for the most effective use of materials in group discussion.

- Clarity reduces unwarranted anxiety.

Explicit directions, unambiguous learning objectives, sample test items, practice and review items, clearly drawn diagrams with appropriate labels, worksheets, and clearly outlined and stated textual material tend to let the learner know exactly what is expected by the author. This frees the limbic system and neocortex from unwarranted anxiety about the requirements of the lesson or course.

- Examples used in instruction can affect the learner's attitude and mood. Effectiveness of examples may also be determined by the mood and attitudes of the learner.

Examples which are clearly pertinent to the subject or to the life goals of the learner provide a realistic backdrop for the information being learned. In many cases, the examples can draw upon aesthetic appeal, empathetic situations, or common positive personal experiences of the learner, all of which can have a positive influence on the limbic system's view of the instruction. The affective portions of instruction must be attended to by the text designer to assist the learner in developing intrinsic motivation to set the information in long-term memory storage. Developing a positive attitude toward learning the material, or at least avoiding alienation of the learner, is important to hippocampal involvement in generating the proteins essential for long-term memory (O'Keefe & Nadel, 1978).

Use of Reward Systems, Novelty, and
Sensory Experiences in Text Design

Reward, novelty, and sensory experiences tap the limbic system. The first two of these are motivators which apparently trigger the hippocampus into generating the short-term and long-lasting proteins necessary to the formation of long-term memory.

Reward Systems

Rewards may appear in many guises for the reader, but mostly they entail the feeling that something new has been learned, that former learning has been reconfirmed, or perhaps that a new application has been found for information learned previously. In each of these situations, the reader has had to reach the conclusion that information has been mastered, something has jelled.

Authors can enhance this process by structuring some of the conditions for reward. One commonly employed method involves questioning the reader, as with practice activities and study questions. These questions may be fact-oriented, analytical, inductive, deductive, or of a synthesis nature. If answers are also provided, or at least references for the answers, the reader can be rewarded (reinforced) for correctly answering the questions.

Much has been made of intrinsic and extrinsic rewards in the past several years. O'Keefe & Nadel (1978) point out that, to the human brain, *all* rewards are intrinsic. When a human senses something is important (or rewarding), the hippocampus activates. Unless that individual consciously or unconsciously senses the reward, the hippocampus remains inactive relative to triggering protein production. Fortunately, most people feel rewarded for learning.

Novelty

The new and interesting seem to be remembered better than things that are old and boring. That bit of common sense will come as no surprise to the reader. Yet building novelty into textual materials can be a mind-bending experience to the author. When constructing a text, the author can keep in mind particular types of presentations in other texts which caught the eye and the imagination, keep in mind tried and true methods, and avoid those which seem so old that they no longer keep a reader's attention. Robert Mager includes parables in his books. They are light, witty, and fanciful and almost seem to be Mager's trademark. Other authors use humorous examples, clever stories, poems, lyrical ditties, interesting graphics, and other novel approaches which catch the interest of the reader.

Sensory Experiences

It is novel to include sensory experiences for readers of text materials. The earlier example involving the volleyball "sun," the "Earth," and the basketball court should come to mind. It allows the reader to play with the information, gain a visual context, and be active in the learning process.

There is some justifiable concern among educators that increasing the number of information channels will interfere with learning. As Hartman (1961) stated:

> "A common practice among multiple channel communicators has been to fill the channels, especially the pictorial, with as much information as possible. The obvious expectation is for additional communication to result from the additional information. However, the probability of interference resulting from the additional cues is very high. The hoped-for enhanced communication resulting from a summation of cues occurs only under special conditions. Most of the added cues in the mass media possess a large number of extraneous cognitive associations. The possibility that these associations will interfere with one another is probably greater than that they will facilitate learning." (p. 255)

For the reasons Hartman gave, it is most important to field test materials to determine whether the clarity of the message has been influenced adversely by the addition of other sensory stimuli.

Outlining, Spacing, and Repetition

Outlining, spacing information on pages, and repetition of key facts, concepts, and principles alert the reader to those items the author considers most important, and help the reader develop a logical mental ordering of the information.

Outlining

The use of outlines assists the reader in recalling information. Categorizing facts within major concepts or concepts within underlying principles allows grouping, as previously mentioned, for readers learning the individual steps in instructional design or cardiopulmonary resuscitation (see Long-Term Memory Storage). Outlining also assists the reader in pyramiding information inductively, as shown below.

I. Cancer Drugs
A. Types of Cancer Treated With Drugs
1. Generic Drugs Used to Treat Different Types of Cancer
For each generic drug: the brand names, manufacturer, indications for use,
contraindications, dosage, method of administration, etc.

The text outline could be structured in a normal outline format:
I. Cancer Drugs—types of cancer treated?
  A. Carcinoma—generic drugs used to treat this cancer?
    1. (generic drug #1)
       a. (brand names)
       b. (manufacturer)
       c. (indications for use)
       d. (contraindications)
          etc.
    2. (generic drug #2)
       etc.

This outline could serve as either an advance organizer or a summary, or both. The discussion of drugs used to treat different types of cancer could then fill in the outline for the reader while keeping the organization clear in the reader's mind.

The outline of material need not be formal, in the sense of that style taught in junior high school. Horn's methods of information mapping, discussed in another chapter of this text, also outline material for the reader. The following example (Figure 5.4) again

GASTRIC AND ABDOMINAL DISTENTION

INTRODUCTION

You have read that an orogastric tube should be inserted to relieve distention of the stomach and intestines in an infant who is in need of prolonged ventilation. This page explains why.

EFFECT OF VENTILATION

During bag and mask ventilation, air is forced into the oropharynx where it is free to enter **both** the trachea and the esophagus. Proper positioning will force most of the air into the trachea and the lungs. Some air will enter the esophagus, however, and be forced into the stomach.

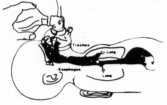

DISTENTION

Air forced into the stomach interferes with ventilation in the following ways:

1. Air in the stomach puts pressure on the diaphragm, preventing full expansion of the lungs.

2. Air in the stomach causes regurgitation of gastric contents which can easily be aspirated during bag and mask resuscitation.

3. Air in the stomach travels through the bowel, producing abdominal distention for several hours. This puts pressure on the diaphragm and makes it more difficult for the infant to breathe.

These problems related to distention can be prevented by inserting an orogastric tube.

Figure 5.4. Example from Neonatal Educational Project text.

from the Neonatal Educational Project, shows how the map title
and side headings provide the reader with an outline of the
material.

Spacing

Information properly spaced on a page can catch the attention
of the reader,

• THIS IS IMPORTANT

and helps the reader keep the concepts separated in his or her
mind. When the material is still in short-term memory, facts and
concepts can become jumbled unless the author makes a special
point of assisting the reader in keeping them separate and distinct.
Visually spacing the information, as below (Figure 5.5), does just
this.

Repetition

The reader has hopefully noted that certain key concepts and
suggestions have been repeated in this chapter, in differing
contexts. If you can recall, at this point, answers to the following
questions, the importance of repetition in text design should be
obvious.

1. Why should an author stress examples which will be
   processed in the locale (contextual) long-term memory?
2. What should be included in discussions and stimulus
   materials to assist the reader in processing information into
   the locale memory?
3. How do the left and right hemispheres of the brain differ
   in their abilities to process information? How can an
   author take advantage of these differences to assist the
   reader in using more centers of his or her brain in learning?
4. In what ways can the R-complex and limbic system affect
   the ability of the neocortex in assimilating cognitive
   material?

As indicated in the section on Long-Term Memory Storage,
repetition strengthens memory in two ways. When information is
practiced in the same way, dendritic spines increase in size and
that particular memory becomes easier to recall. When informa-

IMPROVEMENT

INTRODUCTION   **Improvement** in the neonate is indicated by three signs:

- *Increasing heart rate.*

- *Spontaneous respirations.*

- *Improving color.*

HEART RATE AND RESPIRATIONS
The steps you go through will depend upon the degree of improvement in the infant's condition.

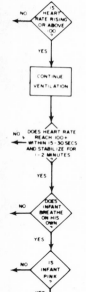

As the heart rate keeps improving toward normal you should continue ventilating the baby at a rate of 30-40 breaths/minute (one every two seconds). Monitor the rise and fall of the chest to prevent over-inflation or under-inflation of the lungs.

Within 15-30 seconds the heart rate should improve to 100 or above. As you continue to bag the infant the heart rate should stabilize above 100 for 1-2 minutes. If this occurs, you should stop ventilating to observe whether the baby can sustain respirations on his own.

The infant who is continuously improving will exhibit spontaneous respirations, in which case you can **discontinue ventilation**. In a short time the color should also improve.

Figure 5.5. Example from Neonatal Educational Project text.

tion is practiced in many different ways, the dendritic spines branch, tying memory to more and more areas of the brain.

Giving the Reader the Opportunity to Be Active in Learning

Hydén (1977) states that, biologically, learning is active not reactive. To take advantage of this, texts should encourage action on the part of the learner: Thought-provoking questions, special projects, physical activities, anything to keep the reader alert and actively working the information. Several text writers have used these techniques in recent years, and the reader is encouraged to seek out examples in his or her subject area. On topics related to instructional design and development, such writers include Mager, Markle, Baker and Schutz, and Davis, Alexander, and Yelon.

Authors are often voracious readers. Because of this they see the wide variety of methods used by others to present information. The reader of this chapter is further encouraged to seek out texts in content areas previously unexplored. Peruse the stacks in your library. Thumb through books and magazines which have never before caught your interest. See what other academic communities are doing to capture the attention of and activate their readers. And, as you do this, keep in mind how the brain functions during learning.

References

Adey, W.R. Models of membranes of cerebral cells as substrates for information storage. *BioSystems*, 1977, *8*, 163-178.

Debes, J. Visuocultural influences on lateralization. *Annals of the New York Academy of Sciences*, 1977, *299*, 474-476.

Diamond, S., & Beaumont, G. Use of two cerebral hemispheres to increase brain capacity. *Nature*, 1971, *232*, 270-271.

Eccles, J. Evaluation of the brain in relation to the development of the self-conscious mind. *Annals of the New York Academy of Sciences*, 1977, *299*, 161-179.

Fifkova, E., & Harreveld, A. van. Long-lasting morphological changes in dendritic spines of dentate granular cells following stimulation of the entorhinal area. *Journal of Neurocytology*, April 1977, *6*(2), 211-230.

Franken, R.E., & Rowland, G.L. Nature and the representation for picture-recognition memory. *Perceptual and Motor Skills*, 1979, *49*, 619-629.

Gazzaniga, M.S., & LeDoux, J.E. *The integrated mind*. New York: Plenum Press, 1978.

Geffen, G. Development of hemispheric specialization for speech perception. *Cortex*, 1976, *12*, 337-346.

Geschwind, N. Language and the brain. *Scientific American*, April 1972, *226*(4), 76-83.

Geschwind, N. Specialization of the human brain. *Scientific American*, 1979, *242*(3), 180-199.

Haber, R.N. How we remember what we see. *Scientific American*, 1970, *222*(5), 104-112.

Hartman, F.R. Single and multiple channel communication: A review of research and a proposed model. *AV Communication Review*, 1961, *9*, 235-262.

Higbee, K. Recent research on visual mnemonics: Historical roots and educational fruits. *Review of Educational Research*, 1979, *49*(4), 611-629.

Holden, C. Paul MacLean and the triune brain. *Science*, 1979, 1066-1068.

Hydén, H. The differentiation of brain cell protein, learning, and memory. *BioSystems*, 1977, *8*, 213-218.

Kimura, D. The asymmetry of the human brain. *Scientific American*, 1973, *227*(3), 70-78.

Kocel, K.M. Cognitive abilities: Handedness, familial sinistrality, and sex. *Annals of the New York Academy of Sciences*, 1977, *299*, 233-243.

Krashen, S.D. Lateralization, language learning, and the critical period: Some new evidence. *Language Learning*, 1973, *23*, 63-74.

Lozanov, G. *Suggestology and outlines of suggestopedy*. New York: Gordon and Breach, 1978.

MacLean, P.D. *A triune concept of the brain and behavior*. Toronto: University of Toronto Press, 1973.

McGeer, P.L., Eccles, J.C., & McGeer, E.G. *Molecular neurobiology of the mammalian brain*. New York: Plenum Press, 1978.

McGlone, J. Sex differences in functional brain asymmetry. *Cortex*, 1978, *14*, 122-128.

O'Keefe, J., & Nadel, L. *The hippocampus as a cognitive map*. New York: Oxford University Press, 1978.

Pribram, K. Hemispheric specialization: Evolution or revolution? *Annals of the New York Academy of Sciences*, 1977, *299*, 18-21.

Pribram, K. Holographic memory. *Psychology Today*, 1979, *12*(9), 71-84.

Sagan, C. *The dragons of eden: Speculations on the evolution of human intelligence.* New York: Random House, 1977.

Webster, W. Territoriality and the evolution of brain asymmetry. *Annals of the New York Academy of Sciences,* 1977, *299,* 213-221.

Section Two:

Explicit Techniques for Structuring Text

6.

Introduction to Section Two: Explicit Techniques for Structuring Text

David H. Jonassen
Paul A. Kirschner

The first section of this book focused on means for structuring the presentation of prose internally. The organizational structure of a passage of expository prose is implicit in the sequencing and presentation of content in the text. In addition to providing a framework for understanding the content of a passage, such structures are often assimilated by the reader into memory. Since a significant proportion of readers find it difficult to organize information as it is presented, they depend upon the author to provide that organizational framework for them. These assimilated content structures may also act as retrieval cues (a point to be discussed in the next few pages).

This second section of the book is concerned with techniques for externalizing that organizational structure, that is, for signaling (to use Meyer's term) the content structure of the prose passage in very explicit ways. These include linguistic, spatial, and typographic cues to the form, function, sequence, content, and importance of segments of a passage. It is important to note that these explicit techniques are usually adjunct to the prose in any passage. They are added to the prose as explicit indicators of the organization of prose presented. They function as "discourse punctuators," to use Waller's and Showstack's term, that is, they punctuate the structure of discourse. Whether we are blocking text, using upper-case, weighted, or italicized type, or diagramming or charting prose, these cues are intended to capture and focus attention during reading. What this introduction and the chapters in this section explore is the need to know what cognitive processes the reader is performing that are benefited by these cues (Wright, 1978). The thread that binds these chapters is the assumption that the nature of complex text and its underlying structure can be indicated to the reader by the way it is displayed on the page.

A Model for the Functioning of Text Characteristics

The first principle of this model is that text characteristics work primarily during the perception and processing of information rather than during retrieval. The characteristics that are used in the text to signal the structure, type, or function of content in any passage are encoded into memory along with the content. This is consistent with the encoding specificity hypothesis: "What is stored is determined by what is perceived and how it is encoded, and what is stored determines what retrieval cues are effective in providing access to what is stored" (Tulving & Thompson, 1973). The spatial or typographic cues suggested by the chapters in this section that are encoded into memory along with the prose they signal will be effective retrieval cues. The more explicit or conspicuous these cues are, the more readily they should be encoded and the more effective they should be during retrieval in accessing the discourse stored in memory. Based on the results of paired associate studies, Tulving and Thompson concluded that contextual information about words can be stored in memory in such a way that it can cue an appropriate response yet not be available for recall itself. Visuals that accompany prose and are available in the same format during retrieval (testing) also have been found to function as retrieval cues, supporting the encoding specificity hypothesis (DeMelo, Szabo, & Dwyer, 1981). Though untested, it seems reasonable to assume that most of the explicit signaling techniques discussed in this section would function in the same way. A variety of information, both semantically related and unrelated, gets encoded into memory with target information. The ability to control the production and use of those cues is an unstated assumption of the techniques described in this section.

An extension of the first principle of this model of text characteristics is that perception (attention to either all or part of the message) and processing are not seen as being two discrete events, but rather as points on an information processing continuum. This process begins with rapid analysis of stimulus material at different levels or stages, and progresses from analysis of physical features to matches with stored abstractions (extraction of meaning) and deeper cognitive analysis (Craik & Lockhart, 1972). This "level of processing" hypothesis eschews traditional multi-store memory models, opting for a series of processing stages which entail "deeper" processing, i.e., more semantic involvement with the information as it is processed. The more semantic involvement, the stronger the memory trace becomes. Among other studies confirming this effect, Zimmer (1979) recently found that when readers were required to attend to the "semantic bases of passages, recall was higher." Each of the text characteristics presented in this section can be thought of as affecting the processing of information at at least one point, but often at more than one point, along this continuum. Put simply, before the reader can process and store the information in text, he or she must first focus on that text and read it, i.e., become semantically involved. The cueing discussed in this book is designed to facilitate that involvement.

Text characteristics affect this process in the following ways. First, certain characteristics may affect the accessibility of that which is to be learned. Second, certain characteristics affect perception of the information either generally (motivational factors) or selectively (attentional factors), depending upon the characteristics. They activate mathemagenic behaviors (the topic of a following section). Once this has been accomplished, processing and eventually storage follow in one or more of the following activities (list does not pretend to be exhaustive):

(1) the learning of specific facts, concepts, or principles (fact retention);

(2) breaking up macro-level text components into smaller, micro-components (segmentation);

(3) expanding on the information in the text (elaboration);

(4)   forming relations between that which is already present in one's cognitive structure with new information (assimilation);

(5)   application of contents to other situations and areas (transfer);

(6)   reviewing of information in the text (rehearsal);

(7)   identifying and discriminating between superordinate and subordinate information (analysis);

(8)   bringing together separate propositions from the text (integration/concatenation);

(9)   drawing of inferences on the basis of information present in the text (synthesis); and

(10) altering one's cognitive representation of things to accept new information (accommodation).

Note: These mental activities roughly relate consistently deeper levels of processing. Each of these activities may be affected by any and all of the previously mentioned characteristics.

The second principle of our model is that by looking only at text characteristics and the learning processes which they instigate and, where appropriate, facilitate, an important part of the learning process is ignored. What has been forgotten is the learning outcome. Simply stated, different text characteristics instigate or stimulate different learning processes, which in turn lead to different learning outcomes.

According to Mayer & Greeno (1972), the use of different text characteristics will result in processing behaviors and learning outcomes which are functionally distinguishable. The question which then arises is not "which characteristic is best?," but rather "which process(es) leading to which learning outcome(s) is (are) desired by the author or publisher?" In this way, the author is required to specify both what it is that he or she would like the reader to learn. After specifying both of these outcomes, it is hopefully possible to select means (text characteristics) which will facilitate those results. Selection of appropriate characteristics requires that we combine the text characteristics with our stated learning processes, arriving at the following matrix construction (see Figure 6.1). The choice of text characteristics and learning

	Process 1	Process 2	,,	,,	,,	,,	,,	Process M
Text characteristic 1								
Text characteristic 2								
,,								
,.								
,,								
,,								
,,								
Text characteristic N								

Figure 6.1. Text characteristic-process matrix.

processes in this matrix must be determined by the needs of each user separately. Reading is a process more naturally individualized than any other.

This matrix, however, is still incomplete, in that an important dimension has been omitted—the learner. The third principle of the model suggests that the writer needs to consider the nature of the target audience. A writer/publisher prepares educational materials for a very broad and heterogeneous target audience. In doing so, the publisher must define the learners' characteristics in terms relevant to that audience and to the text characteristics employed. These may be based upon individual or combinations of characteristics, such as reading ability, general intelligence and maturity, cognitive/learning styles, and general knowledge and prior learning. The issue of individual differences and text processing will be dealt with more extensively in the final section of this book. The three-dimensional matrix presented in Figure 6.2 (Kirschner, 1981; Kirschner, in

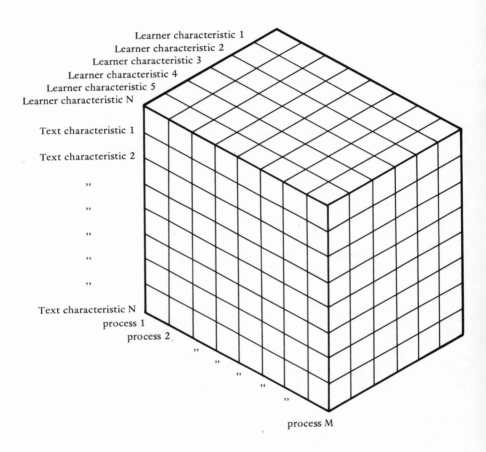

Figure 6.2. *Text characteristic x process x*
learner characteristic matrix.

press) suggests a structuralistic model of instruction (Jonassen, 1978) that requires the matching of the processing characteristics of the task with the facilitative characteristics of text and the processing capability of the learner. The match represents an effective heuristic for the text writer. A fourth dimension, subject matter or message, might be added to our model, as suggested earlier by Solomon (1974). The complexity added by a fourth dimension, however, may not be justified.

How Text Characteristics Affect Learning (Recall)

Our model has developed the conceptual basis for the processing of explicit textual characteristics. It remains only to integrate these individual contributions into the model. To do so, we must refer back to the second principle of our model, which indicates that text characteristics are/should be designed to instigate different mental processes, which result in different learning outcomes. Two such processes readily emerge and shall be used to organize this section of the book.

The first process relates to the application of text characteristics to facilitate learning (recall of information). Learning, as we have stated, occurs on different levels and is facilitated by the encoding of cues and information into memory. The adjunct text characteristics explored in this section of the book facilitate the learning process in at least two ways. First, they function as macro-punctuation (Waller, 1980), that is, they typographically signal or punctuate the macro-structure of any textual passage (for a discussion of macro-structure, see Section Four of this book), just as traditional punctuation marks (commas, periods, parentheses, etc.) signal the structure of a sentence (micro-structure levels). This conceptualization is discussed by Waller in his paper, "Text as Diagram: Using Typography to Improve Access and Understanding." It is placed first in Section Two, because it functions in addition to this introduction as an organizer for the papers subsumed in it. An assumption of all of these characteristics is that by signaling in explicit ways the organization of expository prose, learning will be facilitated. We know from the first section of the book the importance of organization of text to learning.

These explicit textual characteristics facilitate learning in another way; they control the processing of information in a passage. In contrast to the first section of this book, which focused on the internal structure of prose, Rothkopf (1972) proposed that the analysis of structure of text is not the single most important concern for writers. Rather, the analysis of readers' activities while exposed to text is equally important. The mental behaviors which learners use to interpret meaning from text are mathemagenic activities, those that control how an individual attends to and transforms presented material (nominal stimulus) into learning (effective stimulus) (Rothkopf, 1970). Mathemagenic activities, those conducive to the attainment of specified learning objectives, have normally taken the form of adjunct aids to written materials, such as inserted questions, behavioral objectives, advance organizers, note-taking, underlining, etc. All of these mathemagenic behaviors function to control the purposive attention to and processing of text.

The adjunctive inclusion of questions in text is the most heavily researched mathemagenic behavior. Interspersed throughout a medium-length passage, one or two comprehension questions are presented in advance of material (pre-question) or after material (post-question) (Rothkopf, 1965). Generally, adjunct post-questions have been found to produce more intentional (inserted questions repeated) and incidental (not questioned in passage) recall than pre-questions or no questions (Anderson & Biddle, 1975). Other researchers (Rickards, 1977) have concluded that pre-questions are as effective (in some cases, more effective) than post-questions for intentional and incidental learning. The relative efficacy of questions is a function of the level of processing required by the questions—deeper processes benefitting from pre-questions (Rickards, 1980). Of concern to text writers is the lack of ecological validity of these studies, since no textual materials ever present questions like the research studies (text material and related questions on separate pages, the learner being prevented from reviewing material before answering) (Rickards, 1980). This problem has been addressed in studies that have presented adjunct questions and tasks in an ecologically valid setting

(Hamaker & Kirschner 1981a, 1981b; Wouters & Kop, 1981).

Other mathemagenic aids in text include advance organizers and behavioral objectives. The latter technique is not treated in this book because the effects are not specific to text. Neither are some of the other text characteristics, but the use of objectives engenders a larger issue than this book is able to address. Like inserted questions, objectives (normally presented in advance of learning) tend to focus attention on certain aspects of materials, regardless of format. Facilitative effects have resulted from the use of headings and titles also (Dooling & Lachman, 1971), but space does not permit extensive treatment. An important assumption of the text characteristics presented in this section is that learning activities engaged in during the processing of written discourse can be controlled by the text writer/designer.

So, textual display techniques are used to signal text structure and control the mental processes of the learner while interacting with text. In his chapter, "Textual Display Techniques," Philippe Duchastel considers the nature of text and text processing as a context for discussing display techniques that aid that processing. These include labeling, highlighting, and illustrations. Principles for employing these techniques, based upon his research, are provided to help the text designer overcome the problem of focus. The solutions he proposes are grounded in these notions of discourse punctuation and mathemagenic control of processing. Finally, and perhaps most importantly, Duchastel's chapter makes exemplary use of the techniques he discusses.

Those ideas are further elaborated by James Hartley in "Designing Instructional Text." One of the pioneers and leading proponents of textual display methods, he distills years of research into a lucid set of principles for spacing, wording, and evaluating textual materials. His hints on communicating with the printer should prove invaluable to anyone planning to publish text.

Programmed instruction has more consistently and continuously made use of typographic cueing than any other technique. Frames have always blocked and sequenced chunks of information. The requirement of an overt response to presented information is explained in "Programmed Instruction Revisited" as mathemagenic control of the learner's processing activity. Trends in programmed instruction have eschewed traditional behavioral conceptualizations of the processes underlying programming. This combination of features makes programmed instruction one of the most structured methods for presenting text available.

In no instance, with the possible exception of programmed instruction, is the thread of discourse more explicitly or graphically signaled than in the writing of algorithms. Paul Merrill synthesizes a good deal of his own and other research in formulating a set of principles for representing algorithms. In "Structured Outline Representations for Procedures and Algorithms," he shows that for textual exposition of procedures and problem-solving, flowcharting algorithms is one of the most efficient methods available.

Three chapters in this section focus on the supplementation of text with linguistically and spatially oriented forms of adjunct aids. Organizers, diagrams, charts, and pictures supplement text; they are not an integral part of it. While they are not as typographic in nature as the previous topics (although diagrams and charts employ a good many typographic techniques), they are designed to facilitate learning through the comprehension of textual materials. They also function mathemagenically, so they are most appropriately included in this section.

"Advance Organizers in Text" reviews the concepts, principles, and research related to the supplementation of text with advance organizers. Based upon the work of David Ausubel, organizers are probably one of the oldest, yet most under-utilized, mathemagenic supplement. A specific set of procedures for writing organizers attempts to overcome one of the most frequently cited criticisms of the technique, the lack of unambiguous prescriptions for their construction.

Based upon a series of studies, William Winn and William Holliday provide the text designer with a cogent set of concrete "Design Principles for Diagrams and Charts." They conclude that because of the processing demands imposed on the learner by diagrams, they may not be appropriate for all learners. To what degree such a conclusion would generalize to the other techniques presented in this book, only research can tell. Individual differences research related to all these techniques is needed.

So much is available in the perceptual and instructional technology literature on the role of pictures in instruction that at first we thought there was no way the topic could or should be treated by this book. Yet there is no way the topic could justifiably be excluded, since pictures are the oldest form of discourse supplementation. Based upon his analysis of countless textbooks, Philip Brody has attempted to distill the essences of his observations and the available research into a usable set of principles for relating pictures to text. Of most interest to the text designer might be the sections on size and placement of pictures in textual materials. Also, the guidelines on captioning relate well to suggestions by Winn and Holliday regarding the use of study questions. If discourse supplements are not properly attended to, they are of little value. Brody is to be applauded for even attempting such an endeavor in light of the page restrictions imposed on him.

How Text Characteristics Affect Access (Retrieval)

The start-to-finish, once-through conception of reading from text is usually inaccurate, says MacDonald-Ross (1979). Most learners do not interact with text by picking it up, reading straight through, and putting it down, never to read it again prior to being tested on the material. This is the conception that most reading researchers assume in their research paradigms. In reality, we employ text in a variety of ways. Most of the time we are using text to fulfill specific, limited information needs, so we interact with textual materials in ways that most efficiently satisfy those needs. We are top-down processors in the way we access text, that is, we use it to confirm hypotheses, complete schemata, and so on. Explicit signals usually provide readers with enough information to enable them to hypothesize about material without reading it through. The contextual framework that they provide is capable of facilitating top-down processing. One of the most significant contributions of textual display characteristics is to facilitate the accession of information in text. The same typographic cues that signal the structure of discourse may also function as access structures (Waller, 1979). They signal to the reader who is sampling and searching text for information where certain information is contained. Waller, in his chapter in this book, reviews the concept of access structures, which describes one of the most important uses for the three remaining explicit display techniques. In their capacity for providing access structures, these techniques do not primarily function mathemagenically. That is, their purpose is not exclusively to control or facilitate learning processes (recall and retention of knowledge) from text; rather, they facilitate retrieval (location and acquisition) of information from text. This is not to suggest that these techniques are not capable of facilitating learning. It is simply that their strengths or emphasis shift somewhat from retention to retrieval. Tables and flowcharts, as described by Patricia Wright, could easily be subsumed under the previous sub-heading, "Discourse Supplementation," since they share many characteristics with diagrams. However, the way that individuals access information from tables, as reflected in the chapter, is more retrieval-oriented. "Information Mapping" and "Discourse Punctuation" are systems of structured writing as Robert Horn explains in his chapter, "Structured Writing and Text Design," and Richard Showstack demonstrates in his chapter, "Printing: The Next Stage: Discourse Punctuation." These systems are capable of facilitating retrieval of information (Jonassen & Falk, 1980).

The chapters in this section of the book represent a prodigious amount of research and development effort by the authors and others. All would probably readily admit that much more is needed before we can be completely definitive about the application of any of these techniques.

References

Anderson, R.C., & Biddle, W.B. On asking people questions about what they are reading. In G. Bower (Ed.), *Psychology of learning and motivation*, Vol. 9. New York: Academic Press, 1975.

Craik, F.M., & Lockhart, R.S. Levels of processing: A framework for memory research. *Journal of Verbal Learning and Verbal Behavior*, 1972, *11*, 671-684.

DeMelo, H.T., Szabo, M., & Dwyer, F.M. *Visual testing: An experimental assessment of the encoding specificity hypothesis.* Paper presented at the Annual Convention of the Association for Educational Communications and Technology, Philadelphia, April 6-10, 1981.

Dooling, D.J., & Lachman, R. Effects of comprehension on retention of prose. *Journal of Experimental Psychology,* 1971, *88,* 216-222.

Hamaker, C., & Kirschner, P.A. *The effect of adjunct application questions on the recall and application of text information.* Paper presented at the annual meeting of the American Educational Research Association, Los Angeles, April 1981(a).

Hamaker, C., & Kirschner, P.A. Toegevoede vragen en voorbelden bij een biologie-tekst voor middlebare school leerlingen. *Educational Psychology Internal Reports,* University of Amsterdam, 1981(b).

Jonassen, D.H. Structuralism in instructional design. *Journal of Educational Technology Systems,* 1978, *7,* 187-193.

Jonassen, D.H., & Falk, L.M. Mapping and programming textual materials. *Programmed Learning and Educational Technology,* 1980, *17,* 19-26.

Kirschner, P.A. *Manuals for editors and authors.* Paper presented at the annual meeting of the American Educational Research Association, Los Angeles, April 1981.

Kirschner, P.A. *Manuals for editors and authors.* Groningen, Netherlands: Wolters-Noordhof, in press.

MacDonald-Ross, M. Language in texts. In L.S. Shulman (Ed.), *Review of Research in Education,* Vol. 6. Itasca, Ill: Peacock, 1979.

Mayer, R.E., & Greeno, J.G. Structural differences between learning outcomes produced by different structural methods. *Journal of Educational Psychology,* 1972, *63,* 165-173.

Rickards, J.P. On inserting questions before or after segments of text. *Contemporary Educational Psychology,* 1977, *2,* 200-206.

Rickards, J.P. Note-taking, underlining, inserted questions, and organizers in text: Research conclusions and educational implications. *Educational Technology,* June 1980, *20*(6), 5-11.

Rothkopf, E.Z. Some theoretical and experimental approaches to problems in written instruction. In D. Krumholtz (Ed.), *Learning and the educational process.* Chicago: Rand McNally, 1965.

Rothkopf, E.Z. The concept of mathemagenic activities. *Review of Educational Research,* 1970, *40,* 325-336.

Rothkopf, E.Z. Structural text features and the control of processes in learning from written materials. In J.B. Carroll & R.O. Freedle (Eds.), *Language comprehension and the acquisition of knowledge.* Washington, D.C.: V.H. Winston, 1972.

Solomon, G. What is learned and how it is taught. In D.E. Olson (Ed.), *Media and Symbols: The forms of expression, communication, and education.* National Society for the Study of Education Yearbook, Vol. 73, Part 1. Chicago: University of Chicago Press, 1974.

Tulving, E., & Thompson, D.M. Encoding specificity and retrieval processes in episodic memory. *Psychological Review*, 1973, *80*, 352-373.

Waller, R.H.W. Typographic access structures for educational texts. In P.A. Kolers, M.E. Wrolstad, & T.H. Bouma (Eds.), *Processing of visible language*, Vol. 1. New York: Plenum Press, 1979.

Waller, R.H.W. Graphic aspects of complex texts: Typography as macro-punctuation. In P.A. Kolers, M.E. Wrolstad, & T.H. Bouma (Eds.), *Processing of visible language*, Vol. 2. New York: Plenum Press, 1980.

Wouters, L., & Kop, P. Concret iserende elaboraties en tekstbestudering. Tijdschrift voor Onderwijs-*research*, 1981, 113-129.

Wright, P. Feeding the information eaters: Suggestions for integrating pure and applied research on language comprehension. *Instructional Science,* 1978, 7, 249-302.

Zimmer, J.W. *Effects of processing activities on free recall from text.* Paper presented at the annual meeting of the American Educational Research Association, San Francisco, April 1979.

7.

Text as Diagram:
Using Typography to Improve
Access and Understanding

Robert Waller

Texts and diagrams are usually considered opposites. When we think about text in an abstract way—in teaching composition, perhaps, or researching into reading and learning processes—we most often refer to straightforward, continuous prose. But take a look at the actual texts that most people read and use everyday— newspapers, magazines, advertisements, forms, packages, manuals, and handbooks. Within a particular column of type, the prose may be plain enough, but each page (or each text as a whole) will probably be constructed from a range of separate components, including headings, boxed items, tables, illustrations, and so on.

Sometimes these components are arbitrarily arranged to fill the space available, such as in Figure 7.1, but often the layout adds new meaning to the material (Figure 7.2). The designer can use spatial and graphic means—rules, borders, tints, type variations, and so on—to assign qualities to and to display relationships between different components of the text. To put it another way, he or she can *diagram* the text (Figure 7.3).

"Text as diagram" is a useful metaphor because it focuses us on the written-ness of text, mostly ignored by linguists and those who study reading and learning. Diagrams are essentially written, or rather graphic, entities. Many only have existence in spatial terms and cannot be transposed into other media. They use graphic techniques to display or summarize often quite complex relationships between the components of systems, mechanisms, or

Figure 7.1. The juxtaposition of these Victorian advertisements adds nothing to their meaning.

	At home *five-year-olds*	Community *seven-year-olds*	School *ten-year-olds*
TYPE OF PLAY	Playing at having a tea party	Skipping and chanting	Acting a play about going to a new school
SKILLS CO-ORDINATION	Laying table	Skipping	Making costumes, scenery, posters etc Learning words
UNDERSTANDING THE PHYSICAL WORLD	Using yoghurt pots as pretend tea-cups Pouring real liquids into the 'cups'	Keeping rhythm	Using stage lights and props
UNDERSTANDING OTHER POINTS OF VIEW	Taking turns to take the most popular part in the game Sharing out real food and drink Playing at being different people	Waiting for a turn Seeing that some children are more talented than others Showing off	Seeing the range of abilities of others and that everyone has a talent for something Co-operating to get the work done
LEARNING RIGHT FROM WRONG	Pretending to be naughty or to tell off naughty children	Telling off those who don't take turns fairly	Acting out quite complicated ideas about right and wrong in the various situations of the play

Figure 7.2. The use of space is essential to the meaning of this typographic display. A tabular syntax has replaced the normal syntax of prose.

You&Us

This is the page where you have your say—and there's a £5 prize for every letter published

WE THINK

Being a "married woman", says Angela Hooper M.P., is a full-time occupation. We think—we hope—she meant being a mum with very young children is a full-time occupation. Because the married state, as such, is not full-time employment, or if it is for women, so it is for men.

The Government are considering tax concessions for women who make house-wifery a full-time occupation (because they choose to or have to due to the lack of other employment). But perhaps we should not be fooled into thinking this is a kind of recognition of the value of the little lady at home. (They could have done so years ago if they felt so warmly towards this undervalued body of women.) No—it is being considered now because encouraging women to stay at home does a number of things to help the Government:
1. It means unemployment figures.
2. It means more women will be able to take up the responsibilities for the young, the old and the sick, so steadily being dropped by Government.
3. Traditional family pattern will be restored—man at work, woman at home—and while this may be comfortable for men (the majority in Government), it is far from comfortable for women who'd prefer to be out at work.

These days women are educated to expect some choice in how they spend their lives. If they choose to marry why should it be assumed this means staying at home? (Or is this some ghastly plot by men to keep female prime ministers out of office!)

Thanks!

A teacher friend of mine had an unexpected gift, a bunch of flowers given to her by one of her pupils. Delighted, she admired them and thanked her, to which the small girl replied: "I wanted to bring them yesterday only Mum said they weren't dead enough."
—Mrs. A. Willcocks: Durham.

Feeling really ill and being quite alone, I called my doctor and asked him to visit me. It was a miserable, cold and windy night. When he arrived I apologised for getting him out in such terrible weather. "That's all right," he replied. "I've got to see another patient in this area so I'll kill two birds with one stone . . ."
—S. Robertson: Edinburgh.

Females under stress

I've noticed recently that there are many more young women, only in their 20s or early 30s, who have grey hair. Is there a special reason for this which I haven't heard about? Or is it just that people are so confident of themselves that they don't try to disguise it these days?
—N. Cimelli: Merseyside.

Hidden persuaders

Isn't it amazing what influence young grandchildren have on their grandparents? I have

Winning ways

Great snakes!

I wonder if the snakes were fried, boiled or baked!
—Joan Rendall: Launceston.

tried for more years than I care to remember to persuade my mother to give up smoking—and for even more years to fly abroad with us on holiday. But alas, all my persuasion fell on deaf ears. Then everything happened. At the age of 67, my mother has decided to give up smoking after 54 years of doing so—and as a result of much assurance by her grandsons that she will be well looked after by them, she has finally booked up for that holiday abroad. What have my kids got I haven't?
—Joan Harre: Sidcup.

My father was mistaken often for Sir Winston Churchill—and the resemblance was even more marked when he took a puff on his cigar!
—Mrs. E. Eggle: Brockworth.

All contributions to the YOU & US pages must be original, not copied nor duplicated to other editors. Subject to these conditions £5 will be paid for each letter printed. Letters intended for publication should be addressed to YOU & US. Other letters should be addressed to appropriate departments. We can reply only to those readers who enclose a stamped, addressed envelope.

woman

WHO WE ARE

EDITOR IN CHIEF	Jane Reed
ASSISTANT EDITORS	Billie Figg
	George Cannon
ART EDITOR	Nick Overhead
MANAGING EDITOR	Betty Hale
SENIOR EDITOR	Gaythorne Silvester
FEATURES EDITOR	Des Nolan
FASHION	Geraldine Gobby
BEAUTY	Arline Usden
HOME	Jane Graining
KNITTING	Lesley Stanfield
COOKERY	Frances Naldrett
FICTION	Rose Wild
TRAVEL & MOTORING	Jean Barratt
YOU & US	Kate Mahony
PICTURES	Barbara Peevor
CHIEF SUB-EDITOR	Linda Belcher
READERS' SERVICE	Terry Austin

WHAT'S IN IT FOR YOU

FASHION
- **30** Dressing To Kill!—in this year's wildest party outfits
- **22** Breeching The Gap

BEAUTY
- **16** Pressure Points—find yours for soothing self-help
- **43** Your Kind Of Scent?

HOME
- **24** Sofa Beds—elegant seating by day, glamorous bedding by night
- **53** The Christmas Collection

KNITTING
- **44** Principal Girl—step into the limelight in our chenille jacket

COOKERY
- **26** Let Them Eat Steak—and we don't mean beef
- **51** Your Nuttiest Christmas Cake Ever

FEATURES
- **8** "I Don't Want Anyone Watching My Thighs Get Old" —Jackie Bisset
- **12** Gloucestershire . . . By Royal Appointment
- **28** Behind The Gossip
- **32** "It's Just As I Planned"—says Anthony Andrews
- **34** Phobias—is this the breakthrough?

ACTIONWOMAN
- **20** Crackers—Will Your Christmas Go With A Bang?

TRAVEL
- **41** Two Wonderful Weeks In The South Of France

FICTION
- **18** The Wing Walker
- **39** Tilly Trotter Widowed—serial

SUPERSAVERS
- **50** The Woman Diary, 1982

REGULARS
- **54** Star Guide—Jillie Collings
- **55** Problem Page—Virginia Ironside
- Cover—Herb Ritts

WHERE WE ARE

KING'S REACH TOWER STAMFORD STREET, LONDON SE1 9LS. TEL: 01-261 5413.
Advertising inquiries: 01-261 6770
Editorial offers: Medway (0634) 407380
VOLUME 89 NUMBER 2302
Prices—including VAT at current rate—quoted in this issue are correct at time of going to press. © IPC Magazines Ltd., 1981.

please turn to page 7

5

Figure 7.3. This page from a woman's magazine is, in a sense, also tabular. It is divided into three vertical columns, containing an editorial, readers' letters, and the contents list. Two of these columns are further divided with horizontal rules (by kind permission of *Woman* magazine U.K.).

organizations. Writing, too, has a physical and spatial presence as well as abstract meaning. It has to be made and used, as well as composed and interpreted, and in this chapter I shall argue that the opportunities and constraints of its graphic nature affect all of these processes, but that their disparate nature presents obstacles to those seeking simple guidelines for practitioners.

Analyzing Typography and Layout

The books, magazines, packages, and other texts that surround us display a wide variety of formats and styles. What has led to their designers choosing those particular designs? Some (and in some text types, most) result from considerations of fashion and style, but many result from one of three distinct categories of functional imperatives:

- Firstly, the *syntactic* structure of the content is affected by the way in which items are ordered and grouped graphically on the page.
- Secondly, the method of manufacture may result in *artefactual* effects which have no semantic import, but which nevertheless significantly constrain the designer's syntactic options. For instance, page breaks are arbitrary and artefactual but place strict limits on what may be spatially juxtaposed.
- Thirdly, the way the text will be *used* must have a major influence on a designer's decisions.

Textual Communication Is Mediated Communication

These three categories of functional design considerations correspond to three stages in the textual communication process—origination, mediation (editing, design, manufacture, and distribution), and use. There is an obvious contrast between this and direct personal communication.

Text is a static and reflective medium, and it uses language in quite a different way from speech, which is dynamic and reactive. Thus, written language spoken out loud often sounds stilted and flat, and it can be hard to follow complex arguments which were designed to be read; in the same way, spoken language transposed onto paper seems rambling and ungrammatical, although when originally spoken, its listeners had no difficulty understanding it.

The difference is that speakers can see the reactions of their listeners and alter course in response to the immediate feedback provided by puzzled, bored, or surprised expressions, or questions and ripostes. The progress of a conversation, then, depends on both parties. In text, though, the sequence and form in which ideas are presented are up to one party only, the writer, who can only guess at the needs of his or her readers. Readers, though, have a facility not available to (polite) participants in a conversation—they can turn over pages, reread sections, or close the book. That is, although the argument presented can be more carefully controlled by the writer, its reception is controlled by the reader.

This is perhaps rather obvious, but it is not widely reflected in research on prose learning and instructional design. Experimenters often find it methodologically convenient to prevent subjects from rereading portions of experimental materials (or they discard the data from those who do). Nor is it always recognized by readers themselves, who when asked if they have read a particular book will often respond 'Not properly' when they have, quite appropriately to their needs, skim-read it or read it but discarded its argument as trivial, wrong, or out of date.

Reading Is a Selective Process

The confidence with which authors can predict the needs of their readers varies from text to text. Novelists have a self-selecting readership—so long as a hundred thousand people buy their book, it does not matter which hundred thousand it is. At the other extreme, some readerships are tightly controlled. Some courses control for prior knowledge and ability with strict entry tests—unsuitable readers are simply kept out. But the majority of textbooks are open to almost anyone, and their authors can predict comparatively little about their readers—their abilities, purposes, opinions, prior knowledge, or personal circumstances. Perhaps the only thing they can predict is that most of their readers must read selectively.

This view is reinforced by observation of reading styles and strategies by Pugh (1975) and Thomas (1976), who found that a straight-through linear strategy was not typical of efficient readers. Pugh linked selectivity with reading efficiency (defined as having a purpose in reading and achieving it), and found that otherwise fluent readers often had difficulty in using books as resources. Advisors on reading and study skills quite commonly recommend students to read selectively, previewing texts by scanning ahead and selecting particular parts for special attention.

Indeed, there are those who argue that students ought as a matter of course be given more responsibility for the selection of reading material and for determining their educational objectives. This 'gardening' approach to education (gardeners, the metaphor runs, tend their plants occasionally with nourishment or pruning, but mostly let them get on with the business of growing on their own) contrasts with the 'medical' approach (where professional medical staff diagnose knowledge deficiencies in students and, making use of the latest scientific data, prescribe a carefully measured diet of approved material). Both are exaggerations, of course, and in the wrong hands they are equally ineffective. But the carefully controlled texts, produced with the aid of readability formulas and interspersed with objectives, adjunct questions, and the like, which have been the apparent goal of traditional educational technology, have never been a very realistic proposition. And they are likely to become less realistic as, for reasons of politics and changing educational philosophies, mixed ability classes grow and open learning systems are introduced on a wider scale.

It is notable that at lower grade levels efforts are made to improve the textual communication process from both ends. That is, texts are prepared with careful attention to precisely the same factors that are the focus of reading instruction at those levels—vocabulary, grammar, and so on. At the higher levels, and at college level, students are assumed to be fluent readers, and instruction centers around study skills, but the corresponding efforts are not often made by textbook publishers. But what exactly should they be doing? How can textbooks be designed to aid students trying to use selective reading strategies?

Typography as Access Structure

Until recently, little attention was paid by the educational research community to the graphic organization of text. If you were to set out the contents page of this book as continuous prose, there would be remarkably little research in the literature to prove you wrong. After all, each word would be legible, recognizable, comprehensible, and even memorizable, although completely unusable for its intended purpose. The information would be inaccessible.

The purpose of a contents list is to provide an overview of the structure of a book as an aid to both planning a study task and identifying the location of particular information. It works because it uses typographic layout and signaling to display the structure of its contents (usually a hierarchical one). The structure of whole texts can be made accessible in a similar way, both by the provision of special typographically structured devices (such as contents lists) and also by the graphic treatment of the text itself.

Access structures share the two functions of contents lists: they have a global role in assisting the overview of a subject area and the planning of an active reading strategy; and they have a more local role in identifying or characterizing particular units of text, and giving visual structure to an argument. Under these two headings, we can identify a number of access devices in common use.

Global Accessibility

• *Contents lists.* The construction of contents lists seems to be a lost art today. Potentially, they can act as elaborate chapter summaries or even commentaries (see the marvelous contents lists to Henry Fielding's novels, Figure 7.4).

• *Concept diagram.* While contents lists show the structure of a particular linear text, a selection of topics ordered for educational as well as subject-matter reasons, concept diagrams show the author's conceptualization of his or her subject area, freed from the specificity and linearity of the book. See Figure 7.5.

• *Index.* An index is essential for a book designed to be used actively and creatively. It enables students to ask questions of it at

Figure 7.4. Part of the contents list of *Jonathan Wild* by Henry Fielding (1707-1754).

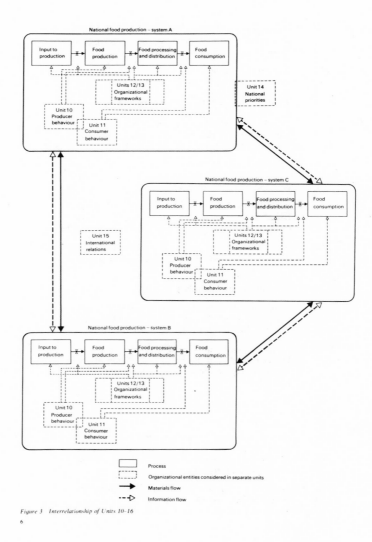

Figure 3 Interrelationship of Units 10–16

6

Figure 7.5. This concept diagram shows how the subject matter covered by six units of the Open University course T273 "Food Production Systems" is structured.

any point without relying on the author having anticipated their problem in advance. Indexes can be constructed to infinite levels of detail—the index to Boswell's *Life of Johnson* is longer than the book itself, and Bible concordances are nearly as long as the Bible. See Figure 7.6.

• *Glossary.* A glossary of special terms and their definitions is also essential for active readers, although if definitions are given sufficiently succinctly in the text, they can be accessed through the index.

• *Objectives.* Lists of objectives, quite apart from the effect they may or may not have on learning, are useful overview devices. However, a problem which all overviews encounter is that the student's needs are different according to whether he or she is treating them as *pre*views or *re*views. Highly specific technical objectives will be meaningless to students who have not yet been introduced to the technical terms they describe. One way around the problem is to provide more general ordinary language aims at the beginning of a text, and a more technically worded 'comprehension checklist' at the end.

• *Summaries.* These again should logically be different according to whether they are preview aids or review aids. The first should introduce the argument that is to follow in terms of that which has preceded it. The second reminds a reader, who is assumed to have read the chapter, of the nature of the argument and its conclusions.

Local Accessibility

The devices discussed above are all summarizations, condensations, or restructured collections of concepts occurring in the main body of text. At a more local level, though, while actually engaging the author's argument, an accessible visually-cued structure is also helpful.

• *Headings.* Although headings may also have an organizing function at the global level (readers can skim-read them to gain an overview), their primary function is an orienting one. That is, they label the text so that readers can locate the information they need and while reading be reminded of the context of the discussion

Figure 7.6. A good index or concordance reorganizes the information contained in a complex book to make it more accessible for readers with special purposes (courtesy Lutterworth Press).

and the point they have reached in a branching or hierarchical argument.

The first problem is 'what should they say.' There is a conflict between the ordinary-language terms that will be useful to the skimming reader (and in the contents list) and the technical terms which may best describe the topic to be discussed. One solution is to use both a technical title and a non-technical sub-title. A second problem is 'where to put them.' Cross-headings interrupt the text, and imply a boundary and a change of subject; they therefore have a role in structuring the argument, often replacing more discursive transitionary techniques. Side-headings, though, allow the flow of discourse to continue, and can be used, in effect, to comment on it or summarize it. Running headings (positioned along the top of the page, as in this book) can be used in the same way to summarize the contents of the page and remind readers of the general context of the specific information on the page.

Although ubiquitous, headings have never been properly incorporated into the mainstream of grammatical analysis or composition teaching. Uninformative or misleading headings are common, and inconsistent or illogical patterns of headings frequently escape comment. One problem is that we lack a vocabulary for discussing them. Publishing manuals tend to assume a hierarchical structure, and refer to A, B, or C headings, or Headings, Sub-headings, and Sub-sub-headings. But just as Eskimos have many more words than us for describing snow, journalists (whose working environment is the production of graphically-organized 'random access' texts—newspapers) have developed a more sophisticated vocabulary for describing headings. Their jargon, which differs from place to place, is a blend of *appearance* words—'eyebrow,' 'multideck,' 'standfirst,' 'skyline,'—and *function* words, like 'thinkpiece,' 'kicker,' or 'screamer.' This latter series hints at a possible alternative to the traditional hierarchical structures. Instead, we can talk about headings in terms of the way they act upon the reader (although, in an educational context, PTAs may be happier if we rephrased some of the journalists' terms!).

- *Layout.* The layout of components on a page, together with the way they are styled (their typeface, size, color, and so on), can be used to make individual items easy to locate—certain items, such as summaries, running headings, or marginal notes, can appear in regular positions, so that a pattern is created and carried over from page to page, chapter to chapter. But layout can also be used to make accessible the structure of the content of a text. Linked items can be clustered together, sequential links can be illustrated with spatial alignments, or boundaries indicated with space or rules.

Typography as Syntactic Structure

This brings us back to the original notion of text as diagram. Layout not only serves as an aid to selective reading, but also as part of the writer's repertoire of syntactic cues for giving a discourse direction and coherence. There are two significant barriers to the reliable implementation of this notion.

The first is the division of the (broadly-defined) writing process into specialisms. Writers are not normally expected to lay out their own material or to specify its typography; nor are the professional editors and designers who are responsible for this task expected to understand and intervene in the content of the books they handle. The second problem is that even if writers did have that opportunity, most would have difficulty with the task.

A solution to the organizational problem would require radically new management structures in the publishing industry. Specialist boundaries may have to be redrawn and a team approach encouraged. Several precedents can be suggested. The British Open University uses course teams of writers, editors, designers, educational technologists, and television producers to produce integrated courses, often without attribution to particular authors. And many of the highly graphic popular handbooks now widely sold—Time-Life and Readers Digest publications come to mind—are produced by large teams of writers, editors, artists, and photographers, who by working closely together gain a wider understanding of each other's skills. In these circumstances, even matters of office layout and other social factors become important.

The second problem is one of integrating graphic factors into our general concept of literacy, of developing a finer awareness of the subtleties of typography and their syntactic effect. If we could define the criteria that lead some layouts to work and others to fail, perhaps reliable guidelines could be developed for use by non-professionals acting as designers.

Typography as Macro-Punctuation

It is sometimes helpful to describe areas of doubt in terms of compatible areas of reasonable certainty. In this case, it might be a good starting point to conceive of spatial and graphic factors as having a similar role at the page or text level to that of punctuation at the sentence level. For example, we often put short interpolations in parentheses; if they get too long, though, we might use a footnote at the bottom of the page instead. The syntactic relationship between the interpolation and the rest of the sentence is the same—only the scale is different. Further, if the footnote becomes too long, we might put it in an appendix at the end of the book, or even in a separate volume altogether—the ultimate spatial distinction. Several functions of punctuation are paralleled at the macro-text level by typography and layout. Four are listed below.

Interpolation

• punctuation	• typography
parentheses	footnotes
dashes	boxed items
commas	marginalia
	indentation

Interpolation is the insertion (either by cross-reference or by actual juxtaposition) of a short component into a longer one in such a way that the continuity of the longer sentence, paragraph, or page is not spoiled. Interpolations within the sentence usually have the purpose of clarifying or commenting on an argument, or a fact mentioned in the course of an argument. At the macro-text level, though, they can also have an accessing role—signaling the main points for the browsing reader. See Figures 7.7 and 7.8.

s2-5 unit 1

blood group system. An individual, heterozygous in possessing both A and B alleles, shows both A and B substances on its cells. In other cases one member of a heterozygous pair may fail to make its presence felt. It is then designated as *recessive* to its *dominant* partner. For example, certain human beings lack pigments in the skin, a condition known as *albinism*. Most albinos are the children of non-albino parents, a situation that can be explained as follows:

The father has one 'albino' allele (a) plus one 'non-albino' allele (−). It follows that half the gametes he produces will carry the albino allele.

The mother is in the same position.

If the offspring of such a union are predicted we should expect one-quarter to have two 'non-albino' alleles (+/+) and to be non-albino in appearance, one-half to have one albino allele only (a/ + like their parents) and to be non-albino in appearance and one-quarter to have two albino alleles (a/a) and to be albino in appearance. This can be represented diagrammatically [7] as:

a/ −	×	a/ +		— parents
a	−	a	+	— gametes
a/a	a/ −	a/ +	+/ +	— offspring

Such inheritance is called *Mendelian* after Gregor Mendel, its discoverer. The Mendelian calculus allows for the prediction of the genotypes and phenotypes of organisms in respect of any number of separate genes.

Mendelian inheritance implies very considerable accuracy in the process of replicating genes during cell proliferation. Yet altered alleles do occur 'spontaneously' rather rarely. They are known as gene-mutations and can take the form of change in part of the DNA sequence constituting an allele, that is, change in the nucleotide base sequence, by loss or substitution. [8] It is characteristic of mutant alleles that their own subsequent replication is also very accurate. Mutations in cells that are destined to give rise to tissues of the body (so-called *somatic* cells) are known as somatic mutations. They will often pass unnoticed. Occasionally the descendants of a somatic cell which has mutated are seen as patches of aberrant skin with different colour or hair form from the rest of the body. [9]

Modern genetics has thus provided an understanding of what lies behind both inheritance and variation in animals and plants. Because DNA contains, in the sequence of the nucleotide bases of which it is largely composed, information which specifies the amino acid sequence in protein, cells with the same complement of DNA molecules have the same repertoire of possible proteins that they could synthesize. Because the DNA molecule can be copied with great precision to produce two 'daughter' molecules with the same base sequence as the 'parent' molecule, any clone of cells (mutation ignored) will have the same genetic information and hence the same range of proteins available to all its members.

This limits the effect of the environment of the cell to controlling or selecting which part of the genetic information present in it should be used (transcribed and trans-

5 The haploid number, that is the number of chromosomes per haploid (gamete) cell, for a species is often given the abbreviation n. Most known diploid (2n) numbers are below 30, but higher numbers are found. The numbers for some favourite genetical organisms are:

fruit-fly (*Drosophila melanogaster*)	—	2n = 8
man	—	2n = 46
mouse	—	2n = 40
maize	—	2n = 20

Two interesting types of chromosomal anomaly may occur spontaneously or be provoked experimentally. Polyploidy is a condition in which a cell has more than two complete haploid sets, such as in triploid (3n) and tetraploid (4n) eggs which may, in some species, develop into adults. Within the mammalian body some tissues (notably liver) have a proportion of polyploid cells.

Aneuploidy is a condition in which the cell does not have a multiple of haploid sets, but has one, or a few, too many or too few chromosomes. Aneuploidy is often lethal, but organisms exhibiting minor degrees of it may be viable.

6 The word gene is used in at least two different ways, and sometimes ambiguously. Often, however, the context makes it clear which of the following meanings is in the user's mind. It is used:
(a) collectively for all the possible alleles that could occupy one particular site (or locus) on a chromosome.
(b) for one specified allele.

7 × is common genetic shorthand for a 'cross', that is, a mating between the individuals indicated.

8 Spontaneous mutation rates in man are estimated, for different genes, to lie between 1 in 10 000 and 1 in 100 000 per allele per gamete.

As you know from Unit 19 of S100, mutation rates can be raised by high temperature, some chemical agents and by ionizing radiation (e.g. X-rays or the radiation from decaying radioactive isotopes). Not all mutations are necessarily harmful, but on balance it is possible to say that in human populations mutagenic agents (i.e. things causing mutations) are hazardous to future generations. Hence great care is taken to minimize the exposure of the gonads (including those of a foetus in the uterus) to X-rays. Nuclear weapon fall-out is, fortunately, a diminishing hazard as overground tests have been largely abandoned.

It is important to stress that the effects of mutation on the organism are not specifically related to the agents provoking them. For example, mutations caused by X-irradiation do not necessarily confer greater or lesser sensitivity to X-rays on the organisms carrying them.

9 Somatic mutation is thought to be responsible for some cases in man in which one eye differs from the other in colour or in which one segment of one iris is different in colour from the rest.

ITQ 1

Will the stage of development at which a somatic mutation occurs affect its final effect?

Now check your answer against that on page 27.

11

Figure 7.7. The design of this Open University text (S2-5, Unit 1, "Genes and Development") is intended to help students employing a skim-read strategy in preparation for a more detailed read. Definitions, commentary, exercises, and figures have all been interpolated in the right-hand column. The use of bold reference numbers in the main (left-hand column) text ensures that readers can move equally easily from the right-hand to the left-hand column.

TOWARDS A SYSTEMS-BASED METHODOLOGY FOR REAL-WORLD PROBLEM SOLVING

P.B. Checkland

INTRODUCTION

Everyone pays lip-service to "systems" ...

The notions of 'systems analysis' of complex problem situations and 'a systems approach' to problem solving have become so modish that few are brave enough publicly to reject them and to argue for a reductionist rather than a holistic approach. One reason for this must be the sheer *generality* of claims made for using 'a systems approach'. The complex problems of organisations private and public, and the yet more difficult problems of society as a whole, are so obviously multi-faceted and contain so many connections that it is 'obvious' that we must somehow embrace 'the whole problem' in seeking to solve it, lest improvements in one area produce effects elsewhere which are inimical to the whole.

But few know how to apply the ideas

But constant lip service to 'a systems approach', and exhortations to use it, do not hide the relative lack of determined persistent efforts both to define what a systems approach consists of and to use it in tackling real-world problems. It is not helpful to make claims for an approach unless it is possible to detail the concept sufficiently for interested persons to grasp it and use it in tackling problems of their own. A recent international symposium on "A Systems Approach to Management", for example, generated much useful discussion [1], but absolutely absent from it was any account of how a systems approach to management might actually be made manifest in the management of an organisation, let alone the 'management' of society.

If 'a systems approach' is to become more than an easily accepted but somewhat irritating concept, there is a need for expressions of it which eliminate any difference between what it is and how we may use it; the need is for accounts of systems-based *methodologies* which describe a systems approach as a way of analysing and hence trying to solve real-world problems.

The challenge: develop methodologies covering the hard–soft spectrum

In a previous paper [2] I has been suggested that the challenge facing those seeking to develop a systems approach is to develop methodologies appropriate across the spectrum from "the relatively 'hard' systems involving industrial plants characterized by easy-to-define objectives, clearly defined decision-taking procedures and quantitative measures of performance...(to)...'soft' systems in which objectives are hard to define, decision-taking is uncertain, measures of performance are at best qualitative and human behaviour is irrational".

This methodology has actually been used in practice

This paper is an attempt to begin to meet that challenge. It presents a general methodology which uses systems ideas to find a structure in apparently unstructured 'soft' problems, and hence leads to action to eliminate, alleviate or solve the problem, or provides an orderly way of tackling 'hard' problems. The methodology was evolved in the course of an action research programme of client-sponsored systems studies during the period 1969-1971, and refined in further projects in 1972 and 1973. It was derived from experience in real-world problem situations and 'tested' in further problems. Tested ideas are rare, and although it is impossible in logic to establish accurately the worth or otherwise of a methodology such as this (a point discussed below), the users of it have found its guidelines helpful.

The methodology is expounded here by means of some account of projects which led to its formulation and reformulation. The aim is to hit a level between the merely anecdotal: "this happened...", and the dubiously academic: "Questionnaires sent to 100 firms showed that...".

Summary of the paper

Section 1 argues the need for ways of using systems ideas which are at once precise yet vague — precise in the sense that the ideas can actually be used to initiate and guide action, vague in the sense that the methodology must not be seen as, must not become, a technique. This section reviews the development of the systems movement and the strands of thinking within it which have led to previous expositions of

Ackoff (1974) argues that there is no such thing in real life as *a problem*. Instead we are faced incessantly with *systems of interlocking problems*. To describe *a system of problems* Ackoff has coined the term "mess". The French word *"problématique"* is more elegant.

Note the implied definitions of "hard" and "soft" systems. Checkland returns to this later.

One of the most important features of the methodology is that it tries to incorporate the insights and concepts of general systems into real-life management consultancy. Lancaster runs a consultancy company (ISCOL) which every year conducts a number of systems investigations. To date upwards of 100 such studies have been carried out.

Figure 7.8. The argument of this text was found to be obscure and hard to follow. In this experimental version, a summary has been added to the left-hand margin and a critique to the right-hand margin. Students strongly favored the new version.

Delineation

• punctuation	• typography
initial capitals	headings
full point	bullets
comma	title-page
semi-colon	space
colon	rules

This term simply refers to ways of marking where a particular unit of text begins and where it ends (or, in the case of non-linear items like pictures, where the boundary is). A sentence begins with an initial capital and ends with a full point, or another punctuation mark of equal status. A newspaper story begins with a bold headline and ends with a rule, space, or perhaps the next headline. See Figures 7.9 and 7.10.

Serialization

• punctuation	• typography
commas	headings, numerals
semi-colon	tabular format
oblique strokes	regular spacing, patterning
bullets	regular styling
numerals	rules, arrows

Serialization refers to the organization of text components into clear sequences and structures. For example, this section is one of a series of four, which are linked by a regularity of treatment—similar headings, tabular displays, and overall layout. Series may be straightforward sequences of items to be attended to in a particular order—technical instructions, for instance—or they may be hierarchical in nature. See Figure 7.11.

Stylization

• punctuation	• typography
quotation mark	size variation
exclamation mark	typeface variation
question mark	distinctive layout
italicization	background tint, colored paper
	symbol, keyword

Figure 7.9. This complex newspaper page uses a wide range of techniques for delineating different units of text (courtesy *London Daily Star*).

3   Looking at the pattern of what you do

A Break the old pattern Alert yourself to what you're doing. For example, if you eat snacks without thinking about it, stick warning notices or pictures on the fridge and biscuit tin.

Set limits on when or where. For example, only have a drink when your partner is with you. Or, only eat when sitting up at a table.

Make it less pleasant. Make it a rule you will only smoke while sitting on a hard chair facing a blank wall.

B Make the new pattern easier For example, if you want to get to work on time, set everything ready the night before! Or, if you are dieting, don't keep any sweets or biscuits in the house.

Joan

A To make sure I don't smoke 'by accident' I will put the pack inside a tin with a difficult lid

I'm limiting my pattern by trying to start smoking a little later each day

B I'll drink orange juice for breakfast, it tastes a lot better if I don't smoke at the same time

Harry

A I'm going to stop myself wolfing down food without thinking when I come in at night by putting a warning notice on the kitchen door

The first week I'll cut out all potatoes. The next week add bread and the following week cake and biscuits, to the forbidden list. The fourth week I'll be brave and change to drinking halfs instead of pints

B I'll get my wife to serve out the meals on to my plate instead of serving myself

4   Help yourself to change

If something good happens just after you've done something then you are likely to repeat the action. You have linked it in your mind with a reward. This will make you more likely to want to do it again.

If something bad happens you link the action with what seems to be a punishment. So make an effort to remember this punishment when you are next tempted and you will be less likely to repeat it.

A What rewards you? If you haven't already done it, turn back and do the rewards activity on page 116. You need your own private list of rewards! Remember it has been proved that small rewards, given at once, make it easier to learn new habits.

B How can you earn rewards? Break your task of changing into very small steps. Plan to give yourself many instant, small rewards, so it makes it easy to earn them. (Keeping your record chart each day deserves a reward.) If you like you can try collecting points towards a bigger reward. In that case it is important to give yourself a visible token reward that you can 'trade in' for the real reward (like green shield stamps!). That way you have something to look at to remind yourself that you are steadily working towards your big reward. Otherwise you may get discouraged.

C Get your friends to help Rewards from friends can speed things up. A kiss from his wife every time he remembered to fasten his seat belt worked best for one man. Look back at your private list of rewards. Use those marked .. as extra rewards when you begin to find that changing is harder than you thought when you started.

D Punishments Watch out! These can be very tricky to use, particularly the punishment of nagging yourself. They can easily make you give up hope. Punishments from your friends may be tricky too. They may agree to confiscate your cigarettes if they catch you with them – and then you get angry with them for doing it. That way you may end up losing friends!

Sicken yourself. Chain smoking for 10 minutes or until you get sick or dizzy is sometimes used at the start of trying to give up smoking. Or eating chips until you are sick may put you off them for a long time (but add pounds to your weight!).

Joan

A The five 'rewards' that I ticked on my list were:

  having a cup of tea
  reading my favourite magazine
  having a bath
  stroking the cat
  buying make-up

B I'll have a cup of tea each time I fill in my chart

If I start to light up but then stub it out again I'll take five minutes off to read magazine

On the days I go a whole extra hour without smoking I will buy myself some make-up

C When I feel desperate I'll ring up or go and see Mum or Anne

D I'd feel silly punishing myself

Harry

A My five pleasures I ticked were:

  doing the crossword in the newspaper
  playing country & western records
  having a quick look at Penthouse
  a cigarette (I'm going to give those up next but I might as well enjoy them while I can)
  eating apples

B I'll take an apple to work and reward myself with it if I don't eat chips

I'll do the crossword when I get in at night instead of going into the kitchen and eating

Instead of taking a snack to bed with me I'll have a quick look at Penthouse magazine

C I'm not going to tell my friends, so I can't get them to help

D If my waist isn't any smaller when I measure it on a Sunday, I'll have a week with no beer at all

Figure 7.10. This page, from an educational text, is also quite complex. However, the same typeface and rules have been used for the main text and the tables, and as a result, the structure is hard to see. From the Open University text, *The Good Health Guide*, Harper and Row, London, 1980.

Target – eat less fats

Why?
Cholesterol is the main constituent of fatty deposits in arteries and of gallstones. Excess amounts are made in the body when high fat foods are eaten. Particularly food rich in 'saturated' fat mainly found in animal foods. Other fats in the diet – called 'poly-unsaturated' fats – tend to reduce cholesterol in the body. This type of fat is found in many foods, particularly in corn oil, sunflower seed oil and soya oil. (NB some vegetable oils and margarines are, in fact, rich in saturated fat.)
   As far as general health is concerned it is more important to reduce the total amount of all fats rather than just to swap animal fats for special vegetable oils or margarine

By how much?
We get more than 40% of the calories we need from fats. It would be better to reduce fats to 30–35%. This is difficult to calculate. You almost certainly need to cut down if you often do one or more of these things. Eat fried food. Put butter or margarine on cooked vegetables. Spread butter thickly on your bread. Eat a lot of the foods listed in the next column. Provided you keep the total amount low you do not need to cut out completely your favourite butter, cream or fried food. If you are not prepared to cut down on the total amount of fat in your diet you should change to special vegetable oils and low fat spreads

Watch these foods
Fat is a major part of: cakes, pastries, biscuits and chocolates, sausages, salami, pork, lamb, cheese, cream, butter and margarine, cooking oils and fat.
   If you love the taste of butter, really savour it on a plain slice of bread and butter.
   Change your cooking habits by
○ Grilling instead of frying
○ Using non-stick pans
○ Using recipes which use less fat
○ Using skimmed (low fat) milk instead of ordinary milk in recipes

Target – eat less sugar

Why?
A high sugar diet encourages dental decay. Sweet foods can spoil the appetite for more nourishing foods. Sugar only provides energy which is also provided by, for example, potatoes and wholemeal bread. Because we become addicted to sweet things we are tempted to overeat and so may put on weight

By how much?
Most people get one fifth of their energy needs (calories) from sugar. About half of this is from the use of packet sugar and jams. The other half might be thought of as 'hidden sugar' which is added to many manufactured foods. *We do not need any sugar at all*

Watch these foods
Sugar is the major part of sweets, soft drinks, cakes, biscuits, puddings and jams. It is also added to many manufactured foods like tomato ketchup, tinned fruit, ice cream and frozen foods. Reading the label will tell you which have sugar added to them. If you have a sweet tooth you could have an occasional treat, eg, jam on your bread or a piece of chocolate

Target – eat more fibre

Why?
There are probably a dozen different kinds of fibres, all with different roles to play. Therefore cereal foods *and* fruit and vegetables are equally important. Extra bran is not the same as 'high fibre diet' and is only good for helping constipation. 'High fibre diets', which may offer protection from a number of digestive ailments, are also low in fat and animal protein

By how much?
You can't really eat too much when it is a natural part of food. You could eat too much bran – but you would be hard put to swallow it. You are probably eating enough if you have regular bulky, but not hard, bowel movements

Watch these foods
Eat more of the bulky foods listed in 'fillers' *and* a variety of fruit and vegetables
   Eat breakfast cereals made from the whole grain
○ Try brown rice or wholemeal pasta
○ Eat wholemeal or brown bread
○ Eat the skins of old potatoes as well as new ones

Figure 7.11. The rhythmic headline writing and typography of this page diagram its structure particularly clearly. From the Open University text, *The Good Health Guide*, Harper and Row, London, 1980.

Stylization here refers to the indication of a mode of discourse differing in voice or genre from the main body of text. For example, exercises, objectives, and study notes might be distinguished by a special typeface or color to indicate that they do not form part of the main argument of the text but have a special function or have been inserted by a different author. See Figure 7.12.

Parallels in the Development of Theory

It is worth pursuing this analogy with punctuation a little further, because there may be an interesting parallel between the way that theories of punctuation were originally developed and the way that theories of 'macro-punctuation' might develop now and in the future.

Until comparatively recently, punctuation practice, and indeed spelling, was erratic and unstandardized. It was not until the seventeenth and eighteenth centuries that 'correct' practice started to be codified by the early English grammarians. They regarded it as an elocutionary aid, denoting breathing spaces, pauses for dramatic effect, and cues for special intonations required of the reader, who was assumed to be reading out loud, or at least sub-vocalizing as he or she read silently. But during the eighteenth century, linguists developed theories about the syntactic function of punctuation. The various kinds of period—full point, colon, semi-colon, and comma—were seen as making distinct kinds of transition between and within sentences, rather than simply denoting different lengths of pauses when 'performing' the text. Cohen (1977) gives a detailed account of these developments. Honan (1960) takes the story further, into the nineteenth century, when the elocutionary theories were completely rejected in favor of elaborate and often pedantic schemes for using punctuation syntactically. These days it is normal to steer a middle course and recognize a combination of the two roles.

Is there any sign that typographic factors will ever be incorporated into the framework of linguistic analysis in a similar way? Some recent developments in linguistics may indicate that they will. It is significant that the early linguists almost all included sections on punctuation in their grammatical treatises, in

Section 5

THE PROBLEMS AND POTENTIAL OF PARTICIPATION

Although most of the forms of participation discussed in the previous sections were aimed at giving a significant amount of power to the user, the worker or citizen, there still remained a definable professional or managerial role. This Section concentrates first on the role and problems of these professionals. Can they aid participation, or should (and could) more power be wielded by the non-expert citizen? Can citizens participate in decision-making given our present complex, social, economic and technical systems and what happens if they cannot? In looking at some of these questions, the central issue that emerges is: can people formulate and articulate goals and priorities autonomously, or must they be constantly aided by experts?

Required reading for Section 4: Reader: 2.6 Stringer.

Many advanced states are experiencing within themselves . . . (a) gap between public opinion and the machinery of government. A paradox of the modern technological society is revealed: the society creates problems so complex that they can be handled only by those with specialist skills and intricate knowledge, and at the same time it produces people who are in general more highly educated and inquiring than previous generations. It centralizes decision-making but spreads the desire to make decisions. How can democracy, in this predicament, satisfy both the need for greater efficiency and the need for wider participation?*

As you have seen, the basic idea of 'social control' of technological policy (and related social and economic policies) can lead to a wide variety of prescriptions for 'participation', 'community socialism', 'advocacy planning', 'community control', and so on. Most of these prescriptions are concerned with overcoming both professional reluctance and public inertia and fatalism. But quite apart from the problems of apathy, and, of course, vested interests and hierarchical control, these are problems which relate to the very nature of our technological society.

For example, it could be argued that given the technological and economic complexity of modern society, direct social control is probably unrealistic and certainly inefficient. As journalist Milton Shulman has said:

participation in complex society

Whether the natural intelligence of people, untramelled by expertise or knowledge will come to a wiser decision about such matters as the floating pound, the deterrent impact of hanging, the third airport, entry into the Common Market, inflation, North Sea gas, Concorde, than a cabal of experts stuffed with information about the subject, is a deduction that, to put it mildly, is highly speculative.†

* Editorial, *The Times*, 27 May 1968.

† Shulman, M., (1973) 'What People Think They Think', *Evening Standard*, 2 May.

55

Figure 7.12. This page, although not exemplary in design, shows several different genres of text components signaled typographically: the headline is capitalized; the summary has a red tint over it; quotations are indented; the required reading is printed between rules; and a special term is flagged in red in the margin. From the Open University course T262, "Man-Made Futures."

contrast to their modern counterparts—it is very hard to find even a mention of it in any modern linguistics textbook. The difference between the two lies partly in their objectives. The early grammarians aimed to investigate, regularize, and improve the communication process, while modern linguists study language primarily as a key to understanding the structure of human thought processes. Recently, though, text linguists have begun to extend grammatical analysis beyond the sentence to whole texts, and some are working together with psychologists to investigate the communication effectiveness of different configurations of macro-textual units. Now graphic factors are emerging in their analyses (although not as a major focus). For example, Werlich's (1976) text grammar deals with headings and other graphically signaled devices, and van Dijk's (1979) list of relevance cues includes typographic along with lexical and syntactic factors.

Problems of a Dual Role

The two roles of punctuation are, in effect, biased—the one towards the writer and the other towards the reader. Syntactic punctuation constitutes part of the writer's expressive repertoire; it helps him or her articulate his or her thoughts precisely. And elocutionary punctuation aids the reader in the performance of reading. In relation to punctuation, that debate is no longer current or meaningful, but it still has a relevance in relation to typography as macro-punctuation. At the micro level, one person, the writer, normally has control of all aspects of the use of language; but at the text level, as we have seen, a range of specialists is involved. Writers typically compose a text before decisions are made about typography and layout, which, when not regarded just as side-effects of the manufacturing process or as a marketing consideration, are seen as solely of relevance to the ergonomics of reading and using books rather than to the articulation of their content.

A text, then, presents a different set of problems to reader and writer. The writer's main problem is to construct a sound *argument*, and many of the devices we have discussed (or the items they signal) augment his or her means of expression—they have a rhetorical function, in the non-pejorative sense of the word. The reader, though, is faced in the first instance with a *book*, a physical artefact through which he or she may gain access to the argument. But the same graphic techniques form part of this means of enquiry for the reader.

Table 7.1 summarizes some of the devices and text components which serve to help writers construct coherent messages, and to help readers read and study effectively. Several have more than one role, and so in many cases it will not be possible to determine an exclusive grammatical or normal role for a particular graphic technique. A looser case-law description of common practices, allowing for variations in style according to circumstances, is likely to be of more help than any attempt to strictly rationalize or regulate the use of typography.

Typographic Semantics

How then can we handle, in analytic terms, the meaning that typography and layout can contribute to a writer's message? Bearing in mind, of course, those factors which may be entirely artefactual, a 'case-law' of typography would have to draw on at least three distinct kinds of sources of visual effects.

Conventional Effects

Some visual aspects of writing have emerged for historical or accidental reasons but have acquired a significance about which there is general agreement within a linguistic or cultural group. There is a visually arbitrary relationship between the graphic effect and its referent or content. For example, the letters of the alphabet bear no relationship to the sound patterns of speech—they have a purely denotative status. Other conventions of our writing system are that we write from left to right in lines from the top to the bottom of the page.

Representational Effects

These are graphic effects which imitate some aspect of visual or phonic experience. For example, bold type can reflect vocal stress, and musical notation reflects the up-down metaphor in the

Rhetorical functions—the writer's means of expression

About the argument	summarization (title, summary)
	introduction (foreword, preface, introduction)
Within the argument	emphasis (underlining, italics, etc.)
	transition (headings, space, etc.)
	bifurcation (alternative options, parallel texts, interpolated sections)
Extra to the argument	substantiation (footnotes, appendices, references)
	addenda (apologia, acknowledgments, etc.)

Access functions—the reader's means of enquiry

About the book	overviews (contents list, abstract)
	definitives (glossary, index)
	identifiers (title, author, style)
Within the book	locators (topical headings, typographic signaling)
	descriptors (functional headings, captions)
Extra to the book	study guidance (recommended reading, exercises)

Table 7.1. The dual role of typography and typographically signaled text components.

description of music. They are, in a sense, pictorial or onomatopoeic. See Figures 7.13 and 7.14.

Associational Effects

Associational effects have a connotative force, and result from stylization, exploiting the aura that becomes attached to visual imagery. Just as a white coat makes the presenter in a toothpaste advertisement look like a scientist, graphic designers can borrow external signs of quality, value, or authenticity and use them in a rhetorical manner. The special offer tokens on breakfast cereal

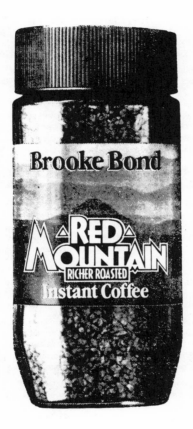

Figure 7.13. The lettering on this coffee jar is clearly representational (courtesy Brooke Bond Oxo Ltd.).

PART I PROPOSITION (i) THE RENAISSANCE IN PAINTING CONSISTED OF A RE-ENACTION OR RECREATION OF CLASSICAL STYLES, MOOD AND SUBJECT MATTER

145   The basic implication of the term 'Renaissance' is that it meant a 'rebirth' of classicism in art. Compare *A scene from the Villa of the Mysteries* (from now on referred to as *The Mysteries*) (Plate 1) painted at Pompeii in the first century A.D. and *Parnassus* (Figure 87), painted around 1509, in Rome, by the painter Raphael. Pause, and ask yourself how thorough Raphael's recreation of classical art was, and whether the sympathy between the two paintings is extraordinary. Because Raphael had not, in fact, seen any classical paintings like this. Can you see any similarities in subject, form, costume or mood?

146   Raphael has treated a classical subject (the poets on Parnassus headed by Apollo and the Nine Muses) in classical form (note the sense of solidity and liveliness in each figure, the use of relief-modelling and the clear sense of space), in classical costume, and, most important though perhaps most evasive, in a classical mood, by which I mean a pervasive equilibrium and tranquillity. Raphael has produced what is not a copy of any particular classical painting, but a classical production in its own right. And this is very extraordinary, because the two paintings were produced in cultures widely differing from one another, and they are separated by fifteen hundred years, during which the principles of classical art were neglected either partially or wholly.

147   How did Raphael achieve his recreation? Since a complete recreation of classical painting involves the assimilation of its forms, subject matter and mood, when did this happen, or did it ever really happen at all? Before answering such questions you must get a clear idea of some of the specific characteristics of classical painting, so that you can gauge its influence on later painting.

148   In the two columns below I have prepared a tabulated comparison between classical and medieval painting. The examples of classical painting are:
The Mysteries (Plate 1); first century B.C.;
The Three Graces (Figure 88) and a Roman wall-painting of a scene from the Odyssey (now referred to as *The Odyssey*) (Figure 89). The examples of medieval painting are:

Figure 7.14. Although legibility research would condemn the use of upper case in this heading, the designer has attempted to reflect Renaissance inscriptional lettering and book design. Unfortunately, the effect is spoiled by the use of a non-contemporary type-face. The decorative border (to denote a place to stop and think) also has Renaissance connotations. From the Open University course A201, "Renaissance and Reformation."

packets imitate the originally functional use of copperplate lettering on banknotes, to gain an impression of value. In textbook design, publishers can sometimes be inhibited from exploring innovative formats for fear of projecting the wrong image, or an unfamiliar one.

Typography—Art or System?

Eric Partridge (1953), whose punctuation manual is one of the most subtle (although considered eccentric by some), talks of "Punctuation an art, not a haphazardry nor yet a perfunctoriness." This is true of typography, and it is true of diagrams. The definition and specification of rules for clear writing have so far eluded us, in spite of enormous efforts. We can recognize and describe it—even measure it—but it remains a skill acquired through hard work and sensitive observation: perspiration and perspicuity. The writer wishing to exploit the full potential of his or her medium—which is a writing system as well as a language—will find further skills to be mastered, and considerable obstacles presented by a publication process that divides the responsibility for the writing/editing/designing process (an essential unified task—see Macdonald-Ross & Waller's (1976) proposal of a 'transforming' communications role) between several individuals. However, the printing and publishing industries are changing fast, and in the not so far future it may well be possible for writers to regain some of the control over their medium that they lost to Herr Gutenberg. Meanwhile, we do need a more subtle understanding of how typography works, and this is likely to come from exactly the sort of combination of approaches reflected in this volume: an appreciation of the cognitive processes used by readers in tackling the study of text, and a 'literary tradition' of practical experience and experiment with real texts and innovative formats.

References

Cohen, M. *Sensible words: Linguistic practice in England, 1640-1785.* Baltimore: The Johns Hopkins University Press, 1977.

Honan, P. Eighteenth and nineteenth century punctuation theory. *English Studies*, 1960, *41*, 92-102.

Macdonald-Ross, M., & Waller, R.H.W. The transformer. *The Penrose Annual*, Volume 69, London: Northwood Publications, 1976.

Partridge, E. *You have a point there*. London: Hamish Hamilton, 1953.

Pugh, A.K. The development of silent reading. In W. Latham (Ed.), *The road to effective reading*. London: Ward Lock, 1975.

Thomas, L. *The self-organized learner and the printed word*. Uxbridge: Brunel University Centre for the Study of Human Learning, 1976.

van Dijk, T. Relevance assignment in discourse comprehension. *Discourse Processes*, 1979, *2*, 113-126.

Werlich, E. *A text grammar of English*. Heidelberg: Quelle and Meyer, 1976.

8.

Textual Display Techniques

Philippe C. Duchastel

1. Introduction

This chapter is concerned with the notion of textual display as it applies to the design of texts, especially textbooks. Textual display is the manner in which text information is presented on a page or in a chapter. The traditional form of text display is sequential prose, often enhanced by headings and sub-headings. An alternate well-known form is programmed instruction; other forms, such as Information Mapping, and Discourse Punctuation, are represented elsewhere in this volume.

All of these are textual display systems, which make use of various textual display techniques (such as typographical highlighting, for instance) as components of the system. I shall examine later in this chapter a number of such techniques, but the theme of this chapter is the broader consideration of how textual display techniques as a whole fit into text design. Textual display is and will remain an art (a point I return to in the conclusion), and various systems of text presentation will continue to be created as instructional designers and publishers consider further the importance for learning of taking into account explicit means of text design.

This chapter explores the foundations for such an orientation in the field of text design. To do so, it initially considers some basic assumptions about the nature of text and text processing. It then briefly turns to problems in learning from text (a vast subject in itself) and from this particular angle, examines a number of specific display techniques that can assist the learner in overcoming text-processing problems.

167

In conjunction with a number of the other contributions in this section of the volume (especially the chapters by Hartley and by Waller), this chapter should help the text designer in establishing a conceptual framework with which to examine, develop, and use explicit means of text design.

2. The Nature of Text

A text is a medium of communication just as any other medium is, such as direct speech, television, radio, etc. At its simplest, then, a text is a process by which an author communicates a message to a reader (Figure 8.1).

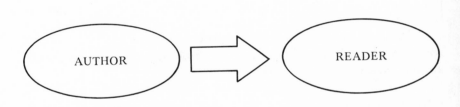

Figure 8.1. Relationship: Author and reader.

A text differs from most other media, however, in its permanence. The message being communicated does not just flick by on a screen (as in television), nor is it merely seen fleetingly as one rushes by (as in the case of advertising posters, for instance). Instead, a text is physically in the hands of the reader; as such, it becomes a resource to be used with discernment by the reader. In writing a text, the author creates a product; in studying a text, the reader uses the product (Figure 8.2). This conception of text, which I have borrowed from Waller (this volume), emphasizes the prime importance to be attached to the activities of the reader in considering textual communication. This perspective is just emerging in the field of text design, as evidenced by many of the contributions reflecting it in this volume. I reiterate it here because it underlies **the notion of text processing**, which I shall be exploring in this chapter.

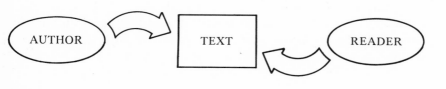

Figure 8.2. Relationship: Author and reader to text.

Of course, it has always been customary for authors to consider their potential readership when writing texts. A secondary school text, for instance, will treat a subject in less detail than will a corresponding college text, and the language used will be simpler. In these matters, the reader certainly is considered explicitly. These issues, however, are content issues, not issues concerning presentation factors. In other words, they relate to the message, not to the medium; they relate to the subject-matter content, not to the text. As such, they are associated with the model in Figure 8.1.

Traditionally, a text was considered to be composed of a message (the subject matter), which was communicated by means of a particular medium (the textbook). The medium itself was simply a convenient way of packaging the message and no more than that (see Figure 8.3, which displays a textbook page from an earlier era). Consideration of the reader was limited to the design of the message, and did not involve the design of the medium. Figure 8.4, which displays a modern text, shows how this state of affairs is changing. **The text is no longer just a package for the message; it is itself being used creatively to support learning.** This is an evident trend in current textbook publishing (although far too many texts are still unresponsive in their design to text-processing needs and still follow the older model.

To summarize the discussion so far, **texts are becoming responsive to learner requirements not only in what they communicate, but also in how they do so** (Figure 8.5). This evolution has largely occurred as a result of a growing awareness in education that **learning from text involves more than passive reading. It involves active text processing.** Editors and instructional designers are increasingly realizing that textual display techniques may be employed constructively to enhance text usage and thus to facilitate learning.

3. Text Processing

While a text is a product that can be used by many people for many purposes, it is usually created with a specific audience and a particular purpose in mind. **Thus, a text can be characterized in functional terms.** Dictionaries, for instance, are used for looking up the meaning of words, reference books for finding out specific information about a subject, novels for entertainment. Textbooks are used primarily for learning.

The importance of this functional perspective lies in the fact that **different types of text (and the specific purposes for which they are used) will influence which processing strategies are engaged in by the reader.** The activity of studying a textbook is rather different from the activity of reading a novel or from that of looking up a word in a dictionary, as is nicely illustrated by Gibson & Levin (1975). **How a text is processed is thus intimately tied to its function.**

Text processing itself is an artful skill that one masters slowly. There is generally more to learning from a textbook than simply

THE SELF. 209

soil was soft, but that the weight of my body was reduced to almost nothing. . . . I had the feeling of being without weight. . . ." In addition to being so distant, " objects appeared to me *flat*. When I spoke with anyone, I saw him like an image cut out of paper with no relief. . . . This sensation lasted intermittently for two years. . . . Constantly it seemed as if my legs did not belong to me. It was almost as bad with my arms. As for my head, it seemed no longer to exist. . . . I appeared to myself to act automatically, by an impulsion foreign to myself. . . . There was inside of me a new being, and another part of myself, the old being, which took no interest in the new-comer. I distinctly remember saying to myself that the sufferings of this new being were to me indifferent. I was never really dupe of these illusions, but my mind grew often tired of incessantly correcting the new impressions, and I let myself go and live the unhappy life of this new entity. I had an ardent desire to see my old world again, to get back to my old self. This desire kept me from killing myself. . . . I was another, and I hated, I despised this other; he was perfectly odious to me; it was certainly another who had taken my form and assumed my functions." *

In cases like this, it is as certain that the *I* is unaltered as that the *Me* is changed. That is to say, the present Thought of the patient is cognitive of both the old Me and the new, so long as its memory holds good. Only, within that objective sphere which formerly lent itself so simply to the judgment of recognition and of egoistic appropriation, strange perplexities have arisen. The present and the past, both seen therein, will not unite. Where is my old Me ? What is this new one ? Are they the same ? Or have I two ? Such questions, answered by whatever theory the patient is able to conjure up as plausible, form the beginning of his insane life.

* De l'Intelligence, 3me édition (1878), vol. II. p. 461, note.

Figure 8.3 A page from William James's **Psychology**, *published in 1910 (copyright 1892).*

flowing clockwise and the corresponding money payments flowing counter-clockwise.

Two sets of markets link households to firms in this economy. Product markets, which appear at the top of the diagram, are markets where households purchase goods and services—bread, television sets, houses, dry cleaning services, entertainment—for their own direct consumption. Factor markets, which appear at the bottom of the diagram, are the markets in which households sell to firms the **factors of production** they use in making the things sold in product markets.

Factors of production are traditionally classified as natural resources, labor, and capital. **Natural resources** include everything useful as a productive input in its natural state—agricultural land, building sites, forests, and mineral deposits, for example. **Labor** includes the productive contributions made by people working with their minds and muscles. **Capital** is all means of production created by people, including tools, industrial equipment, structures, and improvements to land.

In return for the natural resources, labor, and capital that they buy from households, firms make *factor payments* in the form of rents, wages, salaries, and interest payments. As a matter of accounting convention, when firms use land, labor, or capital that they themselves own, they are counted as "purchasing" those factors from the households that own the firms, even though no money changes hands and no explicit factor payment is made. For purposes of macroeconomic analysis, profits are thus considered an implicit factor payment from firms to the households that own them.[1]

Stocks and Flows

Having said this much, let's pause for a moment to concentrate on a word used several times already. Economists call all of the things shown in Exhibit 5.1 **flows** because they are processes that occur continuously through time. Flows are measured in units per time period—for example, in dollars per year, gallons per minute, or tons per month. Measurements of flows are measurements of rates at which things are happening.

The technical language of economics distinguishes carefully between flows and stocks. A **stock** is an accumulated quantity of something existing at a particular time. (The word *stock* in this general sense has nothing to do with the stock market kind of stocks that are bought and sold on Wall Street.)

For an illustration of the difference between stocks and flows, we can think of a bathtub filling. When we talk about how fast the water is running, we are talking about a *flow*, measured in gallons per minute. When we talk about how much water is in the tub at a given moment, we are talking about a *stock* measured only in gallons. Similarly, in the world of economics, we might talk about the rate of housing construction in Buffalo, New York, in terms of new units per month (the flow) as distinct from the actual number of houses in Buffalo as of January 1, 1980 (the stock).

National Income and Product

Two of the flows in Exhibit 5.1 deserve special attention and have special names. The first is **national income**—the total of all wages, rents, interest

---

Factors of production The basic inputs of natural resources, labor, and capital used in producing all goods and services.

Natural resources As a factor of production, everything useful as a productive input in its natural state, including agricultural land, building sites, forests, and mineral deposits.

Labor As a factor of production, the contributions to production made by people working with their minds and muscles.

Capital As a factor of production, all means of production that are created by people, including such things as tools, industrial equipment, structures, and improvements to land.

Flows Processes occurring continuously through time, measured in units per time period.

Stocks Accumulated quantities existing at a particular time, measured in terms of simple units.

National income The total of all incomes, including wages, rents, interest payments, and profits received by households.

---

[1] For certain purposes of microeconomics, profits are not considered factor payments.

Figure 8.4. A page from an economics text that has profited from strong design. Courtesy of the Dryden Press.

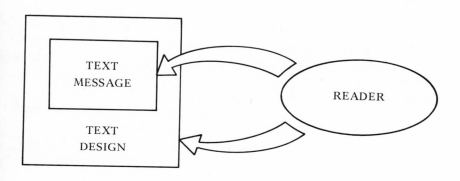

Figure 8.5. Texts becoming responsive to learner requirements.

reading it. Unfortunately, many students do not have well-developed learning strategies and thus often experience great difficulty in coping with textual learning.

One of the central skills of the artful learner is the ability to monitor his or her reading activities and adaptively engage in specific processing strategies according to the demands of the situation. Straightforward reading of a textbook often shows a lack of such an adaptive strategy.

Since many, if not most, students may be deficient in their use of text processing strategies, the text itself should encourage the use of appropriate strategies—largely through the design features of the text itself, i.e., through display techniques. A prime example of this is programmed instruction, which owes a large measure of its effectiveness to the way it forces students to process the text (its deficiencies, on the other hand, are probably due to the rigidity of its form and the consequent lack of adaptiveness it allows).

In summary, the degree to which textual display techniques can and do affect processing strategies is closely tied to the sophistication of the learner and to the primary function of the text. Most educated people can probably handle a dictionary with ease, but many of these same people might experience difficulty in learning from a text such as the one displayed in Figure 8.3. An experienced student would have an easier time of it than a freshman student. Even for the advanced student, however, the use of appropriate textual display techniques would probably make the task pleasanter, if not easier. **Thus, text features can positively influence text processing**.

The function of a particular text will, of course, define to some extent the range of textual features that can be incorporated in it. In functional terms, a dictionary and a textbook have little in common. Consequently, their display features will also have little in common.

4. Text-Processing Difficulties

One approach to the analysis of text processing and to text design is to consider the difficulties that students may encounter in using a text to learn from it. In other words, **it is useful to ask what problems students need to overcome in learning from a text**.

The issue of processing problems can be framed in different ways. One way is to consider the three major elements that enter into learning: attention, comprehension, and retention. In order for a student to learn the basic content of a subject (introductory economics, for instance), he or she must sustain interest in the subject (enough to continue reading the text, if not to get excited about it), he or she must understand what the author has written, and he or she must retain what has been learned. If any of these elements is missing, learning will not occur or it will be imperfect.

Another way to consider processing problems is to examine the level at which they occur. Consider the following processing problems. A student might have forgotten the meaning of a particular technical term, encountered earlier in a text, that is crucial to the understanding of what he or she is currently reading. This is a microlevel problem. At a more encompassing level, a student might read a whole chapter of a text with perfect comprehension of each and every point, but then be unable to summarize the important points of the chapter. This is a macrolevel problem. The reader has been unable to discern the "gist" of the passage (Kintsch & van Dijk, 1978).

Different text-processing capabilities are involved in each case, with the potential for different deficiencies and thus different solutions in terms of text design. The problem of forgetting technical meanings, for instance, can easily be solved by including a glossary, an index, or some other means of singling out technical terms, such as typographical highlighting (see Figure 8.6). Lack of retention of the main points is a subtler problem. It can be reduced through attention in text authoring to implicit means such as those found in elaboration theory (see Sari and Reigeluth, this volume) and through attention in text design to various display techniques to be discussed shortly in this chapter.

It is also evident that the better a subject-matter presentation has been analyzed and structured through implicit means, such as the principles of elaboration theory and component display theory, the less need there is for textual display techniques to overcome processing problems (Figure 8.7). That is, a well-elaborated presentation will engender fewer processing problems and thus be fairly successful even in a text showing few design features. Conversely, the poorer the presentation of the subject matter is, the more scope there is for design features to play a role in enhancing learning. This is not to say, however, that the use of display techniques should be overlooked when dealing with well-elaborated instruction. For one thing, well-elaborated instruction remains rare. For another, implicit and explicit means should always profit from being considered jointly (just as in the case of developing pictures to accompany prose; see Brody, this volume). Textual display techniques, however, become more crucial in a poorly structured and poorly thought-out presentation. This, unfortunately, seems all too often to be the standard rather than the exception in the textbook field, a situation that is illustrated by a sample analysis of textbooks by Anderson, Armbruster, & Kantor (1980). It is also important to note that textual display techniques cannot supplant poor or inadequate text structure; that is, they are not able to produce comprehension from totally incomprehensible text.

The use of a similar but thicker wire will give a generally increased current as in the upper line, while a thinner wire will give lower currents as in the lower one. In the same way, experiments with long wires will give smaller currents while shorter wires will give increased ones. The overall pattern in fact is identical with what you would expect from a series of narrow and wide, long and short pipes with water flowing through them.

For all cases it will be found that the relationship between current and voltage takes the form of a straight line over a reasonably wide range. The line must always pass back through the one experimental point we can be certain of, namely the origin, because no current can flow if there is no voltage. Within the region of this linear relationship, a set of measured current and voltage values $(I_1, V_1), (I_2, V_2), (I_3, V_3)$, etc., taken from a given conductor all fit the equation:

$$\frac{V_1}{I_1} = \frac{V_2}{I_2} = \frac{V_3}{I_3} = \text{constant} = R$$

We call circuit elements which satisfy this equation, *linear elements*. As we shall see, such elements are very convenient for circuit calculation. A knowledge of any one pair of values for current and voltage allows the constant R appropriate to the conductor to be calculated. All other possible relationships can then be calculated using: $V = IR$.

linear elements

This law, that current is proportional to the applied voltage, we call *Ohm's law* and it applies to a wide range of conductors held at constant temperature. It must be emphasized that the value of the constant R describes a property of the conductor. It has the significance that when R is large a given potential difference produces only a small current, and when it is small a relatively large current is produced. The constant can be regarded as describing a tendency of the conductor to inhibit the flow of current, and this is why we refer to it as the *electrical resistance* of the conductor. The unit in which resistance is measured is called the *ohm*, one ohm being the electrical resistance of a conductor which passes a current of one amp when subjected to a potential difference of one volt.

Ohm's law

electrical resistance
ohm

Most metal objects, and many others, show an impressive tendency to obey Ohm's law. It is tempting to think that the law has the weight of one of the major physical laws like conservation of momentum, or mass or electric charge. To do so, however, is to make a very serious mistake. There are numerous exceptions to the law in the conduction of liquids, gases and non-metals. Examples of non-linearity are even more common and arise often because of the heating effect of a current. Household examples include the wires in electric fires and in electric lamps, where the high operating temperature of the wire changes the mobility of the valence electrons so that they drift less readily than when cold. The wire, as a result,

30

Figure 8.6. Highlighting of technical terms in a technology text (partial page). Courtesy of The Open University, England.

5. The Problem of Focus

Before discussing particular display techniques, I want to go into what I consider to be one of the central problems of text processing. The problem is an important one because it is often overlooked and has barely received the attention it should in the instructional literature. It is also the basis for most of the display techniques to be discussed in the next section.

This problem is the problem of selecting important information from the text, i.e., being able to focus in on what is pertinent in order to devote special processing to it, without being overburdened or confused by the larger context within which this information is embedded (Figure 8.8). It is the old problem of not being able to see the forest for the trees.

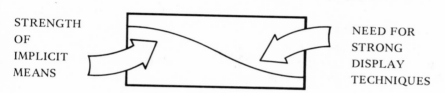

Figure 8.7. The need for display techniques.

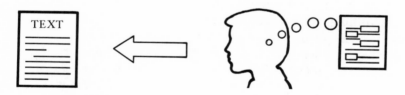

Figure 8.8. The context of information.

A text is not a flat structure in which all ideas are equally important. Rather, it is a highly hierarchized structure in which certain elements are more central than other, supportive or subordinate elements (see Pace, this volume). The entire structure is a mass of interdependent ideas related to one another in any number of ways (indeed, no two authors will treat a given topic identically). The student studying a text is thus faced with the very complex task of focusing on the important points in the text and structuring these in a coherent and memorable whole, while at the same time constantly processing new inputs that may be of only secondary importance. The situation is not unlike the one in which a motorist is trying to follow the signs indicating his or her route when innumerable other signs are also displayed along the way.

The reader of a text must constantly establish the status of the information being read at any given time and appropriately fit this information into his or her own internal representation of the subject being studied. The macrostructure of the text must remain evident to the reader throughout the process. Because of human capacity limitations, this is not always an easy task, unless the text is rather simple. A recent model of text comprehension that explicitly considers these macroprocesses, and that shows much promise for informing text design, is the one developed by Kintsch & van Dijk (1978); see also Vipond (1980).

Recent instructional research illustrates the problem of focus directly. In a series of connected studies, Reder & Anderson (1980) have demonstrated that a text stripped of all incidental information (a summary, in fact) is better remembered than a corresponding text that is fully detailed (such as the usual instructional text). Thus, the main points of a topic are better remembered when learned from a summary than from the full text. The advantage is likely due to the added degree of attention accorded these main points in the summary condition, as compared to the sharing of attention that must occur in the case of the full text.

Likewise, basic research on instructional objectives (Duchastel, 1979; Duell, 1974) and on adjunct prequestions inserted in text (Rothkopf, 1976) has demonstrated that adjunct aids such as these, which help the student focus on relevant information, enhance the retention of such information to the detriment of incidental information.

The point is also made in an interesting study by Smith, Rothkopf, & Koether (related by Rothkopf, 1972) in which various text properties, such as reading ease, frequency of technical terms, etc., were correlated with text recall. The most impressive correlation obtained (-.71) was with the number of incidental facts contained in the texts. **Thus, the more that important ideas in a text are embedded in a mass of secondary ideas, the more difficult they are to remember.**

It thus appears that in learning from text, the problem of focus is a major one, with the implication that **text design should be particularly responsive to the need to facilitate text processing in this area.**

Students are fairly adept at focusing on and remembering the main points of short texts, as the research reviewed by Pace indicates (this volume). Longer texts, however, are likely to cause problems, i.e., situations in which cognitive capacity is more strained. The degree of strain imposed depends largely, of course, on the structure of the text. A well-elaborated text following the guidelines presented by Sari and Reigeluth (this volume) may largely eliminate the problem of focus. Indeed, **this text-processing problem can be considered as the central one that elaboration theory addresses through implicit means.**

As indicated earlier, however, few current texts are well-elaborated, nor can one be optimistic with respect to future texts. Designing instruction according to elaboration theory is an arduous task, probably requiring a strong measure of insight on the part of the author and intensive collaboration from a development team. These conditions are unlikely to be met in many cases of text development, as desirable as they may be. A fallback alternative for the publisher, although much less effective and desirable, is to concentrate on textual display techniques that address the same text-processing problem. Viewed in this way, such techniques are **explicit means that attempt to reduce in some measure the inadequacies of texts that have not been properly elaborated.** Am I being too negative in proposing this view? I do not believe so, especially if we consider Figure 8.7, presented earlier.

6. Display Techniques to Aid Text Processing

Most textual display techniques are aimed at assisting the student in overcoming the problem of focus; i.e., most are concerned with displaying the structure of the text in some way. Some techniques, however, go against this general trend. Programmed instruction is a case in point, as mentioned above. The aim of programmed instruction is to involve the student in responding to the text, and to do this it breaks up normal text into a multitude of small units, or frames. This usually results in an undifferentiated presentation that lacks access in Waller's sense (this volume), and thus forces the students into a sequential processing strategy emphasizing microprocessing at the very real expense of diminished macroprocessing of the text. More seriously, the text becomes nonadaptive to different study strategies: it can accommodate only one study strategy, that of starting at the beginning and going all the way through to the end. Thus in programmed instruction, learner control is totally eliminated, which may account to a large extent for its lack of popularity.

This brings us to **a subsidiary function of textual display techniques, which is to facilitate selective studying on the part of the student,** i.e., to enable the student to skip certain parts of the text and more generally be able to move around in a text according to his or her own plans. Student study strategies vary a great deal and are highly dependent on how much time and effort the student is willing to invest in the particular topic. Many students never completely read or finish a textbook they have started studying, for all too often too many constraints and competing interests interfere with this task. The view that a textbook should be designed only for serious students who devote themselves wholeheartedly to its study is an idealistic view that needs to be replaced by a more realistic one: **students use a text as a learning resource, and their use of it must adapt itself to the students' particular schedules and purposes** (see Duchastel, 1980a, for a consideration of study strategies in this light). If in fact a majority of students will only devote, say, half the time needed to fully study a textbook, the textbook should be designed so as to maximize the benefits to be obtained in that time. **The principle** that design should be responsive to the learners' needs (actual needs at that) comes into play here.

Textual display techniques thus lend themselves to two distinct purposes: (1) assisting the student in the task of focusing on the important points; and (2) enabling the student to selectively process the text when this is necessary.

Undifferentiated texts, such as those displayed in Figures 8.3 and 8.6, do not lend themselves to these purposes. Texts capitalizing on display techniques, on the other hand, do so (to different extents, of course, depending on the particular techniques employed). I will now present and critically examine some of these techniques, grouped for convenience into three general types: labeling, highlighting, and illustrating techniques.

6.1 Labeling

The purpose of labeling text elements is to identify and summarize the different elements that comprise the text. Labeling includes the use of headings, terminology markers, content markers, and marginal notes.

The use of headings is by far the most common labeling technique encountered in textbooks today (see Figure 8.9). Titles of book sections or chapters indicate to the reader what the section or the chapter is about; they identify the content and summarize it in a few words (in a label, in fact). Equally important are subheadings, which perform the same function as titles. Headings permit the student to perceive the organization of the text and thus perform an important access function in the sense presented by Waller (this volume).

Terminology markers (see Figures 8.4 and 8.6) are flags that indicate the appearance of new concepts in a text. They serve both as signals to the student that a definition worth remembering is present in the text and as location markers for later retrieval of the definition if it is forgotten. In this second function, terminology markers can be considered as an embedded glossary. It is desirable, of course, to supplement terminology markers by including an index at the end of the book.

Content markers serve a purpose not unlike that of headings.

force comes in those times when consumer demand for autos and other durable goods fluctuates. (For example, the 1979 gasoline shortages killed off auto sales and helped bring on the 1979 weakness.)

Such *shifts* in the *CC* schedule also contribute to movements in the $C + I + G$ intersections. These shifts, like any other shifts in autonomous factors, involve double-duty multiplier reactions.

A Few Theories of the Business Cycle

When it comes to explanations of why the income schedules shift, an industrious student could easily compile a list of separate theories of the business cycle that would run into the dozens.[5] Each theory seems to be quite different. But when we examine them closely and throw out those which obviously contradict the facts or the rules of logic, or which just appear to be conveying an explanation when really they are not saying anything at all—when we do all this, we are left with only a few really different explanations. Most of them differ from one another only in emphasis.

One scholar believes the cycle to be primarily the result of fluctuations in total net investment. Another prefers to attribute the cycle to fluctuations in the rate of technological inventions and innovations, which act on business *through* net investment. These sound like two different theories, and in most advanced textbooks they might be given the names of two different writers. But from our standpoint they are but two different aspects of the same saving-investment process.

As we shall see, this does not mean there is perfect agreement among different writers.

External and Internal Factors

We may classify the different theories into two categories: primarily *external*, and primarily *internal* ("exogenous" and "endogenous").

The external theories find the root of the business cycle in the fluctuations of something *outside* the economic system—in sunspots or astrology; in wars, revolutions, and political events; in gold discoveries, rates of growth of population and migrations, in discoveries of new lands and resources; in scientific breakthroughs and technological innovations.

The internal theories look for mechanisms *within* the economic system itself that will give rise to self-generating business cycles, so that every expansion will breed recession and contraction, and every contraction will in turn breed revival and expansion—in a quasi-regular, repeating, never-ending chain.

If you believe in the sunspot theory of the business cycle—and no respectable economist today does—then the distinction between external and internal is rather easy to draw. No one can seriously argue that the direction of causation is in doubt—that the economic system causes the sunspots to fluctuate instead of vice versa.

However, when it comes to such other external factors as wars and politics, or even births and gold discoveries, there is always some doubt as to whether the economic system does not at least *feed back* on the so-called "external" factors, thereby making the distinction between external and internal not such a hard-and-fast one.

Purely Internal Theories

As against the crude external sunspot theory, we may describe some simple examples of possible, crude internal theories.

[5]We may mention just a few of the better-known theories: (1) the *monetary* theory—attributes the cycle to the expansion and contraction of bank money and credit (Hawtrey, Friedman, et al.); (2) the *innovation* theory—attributes the cycle to the clustering of important inventions such as the railroad (Schumpeter, Hansen, et al.); (3) the *psychological* theory—treats the cycle as a case of people's infecting each other with pessimistic and optimistic expectations (Pigou, Bagehot, et al.); (4) the *underconsumption* theory—claims too much income goes to wealthy or thrifty people compared with what can be invested (Hobson, Sweezy, Foster and Catchings, et al.); (5) the *overinvestment* theory—claims too much rather than too little investment causes recessions (Hayek, Mises, et al.); (6) the *sunspot-weather-crop* theories (Jevons, H. L. Moore); (7) *political* theories of the cycle (Kalecki, Fair, Tufte). The interested reader should consult G. Haberler, *Prosperity and Depression* (Harvard University Press, Cambridge, Mass., 1958, 4th ed.), or other business-cycle texts for further information.

Figure 8.9. The use of subheadings in a chapter from an economics text. Courtesy of McGraw-Hill Book Company.

They are used in text display systems such as Information Mapping (Horn, this volume) and Discourse Punctuation (Showstack, this volume). Whereas headings generally indicate the substantive content treated in the text, **content markers indicate the type of content treated.** The headings in Figure 8.9, for instance, read "A Few Theories of the Business Cycle," "External and Internal Factors," etc. In contrast, content markers are labels of the following sort: Main Points, Definition, Examples, etc. They serve as category labels, but do not perform the summarizing function that headings do. **They are, in this regard, content-free.**

Marginal notes perform both an access function and a summarizing function (see Figure 8.10). One can view them as **elaborated labels that facilitate access to the ideas discussed at length in the text,** or one can view them as a **running summary that replaces the end-of-the-chapter summary** traditionally included in textbooks (Duchastel & Chen, 1980).

The various labeling techniques discussed above share a similar function: they serve to announce and to point to what is contained in the text (acting in this way as access devices). They also share a similar design feature: they use the space on the page to break up the text into its constituent elements. **They thus structure the text, and by so doing facilitate the interaction between reader and text,** during both initial learning and review.

6.2 Highlighting

The use of highlighting techniques **is aimed directly at helping the reader overcome the problem of focus,** discussed earlier. The reader must at all times decide on the importance of the information being read and gradually build an internal representation of the topic around the core ideas of the text.

Text authors use two implicit means of highlighting the main points in their texts: structural means, such as initial overviews (or advance organizers) and end-of-chapter summaries; and linguistic means, such as semantic signaling (through the use of connectives such as "therefore," "in conclusion," "of particular importance," etc.).

Explicit highlighting, on the other hand, makes use not of the

Payroll tax begun 1937
Benefits paid 1940
1935 SSA contained
1. Old age insurance
2. Unemployment ins.
3. Public assistance
4. Welfare services

Expansion of
old-age ins.
1. Survivors' ins. (1939)
2. Disability ins. (1956)
3. Health ins.--
   Parts A & B of
   Medicare (1965)

SSA today includes
1. OASDHI
2. SSI
3. HI
4. Public assistance
   and welfare
   services

Fed. gov't operates
1. OASDHI
2. Public assistance and
   welfare services

OASDHI in 1979
1. OASDI paying $105
   bil. to 35 mil.
   persons
2. HI paying $30 bil.
3. 113 mil. people
   paying payroll
   taxes

Reasons for late
arrival of SS in U.S.:
1. Self-reliant tradi-
   tion
2. Private philan-
   thropy and public
   charity

Developments leading
to SS in U.S.:
1. Ratio of aged to

1937, and the first monthly social security benefits were paid in 1940. The original Social Security Act established four different programs. Two were social insurance programs: old-age insurance and unemployment insurance. Another was public assistance to the needy aged, needy dependent children, and the needy blind. The fourth program provided services for maternal and child health, crippled children, child welfare, vocational rehabilitation, and public health work.

With respect to old-age insurance, the program was expanded to include survivors' insurance in 1939 and disability insurance in 1956. Health insurance (Parts A and B of Medicare) was added in the Social Security Act in 1965. As a result, social security today is comprised of OASDHI.

I. B. *Social Security Act Today*

The Social Security Act, as amended, includes all the following programs today: Retirement or old age insurance, survivors' insurance, disability insurance, hospital and medical insurance for the aged and the disabled, supplemental security income, unemployment insurance, public assistance and welfare services (aid to needy families with children, medical assistance, maternal and child-health services, services for crippled children, child welfare services).

The first three are OASDI and the fourth is HI. The federal government operates OASDHI and the supplemental security income (SSI) programs. The others are operated by the states with federal cooperation.

In the context of income maintenance and social welfare, OASDHI is only one of the government programs, but it is the most important, in terms of the number of persons covered and the amount of benefits paid. In 1979, about 35 million persons received over $105 billion in cash benefits (under OASDI) as retirees, dependents and survivors, and disabled workers. In addition, Medicare (under HI) is paying nearly $30 billion for hospital and medical insurance reimbursements. Social security payroll taxes are paid by some 113 million individuals, representing more than nine out of ten workers in the country.

I. C. *Background of the Social Security Program*

Social security for the aged was initiated in this country with the passage of the Social Security Act of 1935. The comparatively late arrival of this type of social legislation in the United States may be accounted for by the following considerations.

Prior to the establishment of the social security system, the traditions of independence advocated by the nation's founders emphasized economic security through individual effort. It was assumed that only the unworthy could ever come to want in a new nation blessed with abundant opportunities for earning a living under freedom of choice. The prevailing public opinion before the Great Depression was that Americans could, by and large, provide for their own old age by individual savings and/or by family assistance. In addition, private philanthropy and public charity were factors deferring the emergence of social security schemes.

Several significant developments brought about the consideration and framing of a comprehensive social security system designed to solve a substantial part of the problem

Figure 8.10. The use of marginal notes. From teaching materials dealing with social insurance.

prose itself but of various typographic devices that signal the status of the information through physical means. Various typographic options are open to the text designer: the use of **italics, boldface type, large type, color**, and so on.

An example of a heavy use of typographical highlighting is the set of recent editions of Samuelson's *Economics* (see Figure 8.11), which uses a different printing color to highlight important content. Showstack (this volume) also uses typographic highlighting to good effect in Discourse Punctuation.

Not unrelated to highlighting are adjunct aids, such as learning objectives (Duchastel, 1979) and adjunct questions inserted in text (Rothkopf, 1976). Such adjunct aids, if appropriately used, undoubtedly assist the student in monitoring the importance of what is being read. Typographically, they also stand out from the body of the text itself (unlike an overview or summary, for instance). They are, however, more textual than typographical in nature and might therefore be better thought of as implicit means of directing learning rather than as explicit ones.

6.3 Illustrating

The use of illustrations in text is considered explicitly in the chapter by Brody in this volume. I wish, however, to briefly discuss here **an aspect of illustrations that relates directly to the problem of focus presented earlier**. I have myself elsewhere (Duchastel, 1978) examined illustrations in text from a functional perspective, i.e., by asking **"What roles can illustrations serve in instructional texts?"** I have found it useful to consider **three functions of illustrations in assisting learning: (1) an attentional function**, whereby illustrations enhance the interest of the reader in the text; (2) **an explicative function** (the most common), which assists the reader in comprehending the text; and (3) **a retentional function** (the rarest in current use), through which long-term retention of the material is improved. It is this third function which is of special interest here.

Psychological research has strongly demonstrated that pictures are better remembered than words (Paivio, 1975). And yet, many textbooks fail to capitalize on this important insight in their antisocial act of hoarding at a 10 per cent rate of interest *in real terms*, while the businessman who is foolish enough to give someone a job may find that he cannot even get back his wage outlay, much less earn a profit.

Modern research suggests that the greatest redistribution of income resulting from inflation is from older to younger people. The dollar put aside for retirement at 70 often shrinks in purchasing power: if prices rise at an average rate of about 5 per cent per year, the real purchasing power of a dollar held for 30 years will halve and halve again in that period.

Anticipated inflation   Once an inflation has gone on for a long time and is no longer "unforeseen," an allowance for a price rise will gradually get itself built into the market interest rate. Thus, once we all expect prices to rise at 5 per cent per year, my pension funds invested in bonds and mortgages will tend to pay me 9 per cent rather than 4 per cent. This adjustment of interest rates to chronic inflation has been observed in Brazil, Chile, and indeed in almost all other countries with a long history of rising prices. In the 1970s, one sees a similar inflation pressure in American and European interest rates.

EFFECTS OF CHANGING PRICES ON OUTPUT AND EMPLOYMENT

Aside from redistributing incomes, inflation may affect the total real income and production of the community.

An increase in prices is usually associated with high employment. In mild inflation the wheels of industry are initially well lubricated, and output is near capacity. Private investment is brisk, jobs are plentiful. Such has been the historical pattern.

Thus, many businessmen and union spokesmen, in appraising a little deflation and a little inflation, used to speak of the latter as the lesser of the two evils. The losses to fixed-income groups are usually less than the gains to the rest of the community. Even workers with relatively fixed wages are often better off because of improved employment opportunities and greater take-home pay; a rise in interest rates on new securities may partly make up any losses to creditors; and increases in social security benefits, indexed to adjust for price-level changes, make up losses to the retired.

In deflation, on the other hand, the growing unemployment of labor and capital causes the community's total well-being to be less; so, in a sense, the gainers get less than the losers lose. As a matter of fact, in deep depression, almost everyone—including the creditor who is left with uncollectible debts—suffers.

The above remarks show why an increase in consumption or investment spending is thought a good thing in times of unemployment, even if there is some upward pressure on prices. When the economic system is suffering from acute depression, few criticize private or public spending on the ground that this might be inflationary. Actually, most of the increased spending will then go to increase production and create more jobs and more real income.

But the same reasoning shows that once full employment and full plant capacity have been reached, any further increases in spending are likely to be completely wasted in price-tag increases. (Recall Chapter 13's discussion of "inflationary gaps.")

Figure 8.11. Typographical highlighting. The paragraphs indicated by my arrows are highlighted in green. Courtesy of McGraw-Hill Book Company.

presentation of the material to be learned. Illustrations can be used to advantage (for retention) by embodying in visual **form the essential ideas made in a text.** An example of such a use of illustrations is presented in Figure 8.12. Since pictures are more easily retrievable in memory than are verbal representations, they can serve as valuable memory cues for the learner at a later date when the learned information needs to be recalled. To be most effective, illustrations should probably act somewhat as summaries do, i.e., represent in a concise form the main points in a section of text. In this way, **they can serve in fact as summary statements presented in a graphic form.** Much remains to be explored, however, in this use of illustrations in text, as it has to fit in with other display techniques in the total design of text.

7. Conclusion

The display techniques discussed above have evolved gradually in textbook publishing, mainly in response to a desire for a more attractive product. Much of the current use of illustrations in text, for instance, reflects that concern, rather than a purely peda-gogical one. A concern for attractiveness is not to be scorned, however, if it can be combined in a complementary way with the primary function of a textbook: to assist learning. The art of the text designer is to integrate these two functions to bring out the best of each.

Display techniques in text design are also strongly influenced by tradition, as Williamson (1966) has pointed out, as well as by the constraints of the publishing process. Some techniques, such as the use of headings, are widespread; others, like various forms of highlighting, are employed mainly in specific areas of publishing and seen infrequently elsewhere. This may be in response to the particular requirements of given areas, although it could also be a question of faddishness in many cases.

Some techniques have simply gone out of style. Figure 8.13, for instance, displays the use of marginal notes in a text published in 1923. Rare is the contemporary text that employs marginal notes as did this early textbook.

Why has a technology of text been so long in emerging in education? The main reason is probably the fact that **those who**

creasing the 'dish'. This necessary tolerance was readily recognized by
Sturt as a reason for dishing the wheel.

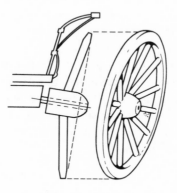

*Figure 1   The 'dish' in cartwheels,
and a section through a waggon
body, wheel and axle*

However, Sturt could not be entirely satisfied with this reason, since
cartwheels had not always had a continuous tyre, and because he knew
that a wheel with an *inadequate amount* of 'dish' would fail in use and
collapse like a gale-inverted umbrella. There must, therefore, be some
structural reason for 'dish'. Sturt eventually realized this more important,
structural reason when he observed the motion of a horse-drawn cart
from behind. The gait of the horse produced a horizontal oscillation of
the cart body on its axles; thus, at each stride of the horse, the cart body
was being thrust, first to one side, then to the other, into the wheel hubs.
Those thrusts must be countered by the inclined spokes of the dished
wheel. If the spokes were not inclined sufficiently—if the 'dish' was
inadequate—then the wheel would fail by the hub being pushed outwards
by the force of the cart body.

However, dishing the wheel had other advantages, and also disadvantages,
which were integrated into a total design of interdependencies. One
immediate advantage to be gained was that the cart body could be wider
across the top of its sides than across its floor, since the wheel rim was
not in the same vertical plane as its hub. This increase in body width was
an advantage in carting loads, and possibly may also have contributed to
the comfort of passengers.

A serious problem was also induced by dishing the wheel, in that the spokes
would be inclined at an angle from the vertical if the wheel was fitted to
the cart on a simple horizontal axle. This would mean that the spokes
would have to carry the weight of the cart by resistance to bending, rather
than by resistance to direct compression. Although the spokes could have
been thickened to cope with this, it was important that the total weight
of the wheel should be kept as low as possible. (Sturt also describes how
the spokes were shaved to their minimum possible section in order to
save weight.)

*Figure 8.12. An illustration serving a retention function. Partial
page from a textbook on design. Courtesy of The Open University,
England.*

134   A STUDENT'S HISTORY OF EDUCATION

'prefects.' immediately subordinate to the rector, but selected by the provincial; and under the inspection of
the prefects are the 'professors' or 'preceptors.'

The Jesuit Colleges.—The Jesuits have never engaged
in elementary education, but have required that pupils
know how to read and write before being admitted to
any of their schools. This may have been brought about
in the first place by the fact that the number of their
teachers was limited, or that the public elementary school
was just coming to be regarded as of importance, and secondary education of the humanistic type was everywhere
The lower
colleges are
secondary and
humanistic, dominant. The Jesuit educational organization has,
therefore, consisted of 'lower colleges' with a gymnasial
course, and of 'upper colleges,' which are of university
grade. Boys are admitted to the lower colleges at from
ten to fourteen years of age, and spend five or six years
there. The first three classes were at first devoted to a
careful study of Latin grammar, and a little of Greek;
in the fourth year a number of the Greek and Latin poets
and historians were read; while the last class, to which
two years were usually given, took up a rhetorical study
with curricu-
lum largely
unchanged. of the classical authors. Only slight variations in the
curriculum have ever been allowed since the *Ratio
Studiorum* was issued, until the revision in 1832. In
that year work in mathematics, natural science, history,
and geography was added in the lower colleges, but the
classics still compose the body of the course.

The full course of the upper colleges lasts seven or
nine years,—the first three in 'philosophy,' followed by
The upper col-
leges furnish
training in
'philosophy'
and theology. four or six in theology. The training in 'philosophy'
now includes not only logic, metaphysics, psychology,
ethics, and natural theology, but also work in algebra,

Figure 8.13. The use of marginal notes in a 1923 text.

select texts are primarily concerned with the content of the presentation (what the author says) rather than with the form of presentation (how it is said and displayed). This is a proper ordering of priorities, of course, for no one would be interested in a well-designed text that lacked substance or in some way misrepresented the subject of study. Textbook evaluation forms used by official selection committees attest to this fact.

Another reason for a disjointed use of display techniques in many texts is **the lack of a solid theoretical underpinning in the field of text instruction.** A few of the display techniques discussed in this chapter have received some attention by instructional researchers, but the research base remains far too limited to build any solid foundation. A case in point is the research that exists on the value of illustrations in text. The consolidated findings amount to little, given the complexity of the problems faced in text design (see Duchastel, 1980b). In the larger area of text design, as in the area of illustrations, **much reliance must be placed on conceptual frameworks such as those presented in this volume, rather than on empirical findings, for the guidance of practice.**

The text designer is thus left with a task to which a good measure of design intuition must be applied. The designer's situation is rather similar in this respect to that of the instructional designer, who can draw on **a set of working principles and a set of conceptual devices that need to be applied judiciously to the situation at hand.** Like instructional design, text design will always remain an art when it comes to practical application.

References

Anderson, T., Armbruster, B., & Kantor, R. How clearly written are children's textbooks? Or, of bladderwords and alfa. *Reading Education Report No. 16.* Center for the Study of Reading, University of Illinois, 1980.

Duchastel, P. Illustrating instructional texts. *Educational Technology*, 1978, *18*(11), 36-39.

Duchastel, P. Learning objectives and the organization of prose. *Journal of Educational Psychology*, 1979, *71*, 100-106.

Duchastel, P. Text learning outcomes and summaries. *Occasional Paper 10*, Research and Evaluation, The American College, Bryn Mawr, 1980a.

Duchastel, P. Textbook illustration: Research and instructional design. In J. Brown (Ed.), *Educational media yearbook, 1980.* Littleton, CO: Libraries Unlimited, Inc., 1980b.

Duchastel, P., & Chen, Y-P. The use of marginal notes in text to assist learning. *Educational Technology*, 1980, *20*(11), 41-45.

Duell, O. Effect of type of objective, level of test questions, and the judged importance of tested materials upon posttest performance. *Journal of Educational Psychology*, 1974, *66*, 225-232.

Gibson, E., & Levin, H. *The psychology of reading.* Cambridge: The MIT Press, 1975.

Kintsch, W., & van Dijk, T. Toward a model of text comprehension and production. *Psychological Review*, 1978, *85*, 363-394.

Paivio, A. Coding distinctions and repetition effects in memory. In G. Bower (Ed.), *The psychology of learning and motivation.* New York: Academic Press, 1975.

Reder, L., & Anderson, J.R. A comparison of texts and their summaries: Memorial consequences. *Journal of Verbal Learning and Verbal Behavior*, 1980, *19*, 121-134.

Rothkopf, E. Structural text features and the control of processes in learning from written materials. In J.B. Carroll and R.O. Freedle (Eds.), *Language comprehension and the acquisition of knowledge.* Washington, D.C.: V.H. Winston, 1972.

Rothkopf, E. Writing to teach and reading to learn: A perspective on the psychology of written instruction. *Seventy-fifth yearbook of the national society for the study of education, Part 1*, 1976, 91-129.

Vipond, G. Micro- and macroprocesses in text comprehension. *Journal of Verbal Learning and Verbal Behavior*, 1980, *19*, 276-296.

Williamson, H. *Methods of book design.* 2nd Edition. London: Oxford University Press, 1966.

9.

Designing Instructional Text

James Hartley

Introduction   In 1967, when I was writing a programmed text on the topic of European Traffic Signs, I was having trouble with the layout of each instructional page. My problem was to decide where on the page to position similar looking signs so that learners could effectively compare and contrast them, and thus learn their different meanings. (For the benefit of non-Europeans, I should perhaps explain that there are over 100 signs in the European system, many of which look alike but have rather different meanings.)

At that time, a colleague told me that Peter Burnhill, a local typographic designer, was going to give a talk about the design of college prospectuses. I duly went along, hoping to get some advice specifically relevant to my own problem. Peter obliged, and, as a result of our discussions, we decided that it would be profitable to collaborate on a more formal basis. So, some 15 years ago, we submitted our first joint proposal to the U.K. Social Science Research Council. In this proposal, we sought to pool the skills of a typographic designer and a psychologist in order to examine how one might set about designing instructional text. Since that date, Peter and I have published, jointly and separately, over 40 publications on the topic. I mention this not to boast but to point out the value of our interdisciplinary approach, and to indicate that in a chapter of this length I can only hope to give the flavor of our research. I shall provide later an Appendix which lists some of our more detailed position papers.

In our work, we are concerned with four related issues:

- We want to argue that the clarity of much instructional text can be improved by manipulating its typographical layout.
- We usually first consider the text we are working with in macro terms, and then more micro-scopically. Thus, we tend to start out with questions like, 'What is this document for?,' 'How is it to be used?,' 'What would be the best size page for a text like this?' We then move on to consider the text in more detail: 'Is this an appropriate sequence?,' 'Is this bit part of that bit, or is it a separate point?' Finally, we might ask more specific questions about particular forms of wording—'Will anyone know what *thixotropic* means?'—or particular forms of typographic detail: 'Wouldn't lower-case bold be better than capital letters?,' 'If we use lower-case bold for headings, should we use italic for the figure captions?'
- Although some of our research has focused on specific issues (e.g., the layout of journal references), we always try to consider as a whole the document we are designing. That is to say we are concerned about the positioning and the design of all the items that make up a particular text (tables, lists, figures, etc.) and not just the words alone.
- Finally, we are concerned to evaluate our prescriptions and to help others to design instructional text.

Our publications, therefore, consist mainly of exhortations, examples, and evidence. As the years have passed, we have found ourselves interested in other issues, e.g., how readers process instructional text, and how we can help them to do it—but these four points have guided much of our work to date.

In this chapter, I shall illustrate each of these four concerns by using one piece of text as a case-history. This means that there will be fewer examples than I usually like to present, but this approach will allow me more room for making comments in the space available. Readers can examine our other publications if they want to see more examples, and, in addition, this chapter is itself (hopefully) presented as an example of our approach. Readers can judge for themselves what they think of it, and see how it compares with other systems provided in this book. (Appendix 2 provides a copy of my instructions to the printer in this respect.)

Spacing text   The first decision typographers make when planning instructional text is to decide on what size page to print the final document. (This decision may be somewhat easier in Europe in the sense that we can choose from a limited set of standard page sizes.) Once this decision has been made, then the nature of the content of the text on this page size constrains all the subsequent decisions—such as the number and width of the columns, the size of the type and the inter-line spacing, the positioning of the figures and their captions, and even where to put the page numbers.

Instructional text is usually (but not always) more complex than straightforward prose. Thus, it offers additional problems for authors, printers, and readers. Furthermore, it is often used in a relatively unpredictable manner—it is read, put down, returned to, scanned, re-read, and so on. The designer, therefore, must produce a layout which is clear and consistent. Things should not change from page to page, and readers should never have to ask themselves 'Where am I supposed to go from here?' Peter Burnhill and I maintain that, given a particular text and a particular page size, one can manipulate the spatial arrangement of the text on that page so as to enhance clarity, retrieval, and comprehension.

To explain just how we do this, I need to provide an example. Figure 9.1 shows the first page of a four-page document, printed in its original format. Figure 9.2 shows the same text printed in a revised format. What have I done to Figure 9.1, and why?

Vertical spacing

Let us look first at the vertical spacing of the text. Our general argument is that units of line-feed can be used in proportion to separate sentences, paragraphs, and headings in text.

In Figure 9.2, the text has been re-arranged so that each sentence within a paragraph starts on a new line. This is not *always* necessary. As in the present text, one might make the paragraph the unit of analysis. However, the text in Figure 9.2 is complex, and our research indicates that opening it up in this way will help readers' comprehension.

Next, between each paragraph, there is one unit of line-feed. (Note: indentation is *not* used to denote the start of new paragraphs: indentation is not appropriate for this function when paragraphs are short. When indentation is used with short paragraphs, then the middles of the sentences stand out rather than their beginnings.)

Then, below each sub-heading is one unit of line-feed, and above it two units. The main heading, Insulating Gloves, could have been placed higher up the page (say four units) if it had been printed in the same typeface, size, and weight as the rest of the text. Here, however, we have used typographic cues (capital letters in bold) in place of space.

In theory then, we start with the smallest unit of the text, and we increase the space proportionally as the size of the units increases. However, this can lead to a cumbersome situation if the text hierarchy is complex. In such situations, one can vary the proportional spacing system (using, for example, 0.5, 1.0, 2.0, and 4.0 units of line-feed instead of 1, 2, 4, 8), or one can turn to using levels of horizontal indentation to convey substructure.

A related consideration here is what to do when we reach the bottom of the page with a system of this kind. In conventional printing, it is usual to stop the text at the same point on every page, regardless of its content. Sometimes, in fact, printers vary the space between the lines, the paragraphs, and the headings in order to achieve this common stopping point. Such a procedure can lead to inconsistencies as far as the readers are concerned. To overcome this problem, we recommend the use of consistent line-spacing throughout the text, and to have what is called a 'floating base-line' on each page. This procedure allows the printer to stop at a particular point with, say, plus or minus two lines in hand. In this way, regular line-spacing is maintained, and there is no need for some of the anomalies that arise in conventional text—such as the last line of a

INSULATING GLOVES

1. GENERAL

1.01 This section covers the description, care and maintenance of insulating gloves provided for the protection of workmen against electric shock, and the precautions to be followed in their use.

1.02 This section has been reissued to include the D and E Insulating Gloves.

2. TYPES OF INSULATING GLOVES

2.01 All types of insulating gloves are of the gauntlet type and are made in four sizes: 9-1/2, 10, 11 and 12. The size indicates the approximate number of inches around the glove, measured midway between the thumb and finger crotches. The length of each glove, measured from the tip of the second finger to the outer edge of the gauntlet, is approximately 14 inches.

2.02 There are various kinds of insulating gloves. The original ones were just called Insulating Gloves. After that B, C, D and E Insulating Gloves were developed. As described below, the D Glove replaced the original Insulating Gloves and the E glove replaced the B and C Gloves.

2.03 **Insulating Gloves** are thick enough to eliminate the need for protector gloves and are intended for use without them. These gloves have been superseded by the D Insulating Gloves.

Figure 9.1. Page one of the original text (figure reproduced courtesy of Bell Laboratories).

INSULATING GLOVES

1.0   General

1.1   This section covers the description, care and maintenance of insulating gloves provided for the protection of workmen against electric shock, and the precautions to be followed in their use.

1.2   This section has been reissued to include the D and E Insulating Gloves.

2.0   Types of Insulating Gloves

2.1   All types of insulating gloves are of the gauntlet type and are made in four sizes: 9-1/2, 10, 11 and 12. The size indicates the approximate number of inches around the glove, measured midway between the thumb and finger crotches. The length of each glove, measured from the tip of the second finger to the outer edge of the gauntlet, is approximately 14 inches.

2.2   There are various kinds of insulating gloves. The original ones are just called Insulating Gloves. After that B, C, D and E Insulating Gloves were developed. As described below, the D glove replaced the original Insulating Gloves and the E glove replaced the B and C gloves.

2.3   **Insulating Gloves** are thick enough to eliminate the need for protector gloves and are intended for use without them. These Gloves have been superseded by the D Insulating Gloves.

Figure 9.2. The same text in a revised layout.

paragraph appearing as the top line of a new page,
or the first line of a new paragraph (or even a
heading) falling on the last line of the page.
With our system, headings and sub-headings are
carried over to the next page without having to vary
the vertical spacing of the text.

Finally, it should be noted that we are using
vertical spacing to group and to separate related
parts of the text. When we do this, we often find
apparent anomalies in the author's original sequencing.
In one tortuous legal text, for example, we found
a sentence on page four that told readers that they
had actually agreed to all of what had gone before
at a previous annual general meeting, and that this
text was really a summary of what had been decided
at that meeting. In our revision, we made this
sentence an introductory statement. I think it
worth observing here that using space along the
lines discussed above has often helped us to
clarify what it was that the original author was
trying to say.

Horizontal spacing

Similarly, horizontal spacing can be used
consistently to group and separate functionally
related parts. Figure 9.1 has "justified"
text—that is, it has straight right and
left-hand edges. This has been achieved by
varying the spaces between the words.
(Compare, for example, the spacing in the first and
second lines of paragraph 1.01.)
Often, text is justified by using hyphenation as
well, and headings in justified text are
typically centered rather than starting at the left.
Occasionally, particularly in newspaper composition
with narrow column widths, the spacing between
the letters of individual words is also varied.

Such varied spacing is irrational and inconsistent, and it can lead to difficulties for young and older readers. Figure 9.2, by contrast, is set in "unjustified" text—that is, it has a ragged right-hand edge. Unjustified text is like typescript: there is an equal space between each word.

Unjustified text is cheaper to typeset, at least with traditional printing methods, and it is cheaper to reset when implementing proof corrections. We prefer to use unjustified text, however, for another reason. As shown in Figure 9.2, unjustified text allows more flexibility in deciding where to end each line.

In terms of consistency and flexibility, then, the argument for regular horizontal spacing is the same as that for regular vertical spacing. There is no need to fill each line and each page with print just because the space is there. In Figure 9.2, the last word on a line is never the start of a new sentence, and clause breaks are frequently used to determine where to stop a particular line. (The observant reader will note with regard to sentences that the rules for horizontal and vertical spacing coincide at this point if one is using the system where sentences within paragraphs start on a new line. However, if, as in this present text, paragraphs are the smallest unit of analysis, then one can still specify to printers—as indeed I have done—that they should never use the last word on the line to start a new sentence.)

Readers might think that procedures such as these would lead to difficulties for printers, wedded as they often are to notions about fixed

depths and widths. This is true. One can
hardly expect typesetters to make decisions
about the meaning of each line in order to
determine where to end it. However, there are
techniques which can help in this respect.
For example, authors:

- can ask for unjustified text;
- can ask for the last word on a line never
  to be the first word of a new sentence;
- can ask for regular units of line-feed to
  be the basis of the underlying vertical spacing;
- can provide a clear specification of what is
  required and mark up the text accordingly;
- can type the manuscript line for line as
  required and ask for it to be photographed.
  One advantage of preparing camera-ready copy in
  this way is that it allows the author almost complete
  control over the presentation of the text and
  the position of the tables, etc.;
- can type the manuscript with the same
  number of characters to a line as will be used
  in the printed version—if it is possible to estimate
  what this will be—and printers can be asked to follow
  it line for line. (This can present some difficulties
  as letter spacing in typescript is regular—whereas
  in print it is proportional—but one can get a good
  estimate of what the final product will look like in
  terms of the amount—and spacing—of the material
  on the page.)
- And, in the future—not very far off—developments
  in computer-assisted typesetting will remove all of
  these chores. Computer programs have already
  been written which allow grammatical constraints
  to determine line-endings.

Figure 9.2, then, illustrates our approach.
It should be clear from this example that we
are opposed to the traditional methods of

balancing a text—either vertically or horizontally—about a central axis on the page. We start from the top left, and we work down and across. We do not fill up the page with print just because the space is there. We use space as our main variable to clarify structure. Typographical variants (such as italic, or bold letters) are used sparingly to enhance or clarify the spatial decisions. Our aim is to seek clarity through consistency: inconsistent spacing and multiple typographic cueing can only confuse the reader.

Re-wording the text

So far I have illustrated with Figures 9.1 and 9.2 what can be done to a piece of text in terms of layout. But what about the language of the text? Much instructional text—and Figure 9.1 is no exception—is more difficult than it needs to be.

There are several guidelines on how to write clear prose, and there are also guidelines which illustrate how to revise existing text in order to make it easier to understand. However, there are no firm rules, accepted by all, and routinely applicable. Nonetheless, it is possible to make useful suggestions that writers can consider with reference to their own work. The guidelines that I currently advocate for re-writing can be considered under two related headings—in addition, of course, to the typographical guidelines just described above. These headings are 'textual' and 'procedural.'

Textual

- Use the active voice where possible.
- Use simpler wording if possible.
- Shorten long sentences (say, over 40 words long), or expand them into two or three simpler sentences.

- Divide long paragraphs into shorter ones.
- List actions and procedures (and put them in temporal sequence).
- When in difficulty, think of how you would explain to a friend what you are trying to say—or actually explain it to one. Write down what you say. Polish it.

Procedural
- Leave each revised draft for at least 12 hours.
- Revise and simplify further the revised drafts.
- Do not look back at the original text (except perhaps to check on ambiguities or points of meaning).
- Ask colleagues to help you to simplify your revised draft—either by simplifying it further themselves, or by pointing out where they think readers less able than themselves will find difficulties.
- Repeat this as often as time allows.
- Try out the text with a sample of the intended readers. Ask them to circle any parts that they think readers less able than themselves will find difficult.
  As already noted above, these guidelines are suggestions, not firm rules. There are, however, some data to support their application.

Figure 9.3 shows what happened to Figures 9.1 and 9.2 when these guidelines were applied. I am not saying here that Figure 9.3 is the only solution. Different readers will be able to suggest other improvements. I myself have been intrigued to notice on coming back to this example after a long period of time that my revised paragraph 1.1 does not convey exactly the meaning of the original paragraph 1.01.

INSULATING GLOVES

1.0   General

1.1   This section describes how to care for
and maintain the insulating gloves
that will protect you from electric shocks.

1.2   The section has been revised to include
the D and E Insulating Gloves.

2.0   Types of Insulating Gloves

2.1   All insulating gloves are made
in the gauntlet style.
There are four sizes: 9½, 10, 11, 12.
The size indicates the approximate number
of inches around the glove across the palm.
Each glove is about 14 inches long
from the bottom of the gauntlet to the top
of the second finger.

2.2   There are various kinds of insulating gloves.
The first kind were originally just called
Insulating Gloves.
After that the B, C, D and E Insulating Gloves
were developed.
As described below, the D Glove replaced the
original insulating gloves, and the E glove
replaced the B and C gloves.

2.3   So **Insulating Gloves** have now been replaced
by D Insulating Gloves.
(Insulating Gloves could be worn without
protector gloves.)

Figure 9.3. The revised layout and the revised text.

I think I would now re-write paragraph 1.1 as
follows:

   1.1 This section tells you how to care for,
         use, and maintain your insulating gloves.
         These gloves will protect you from
         shocks.

Furthermore, in paragraph 2.2, it might be more
helpful to print the words "insulating gloves"
in lower-case bold letters *each time* the
original insulating gloves are mentioned. These
small examples are given to support my point that
it is helpful to try and distance oneself from
the original text if it is possible.

Evaluation   So far I have explained our general procedures,
                 and expressed the opinion that our revised texts
                 (of which Figure 9.3 is but one example) are an
                 improvement over their originals. But is this
                 just an opinion? How can we evaluate the success
                 of our attempts to improve text? And why should
                 we?

There are two reasons why evaluation should be
considered. First of all, it is easy to assume
that because you have done something, there must
be an improvement. Such suppositions must be
tested. For example, I once spent four days
re-organizing a piece of instructional text, and
I was sure that my students would much prefer the
revised version. However, when I asked them, ten
out of 20 students preferred the original.
Similarly, I once re-sequenced the position of some
illustrations in a technical article so that
each one came into line with its textual reference.
I did not think that this would make a great deal
of difference to how people would judge the
effectiveness of the text but, to my surprise, 19
out of 20 students preferred the re-sequenced

passage. So my first point is that designers, typographers, and psychologists all need to test their intuitions against reality.

The second reason for evaluating one's decision making lies with making advances in scientific knowledge. If something works, then we can begin to find out more about how and why this is so. We can begin to refine our experimentation. At the moment, it is probably true to say that opening up text by using a system of proportional spacing will aid the comprehension of complex text. But so will other methods—as argued in other chapters in this book. So what are the critical parameters? Evaluation will help us to decide.

In our research, we have used a number of different ways of testing the effectiveness of revisions to text. We have applied readability measures to "before" and "after" versions. We have asked factual recall and comprehension questions. We have asked users for their preferences. We have timed how long it has taken readers to read original and revised versions. We have timed how long it has taken readers to find specific items in the text. Sometimes we have asked readers to say, once they have found specific items, whether or not they are true or false. We have also attempted to assess the costs of production. In some cases, we have found that costs have risen (because we have used more paper). However, with the increase in costs has come an increase in comprehension—so we have attempted cost-benefit analyses. In other situations, we have found, because of our simplified typography, that costs have been lower for our revised versions.

To illustrate some of these procedures, I will
present the results obtained from five ways
of assessing the effectiveness of Figure 9.3 as
compared with Figure 9.1.

- In terms of *readability*, the first 100 words
  of Figure 9.3 (excluding the headings) have a
  reading-grade level of 10.0, whereas the first
  100 words of Figure 9.1 have a reading-grade
  level of 14.5 (Gunning Fog Index).
- In terms of *preferences*, seven out of ten
  colleagues at the University of Keele chose Figure
  9.3 in preference to Figure 9.1 when asked to
  judge which figure they found 'the clearer.'
  (This difference, while pleasing, is not statistically
  significant.)
- In terms of *reading speed*, ten university
  students took the same amount of time (on average)
  to read three pages of material set in the style
  of Figure 9.3 as for the same three
  pages set in the style of Figure 9.1.
- In terms of *factual recall*, these same ten
  students recalled on average 5.4 out of ten for the
  material set in the style of Figure 9.1, the ten
  others recalled 7.9 out of ten for the same material
  set in the style of Figure 9.3. (This difference
  is statistically significant.)
- In terms of *replication*, when the last
  two studies were repeated with a further 20 students
  using a slightly different test of factual recall,
  the results were almost exactly the same: that is,
  there was no difference in reading speed, but
  a gain in comprehension for materials set in the
  style of Figure 9.3.
  Data such as these, which are quite easily
  obtainable, are encouraging. But—to refer the reader
  back to an earlier paragraph—did they all meet
  with your expectations?

There are, of course, difficulties with evaluation
of the kind described above. Often one feels that
the process of evaluation distorts the very thing

that one is trying to evaluate. People do not read naturally in experiments, especially if they are aware that they are being timed and tested on the outcome. Much more needs to be done with unobtrusive measures: Do people actually read instructions when they are in difficulty—or do they ask a friend? How long do documents actually last before they find their way into the waste-paper basket? How quickly do people give up trying to follow instructions, correspondence course material, etc.? How are sales affected by changes in layout and design? Research workers rarely seem to ask practical questions such as these.

In terms of the kind of material discussed in this chapter (i.e., an extract from a technical manual), perhaps the best data one could gather would come from observing workers actually using such materials and, indeed, from asking them how they would suggest that one might improve the manual further. The suggestions of such people might be surprising. It seems highly likely that users will not take kindly to wordy text, no matter how well written or displayed. In short, the whole idea of an instructional manual needs to be re-thought. What do workers use such manuals for? When do they use them? How do they use them? How, with modern technology, can we help them to achieve their aims more easily? These are perhaps the questions that should be addressed first, before one launches into producing dinosaurs.

Acknowledgments. I am grateful to Colette Paul, David Lewin, and Mark Richards for providing me with some of the data reported in the section on evaluation.

Appendix 1: A Selected Bibliography

General
guides

Hartley, J.
Designing Instructional Text.
London: Kogan Page. New York: Nichols, 1978.

Hartley, J. (**Ed.**)
The Psychology of Written Communication: Selected Readings.
London: Kogan Page. New York: Nichols, 1980.

Hartley, J.
Eighty ways of improving instructional text.
*I.E.E.E. Transactions on Professional
Communications*, 1981, *Vol. P - C 24*, 1, 17-27.

Spacing
text

Hartley, J., Burnhill, P., & Davies, L.
The effects of line-length and paragraph
denotation on the retrieval of information from
prose text.
Visible Language, 1979, *XII*, 2, 183-184.

Hartley, J.
Space and structure in instructional text.
In J. Hartley (Ed.), *The Psychology of Written
Communication: Selected Readings.*
London: Kogan Page. New York: Nichols, 1980.

Hartley, J.
Spatial cues in text.
Visible Language, 1980, *XIV*, 62-79.

Techniques
of
evaluation

Hartley, J., Fraser, S., & Burnhill, P.
Some observations on the reliability of measures
used in reading and typographic research.
Journal of Reading Behavior, 1975, *7*, 3, 283-296.

Hartley, J., Trueman, M., & Burnhill, P.
Some observations on producing and measuring
readable writing.
Programmed Learning and Educational Technology,
1980, *17*, 164-174.

Hartley, J., & Trueman, M.
The effects of changes in layout and changes in
wording on preferences for instructional text.
Visible Language, 1981, *XV*, 1, 13-31.

*Journal
design*

Hartley, J.
Designing journal contents pages: the role of
spatial and typographic cues.
Journal of Research Communication Studies,
1980, *2*, 83-98.

Hartley, J.
Sequencing the elements in references.
Applied Ergonomics, 1981, *12*, 1, 7-12.

*Access
structures*

Hartley, J., & Davies, I.K.
Pre-instructional strategies: the role of
pre-tests, behavioral objectives, overviews,
and advance organizers.
Review of Educational Research, 1976, *46*,
2, 239-265.

Hartley, J., Kenely, J., Owen, G., & Trueman, M.
The effects of headings on children's recall of
prose text.
British Journal of Educational Psychology,
1980, *50*, 3, 304-307.

Hartley, J., Morris, P., & Trueman, M.
Headings in text.
Remedial Education, 1981, *16*, 5-7.

Hartley, J., & Trueman, M.
The role and position of summaries in instructional
text.
In F. Percival and H. Ellington (Eds.), *Aspects of
Educational Technology XV*.
London: Kogan Page. New York: Nichols, 1981.

*Student
activities*

Hartley, J., & Davies, I.K.
Note-taking: a critical review.
Programmed Learning and Educational Technology,
1978, *15*, 207-224.

Hartley, J., Bartlett, S., & Branthwaite, A.
Underlining can make a difference—sometimes.
Journal of Educational Research, 1980, *73*, 218-224.

Appendix 2: Text Specification

This Appendix contains a copy of my typographic
specifications to the printer concerning the
layout of this chapter. It is reproduced here so
that readers can (a) see how it was done,
(b) see that it is not difficult to do, and
(c) see whether or not the printer followed it.

*Horizontal
spacing*

Please indent the main body of the text up to
17 character spaces throughout. Side headings,
printed in bold and italic, are set in this space,
as indicated on the manuscript.

Please set the text unjustified.
Please avoid word breaks—hyphenation—at line ends.
Please do not end a line with the first word of a
new sentence. Carry this word over to the next
line.

*Vertical
spacing*

All line-spaces should be in terms of whole numbers
of units of line-feed—never fractions.
The text is set in sections—broken by two units of
line-feed—and paragraphs within these sections are
separated by one unit of line-feed (as marked on
the manuscript).

Each section is accompanied by a side heading
printed in bold.

If necessary the text may stop short or over run
by two units of line-feed. There is no need to
end the text at the same point on every page.

Please do not start a new section or a new
paragraph on the last one or two lines on the page.
Please do not end a paragraph on the top line of a
new page.
Please put the figures on separate pages, divorced
from the text, at the point indicated in the
manuscript.
Please reduce each figure by the same amount.

10.

Programmed Instruction Revisited

David H. Jonassen

The purpose of this chapter is to revive awareness and interest in one of the best established and most effective means for structuring and displaying prose available—programmed instruction. Its decline in popularity belies its continued efficacy as a medium of and heuristic for designing instruction (see Markle, 1978). The following is a very lean program designed to reacquaint you with the trends in programmed instruction.

---

1. Programmed instruction is traditionally grounded in behavioral psychology. It is based on the two most critical axioms of behaviorism—the laws of the exercise and effect. The former, also known as the law of use and disuse, states that the more a particular stimulus-response connection is used, the stronger it becomes (practice). The law of effect states that when a particular connection is followed by a reward, it is strengthened (reinforcement). If you reward a particular response in the presence of a particular stimulus, the response is more likely to be emitted when next the stimulus is presented.

   In the laboratory, researchers reward a pigeon with a grain of corn after it pecks at a disc. The more times this response occurs, the more likely it is to be repeated. In this case, the consistent pecking in the presence of a disc represents the practice and the kernel of corn the reinforcement.

Programmed instruction presents chunks of information to the learner and then asks the learner a question about it. The active response to presented material made by the reader represents the practice. What do you suppose represents the effect or reinforcement (in your own words)?

Knowing the response is correct. Since most programmed instruction is designed so that the learner makes the correct response to the question, the knowledge that you were correct is *reinforcing*.

2. According to principles of behavioral psychology, is it necessary for the learner to make an overt response to the question presented in programmed materials, that is, write the answer in the blank?

Yes. It is through practice that behavior becomes predictable.

3. Every *frame* in a program (this one is the third in this program) presents some information to the learner (amount varies according to style) followed by a question. The learner is directed or required to make an active response to that question. Confirmation of correctness of that response is provided in that frame or another to which the student is directed. According to behavioral psychologists, why is this

knowledge *of results* or feedback supposed to be reinforcing to the learner?

(In your own words) Success is its own reward, so knowledge of correctness or positive feedback is rewarding.

4. The reinforcement of correct responses insures that the learner in a programmed sequence is practicing the appropriate responses. If a student makes a response that is reinforced, he or she will be (more/less) likely to repeat that response if the same or similar stimulus material were presented again.

----

more

5. Programmed instruction has defined the "associative learning" model, which is essentially a three-component process. Based upon the previous discussion, see if you can identify each component (box) and the relationship between them by connecting the boxes with lines and arrows.

```
┌─────────┐   ┌─────────┐   ┌─────────┐
│         │   │         │   │         │
└─────────┘   └─────────┘   └─────────┘
```

Your model should look something like this:

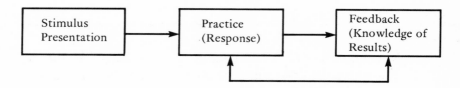

According to behaviorists, this is the way most learning takes place.

Note: As programmed instruction has evolved, it has outgrown the behavioral model. New techniques in programming have made different assumptions about the learning process. Learning is not conceived to be as mechanistic or as subject to direct manipulation. Motivation need not be extrinsic to the learner, i.e., provided through reinforcement. Learning is not synonymous with performance. The mindless copying of verbal responses is not the key to learning all things. These changes have impacted on all three components of the programming process, which will be reviewed in the next several frames.

---

6. Frames or units of instruction have become longer. More information is being presented in a less mechanistic manner. The former *de facto* limit of 30 words per frame is regularly exceeded. Much of the boredom and lack of appeal of early programs resulted from the relentless march of redundant frames and blanks to be filled in. These copy frames (Markle, 1969) only exercised handwriting, not thinking. The learner is now credited with the ability to assimilate and hold in working memory more information before making a response.

These changes in the stimulus presentation have most significantly affected which programming variable?

    a. programming style
    b. step size
    c. sequence of presentation

----

    b. step size. A fundamental characteristic of traditional, linear programming was its small step size

---

7.   Small step size was critical in early programming. Only by incrementing information in abstemiously bite-sized bits could the programmer insure a _____.
_____ .

----

correct response, so to be reinforcing

---

8.   The most significant change in programmed instruction is reflected in the nature of learner responses. Programmers still assume that responding should be active, but it need not necessarily be overt.

The traditional constructed response frame (fill-in-the-blank) required an overt response, i.e., the learner would write his or her answer in the blank.

Alternative response mechanisms, such as discrimination frames (multiple-choice, true/false, yes/no questions) require an active but _____ response.

----

covert (although this frame called for an overt response)

---

9.   The value of programmed instruction is not necessarily in the physical response behavior. Rather, it is in the mental activity stimulated by the question, what the behaviorists called mediated responses. We cannot see them, but we know they take place. This distinction has been one of the more important issues in programmed instruction research.

Do you believe that research evidence has shown that learners forced to write their responses have generally performed (worse than/about the same as/better than) learners who only thought through the answer? Why?

- -

about the same as. In both cases, the mental (learning) behavior was elicited and that is what affected performance.

---

10.   Some psychologists refer to the mental activity stimulated by the questions in each frame as mathemagenic behaviors, those that "give birth to learning." The active response is an integral part of Rothkopf's (1970) "inserted question" paradigm. Questions inserted in text control the way the information is attended to and processed. By controlling the way the learner thinks about textual material, we can determine how learners will convert presented information (nominal stimuli) into encoded information (effective stimuli).

Which of the following additions to text do you believe would also elicit mathemagenic behaviors?
            _____ taking notes while reading
            _____ glossaries in text
            _____ prefacing passage with behavioral objective
            _____ summarizing and outlining passage

    _____ table of contents
    _____ overviews at the beginning of a passage

According to Faw and Waller (1976) and others, note taking, objectives, summarizing, and overviews are all mathemagenic, that is, they control the way the reader thinks about and processes prose.

---

11.   Programmed instruction still assumes that the learner must actively respond in order to be effective. However, the response must be an active intellectual response, a mathemagenic response, that need not always be correct. An important principle of behaviorally oriented programming was errorless performance. In order to accomplish this, the behavior elicited by the stimulus material had to be so simple that the least capable to average learner would always respond correctly to each frame.

Constructed responses in which the learner fills in a blank with information contained in the frame requires the learner to be (active/passive). In completing this type of frame, is the learner actively attending to the meaning of the stimulus material (yes/no)? Would you say the learner is mentally (active/passive)?

----

active. no. passive

---

12.   Reinforcement is predicated on positive feedback to performance. An assumption of cognitive (or information process-

ing) psychology (having replaced behaviorism as the pre-eminent model of learning) is that the learner need not always perform correctly. Many learning tasks require mental processes that are difficult to acquire and easy to misinterpret. Correction of mental errors is a legitimate form of learning, often "the best teacher."

Mentally constructing difficult thought processes often results from _____ feedback to responses that are _____ .

negative. incorrect.

13.   Does making the wrong response to the stimulus material mean the learner was mentally passive?

not necessarily. He or she may have simply misinterpreted information or formed an inaccurate concept.

14.   The most critical deficiency in the behavioral approach to programming relates to the limited levels of learning imposed by having to operantly condition student behavior (requiring overt behavior as a component of the learning process). Effort spent in responding detracts from the amount of effort needed for understanding. The more difficult the learning task, the more mental effort is required. Remembering is a function of the amount of semantic involvement with the stimulus material (Craik & Lockhart, 1972). Different "levels of processing" require more or less attention to the meaning of material. For

instance, analyzing the symbols used by an author in a short story requires closer attention and therefore represents deeper processing than summarizing the plot.

Rank these learning tasks in terms of depth of processing (1 being the shallowest and 4 being the deepest).

    _____ when writing a story, include appropriate foreshadowing

    _____ reciting a definition of foreshadowing

    _____ knowing when to use foreshadowing and why

    _____ recognizing an example of foreshadowing a story

4,1,3,2

---

15. This simple example was included to illustrate that learning tasks require different _____ of mental activity which are (overt/covert).

----

levels or depths. covert.

---

16. The more difficult the task, i.e., the deeper the processing, the more likely learners are to misinterpret a presentation of it. Certainly more mental effort is required. With anything more than the most basic associative learning, it is unreasonable to expect that individual learners will not differ in their ability to acquire mastery of the material.

What individual difference variables are likely to account for differences in learning from programmed (or any) instruction?

Mental ability, including intelligence, reading ability, problem solving skill, etc., normally ranks as the strongest predictor of learning. Brighter students often learn in spite of our instructional interventions. *Motivation* determines the amount of effort that will be applied to any learning task. This may be related to how interested the student is in the topic or general expectations for performance. *Prior learning*, how much the learner already knows about the topic or related topics, provides the necessary knowledge structures for taking in more. Differences in these and other variables will determine how well someone learns from programmed instruction.

17.   Intrinsic or branching programming is a technique that was developed to address the deficiencies of operant, linear sequences. Linear programming controls the learning process by reinforcing the overt performance of limited memory tasks. In a branching program, a body of information is presented (usually longer than linear frames) that the learners must read, understand, and think through. A question that tests that understanding is presented to the learner. A correct response will send the learner to another frame that confirms the correctness, explains *why* it was correct, and presents new information. An incorrect response leads the learner to a separate frame which confirms the response the learner made and discusses *why* it was incorrect by providing an alternate explanation or remedial instruction before retesting. Learning behavior is intrinsic to the material and the learner, not extrinsically controlled by

reinforcement. Branching programs assume that some learners will misinterpret information. Rather than simply confirming their incorrectness, an attempt is made to rectify the thought processes that resulted in the misunderstanding. Separate branches can (should) be written for each possible misinterpretation of the information.

Which form of programming is better able to teach "deeper levels of processing" according to the previous definitions—linear or branching?

> Linear: Proceed to Frame 18A
> Branching: Proceed to Frame 18B

18A. You chose linear programming as being better able to produce deeper levels of processing. As you should recall from Frame 14, "deeper" processing requires more mental effort and more difficult mental processes. These are the processes in which individuals more frequently differ in ability or background (see Frame 16). These types of skills tend to be more frequently misunderstood, indicating the need for alternatives available in branching programs.

Now suppose you had a problem that required new employees to memorize the names for several frequently encountered parts in an assembly process. Would you choose a linear or a branching program?

> Linear: Frame 18C, next page
> Branching: Frame 18D, next page

18B. Branching programming is probably correct. Since levels of processing require more difficult mental processes on which individuals will more likely differ, branching offers the

advantage of correcting those possible misconceptions better than a linear format.
Proceed to Frame 19.

18C. Linear programming is probably all that is necessary, if that. This is a very "shallow" process for new employees, all of whom we may assume, do not know the material. A branching program would work, though there is no reason to assume it would work any better.
Proceed to Frame 19.

18D. A branching program would probably work well for this low-level or "shallow" learning objective. However, since all of the employees are new, we may assume none of them know the information, hence no differences in prior learning. However, a simpler linear program would work just as well. Memorization of labels for objects is more binary—the answer is right or it is wrong, so branching is unnecessary.
Proceed to Frame 19.

Note: Adaptive instruction, such as that afforded by intrinsic or branching programming is at the heart of the Socratic method and represents the conceptual basis for most forms of interactive instruction involving newer technologies, such as computer-controlled videotape and disc and CAI. CAVEAT EMPTOR! Many branching programs do very little branching. Common branch frames often send the learner, armed with a repetition of the principle being explained, back to the original frame to "try again." Even the lowest ability learner knows that the other answer to a two-option question is probably right. Right?

19. Table 1 summarizes some of the characteristics and enumerates some of the advantages of programmed instruction.

*Table 1. Characteristics and advantages
of programmed instruction.*

Characteristic	Comment
Individualized/Self-Paced	Programmed instruction is a self-administered, individually sequenced teaching medium with no requirements for teacher interaction or supplementation.
Interactive/Participative	The learner is actively involved with the material while reading or viewing stimulus material. Participation increases attention and retention.
Active Response/Manipulation of Mental Behavior	Learner's responses are controlled or shaped to facilitate intended learning. Learners are provided the opportunity to evince different types of learning in selecting responses.
Sequential/Progressive Development	Various sequences (forward/backward chaining, RULEG, and

Table 1 (Continued)
Characteristics and Advantages of Programmed Instruction

	branching) are used to increment learning in digestible units or to provide for remediation of learner weaknesses or correction of errors.
Feedback/Reinforcement or Correction	The sequencing increases the likelihood of success to near 100 percent. Success is reinforcing, which increases learning and involvement. Feedback may also correct misconceptions to build accurate knowledge bases.

Advantages	Comment
Validated	Programs are normally tested (using a 90 percent criterion level) as part of the development process to insure reliable, replicable learning results, i.e., they are "automatic and guaranteed" (Bullock, 1978).
Cost-Effective	Since programs are not hardware intensive (machines no more effective than text), they are not as costly to develop as other media. Combined with validation, they are a cost-effective alternative.

Table 1 (Continued)
Characteristics and Advantages of Programmed Instruction

Specific/Need-Related	Programs can be developed to meet very specific training needs. Development begins with a needs assessment.
Time-Saving	Research has indicated that equivalent learning, relative to other media/methods requires less time.
Adaptable	Various strategies (algorithmic, deductive, inductive) and sequences can be used to "fit" the content and/or learner characteristics.

Which of these advantages makes programmed instruction most applicable to training, as is practiced in business, government, military, or school situations?

Your choice—depending upon what your instructional, financial, and temporal constraints are.

Note: Summary

In a broader sense, the characteristics of programmed instruction represent important organizational strategies for instruction. The internal structuring and sequencing (chaining, RULEG, etc.) of information synthesized into frames are consistent with the other techniques presented in this book with regard to the need for organization. Among other myriad variables that designers need to control (Reigeluth & Merrill, 1979), delivery of instruction is equally crucial. The interactiveness and explicit motivation of programmed instruction, coupled with cost-effectiveness, make it a desirable delivery system for instruction. Programming is a strategy for designing instruction, a model for structuring and presenting instruction in any medium, as well as a strategy for delivering instruction to learners.

This chapter was written to underscore the presence of programmed instruction as one of the best established and most verified means of structuring and presenting expository prose that is available. Thoughtfully prepared and executed programs have a broad range of applicability. The strategies and principles of programming have been employed in the design of materials in every medium available. After reaching its zenith of popularity in the sixties, programmed instruction plummeted in the seventies. The eighties suggest a time of pragmatic reappraisal of what programming has to offer.

References

Bullock, D.N. *Programmed instruction* (Instructional Design Library, Vol. 14). Englewood Cliffs, NJ: Educational Technology Publications, 1978.

Craik, F.I.M., & Lockhart, R.S. Levels of processing: A framework for memory research. *Journal of Verbal Learning and Verbal Behavior*, 1972, *11*, 671-684.

Faw, H.W., & Waller, T.G. Mathemagenic behaviors and efficiency in learning from prose materials. Review, critique, and recommendations. *Review of Educational Research*, 1976, *46*, 691-720.

Markle, S.M. *Good frames and bad: A grammar of frame writing*. New York: John Wiley & Sons, 1969.

Markle, S.M. *Designs for instructional designers*. Champaign, IL: Stipes Publishing Co., 1978.

Reigeluth, C., & Merrill, M.D. Classes of instructional variables. *Educational Technology*, 1979, *19* (3), 5-24.

Rothkopf, E.Z. The concept of mathemagenic activities. *Review of Educational Research*, 1970, 40, 325-336.

P.S. WRITING PROGRAMS:

Writing programs employs the classic, systematic instructional model—needs assessment leading to the statement of objectives, for which criterion test items are written. A task analysis is frequently used to identify the nature of learning required by the needs assessment, which in turn suggests specific programming strategies and appropriate sequences for presenting the frames (task description). An elaboration of this process is beyond the scope of this chapter.

11.

Structured Outline Representations for Procedures or Algorithms

Paul F. Merrill

In an earlier paper (Merrill, 1980), I presented several different ways in which procedures or algorithms could be represented in order to improve communication in education and/or training materials. The purpose of this chapter is to present a new mode of representation for procedures: the "structured outline." This new mode of representation was developed based on some recent innovations in the analysis and representation of algorithms in computer science (De Marco, 1979).

Mathematicians and computer scientists have distinguished between two different types of procedures: algorithms and heuristics. An "algorithm" is a procedure or series of steps which is guaranteed to produce the correct result. In contrast, a "heuristic" is a procedure which uses "rules of thumb," that are not guaranteed to produce the correct result. The main difference between algorithms and heuristics is that the steps of an algorithm must be unambiguously defined (Knuth, 1968), while some steps of a heuristic may be somewhat ambiguous. Although a heuristic may not always produce the correct result, it is better than no procedure at all. Many of the procedures that we use every day, and that are taught in our schools, are heuristics, since our current state of the art is not advanced enough to allow us to define each step unambiguously. However, through continued research and experience, we should endeavor to refine our procedures so that they approach true algorithms (Merrill, 1980).

The general term, "procedure," will be used throughout this chapter rather than the more specific terms "heuristic," "algorithm," or Landa's (1974) "quasi-algorithm." Thus, the term procedure will be used to refer to any series of steps for solving a problem or accomplishing a task. Procedures are used in baking a cake, operating a sewing machine, performing long division, determining the correlation between two variables, closing out a cash register, preparing balance sheets, diagnosing diseases, repairing bicycles, etc. These few examples demonstrate that procedures are very common and important in our lives.

The individual steps of most procedures may be classified as either operations or decisions. Operational steps usually involve the manipulation or some apparatus or the transformation of some information or data. On the other hand, decision steps involve the evaluation or testing of the results or outcomes of earlier operations in order to determine if certain specific conditions have been met. Decision steps lead to alternate paths in a procedure. Thus, decision steps are often referred to as branching points. If the specified condition is satisfied, then one path is followed. If the condition is not satisfied, then the alternate path is taken. Each alternate path contains a unique set of steps.

Procedures vary greatly in complexity. Simple procedures involve only a few operations, which are performed in a linear sequence and contain no decision steps. Other procedures consist principally of decision points and contain few operations. The more complex procedures contain many conditional decision steps and many operations. These many decision steps result in a large number of alternate paths. In the earlier paper (Merrill, 1980), I proposed that different modes of representation should be used for the various types of procedures. For example, it was proposed that linear procedures which involve only a few operations performed in a linear sequence could best be represented by a simple sequential list of the operations or by a symbolic formula. On the other hand, decision rule procedures which consist mainly of decision points and very few operations would be better represented by a decision tree or decision table. For complex procedures which involve many decision points and many operations, the flowchart and decision table were proposed as the most promising representations. The purpose of this chapter is to present a new representation for procedures called the "structured outline." This new representation would be most appropriate for complex procedures and has several advantages over both the flowchart and decision table representations.

In a flowchart (see Figure 11.1), the decision steps are represented by diamond-shaped boxes, while the operations are represented by rectangular boxes. The sequence of steps is indicated by the arrows, and the beginning and ending points are shown as ovals. As can be seen from Figure 11.1, a flowchart clearly shows the sequential relationship between the steps of a procedure. Sequential relationships are obviously critical in the performance of a procedure. However, recent research and evaluation of algorithmic procedures in computer science (Yourdon & Constantine, 1979) have shown that complex procedures organized according to sequential relationships have several significant deficiencies. These deficiencies manifest themselves in (1) procedures which will not work properly; (2) difficulty in finding and correcting errors in a procedure; (3) difficulty in modifying or expanding a procedure; and (4) difficulty in reading or understanding a procedure.

In order to reduce these problems, computer scientists have proposed and validated a new approach to the analysis and design of algorithmic procedures. This new approach is called "structured analysis." The structured analysis approach has significantly reduced each of the problems listed above. The "structured outline" representation of procedures to be proposed in this chapter was developed and derived to take advantage of the principles of structured analysis.

Structured analysis gains its name from the principle or guideline that only a small set of sequential structures of operations and decision steps should be used in the analysis and design of procedures and that these few structures should be organized according to part-whole hierarchical relationships.

Bohm & Jacopini (1966) formerly proved that any procedure could be written using only three primitive sequential structures:

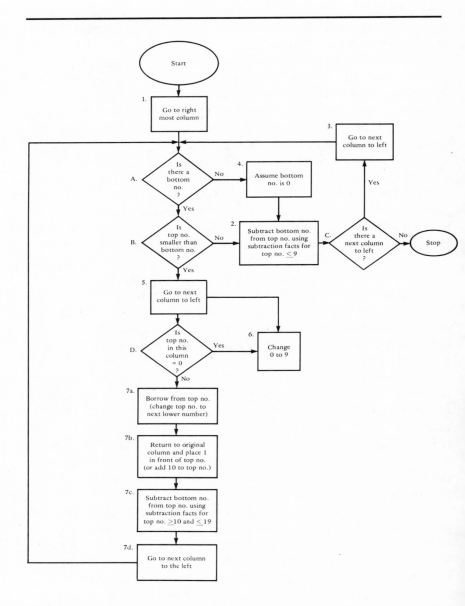

Figure 11.1. Flowchart of a procedure for subtracting whole numbers (from Merrill, 1978).

1. Linear
2. Alternate
3. Repetitive

A flowchart representation of these three structures is shown in Figure 11.2. The linear structure consists of a series of one or more operations. The alternate structure consists of a decision step with two alternate paths of operations. The repetitive structure consists of a series of one or more operations which may be repeated several times. The number of repetitions is controlled by a decision step as shown in Figure 11.2.

Any of these primitive structures may be nested inside any of the others. Thus, each of the rectangular boxes shown in Figure 11.2 represents either a single operation or any of the sequence structures. Figure 11.3 shows the expansion of a simple linear sequence into more detailed flowcharts using nested sequence structures. The dotted lines are not part of the flowcharts, but are included to show the nesting of the structures.

Although any procedure may be written using only the three primitive structures described above, the resulting procedures are not always simple and efficient. The inefficiencies resulting from the exclusive use of these three structures may be eliminated by adding a few variants to the alternate and repetitive structures. The variant to the alternate structure is called the "case" structure. The case structure allows for several alternate paths at a decision step. A flowchart representation of the case structure is shown in Figure 11.4.

There are two permissible variants to the repetitive structure. In the first variant, the decision steps may be made following the operation as shown in Figure 11.5. The placement of the decision step following the operation implies that the operation will be performed at least once. If the decision step is placed before the operation, then it would be possible to exit from the loop without performing the operation at all. The second variant allows for an abnormal exit from a repetitive loop as shown in Figure 11.6. This variant saves considerable time in procedures where a search is being made for a particular item. Without this variant, it would be necessary to search through the remainder of a file or list even after the sought for item had been located.

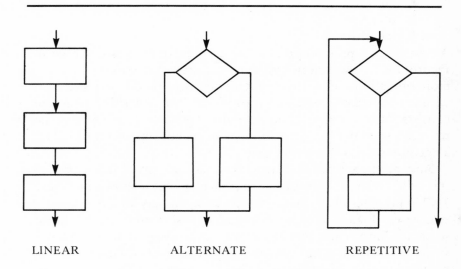

Figure 11.2. Flowchart representations of three primitive sequential structures.

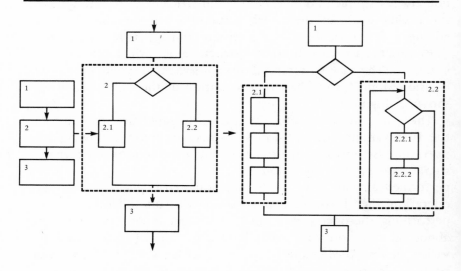

Figure 11.3. Nesting of primitive structures.

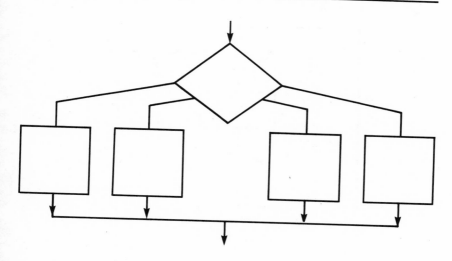

Figure 11.4. Flowchart representation of case structure.

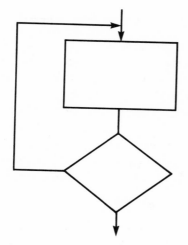

Figure 11.5. Flowchart of variant repetitive structure with decision step following the operation.

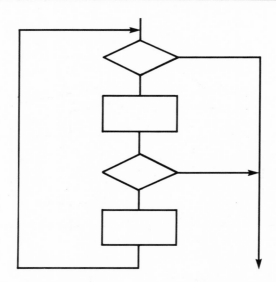

Figure 11.6. Flowchart of variant repetitive structure with abnormal exit.

Why restrict the design and analysis of tasks and procedures to these six primitive structures? Certainly many other structures are possible. How does the use of only these structures reduce errors and facilitate understanding? The key lies in the fact that the complexity of a procedure seems to be proportional to the number of decision steps in the procedure. As the number of decision steps in the procedure increases, the number of paths through the procedure increases geometrically. Errors are difficult to find because of the large number of paths which have to be traced. Procedures with many branching paths are very difficult to follow.

The primitive structures described above significantly reduce the complexity caused by decision steps, since each primitive structure can be treated as a single entity or whole. By considering each structure as a whole, it is possible to design a part-whole hierarchical organization of the procedure, and then represent the organized procedure in a linear fashion. This reduction of complexity is shown in Figure 11.3 by reading it from right to left. The complex flowchart on the right contains several decision steps, but it is composed of only primitive sequence structures. In the successive flowcharts to the left, each primitive structure within the dotted lines is reduced to a single rectangular box, which represents the whole, until a linear sequence is obtained.

The part-whole relationships and underlying linear sequence of a procedure are not readily apparent in a flowchart representation without the dotted lines around the primitive structures. However, these characteristics of a procedure become very clear if we use a different representation called "structured outlines." A structured outline representation is an extension of the common indented outline which is normally used to show the structure and content of a written manuscript (see Figure 11.7). Structured outlines use a limited vocabulary and syntax of normal English to represent the primitive sequence structures and use indention (without Roman numerals, capital letters, Arabic numerals, small letters, etc.) to show the part-whole hierarchical relationships among the primitive structures. Examples of the structured outline vocabulary and syntax for each of the primitive structures are shown in Figure 11.8 (a, b, c, d).

Figure 11.9 shows a structured outline representation of a procedure for generating the "next" numeral in base 3. A flowchart of the same procedure is shown in Figure 11.10 for purposes of comparison. The structured outline is easier to follow than the flowchart, since the outline is simply read from top to bottom as in reading ordinary textual prose; and the parts of the outline (primitive structures) are clearly shown through indention. (The Roman numerals and letters, etc., are included in this example outline for reference purposes and need not be included in all structured outlines.)

Three of the primitive structures described earlier are included in the outline shown in Figure 11.9: linear, repetitive, and alternate. The outline consists of four major sections or parts labeled with Roman numerals. Section "II" is a repetitive

Development of Military Aviation

I. Aviation in World War I

   A. The nature of the early airplane
     1. Its flimsy construction
     2. Its insignificant pay load
     3. Its mechanical unreliability

   B. The uses of aviation
     1. Short-range reconnaissance
     2. Crude bombing
     3. Spectacular but insignificant aerial duels

   C. The reputation of aviation
     1. Generally ignored by military authorities
     2. Regarded as an expensive novelty by public

II. Aviation in World War II

   A. The nature of the modern airplane
     1. Variety of construction to suit purposes
       a. Light, medium, and heavy bombers
       b. Pursuit ships
       c. Transports
       d. Training craft
     2. Structural capacities
       a. Range of flight
       b. Load capacity
       c. Armament and firepower

   B. The uses of aviation
     1. Offensive uses
       a. Long-range mass and precision bombing
       b. Preliminary bombardment before attack
       c. Long-range reconnaissance
       d. Supply
       e. Transport
     2. Defensive uses
       a. Break-up of enemy concentrations
       b. Harassing of enemy movements
       c. Air cover for ships and troops
       d. Submarine reconnaissance
       e. Evacuation of personnel
       f. Interception of enemy planes

   C. The reputation of aviation
     1. Regarded as decisive factor by military authorities
     2. Regarded by troops as aristocratic branch of the services
     3. Highly favored by public opinion
     4. Considered as co-equal with army and navy at end of war

Figure 11.7. Example of an indented outline for a written manuscript (from McCrimmon, 1957).

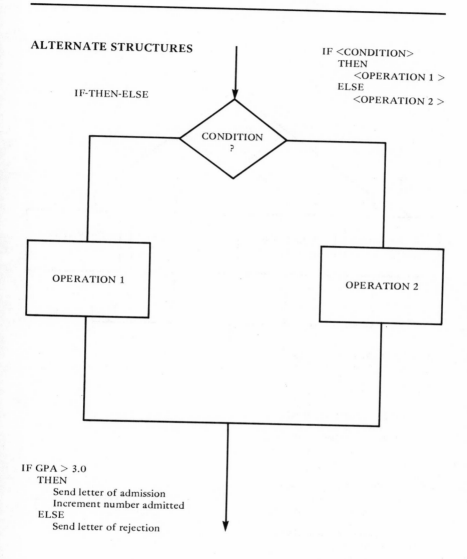

ALTERNATE STRUCTURES

IF-THEN-ELSE

IF <CONDITION>
  THEN
    <OPERATION 1 >
  ELSE
    <OPERATION 2 >

CONDITION
?

OPERATION 1

OPERATION 2

IF GPA > 3.0
  THEN
    Send letter of admission
    Increment number admitted
  ELSE
    Send letter of rejection

Figure 11.8a. Examples of structured outline representations of each of the primitive structures.

Figure 11.8b

CASE

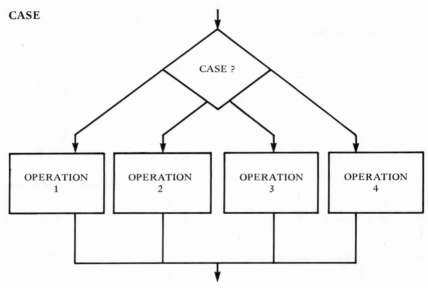

SELECT APPROPRIATE CASE
    CASE 1: <DESCRIPTION>
             <OPERATION 1 >
    CASE 2: <DESCRIPTION>
             <OPERATION 2 >
    CASE 3: <DESCRIPTION>
             <OPERATION 3 >
    CASE 4: <DESCRIPTION>
             <OPERATION 4 >

SELECT APPROPRIATE CASE
    CASE 1: Administrator
             Assign Parking Sticker A
    CASE 2: Faculty
             Assign Parking Sticker B
    CASE 3: Student
             Assign Parking Sticker C
             Fee = $5.00
    CASE 4: Staff
             Assign Parking Sticker D

Figure 11.8c

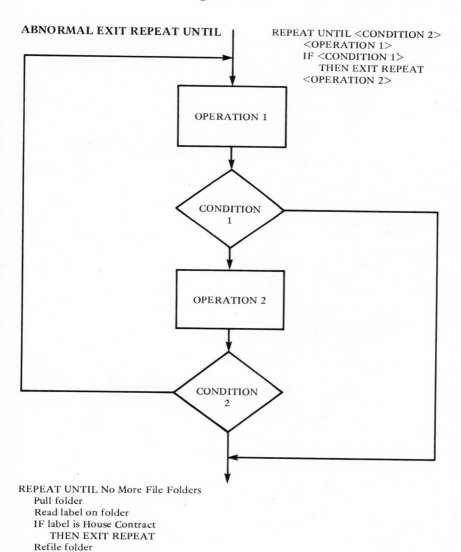

ABNORMAL EXIT REPEAT UNTIL

REPEAT UNTIL <CONDITION 2>
    <OPERATION 1>
    IF <CONDITION 1>
        THEN EXIT REPEAT
    <OPERATION 2>

OPERATION 1

CONDITION 1

OPERATION 2

CONDITION 2

REPEAT UNTIL No More File Folders
    Pull folder
    Read label on folder
    IF label is House Contract
        THEN EXIT REPEAT
    Refile folder

Figure 11.8d

REPETITIVE STRUCTURES

WHILE DO

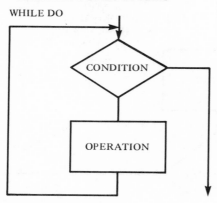

WHILE \<CONDITION\> DO
    \<OPERATION\>

WHILE More Patients DO
    Roll up sleeve
    Swab arm with alcohol
    Give Injection

REPEAT UNTIL

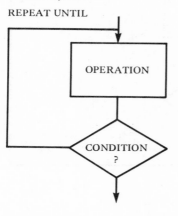

FOR \<CONDITION\>
    \<OPERATION\>

REPEAT UNTIL \<CONDITION\>
    \<OPERATION\>

FOR Each Child
    Comb hair
    Put on boot
    Give kiss

REPEAT UNTIL No More Customers
    Wash windows
    Check oil
    Fill tank
    Collect money

Procedure Next Base Three

I. Read the ones digit of numeral
II. REPEAT UNTIL no more digits

A. IF digit = 2

1. THEN
   a. Change 2 to 0
   b. Write down 0 ◄

2. ELSE
   a. Increment digit by 1
   b. Write down NEW numeral
   c. EXIT procedure

B. Read next digit to left

III. Write "1" in the next position to the left of the last "0" written

IV. END.

Figure 11.9. Structured outline representation of a procedure for generating the "next" numeral in base 3.

structure that is repeated once for each digit until no more digits remain. Nested within the repetitive structure is an if-then-else alternate structure labeled "A." This structure is used to determine if a given digit is equal to 2. If the digit is equal to 2, the operations labeled "a & b" under "1" are executed; otherwise the operations labeled "a, b, & c" under "2" are executed, not both. Thus, if operations "A.1 a & b" are executed, the next operation to be executed would be operation "B." What operation would be executed after "B?" Since section II is a repetitive structure, the operations under "A" would be executed again. In fact, sections "A" and "B" would continue to be executed repetitively until no more digits remain. However, note that the operation labeled "II.A.2.c" is an abnormal exit from the procedure. When this operation is executed, the procedure is terminated. If the procedure is not terminated by "c," then operation "III" is

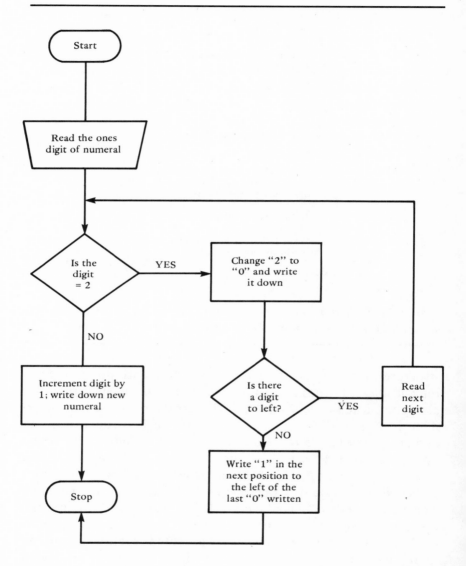

Figure 11.10. Flowchart representation of a procedure for generating the next numeral in base 3 (from Merrill, 1980).

executed only after the repetitive structure under "II" has been completed (no more digits remain).

The flowchart in Figure 11.10 clearly shows the sequential order of the various steps of the procedure. However, the decision points and loops make the procedure difficult to follow. The flowchart does not reveal the part-whole relationships between the various elements of the procedure. This makes the procedure difficult to understand.

Another example of a structured outline is shown in Figure 11.11. This structured outline is an alternate representation of the procedure to subtract whole numbers represented previously by a flowchart in Figure 11.1.

Encode Problem

FOR Each Column

    Encode top number

    IF there is a bottom number

        THEN
            IF the top No. is smaller than the bottom No.
            THEN
                WHILE top No. in column = 0
                    Change 0 to 9
                    Go to next column to left
                Borrow 1 from top No. in next column
                    (Change top No. to next lower number)
                Place a 1 in front of top No. in original column
                    (Or add 10 to top No.)
                Subtract bottom No. from top No. using
                    subtraction facts for top No. ≥ 10 and ≤ 19
            ELSE
                Subtract using facts for top No. ≤ 9

        ELSE

            Assume bottom No. is 0
            Subtract using facts for top No. ≤ 9

    Display complete answer
END

Figure 11.11. Structured outline representation of a procedure to subtract whole numbers.

Summary

The purpose of this chapter was to present a new mode of representation for procedures called the "structured outline." The term procedure was used in a general sense to include any series of steps for solving a problem or accomplishing a task. This definition includes the more specific terms of "heuristic," "algorithm," and "quasi-algorithm." Procedures can be represented in several different ways: sequential list of steps, symbolic formula, decision tree, flowchart, or decision table. The "sequential outline" was presented as an alternative representation for complex procedures which involve many decision points and alternate paths.

A structured outline representation is an extension of the common indented outline which is normally used to show the structure and content of a written manuscript. Structured outlines use a limited vocabulary and syntax of normal English to represent six primitive sequence structures. Structured outlines are superior to flowcharts and other modes of representation since they show both sequential and hierarchical relationships and can be read from top to bottom as with normal expository text. They can also be easily constructed using a standard typewriter or word processor.

References

Bohm, C., & Jacopini, G. Flow diagrams, luring machines, and languages with only two formation rules. *Communications of the ACM*, May 1966, 366-371.

De Marco, T. *Structured analysis and system specification.* Englewood Cliffs, NJ: Prentice-Hall, Inc., 1979.

Knuth, D.E. *The art of computer programming, Vol. I, Fundamental Algorithms.* Reading, MA: Addison-Wesley, 1968.

Landa, L.N. *Algorithmization in learning and instruction.* Englewood Cliffs, NJ: Educational Technology Publications, 1974.

McCrimmon, J.M. *Writing with a purpose* (2nd Ed.) Cambridge, MA: The Riverside Press, 1957.

Merrill, P.F. Hierarchical and information processing task analysis: A comparison. *Journal of Instructional Development*, 1978, *1*(2), 35-40.

Merrill, P.F. Representations for algorithms. *NSPI Journal*, 1980, *19*(8), 19-24.

Yourdon, E., & Constantine, L.L. *Structured design, fundamentals of a discipline of computer program and system design.* Englewood Cliffs, NJ: Prentice-Hall, 1979.

12.

Advance Organizers in Text

David H. Jonassen

CONCEPTUAL FOUNDATION*

Introduction   Learning can be characterized along two dimensions—rote versus meaningful learning and reception versus discovery learning (see Figure 12.1). The type of learning in which an individual engages, as described along these dimensions, is determined by the individual's purpose for learning and the way he or she interacts with instructional materials and sequences. On the first dimension, rote learning consists of remembering discrete, isolated units that are not related to established concepts, i.e., not a part of existing ideational systems. Meaningful learning, on the other hand, occurs when ideas can be related to individuals' cognitive structures, their mental organization of concepts or ideas.

Reception learning results when all of the substance necessary for learning is presented to

---

*The ideas and terminology presented in this chapter were developed and published over a period of years by David Ausubel and associates (Ausubel, 1960, 1962, 1963, 1968; Ausubel & Fitzgerald, 1961; Ausubel, Robbins, & Blake, 1957; Ausubel & Youseff, 1963.

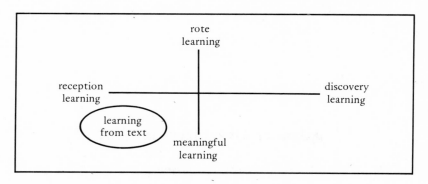

Figure 12.1

the learner. Mental activity is limited to assimilating that material and integrating it with what is known. Discovery learning occurs when all of the material necessary to solve a problem is not presented, and the learner is required to reorganize available information and call upon prior learning for the problem's solution.

Learning from text generally represents reception learning. In order for the material presented in a text to be effective, it should be meaningful. The goal of the text writer/designer is to engage the reader in meaningful reception learning.

SUBSUMPTION THEORY

Expository Organizer

HYPOTHESIS: Rote learning is less resistant to forgetting, because it is not anchored to any cognitive context.

Information becomes meaningful insofar as we are able to relate it to something we know. Knowledge is encoded into memory in a giant network in which all ideas are ultimately related to all other ideas.

ASSUMPTION: Our cognitive structures are organized hierarchically with broader, more inclusive concepts at the top subsuming less inclusive sub-concepts, which in turn subsume more concrete and specific concepts and instances.

Through this process of *progressive differentiation*, we elaborate our knowledge bases from greater to lesser inclusiveness, each idea in the hierarchy linked to the next higher step through a process known as *subsumption*.

ASSUMPTION: Content or subject matter is also hierarchically organized (see Figure 12.2).

What is known about any subject can also be conceived of as a pyramid, with the most abstract or inclusive classes of knowledge subsuming less inclusive classes of knowledge subsuming less inclusive classes of knowledge on down to individual instances.

ASSUMPTION: New material becomes meaningful to the extent that it can be subsumed under relevant existing concepts.

To the degree that we can incorporate material into our existing cognitive structure, i.e., conceptually anchor it to what we know, that new material will be meaningful. In so doing, that material will become more *stable*, i.e., less susceptible to forgetting. Stabilization of new ideas into the learner's cognitive structure is a key concept in *subsumption theory*. Meaningful learning does not entail the mere absorption of an idea, but rather the stable incorporation of that idea into one's ideational foundation. If relevant subsuming concepts are not available in the learner's cognitive structure, the learner will attempt to relate it to the most appropriate concepts available, providing less than optimal anchorage and resulting in less learning and retention.

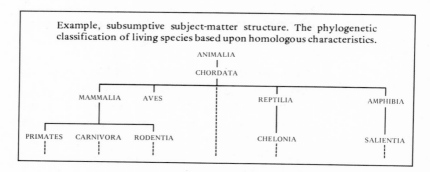

Example, subsumptive subject-matter structure. The phylogenetic classification of living species based upon homologous characteristics.

Figure 12.2

Comparative Organizer

Have you ever struggled with a problem or a unit of novel information, unable to "get a handle on it" . . . or not quite able "to see the point"? After an unsuccessful period of rumination, enlightenment occurred. The intellectual light bulb lit up. You understood the problem or the information. Your sudden understanding probably resulted from your being able to relate the problem in terms of another that you had encountered previously or in terms of ideas or constructs with which you were already familiar. In being able to think about the new material in familiar terms, it suddenly made sense to you, that is, it became meaningful.

The inclusion of advance organizers in learning materials prevents the learner from having to discover the idea that made the information make sense, that lit the bulb, so to speak. Organizers tell the learner how to relate the new material to what he or she already knows, rather than having to discover that context. Organizers short-cut the process of searching for the easiest way to understand novel material. They provide learners with the appropriate context for understanding the ideas that the learner already understands. When you know how to think about a novel idea in terms that you understand, the light bulb comes on immediately. When you do not know how to think about a new problem, you may never complete the circuit that connects the ideas necessary for understanding.

ADVANCE ORGANIZERS

Definition	Organizer: Introductory material in advance of instruction presented at a higher level of abstraction, generality, and inclusiveness than the information presented in the text passage.

Characteristics of Organizers	In order to be considered adequate advance organizers for use in textual materials, the organizer passage must be

- at a higher level of generality

- at a higher level of abstraction

- at a higher level of inclusiveness
  and
- in advance of

the larger, subordinate passage. It is a characteristic (*but not a rule*) of organizer passages, that their length is usually ten to fifteen percent of the length of the primary passage.

Functions of Organizers	Organizers are written to:

- provide advance *ideational scaffolding* for new material at an appropriate level of inclusiveness.

- deliberately introduce relevant and abstract concepts into the learner's cognitive structure to enhance incorporability and *stability* of new, more specific and detailed ideas.

- increase discriminability of the new material presented in the learning passage from similar and/or conflicting ideas already in the learner's cognitive structure.

- provide anchoring points in the learner's cognitive structure for understanding and relating new ideas.

- bridge the gap between what is known and what is to be learned.

Classes of Organizers

Expository Organizers—are used when material is unfamiliar and no concepts are known to which new ones can be anchored, i.e., there are no existing terms in which new material can be explained. They provide more *abstract, contextual* ideas to which the new material can be *anchored*. You are saying to the reader, "in the bigger picture, this is where this information fits—this is how to make sense of it."

> RATIONALE: *ideational scaffolding*—provision of appropriate conceptual foundation, i.e., a building up of the cognitive structure for incorporating new concepts. You cannot add a new room onto your house until you have built the frame (foundation).

Comparative Organizers—are used when learners are familiar with material to which new concepts can be anchored, i.e., which provide an ideational context for new material. They *must* clearly and explicitly delineate similarities and differences between the familiar, contextual material (already in cognitive structure) and the new material.

> RATIONALE: *integrative reconcilia-*
> *tion*—consistently relating new materi-
> al back to concepts existing in cogni-
> tive structure, explaining new ideas in
> terms of old.

Examples   Some examples provided by Ausubel and his
associates in their research studies include (others will be considered in the section on writing
organizers):

New Material: Topic of Presentation	Organizer Topic	Type of Organizer
Metallurgical properties of carbon steel	Major *similarities* and *differences* between metals and alloys, their respective advantages/disadvantages, and reasons for making/using alloys	Comparative
Buddhism and characteristics of the religion	Principal Buddhist doctrine at a high level of abstraction	Expository
	Differences and similarities between Christianity and Buddhism	Comparative
Endocrinology of pubescence	Uniformity and variability of primary and secondary sex characteristics	Expository
Southern interpretation of causes of Civil War	Differences between Southern and Northern positions of causes of Civil War	Comparative
Zen Buddhism	Comparison of doctrines of Buddhism and Zen Buddhism	Comparative

Non-Examples   Organizers are *NOT* overviews or abstracts, which are

- summaries of main ideas of an instructional sequence
- not *necessarily* at a higher level of abstraction.
- meant to simply eliminate specific information and detail.

DO ORGANIZERS WORK?

Introduction

The concept and construction of advance organizers have produced a flood of research which has resulted in differences of opinion and the absence of summative conclusions. Some resolution is possible. This chapter is not intended as a review of advance organizer research. Rather, it is intended to present the rationale and approaches for understanding, writing, and implementing organizers in prose materials. The suggestions included are research-based, but are not always definitive. The applicability and effectiveness of advance organizers have been challenged in a number of reviews of that research base, largely on methodological grounds and the lack of unambiguous instructions about how to write organizers (Barnes & Clawson, 1975; Faw & Waller, 1976; Hartley & Davies, 1976). For replies to these critiques, see Ausubel (1978) and Lawton & Wanska (1977). This brief section will identify the issues and the most generalizable conclusions available.

Original Research

Ausubel, who conceived of advance organizers and the subsumption theory on which they are based (see Expository Organizer, this chapter), published most of the early research on their effectiveness (Ausubel, 1960; Ausubel & Fitzgerald, 1961, 1962; Ausubel & Youseff, 1963; Fitzgerald & Ausubel, 1963). Almost all of these assessed the effectiveness of organizers using novel subjects with undergraduate students (see "Examples" in previous section). All of the studies reported that organizer groups recalled and retained more than control groups, who were usually presented with an historical overview. Although statistically significant, the advantages for organizer-preceded passages were not very large. Ausubel's results were not regarded as adequate substantiation of subsumption theory by many researchers.

Conclusions from Research

Hartley & Davies (1976) summarized the results of several years of research by concluding that:

- Organizers seem to facilitate learning and retrieval, although a number of studies failed to support this conclusion.

- The effects of organizers seem to be specific and cannot be generalized.

- Organizers generally benefit older, more intellectually capable learners than younger, less able students.

- For the less able learners, expository organizers are more effective than comparative.

- Organizers need not be prose passages; effective organizers have taken the form of games, models, and visuals.

- Organizers need not necessarily be presented in advance of instruction in order to be effective. Post-organizers have also facilitated learning.

A recent meta-analysis of 132 studies (Luiten *et al.*, 1980) concluded that organizers do in fact facilitate learning and retrieval.

Criticisms

Reasons for the inconsistent showing of organizers are numerous. Barnes & Clawson (1975) concluded that they simply do not work. Hartley & Davies (1976) attributed the inconsistencies to the problem of generating and recognizing advance organizers, a claim that Ausubel (1978) vehemently denied. Mayer (1979b), in a series of studies, suggested that the wrong questions were assessing the wrong variable. The strongest criticism to date was provided by MacDonald-Ross (1979), who concluded that the entire theoretical framework for organizers was unsound and that organizer research exemplifies, "the tendency of weakly grounded empirical research to produce more confusion, the more experiments are conducted" (p. 252). He claimed that subsumption theory, based on hierarchical models of memory and of subject matter structure, is inaccurate. The most logical structure of cognition is heterarchical, not hierarchical. Knowledge is combined laterally and hierarchically, in different structures. He also criticizes assumptions about start-to-finish, once-through reading as inaccurate, so the rationale for using organizers, particularly in advance of a passage, is untenable.

Comment

The obvious explanation for non-significant effects of organizers is too often overlooked. Organizers do not *always* work, nor should they. Their effect is relative to the learner and the subject matter. If the learner's cognitive structure (schema) for a particular topic is adequate for assimilating (linking) new information, organizers will not have a noticeable effect. It is only when one's schema for a topic is insufficiently developed that organizers will serve the bridging function described by Ausubel.

ORGANIZERS AND ASSIMILATION THEORY

Introduction

Many of the problems encountered in advance organizer research, according to Mayer (1979a), result from the theoretical grounding for their use. In place of subsumption theory, he suggests that assimilation theory is better supported by the existing research base. The assumptions are fairly similar, but the results more consistent.

Assimilation Theory

Assimilation encoding theory (Mayer, 1979a) contends that meaningful learning depends upon:

- reception of the material to be learned
- availability in the learner of a meaningful set of past experiences (assimilative context)
- *activation* of that context during learning.

The key to assimilation theory is the integration of the new information with the learner's prior knowledge. The organizer must encourage the learner to actively integrate the new material with the old. If the learner possesses a large repertoire of past experiences and normally uses such knowledge during learning, the organizers will not facilitate learning.

Research Conclusions

Based on a review of organizer research, Mayer (1979a) concluded that organizers will work:

- when a learner does not possess or normally use an assimilative context for learning new material.

- when material is potentially conceptual and unfamiliar to the learner, thereby lacking the necessary organization for incorporation.

- when the learner lacks related knowledge or abilities.

- when the organizer provides a high-level context for learning.

- when tests of learning measure breadth of transfer rather than recall.

Based on several of his own studies, Mayer (1979b) concluded that organizers facilitate learning when:

- far transfer of knowledge (as opposed to near transfer recall) is measured.

- organizers are presented prior to learning for transfer materials (near transfer facilitated by post-organizer).

- conceptual information is presented that relates material to other ideas (retention of detail facilitated by post-organizers).

- low-ability subjects fail to possess or use an assimilative context.

- textual material is unorganized.

- discovery method is employed to produce far transfer learning.

- presented prior to task requiring storage and integration of premises (post-organizer group retained presented organization).

Comment

The use of advance organizers, according to assimilation encoding theory, effects the structure of recall. They facilitate the retrieval from long-term memory of a relevant assimilative context and the integration of new material into that context. This assumes that the encoding process is an active, conceptual process. Information is not normally encoded in isolation. When it is, learners focus on detail which is soon lost from recall. Organizers activate the conceptualizing process needed to provide an appropriate context for encoding, retrieving, and applying knowledge.

WRITING ORGANIZERS

Utilizing Organizers

Before you begin constructing organizers, you should first determine if they are necessary or appropriate. These research-based heuristics will provide some guidance in making that determination.

- Use organizers when material is novel, when readers are not likely to have encountered the concepts before. Organizers are not needed for familiar material.

- Use organizers when the material is difficult, when you anticipate that readers will have difficulty understanding the material.

- Do not use organizers for short passages with only a single theme; they are not necessary.

- Use organizers when the reader's ability is limited. Facilitating the construction of an ideational framework for understanding is the basis for organizers and the weakness of lower-ability learners.

- If the text passage for which you are writing and organizing is well-organized, with built-in organizers, adjunct organizers are not necessary.

(Ausubel, 1963; Bransford & Johnson, 1973)

Defining Type of Organizers

Once you have decided that organizers will facilitate learning and/or retention from a prose passage, you need to determine the more appropriate type of organizer—expository or comparative.

Ask yourself:
(1) What conceptual models can be used to compare the information presented in the passage?

(2) Are the learners familiar enough with that information to use it as a conceptual model? Such a determination may be based on evidence of prior learning (e.g., pretest, courses completed).

Guidelines:
(1) If relevant conceptual structures (ideas to which new material may be related) are available, write a comparative organizer.
(2) If no relevant conceptual structures are available, write an expository organizer.

Writing Expository Organizers

Step	Procedure
1	Analyze passage to identify the topic.
2	Enumerate main points.
3	Determine level of inclusiveness/ abstraction of points.

4	Determine superordinate class which subsumes the main points. This class should be more inclusive/abstract than that determined in # 3. It should function as a general model for discussing the topics.
5	Discuss in prose form this general model, relating it to the topic and main points presented in the passage. It should explain to the reader where the points in the passage fit in the larger conceptual structure.

**Examples:
Expository
Organizers**

Topic of Prose Passage	Expository Organizer
Subordinated debentures in finance	Transient property of debt
Operant conditioning	Principles of reinforcement theory
Insulation values of building materials	Concept of thermal efficiency and factors affecting it
Concept of "noise" in communication	Properties of media
Arterial sclerosis	Functions of the heart in maintaining adequate blood pressure

**Writing
Comparative
Organizers**

Step	Procedure
1	Analyze passage to identify main topic(s) or concepts.

2	Identify a similar topic with which the readers should be familiar.
3	Identify for the reader and discuss this related concept, relating it to the passage topics.
4	Enumerate the *similarities* and *differences* between the concepts presented in the organizer and those in the passage.

Examples: Comparative Organizers

Topic of Prose Passage	Comparative Organizer
Long Division	Similarities and differences to multiplication process.
Balancing objects on a level with a movable fulcrum	Review actions of a see-saw.
Importance of the Magna Carta	Proposition 13 in California or similar tax revolts.
Human (onto-genetic) development	Review and compare with principles of species (phylogenetic) development.
Democratic Party Platform	Compare with principles of Republican Party Platform.

Suggestions for Writing Organizers

- Organizers should be short (50-500 words), approximately ten to fifteen percent of the passage length.

- You may want to try interspersing organizers throughout passages. Begin each section of the passage with one to two sentence organizers (Rickards, 1976).

- Formulate organizers in question form rather than standard form.

Form of Organizers

According to Mayer (1979a), good organizers are

- concrete models

- analogies

- examples

- sets of higher order rules

- discussions of main themes in general terms.

Poor organizers are

- factual presentations

- summaries

- outlines

- directions to attend to specific portions of text.

Format of Organizers

Effective organizers are not always in prose form. Ausubel, on different occasions, has advocated the use of concrete models or diagrams as organizers. Various spatially oriented material has been successfully used as organizing structures.

- Illustrations were used to establish unavailable knowledge structure into which non-familiar verbal material incorporated (Royer & Cable, 1976).

- Processing a map prior to reading a passage improved performance (Dean & Kulhavy, 1979).

When material is difficult or spatially oriented, the presentation of illustrative material in advance of the prose can function as an advance organizer. In your directions, make certain that the reader interacts with the material, that is, attends to the material and uses it in some way to solve the problem.

REFERENCES

Ausubel, D.P. The use of advance organizers in the learning and retention of meaningful verbal material. *Journal of Educational Psychology*, 1960, *51*, 267-272.

Ausubel, D.P. A subsumption theory of meaningful verbal learning and retention. *Journal of General Psychology*, 1962, *66*, 213-224.

Ausubel, D.P. *The psychology of meaningful verbal learning.* New York: Grune & Stratton, 1963.

Ausubel, D.P. *Educational psychology: A cognitive view.* New York: Holt, Rinehart, & Winston, 1968.

Ausubel, D.P. In defense of advance organizers: A reply to the critics. *Review of Educational Research*, 1978, *48*, 251-257.

Ausubel, D.P., & Fitzgerald, D. The role of discriminability in meaningful verbal learning and retention. *Journal of Educational Psychology*, 1961, *52*, 266-274.

Ausubel, D.P., & Fitzgerald, D. Organizer general background, and antecedent learning variables in sequential verbal learning. *Journal of Educational Psychology*, 1962, *53*, 243-249.

Ausubel, D.P., Robbins, L.C., & Blake, E. Retroactive inhibition and facilitation in the learning of school materials. *Journal of Educational Psychology*, 1957, *48*, 334-343.

Ausubel, D.P., & Youseff, M. The role of discriminability in meaningful parallel learning. *Journal of Educational Psychology*, 1963, *54*, 331-336.

Barnes, B., & Clawson, E. Do advance organizers facilitate learning? Recommendations for further research based on an analysis of 32 students. *Review of Educational Research,* 1975, *45*, 637-659.

Bransford, J.D., & Johnson, M.K. Considerations of some problems of comprehension. In W. Chase (Ed.), *Visual information processing.* New York: Academic, 1973.

Dean, R.S., & Kulhavy, R.W. *The influence of spatial organization in prose learning.* Paper presented at Annual Meeting of American Educational Research Association, San Francisco, April 8-12, 1979.

Faw, H.W., & Waller, T.G. Mathemagenic behaviors and efficiency in learning from prose materials. Review, critique, and recommendations. *Review of Educational Research*, 1976, *46*, 239-265.

Fitzgerald, D., & Ausubel, D.P. Cognitive versus affective factors in the learning and retention of controversial material. *Journal of Educational Psychology*, 1963, *54*, 73-84.

Hartley, J., & Davies, I.K. Pre-instructional strategies. The role of pretests, behavioral objectives, overviews, and advance organizers. *Review of Educational Research*, 1976, *46*, 239-265.

Lawton, J., & Wanska, S. Advance organizers as a teaching strategy: A reply to Barnes and Clawson. *Review of Educational Research*, 1977, *47*, 233-244.

Luiten, J., Ames, A., & Ackerson, G. A meta-analysis of the effects of advance organizers on learning and retention. *American Educational Research Journal*, 1980, *17*, 211-218.

MacDonald-Ross, M. Language in texts. In L.S. Shulman (Ed.), *Review of Research in Education*, Vol. 6. Itasca, IL: Peacock, 1979.

Mayer, R.E. Twenty years of research on advance organizers: Assimilation theory is still the best predictor of results. *Instructional Science*, 1979a, *8*, 133-167.

Mayer, R.E. Can advance organizers influence meaningful learning? *Review of Educational Research*, 1979b, *49*, 371-383.

Rickards, J.P. Processing effects of advance organizers interspersed in text. *Reading Research Quarterly*, 1976, *11*, 599-622.

Royer, J.M., & Cable, G.W. Illustrations, analogies, and facilitative transfer in prose learning. *Journal of Educational Psychology*, 1976, *68*, 205-209.

13.

Design Principles for Diagrams and Charts

William Winn
William Holliday

Over the last few years, we have been involved in research dealing with the instructional effectiveness of diagrams and charts. Our studies have led us to believe that diagrams can be an extremely powerful medium provided they are properly designed and used. It is the purpose of this chapter to explain our research findings in applied terms so educators and technologists can develop diagrams and charts of high quality for textual applications. First, we will describe some of their important characteristics based on our analyses. We will then present specific suggestions, derived from our research, as to how designers might improve the effectiveness of the diagrams and charts they create. To do this, we will describe ways of developing diagrams in isolation, in relationship to accompanying text material, and in terms of how they affect students with different mental abilities.

The words "diagrams" and "charts" are used without distinguishing between the two forms. It is generally understood that charts are the more formal of the two media, usually consisting of single words or short phrases placed in the rows and columns of a rectangular matrix, accompanied by category headings. Diagrams, on the other hand, usually have more of the properties of pictures (e.g., schematic drawings). However, the most psychologically important characteristic of diagrams and charts is one that is common to both. Both diagrams and charts differ from texts in that the logical or syntactical relationships that exist among the concepts they describe are represented spatially on the page rather than in sentence form. For example, Figure 13.1 is a simple diagram describing predator-prey relationships in a typical food chain (Winn, 1980a).

If we look at the right-hand end of the central block, we find "Mice," "Snakes," and "Hawks" arranged one above the other, with arrows between them. "Hawks eat snakes, and snakes eat mice" is the equivalent textual message. In a text, the chain that relates these three concepts, hawks, snakes, and mice, is created by the verb "eats." But this word does not occur in the diagram. In the context of food chains, it is clear from the fact that the word "Mice" is above the word "Snakes," which is in turn above the word "Hawks," and from the direction of the arrows, who is eaten by whom.

This diagram also communicates analogous, and more general, relationships than merely examples of predation. Such relationships among concepts are known as "principles." For instance, biology teachers are concerned that students comprehend the principles "herbivores (mice) are consumed by first-level carnivores (snakes) which are then consumed by second-level carnivores (hawks)" and "all three animals consume energy-rich material in this order." Clearly, such principles are more easily learned when relationships among concepts are presented in ways requiring the least mental effort on the part of the student. Indeed, proper use of diagrams can reduce the complexity of many relationships by allowing students to inspect related pieces of information at a glance. So, while moving down the page describes a sequence of processes that occur in the food chain, moving across the page describes a scheme whereby the animals that play roles in the food chain can be classified.

To understand fully the spatial expression of syntactic or logical relationships in diagrams and charts, it is useful to apply the metaphor of "semantic distance." This term has rather special connotations for psychologists. However, in everyday usage, we refer to one concept being "closer to" a second concept than to a third, "more distant" concept. For example, we might think of cats being "closer to" dogs than to aardvarks, by virtue of the fact

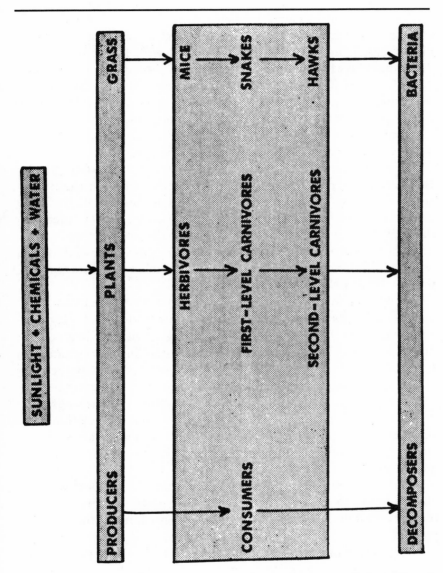

Figure 13.1. A simple block-word diagram (courtesy John Wiley & Sons, Inc., Publishers).

that cats and dogs are domestic pets, while aardvarks are not. It is obvious that the property of being "closer" is conceptual rather than spatial in this case. However, diagrams and charts express this metaphorical proximity in literal spatial terms. In the food chain diagram, "Hawks" is conceptually and literally further from "Mice" than from the concept "Snakes." It is this spatial rendering in layout of the "distance" metaphor that makes diagrams and charts powerful agents of communication.

From all of this, we can conclude that diagrams and charts possess characteristics of both text and pictures. Like text, diagrams explain and describe by means of written words. However, they reduce syntactical complexity through the use of language forms that are considerably abbreviated, usually to single words or short phrases. Like pictures, they convey meaning through the exploitation of two-dimensional space. But they do so to create easy-to-read abstract expressions of syntactic and logical relationships among concepts, not "realistic" representations of the physical world.

In addition to studying the spatial properties of the two forms, our work has been directed to other characteristics of diagrams and charts. We have found that including small drawings within diagrams can facilitate students' understanding of commonly taught concepts and principles. We have also studied how the way in which the sequence of concepts is presented affects learning. Also, we have considered the fact that diagrams and charts usually occur in prose passages. There is a whole host of relationships between them and adjacent text. These complex relationships clearly affect students' understanding of the information presented, according to our research.

Finally, we have learned that diagrams are not the best way for all students to learn. The correct interpretation of diagrams requires various mental skills that designers should not take for granted.

Design principles will be stated at appropriate places throughout the following discussion to stress how our research-based conclusions directly apply to the design of diagrams and charts.

The Design of Diagrams and Charts

Spatial Layout

Since a major characteristic of diagrams and charts is that they express logical relationships among concepts spatially, the first thing the designer must be conscious of is the accuracy with which the diagram or chart captures these relationships. This presents few problems in fairly simple cases like the food chain diagram, where processes ran neatly down the page, and a classification scheme across it. However, in the case of a flow diagram, like the one in Figure 13.2 (Holliday, 1976), things get a little less easy to deal with. Again, the verbal portion is reduced to one or two words printed in various locations on the page. In this case, though, the greater complexity of the information to learn precludes any straightforward vertical and horizontal organization of concepts.

First, notice that the processes are cyclical, centering around the plant. This conceptual organization is expressed in the diagram by placing the word "Plant" at the center of the page. Its importance is heightened by the larger type face, and by surrounding it with a box. The four cycles are placed, quite literally, around this central concept. The effect of this is to draw attention immediately to the most important concept, and then to lead the eye to the other concepts that are related to it.

Second, the concept labels have the same sequential relationships as the processes the diagram describes. For example, the portion of the diagram that describes fossil fuels being created and burned to produce carbon dioxide leads directly into the next process in the cycle, the absorption of carbon dioxide by plants through photosynthesis. Thus, the sequence in the diagram follows the steps in the real process. In terms of semantic distance, the label "Carbon Dioxide" is located further from the words "Fossil Fuels" than it is from "Car." Similarly, the name of the process "Evaporation" is further from the word "Plant" than the word "Transpiration." Our research has suggested that the superior learning observed when such diagrams are used is attributable in part to this spatial differentiation of concepts.

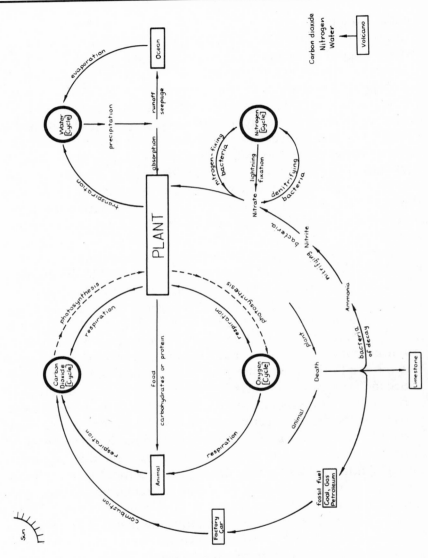

Figure 13.2. A fairly complex flow diagram (courtesy Association for Educational Communications and Technology).

Principle 1

Make sure that the distances among concept labels in the layout on the page correspond to the "semantic distance" between concepts in the content you are teaching. Also, be careful that layout accurately reflects any sequential relationships among concepts.

A third feature of this particular diagram is that arrowed lines are used to indicate the direction of the cycles described in the display. These cycles are descriptions of specific principles. Thus, the burning of fossil fuels (concept) causes (relationship) the creation of carbon dioxide (concept) which enables (relationship) photosynthesis (concept) to take place. In prose, the verbs "causes" and "enables" are used to describe these cause-and-effect relationships. In the diagram, the syntactic conventions are effectively replaced by arrowed lines. Other graphic devices, such as separation, shading, color, grouping, and ordering can also be used to clarify relationships like these.

A final feature of layout is the use of boxes to help students distinguish concepts that belong together from those that do not. For example, the words "Car" and "Factory" in Figure 13.2 appear together in the same rectangle. The effect of placing them so is to isolate them perceptually, and thus conceptually, from the other concepts. The result is that the words inside the box are thought of as belonging together, and distant from the other concepts. This has two results. First, the "semantic distance" effect created by spatial layout is enhanced. Second, placing concepts in the same box tends to emphasize their common characteristics while putting them in different boxes stresses differences.

Principle 2

Use arrows and lines to indicate direction and sequence of concepts within processes. Use boxes and other graphic

> devices to enhance the "distance" effect, and to assist students to generalize and discriminate concepts.

Pictorial Elements

You may have noticed that in Figure 13.2 there is a parallel between the location of concepts on the page and where they might occur naturally in the real world. For example, "Limestone" and "Fossil Fuels" are located in the lower portion (beneath ground level, as it were), while the gaseous components of the Carbon Dioxide cycle are where you would expect the sky to be. This concept is better illustrated in the diagram shown in Figure 13.3. Here we have a different version of the same diagram, incorporating several characteristics of pictures.

Notice that there is indeed a correspondence between the position of a concept on the page and where you would expect to find it in the real world. The water cycle takes place largely above ground level; the nitrogen cycle both above and below ground. This fairly realistic placement of concepts within the diagram increases the ability of students to learn the information, according to our research findings (Holliday, 1976).

Principle 3

Whenever possible, arrange the layout so that concept labels are found in positions corresponding to where they would occur in the real world.

The other very obvious feature of this diagram is that concepts are described by means of small pictures as well as in words and phrases. The technique of illustrating concepts in a diagram with pictures has been shown particularly to help students of low verbal ability (Holliday, Brunner, & Donais, 1977). The matter of how student abilities relate to learning from diagrams and charts will be discussed in more detail below. However, it is worth mentioning at

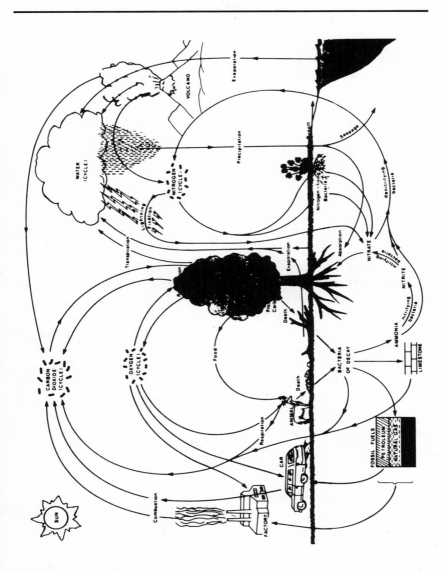

Figure 13.3. A typical picture-word diagram (courtesy Association for Educational Communications and Technology).

this point that if diagrams are designed in such a way as to supplant mental skills in which students are weak, then learning will be improved for those students.

Principle 4

Include small pictures in diagrams to teach concept identification, especially with students of low verbal ability.

Sequence

The sequence of events in cycles or processes often constitutes an important part of the information that diagrams aim to teach. For example, the food chain diagram illustrates sequential predator-prey relationships, and the biogeochemical diagram shows events by which fossil fuels burn, and carbon dioxide is used in photosynthesis. However, in some of our studies, the use of diagrams to teach sequences was studied more specifically. Figure 13.4 shows one such diagram (Winn, in press).

Here, the objective was to teach the evolutionary sequence of dinosaurs. They are shown evolving from left to right, which is stressed by the fact that they also appear to be walking from left to right across the page. The evolutionary sequence is reinforced even further by the use of arrows, and by the time scale at the top of the page. In contrast, we showed some of the students in our study the diagram shown in Figure 13.5.

The order, and the direction the animals are facing, have been reversed, and the diagram has been turned around top-to-bottom as well. Our goal was to determine the importance of displaying pictorial information left-to-right and top-to-bottom. The students were tested for a variety of things, including the evolutionary sequence. Those who saw the first diagram were far more successful in learning this than those who saw the diagram where the sequence had been reversed. In fact, learning the sequence from the reversed diagram proved to be so difficult that the students performed no better on the test than students in a

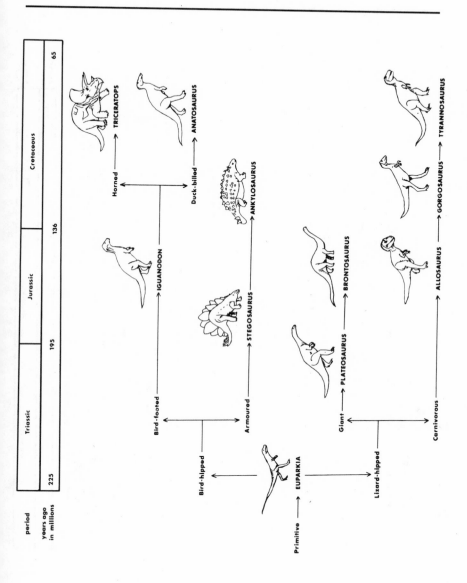

Figure 13.4. Left-to-right, top-to-bottom sequencing.

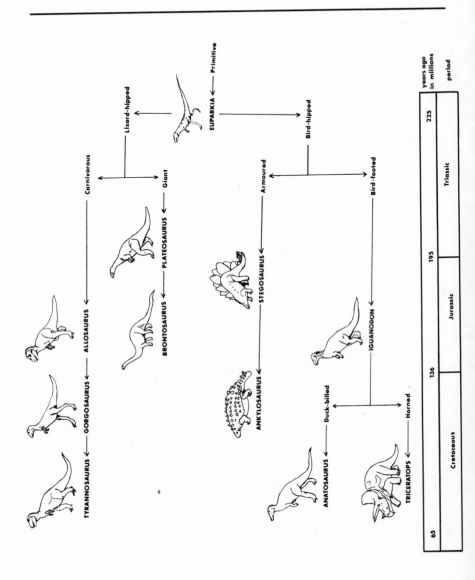

Figure 13.5. Reverse-order sequencing.

control group, who had been given no diagrams and no information about evolutionary sequence at all. We concluded that the reversed-diagram group had learned virtually nothing about the sequence.

We drew two conclusions from our results that have a direct bearing on the design of diagrams. The first was that essentially all students "read" diagrams from left to right and from top to bottom, just as they read prose, and that this habit is so strongly ingrained that they try to learn sequences presented in the opposite direction backwards, even if to do so goes against all logic. Our second conclusion was that the usual techniques for showing direction, such as arrows, are not sufficiently strong to override the conventional way of reading information.

Principle 5

Be sure to arrange any sequences of concepts so that they run left-to-right and top-to-bottom on the page.

A second objective of this study was to have the students learn to classify the dinosaurs into superordinate classes. Looking at Figure 13.4, it is clear that each animal can belong to at least two categories. Triceratops can be classified as a horned dinosaur, and as bird-hipped. On tests of classification ability, we found, once again, that students who had seen the reversed diagram scored poorly. We saw this as evidence that students reading the reversed diagram from left to right would encounter the names of the dinosaurs *before* they read the names of the categories to which they belonged. In the case of the "normal" diagram, the opposite would be true. Students would read the names of the superordinate categories first. Students seeing the normal order diagram would therefore first establish a classification scheme, and then be able to classify the animals quite easily. Students seeing the reversed diagram would not have established such a classification scheme before learning about the animals, and would have greater difficulty assigning them to categories.

This conclusion was confirmed indirectly in another study (Winn, 1981) using the chart shown in Figure 13.6. This chart was used to teach students to identify insects at different stages of metamorphosis.

The row and column headings were the names of superordinate categories to which the various insects belong. In addition, two headings in capital letters embraced two columns each. This chart proved superior to pictures and narration in teaching the type of metamorphosis each insect goes through. Apparently, the headings in capital letters allowed the students to establish a simple two-category classification scheme before they read the other headings and looked at the insects in the chart. (Incidentally, this finding was confined to high-verbal students—more on this later.) This provided further evidence of the need for arranging names of superordinate categories, in this case column headings, so that they were read first by students.

Principle 6

Arrange the layout of diagrams and charts so that the names of superordinate categories of concepts are read first, from left-to-right across the page or top-to-bottom. This is especially important when teaching classification.

Diagrams in Text

Diagrams rarely occur alone. Most often they are found in books adjacent to text materials, which they serve to elaborate. As a consequence, there is often a certain amount of redundancy between diagrams and charts and the adjacent text. It is perhaps because of this redundancy that students sometimes prefer not to look at diagrams at all. We have found (Holliday, 1976) that diagrams are better than text and diagrams plus text at teaching biogeochemical cycles, such as those shown in Figure 13.2 and Figure 13.3. The finding that the addition of a text to a diagram

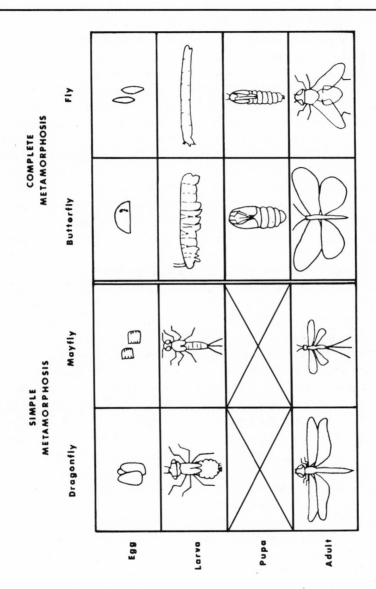

Figure 13.6. Chart with two-level column headings.

reduced its effectiveness as an aid to learning was interpreted as suggesting that students believed they could get all the information they needed from texts, and therefore did not bother to look at the diagrams. This idea is by no means original. It has been discussed by both Anderson (1970) and Samuels (1970), who suggested that students used the least possible amount of effort, and thus the most familiar medium, to learn. Designers can obviously encourage students to look at diagrams and charts by making them eye-catching. But we have tended to study other ways in which students' attention can be directed to particular parts of diagrams and charts.

The technique for directing students' attention that we have given most attention to has been adjunct, or study, questions. Students are asked questions about the material they are studying while working through it. These questions tell the students what is important information in the diagram. As a result, they tend to pay more attention to it, and learn it better. This has been demonstrated particularly well in a study by Holliday (in press), using the diagram shown in Figure 13.3. Study questions improved students' performance on a comprehension test. It was also found that if only some of the information was covered by the study questions, the students performed worse than those who saw the diagram and were questioned on all of the information, and worse than those who simply saw a diagram without study questions. This suggests to designers that while study questions can focus students' attention on important information in a diagram, unless the questions are carefully constructed to cover all of the material to be learned, they can misdirect attention away from important details.

In a similar vein, Holliday & Benson (1981) used the chart shown in Figure 13.7 to teach about vitamins.

Different sets of study questions were used to direct attention to the different columns in the chart, and to column combinations. In addition, some students were told that the study questions were important, while others were allowed to see the posttest before they studied the chart. While the results from this study are varied and complex, it is relevant for designers to know

VITAMIN CHART

Vitamin Letter	SOURCE		EFFECTS	
	One Name	One Food	Can help produce healthy	Lacking or too little can produce unhealthy
A	carotene	red peppers	lungs	night blindness
B_1	thiamine	organ meat	muscle	appetite loss
B_2	riboflavin	almonds	eyes	premature aging
B_3	niacin	rice bran	tissues	swelled tongue
B_4	pantothen	yeast	adrenals	sleep disturbances
B_5	biotin	egg yolks	fats	mental disorders
B_6	pyridoxine	nuts	antibodies	muscle weakness
B_7	choline	peas	nerves	liver problems
B_8	folacin	gland meat	babies	gray hair
B_{12}	cobalamin	soybeans	bones	fragile cells
C	ascorbate	parsley	capillaries	tooth loss
D	calciferol	fatty fish	cartilage	muscle spasms
E	tocophenol	margarine	skin	cell breakdown
K	naphthoquinone	alfalfa sprouts	liver	internal bleeding

Figure 13.7. Chart used with study questions.

that, again, study questions improved student performance on a test of the information given in the chart. In particular, it was found that students whose attention was directed to all the columns learned no more than those who had no questions to study. On the other hand, those students whose attention was focused on particular columns learned much more in those columns than students in other treatment conditions. This again suggests that while study questions are useful in directing students' attention to important parts of diagrams and charts, they should be designed to focus attention only on those places where attention needs to be focused, otherwise learning will not be improved and may even be impaired. Put another way, study questions used with diagrams and charts should be precisely targeted on important information.

Principle 7

Use study questions to focus students' attention on important details of diagrams and charts. Take care that the questions cover all of the material to be learned.

In another study, Holliday (1980) showed that study questions which overprompted students were not as effective as those that did not overprompt them. This suggests that, as with other kinds of materials, a degree of relatively deep mental processing is necessary if students are to learn from diagrams. Again, there is a message for designers here. Study questions used with diagrams should not make the answers so obvious that students need not think about what they are learning.

Principle 8

Make sure that study questions used with charts and diagrams do not overprompt students.

Individual Differences

Something that our research has told us quite conclusively is that diagrams and charts are not equally effective means of instruction for all students. Several of our studies have looked at the way in which various student abilities predict the success with which they will learn from diagrams and charts. The abilities that we have studied in particular have been verbal and spatial ability.

One of our conclusions concerning student ability has already been mentioned. This was the finding that adding pictures to a diagram helped students of low verbal ability to learn the information. What was of more interest to us, however, were the relationships between verbal and spatial ability and the mixed verbal and spatial nature of diagrams themselves—a complex research problem. We felt that the use of a chart or diagram, regardless of whether it contained pictures, would help low-verbal and high-spatial students to learn, because the spatial aspect of either medium would correspond to a way of presenting and processing information that the student would be comfortable with. Surprisingly, this was found not to be the case. It did not matter whether we measured students' verbal or spatial ability. On no occasion did we find that diagrams were of particular help to either low-verbal or high-spatial students. What we did find, though, was that the diagrams seemed to help high-verbals more than the low-verbals.

In retrospect, this finding should not have surprised us. It is increasingly acknowledged that the construct validity of many of the aptitude tests used in this kind of study is low. Aptitude tests are designed primarily to predict performance. They therefore have high predictive validity. But since the main concern of those who design them is with prediction, a precise knowledge of what they actually measure is of secondary importance. This is fine as long as researchers do not assume that just because a test is labeled a test of spatial ability that this is in fact what it measures.

It would be easy to leave the matter there. However, our studies do tend to confirm more precise theories about verbal and spatial processing. For instance, it has been reported (Hunt, 1978) that the speed at which people are able to make judgments about symbols or sentences that they see is related positively to scores on tests of verbal ability. This suggests that these tests measure general intellectual ability and not just skill with language. This interpretation of "verbal ability" would make a lot of sense given our results. First, in some of the studies, the diagram treatments tended to be more information dense and redundant. More generally able learners would be better able to handle these formats. Also, it is likely that learners who are better able to process information in general (not just verbal information) would be better able to use a relatively novel instructional format to its best advantage.

As far as spatial ability is concerned, the situation is not as clear. Construct validity is again a problem, perhaps even more so. Indeed, Cronbach & Snow (1977, chapter 9) conclude that there may not be any current aptitude test that measures visual learning. Be that as it may, in more than one of our studies, a serious attempt was made to select visual aptitude tests that tapped into the ability learners would have to use in order to perform the tasks we required of them. For example, it was expected that a test of the ability to rotate and flip over visual shapes would assist in coping with the reversed order of the diagrams in the dinosaur study. However, even this serious attempt to deal with the construct validity problem was not successful. It can only be concluded that when diagrams serve as abstract schemata to which the information they contain is to be assimilated, they play a role in cognition that goes beyond the visual. Again there is evidence and theory that would suggest this is a viable explanation. Such theory proposes that visual information is processed in word-like propositional forms at those levels in the cognitive system where comprehension and restructuring of schemata take place (Winn, 1980b). This would mean that the comprehension of diagrams and charts does not rely primarily on visual or spatial ability, but rather on more abstract powers of reasoning.

Our results, then, make a great deal of sense when considered in light of the most recent developments in the theory of how people process information. This has implications for design. When diagrams and charts are used with text, as they usually are, there is a degree of redundancy in the materials. It has been shown on numerous occasions that redundant, and consequently information-dense materials, are processed best by more able students. In our case, only high-ability students were able to handle the extra information provided by the diagrams. It also seems reasonable to assume that, since diagrams and charts are less familiar to students than straight text, students need to have attained a certain level of "diagram literacy" in order to be able to extract information from them. High-ability students would be more likely to possess these skills.

So it seems that what predicts a student's success in learning from diagrams is neither spatial nor verbal ability. Rather it is general ability (or intelligence, if you will), which appears to be measured quite well by some verbal tests. This means that designers of diagrams need to bear in mind the general intellectual ability of the students for whom they are designing diagrams and charts. In practical terms, this boils down to the fact that complex and redundant diagrams and charts are not appropriate for low-ability students, while high-ability students will handle them more easily. In short, keep it simple, do not make diagrams and charts too redundant, and give students, particularly those who are less able, enough time to study them.

Principle 9

Do not use complex and redundant diagrams and charts with low-ability students. Remember, understanding diagrams requires certain mental skills. Diagrams are *not* necessarily "easier" forms of instruction.

Conclusion

Often, designers develop diagrams and charts without attending to research findings that suggest ways of improving the chances of student comprehension. Instead, most designers at publishing companies are more concerned about the marketability of their product, whose fate is often decided by textbook adoption committees consisting of educators equally naive about such research findings. Our research, however, has allowed us to come up with several principles for the design of diagrams and charts which have the potential for reducing this problem. One note of caution, though: our work has been conducted with junior and senior high school students, and some of the principles may not apply to younger students. (We are resonably confident that they apply to older people.)

It is hoped that our nine principles, and some of the other comments we have made, will help instructional designers to create diagrams that are effective and suitable for the intended students. However, we feel that for all their potential value, poorly designed diagrams and charts are best not used at all. While we advocate the use of diagrams, we are the last people to recommend their indiscriminate use. But with careful design and moderation in application, we are certain that diagrams and charts can be most beneficial to students.

References

Anderson, R.C. Control of student mediating processes during verbal learning and instruction. *Review of Educational Research*, 1970, *40*, 349-369.

Cronbach, L.J., & Snow, R.E. *Aptitudes and instructional methods*. New York: Irvington, 1977.

Holliday, W.G. Teaching verbal chains using flow diagrams and texts. *AV Communication Review*, 1976, *24*, 63-78.

Holliday, W.G. Selective attentional effects of textbook study questions on student learning. *Journal of Research in Science Teaching*, 1981, *18*, 283-290.

Holliday, W.G. Overprompting science students using adjunct study questions. *Journal of Research in Science Teaching*, in press.

Holliday, W.G., & Benson, G. *Using questions to focus students' attention on non-prose science materials*. Paper presented at the meeting of the National Association for Research in Science Teaching, New York, April 1981.

Holliday, W.G., Brunner, L.L., & Donais, E.L. Differential cognitive and affective responses to flow diagrams. *Journal of Research in Science Teaching*, 1977, *14*, 129-138.

Hunt, E. The mechanisms of verbal comprehension. *Psychological Review*, 1978, *85*, 109-130.

Samuels, S.J. Effects of pictures on learning to read, comprehension, and attitude. *Review of Educational Research*, 1970, *40*, 397-407.

Winn, W.D. Visual information processing: A pragmatic approach to the imagery question. *Educational Communication and Technology Journal*, 1980, *28*, 120-133(a).

Winn, W.D. The effect of block-word diagrams on the structuring of concepts as a function of general ability. *Journal of Research in Science Teaching*, 1980, *17*, 201-211(b).

Winn, W.D. The effect of attribute highlighting and spatial organization on identification and classification. *Journal of Research in Science Teaching*, 1981, *18*, 23-32.

Winn, W.D. The role of diagrammatic representation in learning sequences, identification and classification as a function of verbal and spatial ability. *Journal of Research in Science Teaching*, 1982, *19*, 79-90.

14.

Affecting Instructional Textbooks Through Pictures

Philip J. Brody

A brief glance through most of today's instructional textbooks shows that they are replete with pictures and visual illustrations. Photographs of people, objects, and events, detailed drawings, labeled diagrams, simple line drawings, graphs, and charts can all be found in modern textbooks. In spite of the pervasiveness of pictures in instructional textbooks, an uneasy feeling remains about the reasons for their inclusion. However gratifying it would be to think that pictures are selected on the basis of their instructional value, supported by empirical evidence, pictures are probably most often selected for more mundane reasons such as their attractiveness, cost, and availability. In fairness to text publishers and designers, it must be pointed out that although considerable research has been conducted on various aspects of pictures, research on the effect of learning from instructional textbooks has been limited. Yet, bits and pieces of relevant information from various sources can be used to offer some advice that will enable pictures to be included in textbooks on the basis of their *instructional* qualities rather than on their *decorative* qualities.

Before discussing some of the ways in which text can be affected by pictures, it is necessary to indicate that in the context of this chapter "instructional textbook" will not refer to all books used for instruction, nor will "picture" refer to all visuals found in books. As used here, the term "instructional textbook" will refer only to those books which possess specific, identifiable characteristics. Most importantly, the book must be primarily designed and utilized for the purpose of direct instruction in a specific academic discipline or subject, to an audience with identified characteristics. Not included under this definition are those instructional books, such as basal readers, which are generally free from subject-specific objectives. Similarly, the suggestions offered in this chapter will not refer to all visual forms. While some of the suggestions offered may be appropriate to such illustrative devices as flowcharts and graphs, treated elsewhere in this book, they are primarily related to the more iconic forms of representation such as photographs, drawings, and paintings.

Expanding the Role of the Picture

Probably the most important, yet overlooked, step in using the full potential of pictures to improve learning from text is determining the various functions or purposes a picture can serve. Decisions related to type of picture, manner of representation, complexity of information, size, and location, to name a few, are all secondary to, and dependent on, the instructional functions the picture is to fulfill. With a little imagination, pictures can emerge from their traditional decorative role to a varied, dynamic, instructional element that can make a substantial contribution to the effectiveness of an instructional text.

Not only can pictures repeat the information presented in the verbal portion of the text, but they also can provide additional information, particularly that which can be verbalized only with great difficulty. Since pictures are often remembered better than words, they can help ensure the retention of information. Similarly, pictures can be used as a basis for forming mental images which can also be used for information acquisition and retention. Pictures can serve other instructional functions; they can stimulate recall of previous knowledge and abilities to better prepare students for the information to be presented in the text. They can also provide an introduction to the new materials as well as a review of the material after it has been read.

Probably more exciting is the suggestion of recent research that pictures can affect the internal cognitive processes of the learner.

While the precise relationship between picture elements and cognitive processes has not been clearly delineated, the implications are clear. Through careful analysis, it may be possible to design pictures that will not only help the student gain content competence, but also develop a specific cognitive skill or strategy. For example, not only can graphic techniques be used to help isolate pictorial elements so that the viewer can better acquire the information, but also to better develop the skills related to isolating relevant information.

Once the desired function of a picture has been determined, it is possible to begin an examination of other pictorial variables which may affect learning from instructional textbooks.

Directing Attention

For textbook pictures to be most effective, they must be used in the manner intended by the text designer. Unfortunately, achieving this state of affairs is often difficult and elusive. One reason for this is the fact that skills related to picture utilization and interpretation vary considerably between learners. The dilemma is compounded when it is realized that picture utilization skills are developmental; thus, assumptions made about one group of learners may not be valid or accurate for another group. This problem can be very acute, for instructional textbooks are usually designed for use by a variety of age groups and instructional levels. Even when all members of the textbook's intended audience are at the same developmental level, their varied backgrounds and idiosyncracies reduce the likelihood of the picture being used appropriately by many. The potential difficulties are many: some students may not examine the picture at all, while others may look at it but not understand what they are looking at. Still others may not examine the picture at the optimal moment in the instructional sequence, thereby increasing the difficulty of relating the picture to the written passage. In such a situation, the picture could become distracting, consequently reducing its instructional value. Thus, for a picture to be used most effectively, it is necessary to control both what the learner is looking at and when it is to be examined.

Some of the difficulties associated with directing attention to the picture at the proper moment can either be eliminated or reduced through the placement of the picture on the page. A picture can be placed either before a particular passage or after it, thus increasing the possibility that the picture would be examined at the intended moment. While often useful, this and other techniques based on graphic design and composition cannot always work. It is difficult, for example, to place a picture in the middle of a paragraph; there may be a lack of space for a picture on the specific page or column; the overall attractiveness of the page, probably the prime determinant in picture placement decisions, may suffer.

Though not as elegant as directing attention by graphic design and layout techniques, probably the most effective and efficient way to ensure that a student examines a picture at the proper moment is to direct the student to do so by referring to the picture in the written narrative. This reference can be made as an aside to the written narrative by placing references, such as "see Figure 4.1," inside parentheses. Similarly, the reference to the picture can be integrated with the main narrative by using such phrases as "Figure 1 shows" or "As seen in Figure 1." The exact manner of the reference has been rarely studied, and it is doubtful whether any significant findings would come from such a study. Rather, the point to be made is that a major, and often overlooked, factor in influencing the instructional effectiveness of pictures in instructional textbooks lies in the ability to direct student attention to the picture *at the time most appropriate for learning*.

An examination of current instructional textbooks reveals somewhat systematic, discipline-based biases toward making direct reference to a picture in the narrative; science texts, for example, seem to make reference to specific pictures more often than social science texts. Even within a specific discipline, practices vary considerably between publishers. Some science texts, for example, directly refer to 30 or 40 percent of the pictures, while others refer to less than ten percent. These figures raise serious questions as to whether or not publishers use pictures primarily for their ability to make a book more attractive or for their ability to increase the instructional effectiveness of the book. It would seem that if pictures are to serve a more substantial role than mere decoration, then more of an effort should be made to have the written narrative refer directly to the appropriate picture.

The primary instructional function of directing attention to a picture at a particular moment is to place the picture in an appropriate context, thus reducing the number of possible interpretations. Viewing a picture of a third-world family working together, while reading about extended families, will certainly result in a different set of interpretations than viewing the same picture during a section concerned with the economies of developing nations. In spite of its obvious instructional value, directing attention to a particular picture is a necessary, but not sufficient, condition for the proper integration and utilization of pictorial information; its success is dependent on the extent that viewers possess similar processing strategies as well as share common experiences with the content being represented. Since individuals typically vary greatly in regard to these conditions, all that can be expected is for the picture to be examined at the same moment of instruction, but with interpretations differing between learners.

Captions

It is well established that picture interpretation is closely tied to individual experiences and expectations; even students with similar backgrounds and abilities do not always interpret a picture in the same manner. One possible explanation for this is that while looking at the same picture, each student may focus on a different aspect or component of that picture. When viewing the Victorian mansion in Figure 14.1, I may focus on the interesting roofline, while another may focus on the windows or entryway. Similarly, even when examining the same component of a picture, individuals will vary on the values attached to that component. The mansion may be viewed by some as an instance of the "good old days," while others may view it as a symbol of the power and wealth of a privileged few.

Figure 14.1. Appropriate captions help reduce student ambiguity.

Even though we are somewhat familiar with the content of the above example, it demonstrates the difficulties involved with maximizing the effectiveness of pictures used for instructional purposes in textbooks. The magnitude of this problem is increased when the picture represents something that is relatively unfamiliar, for without the parameters placed by personal experience, the number of possible picture related conclusions expands considerably.

Therefore, in addition to placing the picture in an appropriate context and directing the student to examine it at the proper instructional moment, an effort must be made to provide the learner with more precise and detailed information, information that will help answer many of the questions raised: What is this a picture of? On what aspects of it should I focus my attention? How will I use it? How is this picture related to what I have been reading?

Several of the graphic techniques previously mentioned (e.g., arrows, color, shading, size) can help answer some of these questions. In particular, these traditional techniques are most useful in informing the learner of what is to be examined. However, graphic techniques offer less information regarding the purpose of the picture or how the learner should interact with it.

One of the most efficient ways to answer many of the questions raised upon viewing a picture is to simply and directly inform the learner of picture content and purpose. Rather than placing this information in the body of the text, it is probably more desirable to place it in a separate caption, adjacent to the picture. This will allow for smoother and easier reading and comprehension of both the text and the picture. Numerous captioning techniques are available. Often, the caption includes only a title for the picture; other times it is desirable for the caption to provide an explanation or ask a question of the learner. Additionally, various combinations of the major element of a caption—title, explanation, question—have also been used.

Although little is known about the comparative effectiveness of the various forms of captions, several observations can be made. An examination of textbooks reveals that within a given book, there is little variability in the forms of captioning used. This would suggest that most publishers make their captioning decisions on the basis of noninstructional factors. While a certain degree of similarity is needed for continuity and unity, too much similarity can become uninteresting and boring. When all captions are almost identical, it is likely that students will soon stop looking at many of them, thereby reducing the potential effectiveness of the picture.

While first appearing to be of minor utility, the importance of captions cannot be overlooked. Gombrich (1972) deems captions to be one of the most critical variables in the proper understanding of pictures. So important is the role of captions that Gombrich suggests that they can often compensate for lack of context. The instructional value of captions can only grow when they are placed in instructional textbooks where the information, content, and context are somewhat unfamiliar and the backgrounds of the intended audience diverse.

Pictorial Format

The selection of the appropriate pictorial format is an important consideration when choosing pictures to be included in instructional texts. Among the numerous pictorial formats available, those most commonly found in instructional textbooks are: color and black-and-white photographs; detailed, realistic, colored drawings; highly stylized drawings; labeled diagrams; simple line drawings; and cartoons. While the relative benefits of different formats have been examined by researchers, the often contradictory results make it quite difficult to provide very many explicit recommendations. Perhaps the most that can be said regarding the comparative effectiveness of photographs, detailed drawings, and other pictorial formats is that no single format is best for all occasions. What does seem apparent, though, is that the effectiveness of a particular pictorial format is dependent upon its relationship with assorted contextual components of the instructional system, including, but not limited to, types of learners, objectives, and instructional strategies. Although limited by lack of diversity of content and pictures, Dwyer's (1972) series of studies offers valuable suggestions into the import of contextual factors. Most specifically, Dwyer indicates that realistic photographs were most effective when the learner was able to control viewing time, while line drawings were most effective when viewing time was externally controlled as in television and slide/tape presentations. This is in contrast to the traditional audio-visual belief that realistic visual formats, such as photographs and detailed drawings, are generally more effective than less realistic formats.

Research on student picture preference offers some information that may be useful in the selection of appropriate visual formats. At the outset, it must be pointed out that while adding insight into this problem, the relationship between student and instructional outcomes is rather tenuous; as indicated previously, preference for a particular visual format does not necessarily result in increased learning. Yet, in the absence of more substantial data, information based on student preference has a meaningful role to play in affecting learning from instructional texts. All other things being equal, we should provide formats which are preferred by the viewer, thus making the text more attractive, and hopefully more motivating.

Picture preference pattern is remarkably stable for students of all ages. Generally, students seem to prefer photographs and realistic detailed drawings to the less realistic formats, such as line drawings. In one of the more comprehensive student picture preference studies, Myatt & Carter (1979) examined the picture preferences of 380 students in several different grades, from kindergarten through high school, and concluded that both children and young adults seem to have greatest preference for photographs and second greatest preference for realistic drawings. Similarly, Dwyer (1972) reported that college students also have a preference for more realistic formats.

While using student preference information as a guide, care must be taken that the format is appropriate for the sophistication of the learner and the level of information required to achieve the instructional outcome: jet propulsion could probably be explained better to fifth grade students by including line drawings rather than color photographs of a jet engine. Additionally, it is necessary to remember that learning is often increased when students are presented with relatively novel instructional situations. This would seem to call for the use of several different visual formats within a book, for student interest will soon be reduced if one mode of pictorial representation dominates.

Pictorial Complexity

In addition to decisions related to the selection of appropriate visual formats, the effect of pictures on learning from instructional textbooks can be increased by considering the complexity of the content represented. As demonstrated in Figure 14.2, one of the major factors in determining the complexity of a picture is the number of elements in the picture; as the number of elements increases, so does the complexity. A picture of a world leader surrounded by advisors has more elements and is somewhat more complex than a picture of him or her alone. The use of several variations of standard design elements also leads to greater

Figure 14.2. Adding pictorial elements increases complexity.

pictorial complexity. Variations in the types of lines, shapes, textures, spatial arrangements, and color can all increase the amount of detail represented, thus adding to pictorial complexity.

The importance of providing pictures with the appropriate level of complexity is underscored by research which suggests that children find complex pictures more interesting and will spend more time examining them than relatively simple, less complex pictures. However, caution must be used, for there seems to be a point where too much complexity results in decreased interest and examination time (Wohlwill, 1975). Similarly, it appears that both too much and too little interior detail can reduce the effectiveness of a picture placed in an instructional textbook.

Determining the most appropriate level of pictorial complexity is a difficult task, for complexity is ever-changing and is dependent upon the developmental stage of the learners as well as their previous experiences with the subject matter. What seems terribly complex today may appear rather simple tomorrow. Yet, it seems that some complexity can often be safely added to pictures without reducing their effectiveness. For example, many middle/junior high science texts are replete with pictures of animals or objects taken out of context. Both the polar bear and the praying mantis are shown against similar neutral-colored backgrounds. By carefully adding some background information and detail, such as placing the animals in their natural habitat, the pictures could be made more interesting, and probably more effective. Of course, care must be taken to make certain that the background information does not distract from the main subject of the picture.

The above discussion has referred to complexity in terms of the physical elements in a picture. However, this construct can also refer to the relative complexity of the theme represented by the picture. The major lesson to be learned from considering the complexity of a theme is that young children seem to have considerable difficulty in properly interpreting and integrating pictures which represent themes that need to be examined from several perspectives in order to be understood. That is, the theme will only be understood if the learner is *capable* of understanding it.

Dynamic Quality

Pictorial complexity is not the only factor related to pictorial content which must be considered in order to maximize the effectiveness of pictures in learning from instructional text. One such factor to be considered is the dynamic quality of the picture. Figure 14.3 shows that the major elements of a picture can be represented as being static and somewhat lifeless, or as being in motion, involved with some activity. Although some academic content negates the need for this pictorial quality, the importance of using pictures of a dynamic nature is underscored by the apparent tendency of students to look longer and respond more readily to pictures which show dynamic action (Travers & Alvarado, 1970). Thus, pictures of events would usually be more

Figure 14.3. Dynamic images are more interesting than static images.

effective in instructional texts than would static pictures or portraits. In science texts, for example, a picture of an animal catching its food or climbing a tree should usually be used rather than a picture of the animal standing around, not doing much of anything. Similarly, social studies texts are encouraged to include more pictures of events and activities and fewer portraits. However, when analysis indicates that instructional objectives can best be met by showing a picture of a specific individual or group, it would be desirable to show the individual(s) in a dynamic setting: show Abraham Lincoln chopping wood rather than posing next to a tree.

Size

After many decisions and considerations related to the elements of the pictures to be included in instructional texts, it is still necessary to determine the size of the picture: should the picture be large? small? full page? half page? The importance of picture size grows when it is recognized how closely related are picture size and publication costs—as pictures increase in size, so does cost. Unfortunately, little has been established about the instructional effectiveness of various picture sizes, for most of the research related used projected images rather than printed images integrated into instructional texts. It does appear, however, that appropriate size is dependent on how much inspection time is available; as the amount of time available increases, picture size can be reduced. When reducing the size of the picture, care must be taken to ensure that the relevant pictorial features can readily be discriminated and identified by the target audience, while maintaining the overall attractiveness and interest of the picture.

The relative size of the objects being represented may be more pertinent to the design of instructional texts than the actual size of the picture. Kosslyn (1975) reported that more details of a mental image of an object are remembered when the object is imagined next to a small object. This would seem to suggest if the purpose of a picture is to assist the learner in remembering and recognizing the pictured object and its features, this purpose can be more effectively achieved by juxtaposing the object of interest with a small object, as well as informing the learner, through captions, of the learning task. Thus, it may be possible that details of the frog in Figure 14.4 would be better remembered when the frog is placed adjacent to the spider than when placed next to the squirrel.

Picture Placement

One of the most important, yet least studied, issues related to the use of pictures to improve instructional textbooks is the placement of the picture relative to the written text. For the most part, decisions regarding picture location have been based on aesthetic rather than instructional characteristics. The little that is known about the instructional implications of picture placement must usually be extrapolated from studies that are basically unconcerned with the picture-text relationship.

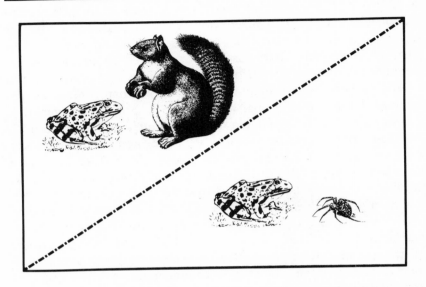

Figure 14.4. The relative size of the frog may affect our ability to remember and recognize it.

Pictures can serve a useful function whether placed before or after a reading passage. When placed before, they can serve as an introduction or overview, preparing the reader for the content to follow. Similarly, when placed before a passage, a picture can serve as a bridge between the learner's previous experiences and the new content. Much as questions placed after a reading passage seem to be somewhat more effective than those placed before the passage, there is a limited degree of evidence which suggests that pictures placed after a passage may cause the reader to covertly review the written text, resulting in increased retention when compared to pictures placed before the passage. One should not infer from this discussion that pictures should always be placed after a reading passage, for this review function can be served by several instructional techniques, including, but not limited to, the use of questions, formal summaries, and outlines.

What needs to be remembered is that students are quick to recognize patterns, and as placement patterns remain unchanged, boredom and lack of interest will increase. In addition to basing placement decisions on aesthetic considerations, it is also possible to utilize information gained from an analysis of the functions to be served by the picture.

Conclusion

Although their instructional value has often been assumed, pictures have the potential to make significant contributions to instructional textbooks. In addition to their traditional decorative role, pictures can excite the learner, explain difficult concepts, and expand the written narrative. Furthermore, there are indications that in addition to aiding in the acquisition of information, pictures can affect intellectual skills and processes.

In spite of the fact that this chapter focused on some of the ways that the potency of instructional textbooks can be increased through the use of pictures, a clear conception of which pictorial elements, either alone or in combination, affect learning from instructional textbooks is missing. For the most part, information concerning these elements must be pieced together from disparate studies which are only tangentially concerned with the picture-text relationship.

Yet, some suggestions for increasing the instructional effectiveness of pictures placed in instructional textbooks can be offered:

1. Pictures should be referred to in the written narrative.
2. Captions can help students understand the relevance of the pictures.
3. Photographs and realistic detailed drawings are usually preferred to simpler formats such as line drawings. However, preference is not always related to student achievement.
4. Within limits, students will spend more time examining complex images.
5. Pictures containing dynamic images are generally more interesting than those which contain static images.
6. Placement of pictures should be based on the function the picture is to serve.

The need is clear: the increasingly visual nature of modern life, new economic realities, and increasing frustration with modern educational practices all demand more effective instructional materials. The question is whether or not instructional materials designers, supported by an expanded research base, will increasingly consider pictures for their instructional, rather than their decorative, capabilities.

References

Dwyer, F.M. *A guide for improving visualized instruction.* State College, PA: Learning Services, 1972.

Gombrich, E.H. The visual image. *Scientific American*, 1972, *227*, 82-96.

Kosslyn, S.M. Information representation in visual images. *Cognitive Psychology*, 1975, *7*, 341-370.

Myatt, B., & Carter, J.M. Picture preferences of children and young adults. *Educational Communications and Technology Journal*, 1979, *27*, 45-53.

Travers, R.M.W., & Alvarado, V. The design of pictures for teaching children in the elementary school. *AV Communication Review*, 1970, *18*, 47-64.

Wohlwill, J.F. Children's responses to meaningful pictures varying in diversity: Exploration time vs. preference. *Journal of Experimental Child Psychology*, 1975, *20*, 341-355.

15.

A User-Oriented Approach to the Design of Tables and Flowcharts

Patricia Wright

Overview

This chapter evaluates some of the design choices available when presenting information in tables and flowcharts. The similarities between tables and flowcharts become apparent when considering the decisions that users must make when looking up information. In both formats, a desire to save space can lead designers to remove "redundant" information which would have been helpful to readers. One critical factor in determining how easily tables and flowcharts can be used is the decision structure selected by the designer. This selection needs to be based on an understanding of how readers will interact with the information. This understanding is also needed to motivate the selection of graphic and typographic options. Although firm design guidelines are inappropriate, general principles based on a user-oriented approach can improve the "user-friendliness" of tables and flowcharts.

Introduction

The suggestion has been made that tabulation schemes are one of the natural functions of *written* language (Stubbs, 1980). Certainly in the history of the development of writing, tables have played a very important role. Inventories of various sorts form a large proportion of what remains of very early writings (e.g., circa 3,500 B.C.). Furthermore, as Goody (1977) has pointed out, such lists have no direct oral equivalent. People rarely enumerate lists of items in the course of everyday conversation. Therefore, the ability to understand and interpret tabulated information requires special reading skills (Wright, 1981a). Appropriate design of the information in tables can help readers who may have only a weak grasp of some of the necessary skills. This is why a user-oriented approach to information design is so important. Design options, which appear to offer comparable alternatives to the information provider, can differ considerably in terms of their ease of use.

Whenever people use a table, they nearly always have to do at least three things:

(1) grasp the logical principles on which the information has been organized;

(2) find the required information within the table; and

(3) interpret the information once it has been found.

Design factors can influence each of these activities that users undertake, but this does not mean that there are simply three groups of design factors. Each of the three user activities will often have several constituent processes. For example, the activity of finding the required information may start with the user making decisions about which page or column to scan. Then perceptual search will be needed before a specific item is located. Similarly, when comparing several values within a table, multiple decision and search processes may be required as part of the activity of interpreting the information. Design factors produce their effects at the level of these constituent cognitive processes (Wright, 1980a).

It is because the user of tables is often faced with making decisions that certain similarities arise in the design factors which influence the ease of using tables and the ease of using flowcharts. Flowcharts usually provide explicit questions which form the basis for the user's decisions (although not always; see Kamman, 1975). In contrast, most tables usually leave these questions for the user to formulate on the basis of information given in the row and column headings.

When looking up information in a table, there are various sorts of questions that readers may ask. Sometimes the reader is looking for a particular numerical value (e.g., a train time or the temperature in Paris). On such occasions, the questions are usually well-specified, in the sense that the reader knows many relevant details (such as what kind of train, where from, where to, etc.). It has been suggested that using tables to answer these well-specified questions draws upon sets of skills which are closely related to those used when reading factual texts and reference manuals (Wright, 1980b). Therefore, many of the design characteristics which are relevant to such texts (see Hartley, 1978) may have their counterparts in the design of tables.

Not all questions that the reader may wish to ask will be well-specified. Sometimes the reader's activity seems more aptly described as browsing or exploring. For example, the reader's interest may center not on particular cell values but on comparisons among cells, trends over time, etc. Tables may not be the ideal way of presenting information that helps readers make these kinds of comparisons. Sometimes diagrams, graphs, or charts may be more appropriate (Ehrenberg, 1975; Macdonald-Ross, 1977a and 1977b). For this reason, the present discussion will not be primarily concerned with these kinds of questions. Instead, it will focus on the design features which can help readers find the answers to specific questions. Even here it must be realized that there will be no universal optimal design for a table. Much will depend upon the reader's ability to specify the problem in a way that maps onto the organization of the table. However, the ease with which readers can do this will depend on how well the designer has anticipated the kinds of questions that readers will want to ask and then selected an appropriate format for providing the answer.

The absence of a single "best way" of presenting information has extremely important consequences. Indeed it applies to all elements of textual presentation, not only to tables and flowcharts. One consequence is that there is no appropriate alternative to analyzing the user's requirements in detail. Recent studies of flowcharts and various alternatives used for designing computer programs have shown that a presentation format which helps people to flow through the information in a particular sequence may make things very difficult for a reader who wants to use the information in some *other* way (e.g., Sheppard, Kruesi, & Curtis, 1980). Flowcharts may be good at taking readers from some general state to one specific option, but people may wish to move in other directions. For readers who identify their starting point as being a terminal node in the tree and who want to know how they got there or how they can get to some other terminal node, tables may be more helpful than flowcharts (Green, 1982).

It is a fact that the user's specific purpose, together with other characteristics of the context in which the information is being consulted, determines the relative effectiveness of alternative information displays. This is why there is a need for a user-oriented approach to designing tables and flowcharts. This emphasis on users contrasts with adopting a text-based approach. The focus of the text-based approach is exclusively on the nature of the information to be provided. On this basis alone, design options are selected and presentation factors determined.

It was shown many years ago that an exclusively text-based approach is inadequate (Wright & Reid, 1973). People were given either a flowchart or a table and were asked to consult this information to solve various problems. Even though the information remained the same and the readers remained the same, the relative advantage of the flowchart compared with the table varied considerably (see Figure 15.1). When problems were easy and few errors were made, then the information was found more quickly in the tables than in the flowchart; but when the problems contained many irrelevant details, then the error rate rose and the advantage of the flowchart lay in the accuracy with which people used it. These results emphasize the need for carefully analyzing the user's needs. These results also indicate that there are likely to be severe limitations to simple guidelines. The most appropriate format for presenting specific information will depend on the precise combination of many factors. These factors include the characteristics of readers—their knowledge and intellectual abilities—which will interact with characteristics of the task such as its complexity. Therefore, the following synopsis of research studies should be taken as indicating some general principles of information design, rather than being findings which can be routinely applied in all cases.

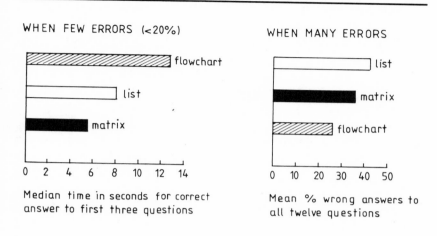

Figure 15.1. Comparisons of alternative versions of the same information, read by the same readers, under different circumstances. When errors were low, the table was read more rapidly than the list or flowchart. When errors were high, the flowchart was read more accurately than the table or list.

The Value of Redundancy

There is a sense in which all tables are essentially lists of items. Some, of course, are cleverly convoluted lists, but there is research evidence suggesting that readers find tables easier to use if the underlying list structure is made more obvious (Wright, 1968; Wright & Barnard, 1975). For example, many people would find it easier to consult the table shown in Figure 15.2a than that shown in Figure 15.2b. The difference is the redundant repetition of the left-hand column in Figure 15.2a. Such redundancy is missing from the conventional matrix arrangement shown in Figure 15.2b.

A similar argument applies to the tabulation scheme shown in Figure 15.3. Many diaries present metrication information in this way because it requires less space. A listing of the pairs of corresponding units would require four columns (two to enable conversions from miles to kilometers and two to enable conver-

Distance in kilometers from

AGADIR		CASABLANCA		FES		MARRAKECH		RABAT		TIZNIT		ZAGORA	
to		to		to		to		to		to		to	
Casablanca	500	Agadir	500	Agadir	791	Agadir	303	Agadir	593	Agadir	88	Agadir	474
Fes	791	Fes	291	Casablanca	291	Casablanca	230	Casablanca	93	Casablanca	601	Casablanca	565
Marrakech	303	Marrakech	230	Marrakech	493	Fes	493	Fes	198	Fes	879	Fes	830
Rabat	593	Rabat	93	Rabat	198	Rabat	323	Marrakech	323	Marrakech	371	Marrakech	376
Tiznit	88	Tiznit	601	Tiznit	879	Tiznit	371	Tiznit	694	Rabat	694	Rabat	658
Zagora	474	Zagora	565	Zagora	830	Zagora	376	Zagora	658	Zagora	534	Tiznit	534

(a)

Distance in kilometers from

	AGADIR	CASABLANCA	FES	MARRAKECH	RABAT	TIZNIT	ZAGORA
to							
Agadir	-	500	791	303	593	88	474
Casablanca	500	-	291	230	93	601	565
Fes	791	291	-	493	198	879	830
Marrakech	303	230	493	-	323	371	376
Rabat	593	93	198	323	-	694	658
Tiznit	88	601	879	371	694	-	534
Zagora	474	565	830	376	658	534	-

(b)

Figure 15.2. Removing the repeated items in the paired list (Figure 15.2a) gives the matrix (Figure 15.2b). People often find it easier to use a list than to read a matrix, particularly as the size of the table increases.

CONVERSION TABLES

The bold figures in the central columns can be read as either the metre or the British measure.
For example: 1 metre — 1.09 yards: or 1 yard — 0.91 metres.

Litres		Pints	Metres		Yards
0.28	**0.50**	0.88	0.91	**1**	1.09
0.43	**0.75**	1.32	1.83	**2**	2.19
0.57	**1.00**	1.76	2.74	**3**	3.28
0.71	**1.25**	2.20	3.66	**4**	4.38
0.85	**1.50**	2.64	4.57	**5**	5.47
0.99	**1.75**	3.08			
1.14	**2.00**	3.52	Kilometres		Miles
1.42	**2.50**	4.40			
1.70	**3.00**	5.28	1.61	**1**	0.62
1.99	**3.50**	6.16	3.22	**2**	1.24
2.27	**4.00**	7.04	4.83	**3**	1.86
2.84	**5.00**	8.80	6.44	**4**	2.48
			8.05	**5**	3.11
Litres		Gallons	9.66	**6**	3.73
			11.26	**7**	4.35
4.55	**1.00**	0.22	12.87	**8**	4.97
6.82	**1.50**	0.33	14.48	**9**	5.59
9.09	**2.00**	0.44			
11.36	**2.50**	0.55	Centigrade		Farenheit
13.64	**3.00**	0.66			
15.91	**3.50**	0.77	−18	**0**	32
18.18	**4.00**	0.88	−15	**5**	41
20.46	**4.50**	0.99	−12	**10**	50
22.73	**5.00**	1.10	−9	**15**	59
27.28	**6.00**	1.32	−7	**20**	68
31.82	**7.00**	1.54	−4	**25**	77
36.37	**8.00**	1.76	−1	**30**	86
40.91	**9.00**	1.98	2	**35**	95
			4	**40**	104
Kilograms		Pounds	7	**45**	113
			10	**50**	122
0.11	**0.25**	0.55	13	**55**	131
0.23	**0.50**	1.10	16	**60**	140
0.45	**1.00**	2.20	18	**65**	149
0.68	**1.50**	3.31	21	**70**	158
0.91	**2.00**	4.41	24	**75**	167
2.27	**5.00**	11.02	27	**80**	176
2.72	**6.00**	13.23	32	**90**	194
3.18	**7.00**	15.43	38	**100**	212

Figure 15.3. Yet another way of removing the repeated items from a list of paired values. People find it more difficult to use a table where the access route is via the center column than to read a matrix.

sions from kilometers to miles). However, there is reason for thinking that people find it difficult to use these tables where access to particular cell values has to be made through a center column that has no constant referential interpretation (i.e., it sometimes means meters and sometimes yards). If designers remove redundancy from tables, this may increase the amount of cognitive processing that the user must undertake when consulting the table. This in turn makes it harder to consult the table if the user has to decide where to look for the missing information.

It has been implied that tables are usually numerical. While this may be true, there are also many listings of verbal information. The index at the back of a textbook would be one example (see Figure 15.4a). Here, as with numerical tables, it is often necessary to combine the information from the main heading with the items listed underneath. Sometimes it may also be necessary to re-order the wording of the phrases at the same time. There does not appear to have been any systematic research into the problems that users have with indexes of this kind; but it scarcely needs research to show that untwisting the phrases and putting the redundancy back into each entry is likely to be found helpful by most users (contrast Figures 15.4a and 15.4b).

The desire to eliminate redundancy takes a different graphic form in flowcharts. Here the designer's objective may be to have as few choice points as possible. As with tables, the advantage of such a design strategy is that it saves paper. However, from a user-oriented approach, there may be good reasons for structuring the decision sequence in some other way. For example, it can be helpful to have the easy questions early and the harder questions later in the sequence. This will often mean that if readers make a mistake, then a wrong decision made late in the sequence will not take them too far away from the correct goal. Consequently, there is less back-tracking necessary in order to rectify mistakes. An alternative decision sequence might be based on a desire to keep the most frequently used path as short as possible. This will obviously require knowing how the information is used in practice. Sometimes diagnostic trees are designed to exactly the opposite criterion in order to encourage the user to consider the

(a)

ignorance, educational, 47-56; alternative to, 55-6; definition, 47-8;
distribution, 48-9; hard-core, 50;
political issue, 47; on reading
process, 50-1; soft-core, 49-50.

(b)

ignorance :	educational ignorance	47-56
	alternative to edl. ign.	55-56
	definition of edl. ign.	47-48
	distribution of edl. ign.	48-49
	hard-core edl. ign.	50
	edl. ign. as political issue	47
	edl. ign. on reading process	50-51
	soft-core edl. ign.	49-50

Figure 15.4. The organization of index entries can sometimes require the reader to untwist the phrases (Figure 15.4a). Designers can help by doing this untwisting for the reader (Figure 15.4b).

unlikely possibilities. Designing an appropriate decision structure is an important element in both tables and flowcharts.

Choosing an Appropriate Decision Structure

Some of the issues about decision structure are perhaps easiest to see when considering the interrogation of a very large data base. The user has to have some understanding of the way in which the data base, or the retrieval system, is organized before starting to search for the answer to a specific query. This is obvious if you consider using information such as that given in the *Yellow Pages* telephone directory. You have to look for Mr. Smith the butcher under B for butcher (or perhaps M for meat) not under S for Smith, as you would in other kinds of telephone directory. The need for the reader's prior understanding applies not only to very large data bases, including those held on computer systems, but also to the smaller data bases that will fit within a single printed page. Sometimes people may have strong assumptions about the likely organization of the information within a table. If the designer chooses some other organization, then readers easily become confused and make many mistakes (Wright & Threlfall, 1980).

The need for the decision structure to be "natural" to users was also evident in a study by Barnard, Morton, Long, & Ottley (1977). They measured the time it took readers to find a piece of information in a 36-item list. This list was presented either as a single alphabetic sequence or was subdivided into six familiar categories, such as *fish, meat, vegetables*. The results of this comparison showed that people were able to find items more quickly within the categorized list than within the single alphabetic sequence. However, from a subsequent experiment, Barnard *et al.* concluded that it was not just the display of six categories which created the improvement, but the choice of categories that were already familiar to the users. The creation of six categories on the basis of some arbitrary criterion (such as number of letters in the word, or relative size of the product) would not have been likely to facilitate performance in the same way. Much remains to be done to make more explicit this notion of a "natural" decision structure and to relate it to characteristics which may be inherent in different kinds of data base. Wason (1968) has suggested that one advantage of flowcharts is that they help *writers* to appreciate the structure of the material and to make an informed choice about the presentation of the material, even though this choice might be for something other than a flowchart.

Flowcharts always require a series of decisions. This is sometimes also the case for tables. Making successive decisions (e.g., two binary decisions rather than one decision among four options) has both advantages and disadvantages. One of the advantages can be seen when the successive decisions are formatted on the page in the way illustrated in Figure 15.5b. Several alternative displays are possible and include that shown in Figure 15.5a, which is a conventional two-sided matrix. People often have problems with matrix tables (Wright & Fox, 1972). Part of the difficulty may arise because users need to integrate a row heading and a column heading simultaneously in order to specify a particular cell. Decisions about which is the relevant row and which the relevant column are taken independently and successively. Therefore, readers must remember the result of one 'decision while making the next. This memory factor is eliminated by the display shown in Figure 15.5b. Once the reader has made the first decision, the page layout does the "remembering" and there is no need to check back after the second decision because the necessary integration of the two decisions has been taken care of already.

Experimental studies have compared people's performance with 16 cell tables which were presented either as Figure 15.5a or Figure 15.5b. Tables corresponding to Figure 15.5a are used more accurately than those corresponding to Figure 15.5b (Wright, 1977). The organization of column headings in Figure 15.5a has several characteristics in common with flowcharts. Both require users to make successive decisions. So it is relevant to consider what effect it might have on performance if the number of decisions is increased. Increasing the number of decisions reduces the size of the number of items in a table which must be searched to locate a particular cell. Instead of hunting for one of 40 *living things*, it is only necessary to hunt for one among ten if they are

Average daily temperature (^{O}F)

	BALI	CAIRO	PEKING	SYDNEY
Jan-Mar	82	59	32	71
Apr-Jun	82	76	67	59
Jul-Sep	83	82	77	59
Oct-Dec	84	68	43	67

(a)

Average daily temperature (^{O}F)

BALI				CAIRO				PEKING				SYDNEY			
Jan-Mar	Apr-Jun	Jul-Sep	Oct-Dec	Jan-Mar	Apr-Jun	Jul-Sep	Oct-Dec	Jan-Mar	Apr-Jun	Jul-Sep	Oct-Dec	Jan-Mar	Apr-Jun	Jul-Sep	Oct-Dec
82	82	83	84	59	76	82	68	32	67	77	43	71	59	59	67

(b)

Figure 15.5. Sometimes the row and column headings of a matrix (Figure 15.5a) can be combined to give a linear decision sequence (Figure 15.5b). There is evidence that people find formats such as 15.5b easier to use than a conventional matrix such as 15.5a.

divided into *birds, mammals, reptiles* and *butterflies*. Alternatively, readers could start by making a decision about whether the item being sought could fly. This would halve the search task and a subsequent decision could halve it again. Frequently, flowcharts use binary questions which provide the user with only two alternatives. This is not always a necessary limitation. It is often a constraint of computer languages (an area where flow diagrams are widely used), but a larger number of options can be implemented in many other flowcharts.

As has already been mentioned, it is not possible to achieve design solutions without considering the characteristics inherent in the data base itself. The range of meaningful design options will vary with the nature of information being presented. For example, a table showing the weather in various parts of the world might be categorized into continents, or a time table might be categorized into morning and afternoon services. Few studies have examined the effect on performance of reducing the size of the number of alternatives (e.g., from 4 to 2) but increasing the number of decisions which must be made (e.g., from 2 to 4). However, at least one study has suggested that requiring more decisions would in some instances slow people down and result in more errors being made when consulting the table (Wright, 1977). Therefore, the frequent use of successive binary decisions in flowcharts or tables may not be the most useful to readers, if the decisions could have been structured to consider more options at the same decision point.

Even after the relevant cell within a table has been found, the user may still need to make decisions, and the information designer can either help or hinder these decisions by the way the material within the table is presented. For example, the use of a 24-hour clock notation often leads to errors when people consult timetables (Sprent, Bartram, & Crawshaw, 1980). On other occasions, users will wish to compare tabulated values with other known values. If the tabulated information can be presented so that the user is making comparisons in the direction of "more" rather than "less," this will be very helpful. Obviously, this will not always be possible; but consider a table which is given in a text alongside a map that is colored to indicate the distribution of income in various parts of the world. The table can give more precise numerical information than can the map. Suppose that the writer chooses to categorize the table into income bands. Readers will almost certainly find it easier to use the table if it is subdivided on the basis of places where the average income is *more than* X per year; *more than* Y per year; *more than* Z per year, rather than use the alternative phrasing *less than*. Although there is a logical symmetry to *more* and *less*, research by psychologists has shown that sentences with the word *more* are easier to understand than those with the word *less* (see Clark & Clark, 1977). This distinction also applies to performance when people consult numerical tables (Wright & Barnard, 1975). The results of the Wright and Barnard study for four different tabulation schemes are shown in Figure 15.6. Different people worked with different tables. For each of the tables, answers were more accurate when people made *more than* decisions rather than making *less than* decisions.

The design issues that are important for the design of tables and flowcharts also have a great deal of relevance to some of the other written materials which are encountered as part of daily life. For example, application forms often include questions which are structured on the principle of a matrix (see Figure 15.7). The questions are provided by row and column headings; answers are supplied by the form-filler as cell values. The importance of appropriately designing such matrices was illustrated in a study by Wright & Barnard (1975). They found that a simulation of a published matrix question produced 26 percent errors in their tests. Altering the decision structure by changing the layout of the information on the page, without changing the wording of the questions, reduced the error rate to eight percent. A fuller discussion of research relating to the design of forms can be found in Wright (1980c).

Whatever choice the designer may make about the decision structure of a flowchart or a table, there remains a variety of options about how this structure is physically depicted on the page. Both tables and flowcharts present designers with novel

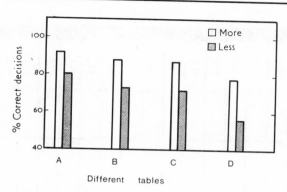

*Figure 15.6. Designers need to consider the decisions that users will make **after** finding a cell value. Presenting information in a way that is compatible with these decisions makes the table easier to use. The vertical bars show that for a variety of tabulation schemes people found it easier to decide that a given numerical quantity was **more than** that shown in the table, compared with having to decide whether or not the quantity was **less than** that shown in the table.*

problems and spatial constraints that do not apply to many other kinds of textual materials. For example, in Figure 15.8 the headings were printed in the usual horizontal orientation on the page. However, the table itself had to be turned through 90°, so these headings were upside down for the user of the table. Again, this emphasizes the need for a user-oriented approach to design decisions.

Presentation Factors

Ehrenberg (1977) has suggested that the following three principles should be applied to the presentation of numeric information in tables.

1. The numbers should be rounded to just two or three figures. This will help readers make comparisons easily.
2. Averages, of rows or columns as appropriate, help readers

Mr Mrs Miss Mstr	Initials	Surname (Block Capitals Please)	Age if under 16 years or over 60 years*		Child reduction ref.*	Insurance* See booking conditions
			Age	Date of birth		
First room occupied by						YES
						YES
						YES
						YES
Second room occupied by						YES
						YES
						YES
						YES
Third room occupied by						YES
						YES
						YES
						YES
Fourth room occupied by						YES
						YES
						YES
						YES

Figure 15.7. Tables and flowcharts can be used for giving information and for collecting it. Here is a very common use of a matrix on an application form.

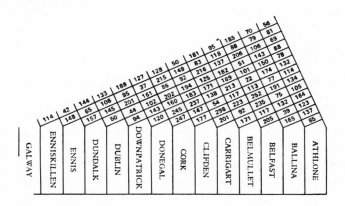

Figure 15.8. The column labels are upside down for those using this table. They have been printed in the conventional horizontal orientation for a normal printed page.

evaluate individual cell values. Often, readers may wish to know whether a particular item is above average or below average. The inclusion of these average values also helps the reader appreciate the scatter among the cell values.

3. Where practicable, the numbers should be arranged in some meaningful order, such as decreasing size from the top of the column. Obviously, such a rule cannot apply to tables that have an inherent ordering determined by row or column headings (e.g., a chronological order); but many tables in educational texts present data concerning lists of items that have no intrinsic structure, and Ehrenberg's principle can be helpful here.

It is quite common to find tables in which the printer has spaced all the columns at an equal distance from each other. Presumably, the reason for this is to satisfy some aesthetic criterion. Nevertheless, readers will find it more helpful to have functional groupings, so that those items which belong together are spatially closer than those items which do not. Hartley, Young, & Burnhill (1975) have argued that there is no need for column headings to be centered over the column. Typists find it easier to align the left-hand edge of a column. Readers seem not to be disrupted by this (Burnhill, Hartley, & Young, 1976), but the spacing between columns may be an important factor to consider here. Simple "guidelines" always have exceptions.

One way of misusing the space in tables is by the introduction of unnecessary gaps. This is common in many tables of contents, where the page numbers on the right of the page are a long way from the chapter titles on the left. Another misuse of space is the failure to provide gaps which would be helpful to readers. For example, Tinker (1965) recommended that there should be a perceptible gap every four or five rows in a table. This gap helps readers to look along rows without the eye "slipping." When adequate functional grouping is achieved by the use of space, then the addition of ruled lines appears superfluous. A splendid example of the use of space to clarify the structure of a college prospectus can be found in Burnhill, Hartley, Young, & Fraser (1975). When tables become very wide, it can help readers if the new headings are given on both the left and right sides of the table (Hartley, 1978).

Another way of creating perceptible grouping within a table is by the use of typographic variation. The success of this technique may depend in part on how well the typographic conventions are understood by users. Marland (1978) has reported that, when reading plays, children will often read the stage directions instead of acting upon them. Here the significance of the italic cue in the text is not being noted by readers. Certainly, there are tables which have so many typographic signals that the reader is almost overwhelmed by the amount of information. Among the examples of this are some train timetables, which differentiate fast trains from slow ones, as well as through trains and trains where changes must be made, and trains with dining or sleeping facilities. The trade-off between using space and using other typographic cues in tables such as indexes has been explored by Spencer, Reynolds, & Coe (1975).

Typographic differentiation within flowcharts takes a rather different form from the choice of font or weight, as Merrill (1980) has pointed out. Often the text of flowcharts is confined within a geometric outline, and the shape of this outline indicates the nature of the contents. For example, tests and questions are often enclosed in diamonds, whereas sequential stages are enclosed in rectangles. Although this convention has become widely established, particularly in computer circles, its value to users has been challenged (e.g., Richards & Johnson, 1980). There is a risk that these outline shapes will reduce the legibility of the text inside them. One solution might be to retain the signaling function of the shapes but make them smaller and place the text outside them. This solution is easier to implement with small flowcharts, where the appropriate space can be introduced between shapes and text. With large flowcharts, the assignment of the text may be ambiguous for the reader if the front of the text is adjacent to one shape and the tail adjacent to another. A quite different solution is to dispense with the shaped boxes altogether (e.g., Coe, 1977). For many readers' purposes, since the text makes it quite clear that a question is being asked, there is nothing to be gained from over-emphasizing this fact.

In spite of the conventions which have become accepted in the computer world, there are a great many different ways of graphically depicting a flowchart (e.g., see Kamman, 1975). Certainly, there is no need for them to look like electrical circuit diagrams. Sometimes tables and "flowcharts" may be combined, as for example, when presenting information about bus routes alongside a bus timetable (e.g., Bartram, 1980). Adequately meeting the full range of user requirements may require inventing compromises of this kind.

One problem, common to both tables and flowcharts, arises from the constraints of getting the information to fit into the available space. This problem is sometimes solved by the use of "telegraphese" or abbreviations. On other occasions, the designer may resort to a footnote to explain in more detail what was meant by the heading of a particular column in a table or a particular question on a flowchart. All these solutions have disadvantages. Telegraphese and abbreviations can lead to ambiguities, or even complete failure to understand if the reader is unfamiliar with the particular contraction being used. Footnotes may mean that the reader has to integrate disparate pieces of information. This had seemed to be part of the problem that readers had when using matrices. Inevitably, having left the table to find the footnote, it is necessary to remember where to go back to. At best, this can be inconvenient.

Readers are sometimes unwilling to abandon the textual information when they are reading, and may disregard the accompanying illustrative material altogether (Whalley & Fleming, 1975). Even though the illustration, a circuit diagram, was on the same page and was essential for a thorough understanding of the text, many people chose to ignore it when it was positioned at the head of the second column, although referred to in the text about halfway down the first column. More people attended to the diagram when it was positioned on the page immediately after it was first referred to in the text. This finding has two implications. It implies that tables, charts, graphs, and other illustrative material must be located carefully on the page. It also implies that readers may choose to deal with the text and the "illustrative" materials on separate occasions, rather than integrate them into a single linear sequence as the writer may have intended. If this second implication is correct, then there is clearly a need for the "illustrative" materials to be fully self-explanatory. They need to be accompanied by legends that will enable readers to grasp the essentials of the information being presented without further reference to the text. Tables in which the columns are headed Group I, Group II, and Group III may require further annotation by the reader before the table becomes easily usable.

Conclusions

It is not possible to summarize the findings of research on tables and flowcharts in a neat list of guidelines. Specific design decisions have to be taken in a way that is sensitive to the internal structure of the data being presented, the needs of the readers who want to use the information, and the constraints of the production system being used to print the material. Therefore, as was pointed out earlier, there is no universally "best" way of communicating a specific piece of information. Nevertheless, there are some general principles which can be helpful for designers to bear in mind. These principles have been discussed in greater detail in the three main sections of this review. They are summarized below:

1. REDUNDANCY. Eliminating redundancy can be a false economy. When designers remove information from a table, so that it requires less space, this can often mean that users have more problems in trying to extract information from the table. This increased difficulty can generate errors when people are looking up information in tables.

2. DECISION STRUCTURE. Designers need to be able to provide the users of tables and flowcharts with a decision structure which is "natural" in the alternatives it specifies and "error reducing" in the sequence through which it takes users. The sequencing of decisions for tables is not confined to the design of the headings for columns and rows. It extends to considering what the user will do with the cell value in order to answer the question which was the reason for consulting the table.

3. PRESENTATION. Designers of tables and flowcharts need to be able to use space to help readers perceive the functional groupings within the material. Failure to use space appropriately can result in legibility problems, particularly in flowcharts and in large tables. Even the physical location of the table or chart in relation to references to it in the text can critically determine how effectively the information is used.

The research findings which support the principles outlined above have shown that it is not sufficient for the information to be physically present on the page. Ease of use requires much more than this. In particular, it requires that the designer be aware of how readers interact with printed materials. Designers need to be able to make explicit, as part of their predesign analysis (Felker, 1980), how readers proceed on a step-by-step basis from formulating the question that motivates their turning to the table or chart, through to arriving at an answer. Detailed discussion of how such an analysis can be undertaken for texts in general is provided elsewhere (e.g., Wright, 1980a, 1981b). The present review has simply tried to extend the currently popular notion of "user-friendliness" from the computer domain to the realm of highly formatted information. Many of the problems of information design are similar in both areas. Detailed consideration of the user's needs provides an approach that can increase the effectiveness of textual communication.

References

Barnard, P.J., Morton, J., Long, J.B., & Ottley, E.A. Planning menus for display: Some effects of their structure and content on user performance. In *Displays for man-machine systems,* Conference Publication No. 150, Institute of Electrical and Electronics Engineers, 1977, 130-133.

Bartram, D.J. Comprehending spatial information: The relative efficiency of different methods of presenting information about bus routes. *Journal of Applied Psychology,* 1980, *65,* 103-110.

Burnhill, P., Hartley, J., & Young, M. Tables in text. *Applied Ergonomics,* 1976, 7, 13-18.

Burnhill, P., Hartley, J., Young, M., & Fraser, S. The typography of college prospectuses: A case history. In L. Evans & J. Leedham (Eds.), *Aspects of educational technology.* London: Kogan Page; New York: Nichols, 1975.

Clark, H.H., & Clark, E.V. *Psychology and language: An introduction to psycholinguistics.* New York: Harcourt Brace Jovanovich, 1977.

Coe, B. A guide to the rules of squash. London: North West Middlesex Squash League, 1977.

Ehrenberg, A.S.C. *Data reduction.* London: John Wiley & Sons, 1975.

Ehrenberg, A.S.C. Rudiments of numeracy. *Journal of the Royal Statistical Society A,* 1977, *140,* 277-297.

Felker, D.B. Document design: A review of relevant research. Technical Report AIR-75002-4/80-BR of the Document Design Product, American Institutes for Research, Washington, D.C., 1980.

Goody, J. *The domestication of the savage mind.* London: Cambridge University Press, 1977.

Green, T.R.G. Pictures of programs and other processes, or how to do things with lines. In T. Duffy & R. Waller (Eds.), *Designing usable texts,* in preparation, 1982.

Hartley, J. *Designing instructional text.* London: Kogan Page; New York: Nichols, 1978.

Hartley, J., Young, M., & Burnhill, P. On the typing of tables. *Applied Ergonomics*, 1975, *6*, 39-42.

Kamman, R. The comprehensibility of printed instructions and the flowchart alternative. *Human Factors*, 1975, *17*, 183-191.

Macdonald-Ross, M. Graphics in text. In L.S. Schulman (Ed.), *Review of research in education*, Vol. 5. Itasca, IL: Peacock, 1977a.

Macdonald-Ross, M. How numbers are shown: A review of research on the presentation of quantitative data in texts. *Audio-Visual Communication Review*, 1977b, *25*, 359-409.

Marland, J. Responsibility for reading in secondary school. In L.J. Chapman and P. Czerniewska (Eds.), *Reading from process to practice*. London: Routledge and Kegan Paul, Ltd., 1978.

Merrill, P.F. Representations for algorithms. *National Society for Performance and Instruction Journal*, 1980, *19*, 18-24.

Richards, C., & Johnson, R. Graphic codes for flowcharts. *Information Design Journal*, 1980, *1*, 261-270.

Sheppard, S.B., Kruesi, E., & Curtis, B. The effects of symbology and spatial arrangement on the comprehension of software specifications. TR-80-388200-2, General Electric, Arlington, Virginia, 1980.

Spencer, H., Reynolds, L., & Coe, B. Spatial and typographic cueing with bibliographical entries. *Programmed Learning and Educational Technology*, 1975, *12*, 95-101 (London).

Sprent, N., Bartram, D., & Crawshaw, C.M. Intelligibility of bus timetables. In D.J. Oborne & J.A. Levis (Eds.), *Human factors in transport research*. London: Academic Press, 1980.

Stubbs, M. *Language and literacy: The sociolinguistics of reading and writing*. London: Routledge and Kegan Paul, Ltd., 1980.

Tinker, M.A. *Bases for effective reading*. Minneapolis: University of Minnesota Press, 1965.

Wason, P.C. The drafting of rules. *The New Law Journal*, 1968, *118*, 548-549.

Whalley, P.C., & Fleming, R.W. An experiment with a simple recorder of reading behavior. *Programmed Learning and Educational Technology*, 1975, *12*, 120-123 (London).

Wright, P. Using tabulated information. *Ergonomics*, 1968, *11*, 331-343.

Wright, P. Decision making as a factor in the ease of using numerical tables. *Ergonomics*, 1977, *20*, 91-96.

Wright, P. Usability: The criterion for designing written information. In P.A. Kolers, M.E. Wrolstad, & H. Bouma (Eds.), *Processing of visible language 2*. New York: Plenum Press, 1980a, 183-206.

Wright, P. The comprehension of tabulated information: Some similarities between reading prose and reading tables. *National Society for Performance and Instruction Journal*, 1980b, *19*, 25-29.

Wright, P. Strategy and tactics in the design of forms. *Visible Language*, 1980c, *15*, 151-193.

Wright, P. Tables in text: The subskills needed for reading formatted information. In L.J. Chapman (Ed.), *The reader and the text.* Proceedings of the 17th UKRA Conference, Warwick. London: Heineman, 1981a.

Wright, P. Five skills technical writers need. In *IEEE Transactions on Professional Communication*, 1981b, *24*, 10-16.

Wright, P., & Barnard, P. Effects of "more than" and "less than" decisions on the use of numerical tables. *Journal of Applied Psychology*, 1975, *60*, 606-611.

Wright, P., & Barnard, P. Asking multiple questions about several items: The design of matrix structures on application forms. *Applied Ergonomics*, 1978, *9*, 7-14.

Wright, P., & Fox, K. Explicit and implicit tabulation formats. *Ergonomics*, 1972, *15*, 175-187.

Wright, P., & Reid, F. Written information: Some alternatives to prose for expressing the outcomes of complex contingencies. *Journal of Applied Psychology*, 1973, *57*, 160-166.

Wright, P., & Threlfall, S. Reader's expectations about format influence the usability of an index. *Journal of Research Communication Studies*, 1980, *2*, 99-106.

16.

Structured Writing and Text Design

Robert E. Horn

OVERVIEW OF STRUCTURED WRITING

Roots in
critique of
programmed
learning

The line of research, development, and implementation of the technology of text described in this chapter has been under continuous development since 1965.

It began as an attempt to improve programmed instruction (P.I.), which suffered from a number of significant problems. Some of P.I.'s problems included the difficulty learners experienced in trying to use P.I. for reference and the difficulty self-directed learners had in scanning to identify what they really needed to know in a programmed instruction book and to be able to skip what they did not need to know.

Now a
mature
technology

The structured writing methodology gradually evolved to incorporate the comprehensive technology of instructional materials and reference book design that is suitable for a very large number of subject matters in academia and in business and industry.

OVERVIEW OF STRUCTURED WRITING

Today a large user group	Today there is a community of several thousand people who have learned structured writing and who have written training manuals, procedure manuals, courses, reference manuals, and computer documentation in several thousand subject matters.
Terminology in the field: tradename	We at Information Resources, Inc., have been calling what we do the Information Mapping ᵗᵐ seminars and writing services. We have used this term as a trademark in the ancient legal tradition that artisans and organizations have used to identify their products and services.
Generic names are many	A variety of generic names have been suggested for the field: "information simplification," "the technology of text," "structured writing," "performance-based instructional materials," "behaviorally oriented design," and, quite simply, "better writing."
Structured writing is preferred generic name	We have preferred using the term "structured writing" as the generic name for the field, because our research suggests that the properties of organization and structure are the most important factors in improving text and in making it a uniform, high performance product that a learner can always count upon.

Continued on next page

OVERVIEW OF STRUCTURED WRITING

Structured
writing is
preferred
generic
name
(Continued)

We have taken that one aspect—"structure"—to focus upon in designating our preference for the generic name for the field.

But we recognize that the community of workers in the field—researchers, teachers, and practitioners—will determine over time what the generic name will be.

Definition of
Information
Mapping tm
writing
services

Structure when applied to *writing* refers to different properties of the text that permit the structure of the subject matter and the document to be perceived by the reader.

Structured writing, using the standards of the Information Mapping writing services, refers to a process that has:

- a specific set of methods for analysis of subject-matter content for different kinds of documents

- a specific set of principles and criteria to guide major writing and graphic choices

- labeled Blocks (each with its own standards) to chunk information into organizable, modular units

- groups of Blocks that form Maps (each with its own standards) and aggregate hierarchically into documents

Continued on next page

OVERVIEW OF STRUCTURED WRITING

Definition of
Information
Mapping ™
writing
services
(Continued)

- specified formatting standards that fit "hand-in-glove" with the context analysis for

  - texts, procedures, reference books, and manuals

  - reports, memos, and other administrative documents

  - computer displayed text (e.g., videotext, computer-assisted instruction)

- specific graphic components (each with its own standards)

- specific guidelines and standards on style, sentence length, type, and word choice (for different readers and user groups)

- specific guidelines and standards for organization and sequencing of different types of text.

Examples

We provide examples of some pages from text and procedure manuals used in industry at the end of this chapter.

Several
hundred
structural
dimensions
synthesized

Guidelines for analysis of several hundred properties of structure in text are used in structured writing.

Continued on next page

OVERVIEW OF STRUCTURED WRITING

Several
hundred
structural
dimensions
synthesized
(Continued)

Some of these are very common and have been used by writers for several years. Four of these structural properties are covered in chapters in this book:

- algorithms and decision tables (see Chapter 11)
- tabular material (see Chapter 15)
- certain types of illustrations (see Chapter 14)
- using marginal labels to identify information and improve access (see Chapters 7 and 8)

References
to major
topics in
structured
writing

It is impossible to summarize several hundred properties of text in a short article.
The reader will find elsewhere reviews of the history, goals, and technology (Horn, 1974, Horn, 1981, Horn *et al.*, 1967), the principles and methodology (Horn, 1976), applications to text design (Horn, 1981), computer-assisted instruction (Horn *et al.*, 1971), management reports (Bixler, 1979, Horn, 1977), computer documentation (Horn, 1980a), large-scale knowledge base design (Horn, 1980b), chemistry courses (Olympia, 1979), management courses (Fields, 1981), and computer languages (Cheung, 1981).

Later in this chapter we will note the progress in evaluation.

This
chapter

This chapter will identify the major criteria for a technology of text and review the progress that has been made in the development of a technology of structured writing.

OVERVIEW OF STRUCTURED WRITING

Concern
for
standards

As may be noted from the definition, our overriding concern in this research and development phase has been to develop criteria, rationale (evidence where available and possible), and standards for each important decision that the writer has to make.

Applications
to books
and manuals

These standards now have been developed for a wide variety of documents ranging from reports and memos in industry to the writing of procedure manuals, policy manuals, and textbooks.

Types of
maps

The method of content analysis for instructional and procedural manuals depends on identifying whether any given sentence or graphic in a subject matter pertains to

- process
- procedure
- structure
- classification
- concept
- fact
- principle

or to specific document functions, such as the overview function.

OVERVIEW OF STRUCTURED WRITING

Matrix of
content
gives
unique
location

The content analysis method further permits the subdivision of almost all subject-matter sentences and/or graphics chunks into large subject-matter matrices, and specifies that any important sentence in a subject matter has a unique place in a particular cell of this matrix.

The matrix below illustrates:

SUBJECT MATTER TERMS

SUBJECT
MATTER
INDEPENDENT
TERMS

	A	B	C
Defi-nition	unique sentences/ or graphic chunks in each cell		
Example			
etc.			

With uniquely identifiable locations for sentences and graphics in a subject matter, users can access the material quickly and writers can do a variety of completeness tests that significantly improve analysis.

OVERVIEW OF STRUCTURED WRITING

Labeling

Our research has also yielded a theory of labeling the chunks of subject matter we call Blocks and Maps.

The importance of a labeling system cannot be overestimated.

The theory of labeling provides guidelines for naming each block of information (each one to seven sentences) in a subject matter the content analysis has yielded.

Our approach to standards has been to determine when to use specific labeling guidelines for each type of subject-matter content and user interaction.

Linking units

Precise identification of small labeled Blocks of information permits one to have an explicit sequencing and interlinking theory for larger aggregations of Blocks.

Formatting

The use of specific formats with particular places for the names of Maps and labels for Blocks permits the reader to feel great confidence in scanning and acts as a kind of checklist and outline for the writer.

Continued on next page

OVERVIEW OF STRUCTURED WRITING

Formatting
(Continued)

It also permits uniform, evaluative research on properties of chunking across widely different subject matters.

Graphic
components

Just as a numerical table is nearly always a superior method of presenting information than a paragraph, so there are other situations when "a picture is worth a thousand words."

The important question for a technology of text is when and where to put in what kind of graphic components.

Our approach is to work with specific, testable guidelines indicating exactly when graphics should be included.

Style

Finally, at the level of words and sentences, it is important that a technology of text specifically identify those components which have to do with clarity and ease of use by different kinds of users.

Different styles have been used in structured writing from highly academic ones written for researchers to highly informal styles in business memos.

Evaluation suggests that one can identify with reasonable accuracy distinct styles and incorporate them into structured writing.

Criteria for a Technology of Text (From a Reader's Point of View)

CRITERIA FOR A TECHNOLOGY OF TEXT
(From a Reader's Point of View)

Introduction	The following pages suggest the criteria that a methodology would have to meet in order for something to be called a true technology of text and the degree to which this can be achieved by present structured writing methods.
Improve learning	A technology should improve learning of subject matter and jobs, measured by fewer errors and/or faster learning.

It should do so at least as well as current programmed training methods and, if possible, improve upon them.

Five recently published studies all comparing structured writing to conventional prose presentations have indicated superiority of structured approaches by ten percent to 50 percent (Romiszowski, 1977; Soyster, 1980; Stelnicki, 1980; Stuart, 1979; Webber, 1979).

Numerous unreported industrial evaluations support these findings. |
| Quick precise access required | Text should unfailingly permit the readers to find what they were looking for in any report or document that came across their desks quickly, easily, consistently, and precisely. |

Continued on next page

CRITERIA (READER'S POINT OF VIEW)

Quick
precise
access
required
(Continued)

This is absolutely essential in today's era of information overload. As one cyberneticist has said, "An interpretation of entropy theory suggests, 'The more you know and the more information you have the more disorganization there is—in the absence of higher organizational principles and methods.'"

Typical values for improved search time in our unpublished studies have indicated superiority of structured writing to conventional methods of representing text by a factor of four to ten times.

Better big
picture and
detail
access

A technology of text should enable the reader to get the big picture or the context accurately and quickly by skimming only a small part of a page and yet have rapid access to the lowest level of detail.

Our page and book formats standards have been designed with this in mind.

Only informal research on this criteria has been performed, although it may be a factor in the research results of Romiszowski (1977), Stuart (1979), Webber (1979), Stelnicki (1980), and Soyster (1980).

Wide
applicability

A technology of text should work for any subject matter in any job that you have to do. It should not be a narrow one-application method.

Continued on next page

CRITERIA (READER'S POINT OF VIEW)

Wide
applicability
(Continued)

Structured writing is now (mid-1981) used by about 4,000 analysts and writers in industry. They have applied it with success to thousands of subject matters. In some large companies, all of the training courses use structured writing (over 80 courses in one case). While it has been used less in academic textbooks, tryouts in at least three dozen subject matters reveal no major difficulties to be surmounted.

Decisions
management
systems

Recent work suggests that structured writing may have significant impact upon the design of large-scale computer-based decision management systems.

These are systems where there is a requirement for large-scale file management and multi-person use.

It appears that structured writing permits managers to avoid being swamped by detail and see the large picture (because the role of the individual page in the document is always apparent) and still have as much detail accessible as they need when they want to analyze a particular point more deeply.

Importance
of costs

A method can be effective, but if its costs outweigh its benefits, it will not be widely used. So the question of costs has been routinely addressed by the evaluation community for the past 20 years.

Continued on next page

CRITERIA (READER'S POINT OF VIEW)

Importance
of costs
(Continued)

It is imperative that the proponent of a new methodology demonstrate its cost-effectiveness.

Recent cost
benefits
analysis:
Procedures
reference
manuals

Recently, several major industries have done cost-benefits assessments of the use of structured writing in large systems environments.

Case One: Order Entry. In one analysis, a large utility found that it would save approximately $850,000 a year in operating an order entry system.

The application involved the basic user procedure documents that are close to 2,000 pages long and are used by 300 order takers and 130 checkers and their supervisors.

A group of eight writers working full time were required to keep this document up-to-date.

The company chose structured writing initially as the only vehicle for permitting standardization and rapid updating in the reformulation of the document when the new system was installed.

However, later cost-benefits analysis showed that, in addition to serving these important purposes, the system would result in

- reduction in user questions
- reduction in user errors
- reduction in training time
- reduction in writing time
- increased productivity of users,

Continued on next page

CRITERIA (READER'S POINT OF VIEW)

Recent cost benefits analysis: (Continued)	resulting in the major cost savings indicated above (Horn, 1981b).
Recent costs benefits Analysis: Training	*Case Two: Training.* In another study done for a company with over 100,00 employees, the consulting group estimated that the company would save approximately 14 million dollars in training costs alone when structured writing was fully implemented. This company is now engaged in a major effort to train all people whose job is primarily writing or analysis in structured writing methods.
Pre-process information for reader	A technology of text should pre-process the information that a reader needs. It should save the reader the work of deciphering or discovering the structure of each new document. It should permit readers to work on what they are already interested in in the first pass of the reading, rather than having to repeat the reading process several times. This is an important criterion, but to our knowledge, no research has been done on it.

CRITERIA (READER'S POINT OF VIEW)

Better
decision-
making

A technology of text should make the organization of a decision-making report instantly visible to readers and enable them to spot the recommendations and the supporting data and to aid the thinking and evaluation process in deciding whether to go ahead with the options recommended.

Significant opportunity for research in decision-making (using in-box appraisal techniques) opens up with structured writing. No studies in this area have come to our attention.

More
creative
use of
information

In relieving readers of the necessity to mentally chunk and label information, a technology of text would enable readers to pay attention to how to combine the information into larger and more incisive context for larger purposes—an important factor according to some researchers in the field of creativity.

Only anecdotal evidence exists to date in this area. Users have reported that it is easier to integrate larger wholes and recognize analogical connections.

SUMMARY OF RECENT EVALUATIONS OF STRUCTURED WRITING
IN INSTRUCTIONAL SITUATIONS

INVESTIGATOR AND DATE	VARIABLES	RESULTS	SUBJECTS
Stuart (1979)	Structured Writing vs. Conventional Prose	Structured writing • resulted in better test performance in knowledge gain *and* • was preferred for readability, understandability, and acceptability.	University Students
Stelnicki (1980)	Structured Writing vs. Conventional Prose	Structured writing produced • higher gain scores for facts • higher gain scores for learning concepts.	Undergraduate College Students
Webber (1979)	Structured Writing vs. Conventional Prose	With structured writing, training time was reduced by 50 percent, and subjects performed nearly twice as well on criterion tests.	Clerical Workers
Romiszowski (1977)	Structured Writing vs. Conventional Prose	With structured writing, subjects learned significantly more mathematics in less time.	High School Adult Learners
Soyster (1980)	Structured Writing vs. Conventional Prose	Subjects using instructional materials in structured writing achieved significantly higher levels of learning.	High School Students Ranging from Low to High Mental Ability

CRITERIA FOR A TECHNOLOGY OF TEXT
(From a Writer's Point of View)

Introduction Most of the research on the technology of text has taken the consumer's point of view (the reader or referencer or browser). Less studied from a formal research point of view is the writer's job. Yet, if a technology of text is to become widespread, the writer's job must be made easier, quicker, and more pleasant. And the transition from writing conventional text to structured writing must be smooth.

In the following, we list important criteria from the standpoint of the writer, analyst, editor, course developer, and manager of these jobs. For brevity, we combine these job functions into the single word "writer."

Formal
research
lacking

No published formal research effort has been devoted to evaluations from the writer's point of view. However, evaluations for industry and government applications have frequently supported structured writing, especially when the need for rapid updating is significant. We present below a list of criteria and an appraisal of the degree to which they have been met.

Writing
process

A technology of text should make it easier for the writer to get started, to handle transitions, to make it flow, to know where and when to put in detail, where to put the big picture, and to know when to

Continued on next page

CRITERIA (WRITER'S POINT OF VIEW)

Writing
process
(Continued)

stop. We have only anecdotal evidence to suggest that writers generally find their jobs easier to do when they use structured writing. Some do complain that the level of analysis required is more demanding, but they concede that the result is better.

Graphics

A technology of text should enable writers to know just when to integrate simple graphics into their writing and enable them to do it or to instruct a typist or artist to do it. The guidelines of structured writing provide this specification.

Formatting

A technology of text should provide writers with ready-made formats that are easy for them and their typists to use to put the document together. The implementation methods provide this writer and typist aid routinely.

Editorial
review

A technology of text should provide writers with methods by which they can *agree* with their editors or bosses who edit their work—not create pitfalls that ensure disagreement. No systematic surveys have been done, but anecdotal evidence suggests that there are fewer editorial controversies.

Team
writing

On large projects to which several writers contribute, a technology of text should provide writers

Continued on next page

CRITERIA (WRITER'S POINT OF VIEW)

Team writing (Continued)	with easy task assignments and with clear guidelines so that all contributors' work looks as though it were written by one person on the first draft—not after extensive revisions. Many large organizations routinely accomplish this without difficulty when writers and managers have been properly trained in structured writing.
Organization of writing	To warrant the name, a technology of text should enable writers to organize their thoughts more easily. A technology of text should give writers carefully labeled chunks of information that would permit them to see what data are there and what is missing so that they can complete their analysis and begin writing in the more precise fashion. This criterion is, of course, the very basis of the structured writing method.
Outlining procedures	A technology of text should permit writers to outline many documents without any further effort than looking them up in a reference book of outlines. Writers should not have to create an outline for every single document that they write. And for any document, it should provide writers with at least half of the outline.

Continued on next page

CRITERIA (WRITER'S POINT OF VIEW)

Outlining procedures (Continued)	The content analysis and labeling methodology of structured writing provides this tool.
Helps spot omissions	A technology of text should aid writers in identifying what has been left out of a piece of writing early in the writing process. Writers report that they routinely spot important omissions and gaps in systems designs—even those that have been carefully checked by normal quality assurance methods.
Methods for subject-matter expert debriefing	A technology of text should enable writers to get from the subject-matter expert what they need in order to write up a document quickly and efficiently.

The technology should help organize the interview with the subject-matter expert.

Writers and managers surveyed indicate that this has been accomplished by structured writing methods. |
| Indexing | A technology of text should provide for the creation—virtually automatically—of indexes at different levels.

It should provide indexes of superior quality that |

Continued on next page

CRITERIA (WRITER'S POINT OF VIEW)

Indexing (Continued)	direct the readers without including too much detail to select from. Methods now exist to do this routinely.
Computer-assisted instruction (CAI)	A technology of text should make CAI instructional "courseware" more transferable from one computer system to another. It should enable writers to organize large training courses easily. Structured writing's accomplishments under this criterion have been documented by Horn *et al.* (1971).
Writer productivity	A technology of text would give writers higher productivity in terms of hours per finished page not only of their own writing but of those managers and writers who work for them. Increasing writing efficiency up to 50 percent has been reported by practitioners. Most reports are in the ten percent range and mention that they would be higher except that structured writing requires more analysis and organization than conventional approaches.
Efficient updating	A technology of text should permit writers to update a document much faster, no matter how complex or lengthy. Wide experience in many industrial settings with all

Continued on next page

CRITERIA (WRITER'S POINT OF VIEW)

Efficient updating (Continued)	types of word processing has been reported at convention panels and discussions.
Electronic filing and retrievability	A technology of text should overcome the problems of the forthcoming paperless office by having electronic filing cabinets in which the writer can find documents and can identify the parts of them easily and quickly when scanning a terminal screen. Research focused on these problems is underway.
Method gets better as complexity and length increase	A technology of text would help writers in all of the areas mentioned above. But as the complexity and sheer volume of the written material increase, a technology of text should also help writers even more. The help it gives should increase as the size and complexity increase. It should help writers analyze what to include when the readership becomes wider and more diverse. This is a difficult criterion to evaluate. Success has been reported on several large courses and knowledge bases (Horn, 1981; Webber, 1979).
Conclusion	Does a true technology of text exist? We believe it

Continued on next page

CRITERIA (WRITER'S POINT OF VIEW)

Conclusion
(Continued)
does exist in the form of the standards of structured writing used by the community of writers and researchers who have been contributing to this field.

References

Bixler, S. *Using structured writing for writing management reports.* Paper presented at the NSPI Conference, Washington, D.C., April 1979.

Cheung, R.Y.-M. *Development and evaluation of an information mapped text on "BASIC."* Unpublished master's thesis, Concordia University, 1981.

Fields, A. A test of an information mapped programmed text. *NSPI Journal,* May 1981, 26-28.

Horn, R.E. Information mapping^{tm}. *Training in Business and Industry*, March 1974, *11*(3).

Horn, R.E. *Writing reports: An information mapping^{tm} course.* Lexington, MA: Information Resources, 1977.

Horn, R.E. *How to write information mapping^{tm}.* Lexington, MA: Information Resources, 1976 (Out of print and replaced by later course materials entitled, *Developing Instructional Materials and Procedures, an Information Mapping^{tm} Course*, 1979, 1980).

Horn, R.E. *Results with structured writing using the information mapping^{tm} writing service standards.* Paper presented at a conference on Designing Usable Texts at the Open University, Institute of Educational Technology, November 3-7, 1980a.

Horn, R.E. Structured writing—possible solution to documentation problems. *Proceedings of the IBM Guide Users Conference*, Miami, Florida, November 13, 1980b.

Horn, R.E. *Update on structured writing.* Paper presented at the NSPI Conference, Montreal, May 12-14, 1981a.

Horn, R.E. Information and decision management through structured writing, a concept paper prepared by Delta Force, U.S. Army War College, Carlisle Barracks, PA, 1981b.

Horn, R.E. *et al.* Information maps and computer-based learning and reference—a research proposal for Hq electronic systems division. U.S. Air Force Systems Command, Bedford, MA, May 8, 1967.

Horn, R.E., Nicol, E., Kleinman, J., and Grace, M. *Information mapping^{tm} for learning and reference.* Cambridge, I.R.I. (A.F. Systems Command Report ESD-TR-69-296.), 1969.

Horn, R.E., Nicol, E., Roman, R. *et al. Information mapping^{tm} for computer-based learning and reference.* Cambridge, I.R.I. (A.F. Systems Command Report ESD-TR-71-165.), 1971.

Continued on next page

Olympia, P.L. Information-mapped chemistry. *Journal of Chemical Education,* March 1979, *56*(3), 176-178.

Romiszowksi, A.J. *A study of individualized systems for mathematics instruction at the post secondary levels.* Unpublished Ph.D. Thesis, Loughborough University of Technology (U.K.), June 1977.

Soyster, T.G. *A comparison of the effects of programmed instruction and the information mapping*tm *method of instructional design on learning and retention of students with different mental abilities.* Unpublished Ed.D. Thesis, Temple University, 1980.

Stelnicki, M. *The effects of information-mapped and standard text presentations with fact and concept levels of learning on low general ability adult learner cognition.* Unpublished Ed.D. Thesis, Northern Illinois University, 1980.

Stuart, T.H. *The effectiveness of information mapping compared with the conventional paragraph in communicating technical information.* Unpublished Master's Thesis, University of the Philippines at Los Banos, October 1979.

Webber, N. *Some results of using the information mapping*tm *writing service standards at Pacific Telephone Company.* Paper presented at National Society for Performance and Instruction, Washington, D.C., April 12, 1979.

EXAMPLE OF STRUCTURED WRITING

HOW TO PREPARE DATA FOR AN AUDIT

Introduction Completing the steps outlined in the procedure below insures that the data

- are current *and*
- all auditing steps are complete.

Procedure

STEP	ACTION
1	Obtain both run data and source document samples of the data items selected for audit.
2	Verify the source documents sample by comparing the sample to the original list.
3	Using the space provided on the worksheets, write down all important descriptive information about the sample.

MINIMUM INFORMATION REQUIRED	EXAMPLES
Description of each data item	● Account Name ● Account Number ● Type of Business
Attribute description	● Sales Territory ● Effective Date

STEP 4

YOU COMPARE. . .	TO. . .	AND. . .
Sample Data	● programming instructions when the source document originated ● company requests ● statistical guidelines	Record any ● errors ● differences and their source on the worksheet
Source Data	Run data printouts	

STEP	
5	After you complete Steps 1-4 ● List differences or errors on Summary Sheet. ● Compute accuracy ratios for data items.

Final Step You and the company management discuss your audit findings. These discussions are important to help

- point out the errors and differences in your report *and*
- correct the discrepancies.

EXAMPLE OF STRUCTURED WRITING

AUDIT ACCURACY RATIOS

Introduction	In order to compare one audit to the next, the audit statistics must be the same. The following accuracy definitions are part of every audit.

Definitions

TERM	DEFINITION
Data Item Verifying Ratio	The number of times a data item is correct, divided by the total number of times the data item is reviewed.
Transaction Ratio	The number of times all data items reviewed on a transaction are correct, divided by the total number of transactions audited.
Account Ratio	The number of times all data items examined are correct on all transactions relating to a single account, divided by the total number of accounts examined.

Rule 1	In your audit report, you must list which data items are included in the Data Item Verifying Ratio.

Rule 2	If the company requests changes or additions to the Data Item Verifying Ratio list, you must note these changes in your Audit Report.

Rationale:

- Any changes will affect the results of the Transaction Ratio. The more fields reviewed per transaction, the lower the accuracy ratio.

- Comparison of audits would be impossible unless the changes were listed.

Rule 3	If you are comparing transaction ratios over a specific time period, the transaction definitions must be the same.

Example:

If the transaction, Cash Receivables, contained international receivables as well as domestic during the first audit, then you must include international receivables in the next audit.

17.

Printing: The Next Stage: Discourse Punctuation

Richard Showstack

<table>
<tr><td colspan="2">Outline: Printing: The Next Stage: "Discourse Punctuation"</td></tr>
<tr>
<td>Introduction</td>
<td>

1. Battle between print and other media
2. College underlining example
3. Gutenburg
</td>
</tr>
<tr>
<td></td>
<td>

I. **Main Points**
  A. Printing is two-dimensional, but ideas are multi-dimensional
  B. Writer and publisher should give the reader help in reading
  C. From sentence punctuation to discourse punctuation
</td>
</tr>
<tr>
<td></td>
<td>

II. **Reasons**
  A. To increase the reader's understanding
  B. To increase reading speed and efficiency
  C. To get the author's intended message (and force him or her to organize it)
  D. To make it easier to choose what to read, to skip around, and to review
</td>
</tr>
</table>

O U T L I N E

III. Examples
   A. Layout
   B. Give the book a trial run

IV. Summary
   A. System should become standardized
   B. Will become popular by "Natural Selection"

V. Conclusion
   A. Reading should be made as easy as possible
   B. Printing must change if it is to compete with other media

I
N
T
R
O
D
U
C
T
I
O
N

A battle is being waged around us every day. It is a battle for the minds of men (and women). Which side eventually wins this battle is a matter which will affect every one of us.

It is the battle of the media.

For hundreds of years, people had no way to permanently record their ideas and transmit their ideas to others except through the printed form. Since it had no competition, this form of communication evolved very little.

Come the twentieth century, however, **printing** has been assaulted on all sides by other media. Now it **is in danger of losing the battle** entirely, unless something is done by those who believe that printed communication has something to offer that radio, television, tape recordings, records, etc., do not offer.

The various electronic media have the advantage of being more "true-to-life" and also much easier on the mind of the receiver. He or she can just lay back and let his or her TV set or tape recorder do all the work.

(1)

Reading, on the other hand, requires relatively greater effort and thought. **Printed matter does have the advantages,** of course, of being more precise, permanent, and convenient in some ways than the other media, **but these advantages are outweighed** by the relatively greater mental strain required by reading than by the other media.

Let us look at **the example of a college student studying a textbook.** Most college students who are serious about their studies inevitably develop a method of marking up their textbooks to make the meaning more apparent. Then one day a student will buy a used textbook and will discover, to his or her puzzlement, that the previous owner of the book has already marked it up, but in a much different way than he or she would have marked it up. This must cause him or her to wonder whether he or she or the other owner of the book understood the book's message, since both of them chose different parts to underline. ②

The question that arises out of this example is: **Why didn't the writer and publisher print the book in some way to make the organization and meaning more clear?** This would not only insure that the author's intended message got across to the reader but also would save the reader a lot of time.

The answer to this question is that ever **since** movable type was invented by **Gutenburg,** the art **of printing has evolved practically not at all** as a way of presenting information on paper. ③

Now, with tremendously increased capabilities in printing technology making use of computers and various photographic copying techniques, and considering the challenge of other forms of media, **isn't it time that printing evolved to the next stage?**

What is the next stage? Before we answer this question, let us consider what printing and writing and reading are.

Printing is a way of permanently recording language on paper. Language, however, is merely a representation of thought. And although thoughts in a person's mind can be incredibly complex, language, whether it be oral or written, is two-dimensional. That is, at any one point in time only one symbol or sound can be expressed in sequence. It is then up to the reader (or listener) to try to reconstruct the original thoughts (meaning) of the writer or speaker in his or her own mind.

I.

M
A
I
N

P
O
I
N
T
S

Until now, a writer would try to convert his or her complex thoughts in the two-dimensional form of communication known as writing; this writing would then be printed and presented as-is to the reader. Important thoughts and not-so-important thoughts, examples and main points, and major divisions and minor divisions in the writer's ideas all looked exactly the same on the printed page: like an endless uniform series of printed symbols.

To make the writer's ideas more easily reconstructible, however, certain techniques were developed, the principal ones being punctuation, paragraphing, and certain writing conventions, such as transition words. Compared to the graphicness of movies or television or radio, however, these techniques are no longer sufficient.

So what is needed is for the writer and publisher to take the process one step further. That is, instead of making printed matter a copy of typed matter, printing should be used itself as a means of communicating ideas. That is, the very way the written matter is set out on the page should communicate something to the reader, and thus

Ⓐ

Ⓑ

make reading (the deciphering of the writer's message) easier and more enjoyable to the reader.

What I am proposing is the development of a kind of "Discourse Punctuation" to be expressed in printing in the same way that sentence and paragraph punctuation were developed for writing. That is, in addition to being able to see (through spacing, commas, periods, etc.) how ideas in a sentence are divided or related, the reader should also be able to see the organization of the ideas of the discourse in its entirety. ⓒ

Printing in the present day has lost all of its flavor as an art form in itself which can communicate information. But as McLuhan reminded us, different media have different kinds of potential for communicating messages in different ways. Unfortunately, printed media are not living up to their potential.

There are several reasons why printed information could and should be presented more efficiently.

II. First of all, it will increase the reader's immediate understanding of what he or she is reading. For example, comparisons and contrasts, emphases, **R** relationships between ideas, the importance of **E** ideas relative to each other, etc., will not only be **A** decipherable, they will be *visible*. ⓐ
S This, in turn, will increase the speed and **O** efficiency of reading. In the present information **N** explosion which we are all facing, it is vital that we **S** find a way to process written information in our minds more quickly. ⓑ

Thirdly, it will insure (or at least make it more likely) that what we think we are reading is the same as what the author thought he or she was writing. That is, we will be able to get the author's ⓒ

intended message more easily. (This may also have the welcome side-effect of forcing authors to organize their thoughts better as well.)

Last, it will make it easier to choose what to read, to skip around to points of interest while reading, and to remember and review what was written afterwards. This is a very important point, for reading does not just entail starting at the first word of an article and reading straight through to the last word; at least, it should entail more than this. A skilled reader will attack a piece of writing and try to use it for his or her purposes. He or she will decide what to read, how much of it to read, how much of it to remember, and how much of it to forget. The problem now is that the writer and publisher normally only put the words down on the paper; they do not give the reader any help in how to read them.

D

So, now let's look at some examples of how the writer and publisher *could* give this kind of help.

The first and most obvious example is to provide a brief outline at the beginning of any piece of printed matter which shows the organization of the contents. If provided with this, the reader can choose the parts of the article to give special attention to (or can choose to skip the article entirely).

However, other aspects of layout could also be used. For example, important ideas could be underlined with a thin line, more important ideas with a thicker line. Boxes and brackets surrounding sentences and paragraphs could also be included to show how different parts of the discourse are related to each other. Along with these, marginal notes and markers could also be used.

In addition, various kinds of printed styles could

A

III.

E
X
A
M
P
L
E
S

be developed to mark different kinds of ideas or sentences. Also, different **color and type sizes** could be used to convey information.

In order to find the best way to mark a particular book or article, the publisher could send it out to several "**discourse markers,**" in addition to proofreaders. These discourse markers could each independently suggest how the manuscript could be printed and, based on their various opinions, a general editor could decide how to print it. (Of course, all the "punctuation" in the world will not help make an unorganized, unclear manuscript into a lucid book. It will be the author's responsibility to *organize* his or her ideas so that the "discourse organization" is so self-evident that two people seeking to "punctuate" a text would agree most of the time on what the important ideas are.)

B

Through time and trial-and-error, **a standardized system of "Discourse Punctuation" would come to be agreed upon,** just as we now have rules of sentence punctuation. Once these rules become accepted and generally known, and practiced, **printing will have moved on to its next stage.**

A

IV.

S U M M A R Y

Of course, the pressure to move toward such a system will not come from authors or publishers. They will see it as a way of increasing their work without increasing their return on their investment of time and money. Therefore, **the push will have to come from the reading** (and publication-buying) **public.** If a few publishers *do* accept such a system, their publications will no doubt become more popular with the public and this will, in turn, increase the economic pressure on the more conservative publishers.

B

V.

C O N C L U S I O N

The net effect, however, will be to make reading both more enjoyable as well as easier. And if the writer would spend, let's say, ten extra hours preparing a manuscript for printing using Discourse Punctuation, it might save readers cumulatively thousands of hours when reading.

Reading something should be neither a logic problem nor a problem in deciphering ideas. The organization of the author's ideas should be made as clear as possible so that the reader can devote his or her mental energy to more important matters, such as *thinking about* the author's ideas, rather than merely trying to understand them. Reading can, and should, be as enjoyable a way of getting information as any other way.

Printing must change and evolve if it is to successfully compete in the battle with the other media. If we start using a new technique of "Discourse Punctuation," then perhaps we will literally be able to begin to "read between the lines."   □

Section Three:

Electronic Text

18.

Introduction to Section Three: Electronic Text

David H. Jonassen

In a decade or so, the book as we know it will be as obsolete as is movable type today. Information is expanding at an exponential rate. Toffler (1970) wrote over a decade ago that at current rates of growth, our knowledge base is expected to expand at least 32 times within five decades. Hard copy print cannot survive long as the primary medium for information storage. Computer data banks have already supplanted this function in many areas, especially those related to financial institutions. Microforms will probably have a minimal impact on the problem; storage limitations and retrieval problems will soon make them obsolete. Emerging technologies, based on the diminishing (size) computer chip, bubble memory, and videodisc, offer enhanced potential for the storage of mammoth quantities of information. Displaying them becomes another problem. With the exception of microforms, most non-print display of textual information is via a television monitor or cathode ray tube. The peculiarities of reproducing high-resolution images on a TV screen pose some significant problems for text designers. The computer, however, can greatly facilitate the production and generation of text. The three articles in this section on electronic text relate to state-of-the-art techniques for producing and/or displaying text via the computer/television interface. Future technologies may engender a whole new set of problems.

As Esther U. Coke explains in "Computer Aids for Writing Text," computer programs for generating text from information bases will not be available for some time. Numerous programs are available for assembling text, and computer assistance or word processing systems are becoming as common as the typewriters they are replacing. The functions and limits of each are carefully treated in this excellent chapter.

As large main-frame computers are supplanted by the smaller, but increasingly powerful, microcomputers, their applications are expanding in all areas of instruction (including word processing). Paul F. Merrill considers a number of constraints in "Displaying Text on Microcomputers." Guidelines for writing text—considering the screen format, paging, and facilitating use of computer stored text—are provided. The primary advantage of computer-delivered instruction via text over hard copy print is the interactive nature of the medium. Controlling the interaction of the learner with the computer is one of the most important functions of any instructional program. Some useful heuristics for the text programmer/designer are also provided.

The newest means for displaying computer-stored text broadcasts or transmits signals from remote data bases to the television in your home or office on demand. Teletext and viewdata networks are emerging world-wide. Both are available in England. Currently, only viewdata systems are available in the U.S. Simply by dialing a phone and connecting it to your microcomputer or television set, you have instant access to myriad amounts of information, including news wire services, commodity and stock quotations, current (to the hour) travel information, electronic mail service, sports scores, and more. The screen limitations and large number (hundreds of thousands) of pages of information available pose serious problems for the Videotex designer. Based on her experience with the British teletext and viewdata systems, Linda Reynolds reviews "Display Problems for Teletext," offering guidelines for information display which should be applicable to developing systems world-wide.

Electronic display of text as a common medium of communication is still in its infancy, the time when information design problems should be corrected. Maturity of this medium should find us all relying heavily on our home video displays for a constant variety of information needs.

Reference

Toffler, A. *Future shock.* New York: Random House, 1970.

19.

Computer Aids for Writing Text[1]

Esther U. Coke

Two approaches have been taken in applying computer technology to the production of written materials. The goal of one approach is to replace the human writer with computer programs that generate the written materials themselves. The goal of the other approach is to develop computer programs that will assist human beings in the writing task.

Work on programs that actually write texts is in the developmental stage and will be noted only briefly in this chapter. The main discussion will be of programs that assist the writer rather than replace him or her. These programs perform well-defined, repetitive tasks or tasks that involve the retrieval and assembly of quantities of information that strain human capacity. Decisions that are not easily programmed are left to the writer, who can draw on real-world knowledge not easily stored in the computer. Such an approach to the writing enterprise assigns to the computer and the human the activities that each does best (Martin, 1973).

Computer Generation of Text

A true computer authoring system should be able to take information from a knowledge base and transform that information into syntactically correct sentences that form a well-structured text. An example of such a program is TALE-SPIN (Meeher, 1976). This program produces Aesop-like fables in English from information that a user provides about the characters, their relationships, and their personalities.

383

Programs such as TALE-SPIN that generate a text should be differentiated from those that assemble segments of text. Programs that manipulate already written materials are really writing aids, not text generators. Such programs do not replace the human writer. They assist him or her. An example of such an authoring aid is a system being developed by the Navy (Brady & Kincaid, Note 1). This system constructs instructional material "from basic job-task information stored in a data base" (Brady & Kincaid, Note 1, p. 1). Job-task information includes text segments of the instructional document that the computer rearranges or merges with other material such as word lists or illustrations. The final instructional document is assembled by the computer according to a sequence and format specified by the human author.

Computer programs that actually compose a variety of documents on different subject matters will probably not be available in the near future. Text generation algorithms require detailed specifications of what constitutes a well-formed sentence and a well-structured text. The knowledge needed for these detailed specifications will come from research in artificial intelligence, psycholinguistics, and related fields.

Computer Assistance for the Writer

To understand how computers can assist the writer, it is helpful to define some of the activities involved in writing. The present discussion reflects the approaches outlined in articles by Hayes & Flower (1980), Flower & Hayes (1980), Gould (1980), and Bereiter (1980).

Components of the writing task that are particularly amenable to computer assistance are shown in Figure 19.1. The labels in the right margin of the figure refer to the general labels that appear in the Hayes & Flower (1980) model of writing. Figure 19.1 is organized vertically to suggest that some activities have logical priority over others. For example, an author has to decide about the topic of a text before gathering pertinent information. However, the organization of Figure 19.1 is not meant to imply that writing is a fixed sequence of steps. Observations of writers, such as those by Stallard and Emig (as cited in Bereiter, 1980),

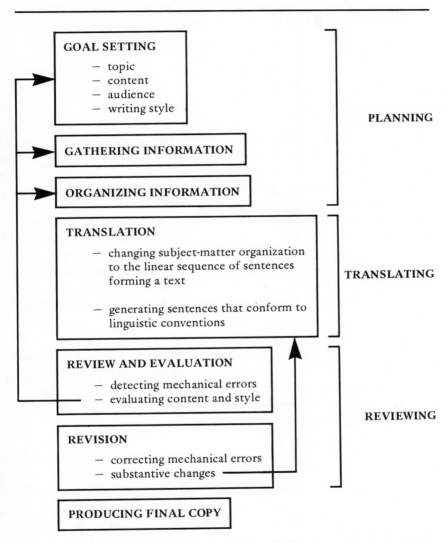

Figure 19.1. Components of the writing task with arrows suggesting optional return to other components from review and revision. Notation from the Hayes & Flower (1980) reading model is shown in the right margin.

suggest that a writer may engage in some or all of the activities shown in Figure 19.1. Furthermore, these activities may be carried out in almost any order any number of times either simultaneously or successively.

The writing activities shown in Figure 19.1 are described briefly below:

Goal Setting. These activities include choice of topic, specification of content, definition of intended audience, and selection of writing style. Goal-setting decisions are often made at the start of the writing task. They set up a frame of reference for the writer and provide constraints for his or her decisions while writing.

Gathering Information. The author must think about the subject matter and gather whatever information he or she needs to construct a coherent text. These activities include storing ideas as mental notes or as external records on paper or in computers.

Organizing Information. As a result of these activities, the author "understands" the subject matter. His or her knowledge may be represented as a knowledge structure in his or her mind, or it may include something external, such as an outline. The organization resulting from this activity need not be identical to that of the completed document.

Translation. This activity transforms the writer's understanding of the material into the linear sequence of sentences that make up a text. Translation involves such decisions as what to write first, how to structure paragraphs, and whether certain information should be presented in tabular or graphic form. The writing itself is guided by the author's choice of discourse type and rhetorical strategies and is carried out according to the conventions of the language.

Review and Evaluation. These activities involve both detecting mechanical errors and evaluating a document's content and style. In detecting mechanical errors, an author looks for misspellings, grammatical mistakes, and typographical errors. In evaluating the document's content and style, an author may ask whether he or she has covered the topic adequately and organized the information effectively. He or she may ask whether he or she has chosen a style that is appropriate for the intended audience. These evaluation activities may cause the writer to return to the goal-setting, information-gathering, or information-organizing activities shown in Figure 19.1.

Revision. During revision, mechanical errors are corrected and more substantive revisions to the document are made. Substantive changes may involve rearrangement or deletion of already written material and insertion of newly written material, including major rewording of existing text segments.

Producing Final Copy. Until recently, the production of final copy almost always involved either hand-written or printed paper documents. Now that written material is being stored in computers, other media for final copy can include displays on computer terminals, computer-produced speech, or computer-produced microfilm.

Word Processing Systems

The most widely available computer aids for writers are the editing and formatting capabilities of word and text processing systems.[2] For simplicity, these systems will be referred to as word processing systems. The basic purpose of a word processor is to automate the production of documents—to store the written word and produce final copy. A word processor performs three basic functions:

1. It stores text in computer-readable form. Input is primarily from typewriters or similar devices. But voice decoders, optical scanning devices, and other hardware are being developed that will make spoken and handwritten input generally available.
2. It allows a user to edit the stored input. Letters, words, lines, and even larger units can be altered and the material rearranged without the need for extensive reentry of material (e.g., retyping).
3. It produces final copy from the stored input. Most systems allow users to specify the format in which the stored input will be printed. Format options include choices about margins, headings, justification of lines, and page numbering.

A word processing system is not necessarily the optimal writing aid, since it is usually designed to automate the production of printed output rather than to help writers. However, these processing systems can make writing easier by helping the author in three of the last stages of writing shown in Figure 19.1—translation, revision, and producing final copy.

During the translation stage of writing, the ease of making corrections with a word processor may free the writer from concern about such details of writing as spelling, choosing appropriate words, or generating well-formed sentences. Freed of the constraints of the mechanics of writing, the author can concentrate more on the expression of content. Most word processors now find spelling errors, and some will soon be able to find grammatical errors (Miller, Heidorn, & Jensen, Note 9). With a word processor, it is reasonably simple to substitute one word for another or to complete a sentence properly. Flower & Hayes (1980) have discussed the "cognitive strain" on the writer while generating text. The availability of a word processor may reduce this strain.

The editing capabilities of a word processor may also facilitate writing by making it easy for the writer to experiment with different ways of expressing ideas. Paragraphs or other portions of the text can be moved by typing editing commands rather than by retyping the text. Some of the more expensive word processing systems, such as Interactive Systems Corporation's IS/1 (The Seybold Report, 1980), allow the writer to view more than one piece of text at a time. This facility could be used to compare ways of expressing ideas. It could also help in the cutting and pasting that often go on when a text is being revised.

The formatting capabilities of a word processor free the writer from concern about the final form of a text as he or she writes. When the author is ready to request final copy, he or she may specify the format with formatting commands. Some word processing systems can insert these commands automatically. For example, word processors often automatically format letters or technical writing so that they conform to prescribed standards.

Writer-Oriented Systems

Computer systems are now being developed specifically to assist writers rather than to automate the production of final copy. Examples of two such systems are (a) CRES—a computer readability editing system developed for the Navy that is written in Wang Basic-2 and implemented on a Wang-2200MVO Computer (Kincaid, Aagard, O'Hara, & Cottrell, 1981)—and (b) the Writer's Workbench—a UNIX[3]-based system developed at Bell Laboratories (Frase, Note 5, Note 6; Macdonald *et al.*, in press).

CRES.[4] This writing aid provides the author with an estimate of his or her text's difficulty and information about word choices. CRES uses a readability formula to estimate text difficulty. In addition to advising the writer about the overall difficulty of his or her text, CRES also identifies sentences that might be difficult because they exceed a specified length. CRES flags words in the text that are likely to be unfamiliar to its readers by comparing the text's words with lists of common and technical words that the audience is presumed to know. The CRES programs can also suggest simpler replacements for difficult words and phrases. The programs' output consists of the original text with computer-produced editorial suggestions inserted in the body of the text. The author makes corrections using the Wang word processor. The CRES system is part of a more general computer-based publishing system being developed by the Navy which will include the authoring aid described in a previous section (Brady & Kincaid, Note 1). Although the CRES word lists are particularly suited to Navy personnel, this system has the facilities for adapting these lists to the needs of any audience.

Writer's Workbench (WWB). This system is a collection of writing aids that the author can call upon as needed. The system is modular in design so that it can easily incorporate new features as they are developed. In its present version, WWB can look for misspellings and some kinds of punctuation and typing errors, calculate a readability index, and flag words and sentences that exceed prescribed lengths. Based on a comparison of the text's words with lists of words and phrases, WWB can advise authors about the abstractness of their documents, flag sexist terms, and suggest replacements for difficult or unnecessary words and phrases. WWB also has programs that assign parts of speech to text words (Cherry, Note 2). Using these assignments, WWB can advise readers about some aspects of their writing style, such as the use of nominalizations and passives, that are associated with text difficulty.

WWB has scripts for its advisories so that its suggestions sound like those of a human editor. Advisories are issued based on standards for a particular audience. For example, an author's use of passive sentences might be assessed against a standard for the use of passives in documents read by engineers. WWB has facilities that allow a writer to set up his or her own standards based on his or her own knowledge of an audience.

Other Systems. Companies that publish large amounts of material often have their own in-house computer-aided publication systems incorporating both a word processor and writing aids. Berman (1977) has described a number of publishing systems available to the aerospace industry that have facilities to aid multi-authoring of a text, to do bibliographic searches, and to help authors keep track of notes. These publishing systems often offer sophisticated word processing systems that can automatically assemble material for final publication according to specified formats.

Specific Aids for Writers

Spelling Aids. Programs that detect spelling errors are becoming standard software in many operating systems. Peterson (1980) describes in detail the spelling programs that have been developed since the earliest ones in 1957. The level of assistance offered by these programs varies in sophistication. The simplest provide alphabetized lists of all the different words in a text and leave it to the user to decide which words are misspelled. The most sophisticated programs compare dictionary entries with text words and report as misspellings all words not found in the dictionary. A few spelling programs not only direct the writer's attention to words that are likely to be misspelled but also provide the correct spellings of words.

All of these spelling programs rely on the writer to decide how to spell a word correctly. Some writing aids can help the writer with this decision. For example, the Writer's Workbench has a program that accepts a few letters of a word, such as the first three, and gives the writer all the words that would have those letters as part of the word.

Calculation of Readability. Computer programs that calculate a readability index for a text are becoming widely available (Klare, 1974-75). A readability index is an estimate of the stylistic difficulty of a text. It indicates how much reading skill is needed to cope with the *way* a document is written. The best predictors of readability (Klare, 1963, 1971, 1974-75) are formulas that combine measures of sentence complexity and word difficulty. Sentence complexity is commonly estimated by calculating the average number of words in the sentences of a text. Word difficulty is estimated either by calculating the average length of a text's words or by finding out how many text words occur in a list of easy words.

Estimating the readability of a document is simple once the copy is in machine-readable form. Old formulas, such as the Flesch (Coke & Rothkopf, 1970; Kincaid *et al.*, 1981; Klare, 1969), have been adapted to computer calculation, and new formulas have been developed whose elements are easily calculated by computer. Readability formulas are good barometers of the overall difficulty of a document for a specific audience. For example, a document written at the 11th reading grade level is very likely to be difficult for the average fifth grader.

Readability formulas were intended to aid in assessing text difficulty. They do not prescribe remedies for unclear or difficult writing. Used properly, a readability index can help the author decide whether his or her writing style is consistent with what he or she knows about the reading skill, knowledge, and motivation of his or her intended audience. Revision of a text to make it easier usually involves such activities as reevaluating writing goals, collecting more information, or reconsidering the organization of the subject matter and how it is translated into text.

Unfortunately, many writers are tempted to misuse readability indices, and this misuse has lead to considerable controversy about the formulas themselves ("Forum, Readability formulas: Used or abused?," 1981). Shortening sentences and replacing difficult words with easy synonyms will make a text easier according to a readability formula. But these cosmetic changes are unlikely to make the text easier to understand.

Computer calculations of readability may increase this misuse of formulas. Writers who know nothing about readability formulas tend to believe that the number provided by the computer is an absolute measure of difficulty. Without any more information than the index value itself, these writers are tempted to revise their writing in ways that affect the readability index but not the reading ease of their text. One solution to this problem is to design computer aids that encourage the writer to use a readability measure correctly. For example, the Writer's Workbench compares the readability level of a text against a readability standard. This standard is set in terms of the reading skills of a particular audience or the standard can be set by the author. The author is told how difficult his or her text is relative to this standard. This approach to readability encourages the writer to consider his or her text's difficulty in terms of the document's audience and not in terms of some absolute standard.

Evaluation of Word Choices. Another writing aid that can be easily implemented on a computer is the evaluation of the writer's choices of words and phrases. This evaluation is accomplished by comparing the text's words and phrases with a stored list. Advice is given to the writer on the basis of this comparison. A list usually consists of words and phrases thought to have some influence on text comprehensibility or clarity of style. CRES programs can flag unfamiliar words. These are words that are not on a list of familiar words. Other writing aids have programs that advise the writer about such text characteristics as abstractness. This characteristic is estimated from the occurrence of words in an abstract word list (Frase, Gingrich, & Keenan, Note 7). Programs can also flag words and phrases that are considered poor usage by style guides (Cherry & Vesterman, Note 3).

Some programs have the ability to suggest replacements for the words and phrases that have been found in a text. The CRES program can suggest simpler words for some of the uncommon words it finds. The Cherry program suggests changes that are thought to improve writing style.

Although computer programs can evaluate word choices and even suggest replacements, the writer must make the final decisions about changes. Replacement of flagged words or phrases does not necessarily lead to a more understandable text (Davison, Kantor, Hannah, Hermon, Lutz, & Salzillo, Note 4). In fact, substitutions can sometimes make a text less comprehensible. Kincaid, Aagard, & O'Hara (Note 8) found that the common words that CRES suggested as replacements were often less specific in their meaning than the unfamiliar words originally chosen by the author. The substitution of these more general terms could obscure the meaning of an expression and make it more difficult for readers to understand what the writer intended to say. Computer aids that evaluate word choices should encourage the writer to reevaluate his or her writing at a more global level before making local changes.

Assessing Writing Style. An author's writing style results from all his or her choices among the optional features of the language. As mentioned previously, computer programs can evaluate the author's specific word choices in terms of a number of word characteristics and can estimate the general level of stylistic difficulty with a readability formula.

Even more complex evaluations of writing style can be made by programs that identify parts of speech or parse sentences. At the present time, parsers that handle writing in general have not been perfected (Miller *et al.*, Note 9). But a program that assigns parts of speech (Cherry, Note 2) has been incorporated into a writing aid (Cherry & Vesterman, Note 3) for the Writer's Workbench (WWB).

The WWB programs can find expressions that fit general patterns rather than expressions that match specific words and phrases of a list. For example, these programs identify passive sentences by looking for sentences with a verb phrase consisting of a form of the verb, to be, and a past participle. The programs recognize complex sentences by looking for sentences with subordinate conjunctions.

The WWB programs issue advisories about constructions associated with text difficulty, such as passive sentences. They also suggest aesthetic changes to the text. For example, the programs might urge the writer to start sentences with fewer nouns and more subordinate clauses and prepositional phrases in order to make the text more interesting.

These computer-produced suggestions can help the writer improve his or her style. However, the writer should be sure that the specific changes suggested by the computer program are consistent with his or her own stylistic decisions. For example, scientific papers are traditionally written in an impersonal style, and the writer who adheres to this tradition will frequently write sentences in the passive voice. A computer program may advise this writer to use more sentences written in the active voice. Before heeding such advice, the writer should reexamine his or her general stylistic decisions to see that his or her specific changes are consistent with these decisions.

Perspectives

The computer aids that have been discussed in this chapter assist the writer once he or she is ready to review and revise the text and prepare a final copy. Few if any computer aids now exist that help the writer during parts of the writing task that are labeled planning and translating in the right margin of Figure 19.1.

Presently, writers themselves can adapt the file manipulation facilities of a computer operating system such as the UNIX/3 system to help them gather and organize material. For example, a writer might record pertinent information and ideas in files whose names denote their content. He or she could list these file names and use this listing as a memory aid for the information he or she has gathered. By printing the contents of the files in a prescribed order, the writer could also experiment with different organizations of the information. Programs that exploit such features of an operating system for the benefit of the writer are being developed.

Programs are also being developed that will directly intervene in the process of translating the writer's ideas into text (Figure 19.1). Woodruff & Bereiter (Note 10), for example, have experimented with programs that provide writers with information about elements of an essay as they are writing. Using student writers assigned to write essays about their opinions, two studies were run. In one study, the writer was allowed to ask for help when he or she needed it. In response, the program explained elements of the opinion essay genre such as statements of belief, reasons, and examples. The program also suggested sentence-openers that might be used to introduce an essay element. In the second study, the computer intervened automatically with a question as soon as the writer completed a sentence. These questions directed the writer's attention to the essay elements. The questions, such as "Do you have a reason for your opinion?," were designed to help the students "compose more carefully considered and more fully developed opinion essays" (Woodruff & Bereiter, Note 10). While these programs did not seem to have much effect on writing quality, students did feel that the computer assistance was helpful when they would ask for it themselves. The unprompted intervention of the computer with questions was found to have a disruptive effect on essay production. These studies suggest that designing effective interactive computer aids for the writer as he or she composes is not a simple matter.

The advantages of using the computer to assist in writing are numerous. The computer can search word lists, compute readability indices, and carry out other repetitive tasks that error-prone human beings find onerous. The computer can free the writer from concern with many of the mechanics of writing so that he or she can concentrate more on content and less on form. The computer can help the writer adhere to standards of word choices or format with unflagging perfection. And computers are impersonal evaluators that are likely to be available when the human writer needs them.

Computer aids can also have certain disadvantages. An uncritical acceptance of a computer's advice may lead the writer to make superficial changes in a text when a reevaluation of his or her goals and plans would result in more effective writing. In addition, the computer's advice may not be appropriate. Computer writing aids, such as the Writer's Workbench, base some of their advice on guides for writers of literary prose (Strunk & White, 1959). This advice may not be appropriate for other types of writing, such as technical writing. For example, the advice to create interest by varying sentence length may not apply to such technical writing as procedural documents. For these texts, short simple sentences may convey information much more effectively than a varied mix of short and long sentences.

Frase (Note 5) has written insightfully about the implications of automated text assessment for text research, product evaluation, writing instruction, and a science of text design. But what is needed now are more computer aids that will help the writer plan what to write and transform these plans into writing. Gould (1980) has found that writers spend about two-thirds of their total writing time planning what they will write. Research is needed to discover how computer aids can help at this stage of writing.

Exactly how helpful computer assistance is for writers is difficult to assess. Writers' acceptance and enthusiasm for computer aids are not adequate criteria for evaluating the help they afford writers or the improvements in texts that result from their use. As Gould & Boies (1978) and others have shown, writers are not good at appraising the quality of their writing. In the study by Woodruff & Bereiter (Note 10), 75 percent of the students thought the computer was helpful. But no differences in ratings of quality were found between essays written with and without computer assistance. Objective comparisons of computer-aided and conventional writing are needed to assess the effects of computer aids on writing quality. But perhaps the most critical need is for studies of the writing task itself to discover how and when the writer might best use computer aids.

Notes

1. I wish to thank M.E. Koether and E.Z. Rothkopf for their helpful comments and suggestions.
2. According to The Seybold Report on Word Processing (1980), the major distinction between word processing systems and text processing systems has to do with when the written material in the computer is formatted to

appear in its final form. A typical word processing system always displays the written material in its final format; a text processing system formats the material as a separate operation. In addition, word processing systems tend to have more office-related functions as opposed to the more general-purpose text processing systems.

3. UNIX is a Trademark of Bell Telephone Laboratories, Inc.

4. At the present time, the hardware and software for a system such as CRES is not inexpensive. The current cost of the CRES hardware is $25,000 (Kincaid *et al.*, 1981).

Reference Notes

[1] Brady, R., & Kincaid, J.P. *Computer aided authoring and editing.* Paper presented at the meeting of the Society for Applied Learning Technology, Orlando, February 1981.

[2] Cherry, L.L. *PARTS—A system for assigning word classes to English text* (Computing Science Technical Report #81). Murray Hill, NJ: Bell Laboratories, 1980.

[3] Cherry, L.L., & Vesterman, W. *Writing tools—The STYLE and DICTION programs* (Computing Science Technical Report #91). Murray Hill, NJ: Bell Laboratories, 1980.

[4] Davison, A., Kantor, R.N., Hannah, J., Hermon, G., Lutz, R., & Salzillo, R. *Limitations of readability formulas in guiding adaptations of texts* (Technical Report #162). Urbana-Champaign, IL: Center for the Study of Reading, 1980.

[5] Frase, L.T. *Writer's workbench: Computer supports for writing and text design.* Paper presented at the annual meeting of the American Educational Research Association, Boston, April 1980.

[6] Frase, L.T. (Chair). *Computer aids for writing and text design.* Symposium presented at the annual meeting of the American Educational Research Association, Boston, April 1980.

[7] Frase, L.T., Gingrich, P.S., & Keenan, S.A. *Computer content analysis and writing instruction.* Paper given at the annual meeting of the American Educational Research Association, Los Angeles, April 1981.

[8] Kincaid, J.P., Aagard, J.A., & O'Hara, J.W. *Development and test of a computer readability editing system (CRES)* (TAEG Report #83). Orlando, FL: Training Analysis and Evaluation Group, 1980.

[9] Miller, L.A., Heidorn, G.E., & Jensen, K. *Text-critiquing with the EPISTLE system: An author's aid to better syntax* (Research Report RC8601). Yorktown Heights, NY: IBM Thomas J Watson Research Center, 1980.

[10] Woodruff, E., & Bereiter, C. *Experiments in computer assisted composition.* Paper presented at the annual meeting of the American Educational Research Association, Los Angeles, April 1981.

References

Bereiter, C. Development in writing. In L.W. Gregg & E.R. Steinberg (Eds.), *Cognitive processes in writing.* Hillsdale, NJ: Lawrence Erlbaum, 1980.

Berman, P.I. *Survey of computer-assisted writing and editing systems* (AGARDograph No. 229). London: Technical Editing and Reproduction, Ltd., Hartford House, 1977 (NTIS No. AD-A045010).

Coke, E.U., & Rothkopf, E.Z. Note on a simple algorithm for a computer-produced reading ease score. *Journal of Applied Psychology,* 1970, *54,* 208-210.

Flower, L.S., & Hayes, J.R. The dynamics of composing: Making plans and juggling constraints. In L.W. Gregg & E.R. Steinberg (Eds.), *Cognitive processes in writing.* Hillsdale, NJ: Lawrence Erlbaum, 1980.

Forum—Readability formulas: Used or abused? *IEEE Transactions on Professional Communication,* 1981, *PC-24,* 43-54.

Gould, J.D. Experiments in composing letters: Some facts, some myths, and some observations. In L.W. Gregg & E.R. Steinberg (Eds.), *Cognitive processes in writing.* Hillsdale, NJ: Lawrence Erlbaum, 1980.

Gould, J.D., & Boies, S.J. Writing, dictating, and speaking letters. *Science,* 1978, *201,* 1145-1147.

Hayes, J.R., & Flower, L.S. Identifying the organization of writing processes. In L.W. Gregg & E.R. Steinberg (Eds.), *Cognitive processes in writing.* Hillsdale, NJ: Lawrence Erlbaum, 1980.

Kincaid, J.P., Aagard, J.A., O'Hara, J.W., & Cottrell, L.K. Computer readability editing system. *IEEE Transactions on Professional Communication,* 1981, *PC-24,* 38-41.

Klare, G.R. *The measurement of readability.* Ames, IA: Iowa State University Press, 1963.

Klare, G.R. Automation of the Flesch reading ease readability formula with various options. *Reading Research Quarterly,* 1969, *4,* 550-559.

Klare, G.R. Some empirical predictors of readability. In E.Z. Rothkopf & P.E. Johnson (Eds.), *Verbal learning research and the technology of written instruction.* New York: Teachers College Press, 1971.

Klare, G.R. Assessing readability. *Reading Research Quarterly,* 1974-75, *10,* 62-102.

Macdonald, N.H., Frase, L.T., Gingrich, P.S., & Keenan, S.A. The writer's workbench: Computer aids for text analysis. *IEEE Transactions on Communication,* in press.

Martin, J. *Design of man-computer dialogues.* Englewood Cliffs, NJ: Prentice-Hall, 1973.

Meeher, J.R. *The metanovel: Writing stories by computer.* New Haven, CT: Yale University, September 1976 (NTIS No. AD-A03162517).

Peterson, J.L. Computer programs for detecting and correcting spelling errors. *Communications of the ACM,* 1980, *23,* 676-687.

The Seybold report on word processing. Media, PA: Seybold Publication, 1980, *3*(2).

Strunk, W.L., & White, E.B. *The elements of style.* New York: Macmillan, 1959.

20.

Displaying Text on Microcomputers

Paul F. Merrill

As paper costs increase and electronic communication and display costs decrease, the use of computer video displays is becoming more prevalent in our society. In spite of this expanding use of computer display screens, very little research has been done to provide guidelines on how to maximize the utility and effectiveness of electronic screen displays. The purpose of this chapter is to propose some preliminary guidelines for constructing computer screen displays. Many of these guidelines will be based on the experience of practitioners in the field rather than on firm empirical evidence. Therefore, many of these guidelines should be viewed as hypotheses which will need future empirical verification. Although the guidelines presented should generalize to most types of computer screen displays, the focus of this chapter will be on displaying text and graphics on microcomputers. The guidelines will be organized into five major categories: screen format, paging, ease of use, interaction, and formative evaluation.

Screen Format

Initially, it would seem that many of the principles discovered through research and practice related to the design and layout of print materials would also apply to the design of computer video displays. Although many of these principles are clearly relevant, they cannot all be applied indiscriminately, since there are significant differences between the printed page and the video screen. The resolution of most video screens severely restricts the quality and quantity of the text and graphics which can be displayed as compared to print material. The quality of the text on video screens is generally quite poor, due to the use of a dot matrix to form the letters and minimal space between lines. On some microcomputers, the quality of text is further reduced by restricting the display to only upper case letters. Often, when lower case letters are provided, they do not have descenders. Most video screens are also limited in the number of characters which can be displayed on the screen at one time. For example, the Apple II microcomputer will only display 24 lines with 40 characters per line, all in upper case. However, with optional firmware boards, the Apple II will display 80 character lines in upper and lower case. Most microcomputers also have some graphics capabilities. However, the resolution is again fairly limited. For example, the Radio Shack TRS-80 microcomputer has a graphics resolution of 128 horizontal by 48 vertical points, while the Apple II has a resolution of 280 horizontal by 192 vertical points. Several microcomputers also have some color display capabilities. Generally, these can display up to 16 different colors.

Because of the limitations described above, the format of the screen can significantly affect the readability of the display. Great care must be taken to avoid making the screen too cluttered or busy. Full screens of text are difficult to read and quite annoying to users. Blank space should be used in a liberal fashion with video displays. Bork (1980) has pointed out that the economics of blank space are quite different for computer video displays as compared to print. Blank space in printed material increases costs, since more paper is required. However, blank space on the computer screen is essentially free. Double spacing lines of text and/or spacing between paragraphs can increase readability.

The limitation in the number of characters that can be displayed on the screen leads to the use of very cryptic abbreviations or codes. These abbreviations and codes are often uninterpretable. This and other problems related to limited space can generally be solved by using more than one screen page to display information. This topic will be discussed in detail in the next section of this chapter.

If several textual and graphic elements are to be combined in the same display, care should be used to insure that the elements are organized on the screen in such a way that the viewer's eye moves naturally from one element to the other in the desired order. Eye movement may be controlled by the positioning and shape of the elements themselves. Whenever possible, the elements of the display should be structured in natural eye movement sequences, such as from top to bottom and left to right (Niekamp, 1972). The elements of the display should not require the user's eyes to jump all around the screen.

Careless programmers often make the mistake of splitting words at the end of lines. This is caused by typing information into a program in free form without paying attention to line length. The resulting displays are obviously difficult to read and reduce the credibility of the program. Spelling and grammar errors have a similar effect. In general, hyphenating words at the end of lines also reduces readability. On the other hand, it has been demonstrated that ragged right lines are easier to read than right justified lines (Bork, 1980).

Particular items in a textual display can be highlighted or emphasized in several different ways depending on the capabilities of a given microcomputer. The standard print highlighting techniques of underlining, boldface type, and all capital letters may be used on some microcomputers but not on others. If only upper case letters and a single type font are available, then these techniques cannot be used. Inverse video (black letters on white background) and/or flashing text can be used for emphasis on some microcomputers. A few microcomputers also have the capability of displaying text in different colors.

Flashing text can be obnoxious and should be used sparingly. When colored text is available, there is a strong temptation to over-use it. Many computer programs use several different colors of text on the same screen. When this is done, it is not always clear what the user is supposed to notice. In fact, if any kind of highlighting is over-done, the point of emphasis may be lost.

Paging

When a person finishes reading a page of printed material, he or she may proceed to additional material by turning the page. With computer video displays, a variety of techniques may be used for paging to additional material. One technique is to clear the screen by erasing all the old material on the screen and then displaying the new frame or page of information. Another common technique is to display the new information at the bottom of the screen one line at a time while scrolling the old information off the top of the screen. This scrolling technique should be avoided, since it is extremely difficult to read the text while it is scrolling.

In addition to paging by erasing the entire screen, it is possible to erase only a portion of the screen and display new information in the erased section. This approach is quite useful when you want to maintain a table or graphic on the screen while presenting several different textual descriptions concerning the graphic, which will not all fit on the screen at the same time. When using this approach, a slight pause should be placed between erasure and redisplay of the same section of the screen. This pause will allow the viewer to notice that the display has changed and that new information has been displayed which should be read.

In some applications, additional information to be displayed may also take the form of computer generated graphics, animated text, or animated special graphic characters. Each of these types of displays involves some movement on the screen. Since movement is very powerful in attracting attention, care must be used to avoid requiring the user to read a textual description and watch an animated display simultaneously. The text should be displayed first; then, when the user has finished reading the text, he or she can press a key to signal readiness to attend to the animation. In some applications, it may be more appropriate to display the animation first and then display the text. In either case, the user should not be expected to attend to two things at once.

New information may be presented on the video screen using any of the techniques described above under either computer control or user control. Under user control, the viewer is required to take some overt action, such as pressing a key on the keyboard in order to signal that new information should be presented. Under computer control, a given display only remains on the screen for a fixed period of time, then the computer automatically proceeds to present the next piece of information. This is accomplished by placing a fixed time delay into the computer program.

In general, computer control of display time should be avoided. It is difficult to determine an optimum display time for a broad range of users. Some people read slower than others. A display time which is just right for the author may be too short for some users and too fast for others. It is frustrating to have the computer display a new page of information when the user has not finished reading the previous page. It is just as frustrating to sit and wait for the computer to go on to new material when the user has already finished reading the current page. It is a simple matter to display a message at the bottom of the screen for the user to press the space bar or some other key when he or she is ready to proceed. It is recommended that the program specifically state which key should be pressed rather than say: "Press any key to continue." Such a message leaves users in a quandary as to which key they should actually press. This is especially important for new users.

When new information is presented on the computer screen, it is generally necessary to erase the old information. This old information is irretrievable unless some mechanism is built into the computer program for it to be redisplayed. A mechanism should be included in computer programs which present several consecutive pages of text to allow the user to page both forward and backward through the text. One way this can be done is to simply place a message at the bottom of each screen page to prompt the user to press one key to page forward and a different key to page backward. In the following example, the user is prompted to type a "B" to go back one page or a "C" to continue to the next page:

B)ack   C)ontinue

If the computer screen is going to be used to present test items, it is critical that the entire test item be displayed on a single screen. If a test item is too long to fit on one screen, every effort should be made to reduce its length or select a different item. If a test item must be displayed across two or more screens, then a mechanism for paging back and forth between the different pages of the item is mandatory.

Ease of Use

Historically, ease of use has not been a major issue of concern with respect to print materials. Most print materials other than reference books are designed to be read in a linear fashion from front to back. Going from one part to another in such material is relatively simple. Ease of use is of greater concern with respect to materials that are used for reference. Such materials need to be designed so that users can quickly find information in which they are interested. Ease of use is of major concern in the design of computer-based materials, since the entire set of materials is not physically visible at one time. It is very easy for users to get lost in a set of computer materials and not know where they are or how to get where they want to go in the materials. Therefore, various mechanisms should be built into computer materials to assist the users in identifying where they are in the materials and how to easily get from one place to another.

The issue of getting from one place to another was addressed briefly in the previous section on paging. It was mentioned that users should be able to go back and review previous screen pages if they desire. However, this technique needs to be expanded to allow users to go to other sections of the materials without having to page through all intervening material. This can be accomplished through the use of menus and/or special commands.

A menu is simply a screen page listing the various options open to the user, much like a menu in a restaurant, which lists the meal items which may be ordered. A menu is also similar to the table of contents in a book. However, in computer materials, when users select a given option in the menu, the computer automatically branches to the section of materials corresponding to the selected option. In order to increase the ease with which users can traverse through a set of computer materials, it is often useful to provide several menus organized in a hierarchical fashion. A main menu would list the major sections of the materials. On selecting one of these major sections, the user would then be presented with a submenu, which would list specific options related to the selected topic. Selections from a submenu could further lead to a sub-submenu, if necessary.

In addition to the menus described above, computer materials could also include provision for the user to enter special commands in order to branch to desired sections or pages of the computer materials. Such commands could be entered by using special function keys built into the keyboards of some computers, such as the PLATO and TICCIT computer-assisted instruction systems. Although most microcomputers do not have special function keys, any of the standard alphanumeric keys can be used for the same purpose.

If the special command feature is included in computer materials, it is important that the purpose of each command and its corresponding function key be made clear to the user. The name of the function key or the alphanumeric key should be as mnemonic as possible by clearly relating to the command to be performed. For example, a function key for the command to return to the menu could be labeled "MENU." If function keys are not available, the letter "M" could be used for the same purpose. The letter "D" would not be a good choice, since it does not relate mnemonically to the command.

If several options are made available to the user as to where to go next, the action required in order to execute each command should be made clear. For example, if the message:

Press "M" to Return to the Menu

appeared at the bottom of the screen, users might wonder what to do if they do not want to return to the menu. In contrast, the following message would indicate that three options are available and which keys to press in order to select each alternative:

M)enu   C)ontinue   B)ack

If there is no room for all alternatives to be displayed on the screen simultaneously, one of the commands could erase the given options and display the remaining options in the same location on the screen. The following example indicates that the user would press "R" to see a statement of the rule, "E" to see an example, "P" to see a practice item, and "O" to see other possible commands.

R)ule   E)xample   P)ractice   O)ptions

In some cases, there may be too many commands to place at the bottom of the screen using the techniques described above. In such cases, the user could be allowed to enter one command which would cause a full screen of possible commands to be displayed. After reviewing the available commands, the user would then return to the previous screen where the initial command was given. When a large number of commands are used, it would also be helpful to provide a printed sheet or card as a job aid which lists the available commands, their purpose, and the keys which should be pressed to execute each command. This off-line job aid would reduce the need for the user to continually page to and from the command list on the computer. If the commands are mnemonic, the user should be able to memorize the commands after a short period of use and eliminate the need to refer to any command list at all.

The commands used should be relatively easy to execute. Where possible the user should only be required to press one or two keys to execute a command. The relationship between commands and the action required by the user to execute the command should be consistent throughout a given computer program or system of programs. It can be very confusing to users if they are required to press the letter "G" to go to a glossary of terms in one part of a program and the letter "T" in another part of the same program.

Another factor which significantly affects ease of use is the provision of clear, simple, and concise instructions. These instructions should be available both on-line and off-line. The off-line instructions could go into greater detail than the on-line instructions. If a computer program is designed to be used several times, there should be provision for the user to skip the instructions on successive executions of the program. However, users are notorious for not reading instructions carefully. Therefore, it would be very helpful if users could enter a command to return to the Instruction page from other points in the program where they might get stuck and not remember what to do next. Where possible the instructions could be broken into sections, with appropriate sections placed throughout the program where they would be immediately relevant. This technique would prompt users as to what to do next at each critical point in the program. Such a technique would reduce the likelihood that users would forget the instructions and would also reduce the number of response errors.

Some authors like to place fancy title pages at the beginning of their programs. These title pages often include computer-generated graphics and music or special sound effects. The use of generated graphics and sound generally requires a significant amount of time for the computer to create the title page. If the program is used frequently, this noticeable time delay can turn out to be quite annoying to the user. Therefore, such title pages should be kept to a minimum.

Many microcomputer programs require that data or graphic information be read off the disk into memory at the beginning or at other points in the program. These disk-reads can cause a noticeable pause in the program. Significant program pauses can also be caused by extensive calculations, sorts, searches, etc. When such pauses occur, the program should print out a message on the screen to inform the user of the delay. Without such a message, users may become quite anxious and think that the program or computer is malfunctioning. If the pause is too long, the user may actually terminate the program or turn off the computer. The pause messages can often be quite creative and humorous in nature, thereby reducing users' annoyance at the delay. If the pause is going to be quite long, it would be useful to inform the user of the approximate duration of the delay. Another possible approach would be to display some kind of simulated clock which would count down the time till action resumes. With a little creativity, a time delay can often be masked from the user by displaying text or graphics just before the delay. The user could then read or study the information on the screen during the delay.

Interaction

One of the major advantages of the computer as a display device is its interactive capability. Users do not have to be just passive receivers of presented information. They may also respond to the information in an interactive fashion. Computer programs should capitalize on this capability as much as possible. Programs which just page through several frames of information without requiring some significant response from the user have little added value over a book. In fact, a book is likely to be more flexible and convenient. In general, the more interactive a program is the more interesting it is. However, the nature of the interaction should be relevant to the purpose of the program. Interaction for interactions sake has little value. Copy frames (Markle, 1969, 1978), user entry of information presented in a frame of instruction, are of no more value in a computer program than they are in a programmed text book.

When the user is required to make a response, the program should display a message which clearly specifies the nature of the expected response. This can often be done with a very simple prompt:

Do you want irregular verbs included (Y/N)?

In the above example, the user is prompted to enter the letter 'Y' for yes or the letter 'N' for no. In the following example, the user is prompted as to the format expected when entering the date:

Please enter todays date (e.g., 08 Sep 85):

Most computer programs require the user to press a special key to signal the computer when a response of several characters has been completed. This key is often labeled as the "ENTER," "RETURN," or "NEXT" key. Before this "ENTER" key is pressed, users may make any corrections to their response they desire. However, it is possible to write computer programs that do not require the pressing of the "ENTER" key to signal the end of a response. This is often done when only a single character response is expected. In general, the elimination of the "ENTER" key requirement is not recommended. Although the "ENTER" key requires an additional key press in making a response, it also allows the user to easily correct any inadvertent mistakes.

Even with the best of efforts at prompting the expected response and allowing for typing corrections, users will still make incorrect responses. Therefore, it is necessary for the program to include error traps. An error trap is a set of computer program code which examines a user's response for possible errors. If an error is found, the program then prompts the user to enter an appropriate response. For example, if the computer asks the user to enter the date, and the user enters his or her name instead, the program should display an error message and ask the user to enter the date correctly. Without such error traps, the program may terminate abnormally when it tries to process the user's response at a later point in the program.

In educational programs, it is important to give users feedback when they enter the incorrect answer to a question or problem. Practice makes perfect only with feedback. The feedback should do more than just inform users that their response was correct or incorrect. When an incorrect response is made, the feedback should also provide the correct response. However, research has shown that it is not necessary to require the user to copy the correct response before proceeding (Atkinson, 1974).

For some reason, many authors enjoy putting sarcastic feedback in their computer programs. Sarcastic feedback to a student is no more appropriate in a computer program than it is in a classroom. Comments such as, "Hey dummy, can't you do any better than that?," are clearly out of place in any instructional interaction.

When students answer a question or problem incorrectly, some authors like to require them to try again. Try-again loops in a computer program are often frustrating for the user. This is especially the case when no additional information or hints are provided to help students determine the correct response. Try-again loops should terminate after students make a mistake several times in a row. If a student makes repeated unrecognizable responses to a free-form response question, the computer program should exit the loop and ask the student to choose from several possible alternatives.

Formative Evaluation

Even if all of the guidelines described in this chapter are followed, success is not guaranteed. Many of the guidelines presented have not been empirically validated. Even those which have some empirical support will not apply in all situations.

Therefore, common sense and formative evaluation are extremely important. All computer programs intended for a wider audience than the authors themselves should be subjected to review by individuals from the target audience. A review by a subject-matter specialist is not sufficient. *Actual users* should go through the program to help identify any ambiguities, difficulties, or deficiencies. This information should then be used to modify and improve the program. The procedures to be used for the formative evaluation of computer programs are basically the same as those used to evaluate other types of materials (Gagne & Briggs, 1979).

Summary
A review of the principles for displaying text on microcomputers includes:

A. Screen Format
    1. Use blank space liberally and avoid a busy, cluttered screen.
    2. Avoid cryptic abbreviations and codes. Use another screen page, if necessary.
    3. Organize screen elements to take advantage of natural eye movement.
    4. Use correct spelling and grammar; do not split words at the end of a line.
    5. Use flashing text and other forms of highlighting sparingly.
B. Paging
    1. Avoid scrolling when paging to new material.
    2. Use a slight pause when erasing and redisplaying the same section of the screen.
    3. Do not require the user to attend to two different things on the screen simultaneously.
    4. Require some user response before proceeding to a new page. Avoid display time outs.
    5. Allow the user to page forward and backward through several pages of text.
C. Ease of Use
    1. Provide menus and/or special commands that enable the user to go from one part of the program to another easily.

  a. Keys used to implement a command should be mnemonically related to the purpose of the command.

  b. All possible alternative commands should be made clear.

  c. A minimum of key strokes should be required to execute any command.

  d. Keys used to execute commands should be consistent throughout the program.

 2. Provide clear, simple, and concise instructions.

  a. Instructions should be available both on-line and off-line.

  b. Allow the user the option to skip lengthy instructions.

  c. Prompt users as to what to do next at critical points in the program.

 3. Minimize the time required to generate title pages.

 4. Provide messages to inform the user of noticeable pauses in a program. Mask pauses where possible.

D. Interaction

 1. Capitalize on the interactive capability of the computer.

 2. Prompt the user on the nature of the expected response.

 3. Allow the user to correct typing mistakes by requiring the pressing of the 'ENTER' key to signal the end of a response.

 4. Use error traps to test the appropriateness of users' responses.

 5. Provide the correct answer as feedback when students enter the incorrect answer to questions or problems.

 6. Avoid sarcastic feedback.

 7. Minimize the number of times students must iterate through try-again loops.

E. Formative Evaluation

 1. Individuals from the target audience of a computer program should go through the program to help identify any ambiguities, difficulties, or deficiencies.

 2. Information from the formative evaluation should be used to modify and improve the program.

References

Atkinson, R.C. Teaching children to read using a computer. *American Psychologist,* March 1974, 169-178.

Bork, A. *Textual taxonomy.* Irvine, CA: Educational Technology Center, University of California, Irvine, 1980.

Gagne, R.M., & Briggs, L.J. *Principles of instructional design*, 2nd Ed. New York: Holt, Rinehart, & Winston, 1979.

Markle, S.M. *Good frames and bad: A grammar of frame writing*, 2nd Ed. New York: John Wiley & Sons, 1969.

Markle, S.M. *Designs for instructional designers.* Champaign, IL: Stipes Publishing Co., 1978.

Niekamp, W.E. An Exploratory Analysis of Selective Factors of Pictorial Composition Through the Ocular Photography of Eye Movements. Doctoral Dissertation, Indiana University, 1972.

21.

Display Problems for Teletext

Linda Reynolds

1. Introduction

Teletext, like viewdata, is a system whereby information held in a remote computer database can be displayed in the home or the office on any domestic television receiver which has the necessary decoding device. The information is displayed in alphanumeric or simple graphic form, and the viewer is able to call up specific "pages" of information from the database using a small remote-control keypad. These kinds of systems are known collectively as videotex systems. The main difference between teletext and viewdata is the way in which the information from the computer reaches the television receiver. Teletext is broadcast from a television transmitter, whereas with viewdata the information is transmitted via a telephone network.

Both teletext and viewdata are publicly available in Great Britain. The two teletext systems, Ceefax and Oracle, are operated by the British Broadcasting Corporation and the Independent Broadcasting Authority, respectively. The British viewdata system, known as Prestel, is run by British Telecom. The most obvious difference between the two kinds of systems as they exist in Britain are the results of the different methods of information transmission. Teletext is broadcast in coded form on four of the 625 lines which make up the normal television picture. The pages of information are broadcast sequentially in a continuous cycle, and the user must "capture" the page he or she requires by requesting the page number on his or her keypad. When the chosen page is

415

next transmitted, perhaps several seconds later, it will appear on the screen and will remain there until another page is selected. This sequential method of transmission means that the total number of pages available on Ceefax and Oracle must be kept to a few hundred only, or the user will have to wait an unacceptably long time for each page requested. This limitation does not apply, however, to viewdata systems such as Prestel. The two-way nature of the telephone link allows specific pages to be transmitted to individual users on request. As a result, the total number of pages available in the system is limited mainly by the storage capacity of the computer, and requested pages are written up almost immediately.

In spite of these operational differences between Ceefax and Oracle on the one hand and Prestel on the other, they are nevertheless similar in terms of the visual characteristics of the displays. This is because the various organizations concerned agreed on a joint standard for the two kinds of systems so that they could both be viewed on the same television receiver. Most of what is said in the following discussion of British teletext, therefore, is also true for Prestel. Indeed, even though some of the teletext and viewdata systems being developed elsewhere in the world do differ visually from the British systems in certain details, they all present similar kinds of problems as far as information design is concerned.

The display problems associated with systems such as teletext are of two main kinds. First, there is the fact that the image consists of transmitted light, as opposed to reflected light, in the case of a printed image. This has a number of very important implications for legibility. Second, the letter forms are crude, and there is a limited range of possibilities in terms of typographic variations and information layout. There is, however, the possibility of using seven colors at no extra cost. Teletext displays, therefore, have characteristics which are quite different from those of the printed page, and it cannot be assumed automatically that design conventions which have been shown to be appropriate for print will necessarily be applicable. The design of teletext pages must be based on a careful consideration of the limitations and possibilities of this particular medium, drawing on experience in other media only where it can be shown to be appropriate.

The aim here is to summarize the visual characteristics of teletext displays, to examine their implications for the legibility and "readability" of the displayed information, and then to look at ways of presenting various kinds of information such as text, tables, indexes, and graphics of various kinds.

2. Visual Characteristics of Teletext Displays

2.1 The Character Grid

Each page or frame of information on teletext displays consists of a maximum of 24 lines of up to 40 characters each, making a total of 960 character positions in all. Each of these positions can be occupied either by a standard alphanumeric character or a graphics character.

2.2 Standard Alphanumerics

Each alphanumeric character is formed on a 10 x 6 dot matrix. This is shown diagrammatically in Figure 21.1. The characters themselves are a maximum of seven dots high by five dots wide for capitals and for lower case letters with ascenders or descenders, and five dots high by five dots wide for lower case letters without ascenders or descenders. The additional dot spaces serve to create space between adjacent characters and between successive lines of characters.

On some receivers, the basic character set can be extended vertically to produce double height characters. Only 12 lines of such characters can be displayed on any one page.

2.3 Graphics

In the graphics mode, each of the 960 character positions is divided into six cells, as shown in Figure 21.2. It may be seen that the two central cells are slightly larger than the top and bottom cells. This is because each character position occupies 20 TV scan lines, and this number is not divisible by three. Any combination of these six cells can be displayed, and each cell will appear as a

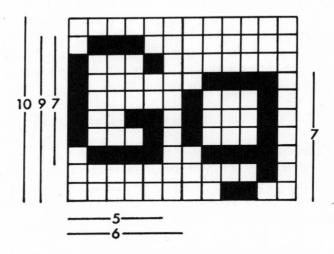

Figure 21.1. The alphanumeric character matrix.

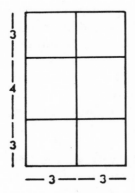

Figure 21.2. The graphics mode character matrix.

Figure 21.3. Alternative cell configurations in the graphics mode.

solid block of color. The variety of shapes which can be generated is illustrated in Figure 21.3. They can be used to construct character fonts for titling, for drawing simple graphs, charts, and diagrams, and for rules and decorative borders. A standard alphagraphics font is available from the editing keyboard, but other fonts can be devised at will.

2.4 Color

Both alphanumeric and graphics characters can be displayed in any one of seven colors. These are the three primary colors, red, blue, and green, the three complementaries, cyan, yellow, and magenta, plus white. Each of the three primary colors is produced by one of three separate electron guns. Each complementary color is obtained by mixing two of these primary color signals. Thus, cyan is a mixture of blue and green, yellow is a mixture of green and red, and magenta is a mixture of blue and red. White is a mixture of all three primaries.

Both kinds of characters can be displayed either on a black background or on a colored background. In the case of the graphics characters, this means that two different colors can be distributed at will among the six cells in each character position.

2.5 Flashing

Groups of characters can be made to flash on and off in order to attract attention.

3. Implications for Legibility and "Readability"

3.1 The Character Grid

The fixed nature of the character grid has a number of important implications.

First, the characters are uniformly spaced, regardless of their width; proportional spacing is not possible. This means that narrow letters, such as i and l, tend to become isolated. This is less than satisfactory from an aesthetic point of view, but it has not been shown that proportional spacing would significantly improve legibility.

The uneven texture which results from monospacing is more marked with lower case letters than with capitals, and for this reason it has been suggested that capitals may be preferable. There is no doubt, however, that capitals are less legible than lower case letters for continuous printed text[1]. This is because they are of uniform height and, therefore, they create less distinctive and less easily recognized word shapes than lower case letters with their ascenders and descenders. There is no reason to suppose that this argument does not also hold for teletext displays. Capital letters also tend to give large blocks of text a very solid and daunting appearance, whereas lower case letters appear to create more space between successive lines of text.

The second important implication of the fixed grid is that word spacing is also invariable, except in whole character units. This means that justification of the right-hand margin is very difficult to achieve without resorting to uneven word spacing or excessive hyphenation. The value of right-hand justification is questionable, however, and it should certainly not be achieved by the omission of punctuation or the use of non-standard abbreviations.

The third consequence of the grid is that line spacing can only be varied in units of a whole line. This means that space cannot be as freely used to separate information as it often is in printed materials, or the information content of each frame would be reduced to an unacceptably low level.

3.2 Standard Alphanumerics

The use of a dot matrix for character generation severely limits the possibilities for character design. Research on similar kinds of display suggests that a matrix of the size used for teletext is likely to give adequate legibility, though a larger matrix (in terms of the number of vertical and horizontal elements) would undoubtedly permit the design of more aesthetically pleasing characters and possibly of alternative fonts.

The exact configuration of some of the characters varies slightly according to the manufacturer of the receiver. There would appear to be no published data, however, on the relative legibility of these different shapes. Research on other kinds of electronic displays has suggested that as long as dot matrix characters are designed to look as much as possible like roman characters, it is almost inevitable that some of the characters will be confused with one another. Redesigning certain characters, however, can often result in a favorable redistribution and reduction of possible sources of confusion. The design of dot matrix characters for optimum legibility is not a simple matter, and it is important that manufacturers should be persuaded to draw upon the expertise of typographic designers in any future modifications to their character sets.

3.3 Graphics

The crude nature of the graphics mode presents problems in the design of both graphics alphabets for headings and diagrammatic or decorative devices. The fact that each character position is divided into only six cells means that it is impossible to represent diagonals and curves satisfactorily, and the unequal size of the cells is often very apparent.

In the case of graphics fonts in particular, it is extremely difficult to create acceptable shapes for letters, such as K and X, which contain diagonals. The expertise of the typographic designer is badly needed here, in order to obtain the best results possible under the circumstances.

A further difficulty with graphics fonts is the amount of space which they occupy. The alphagraphics font which is available direct from the editing keyboard occupies three lines, and allowing for a line space above and below, this means that a considerable proportion of the available information area is lost. What is needed, therefore, is a more sophisticated graphics mode, which would allow the design of acceptable fonts using less space.

3.4 Color

3.4.1 Definition and luminance. The method of color generation used has two important consequences. First, images in complementary colors or white will tend to be less sharp than images in primary colors. Colored rims around the symbols and an uneven internal distribution of color can often be seen, particularly if the color registration on the receiver is not perfectly adjusted. Second, the colors differ considerably in luminance. If white is regarded as having a luminance of 100%, then green has a luminance of 59%, red 30%, and blue 11%. Thus, yellow has a luminance of 89% (green plus red), cyan 70% (green plus blue), and magenta 41% (red plus blue). The contrast which these colors make with a dark background, therefore, varies considerably. In terms of luminance alone, white, yellow, cyan, and green, in that order, are likely to be the most legible colors, on a black background and magenta, red, and blue the least legible.

3.4.2 The sensitivity and acuity of the human eye. The relative legibility of the colors is also affected by the fact that the human eye is not equally sensitive to all wave lengths of light. When the eye is light adapted, as it normally would be when looking at teletext, it is maximally sensitive to wave lengths in the yellow/green area of the spectrum[2]. Yellow is only 90% as efficient a stimulus as green, orange 80%, and red only 6%. Blue in particular tends to have a lower subjective brightness than other colors, especially when viewed against a dark background[3].

The ability of the eye to resolve fine detail also varies with the wave length of light. Acuity is highest for white and green light. Our resolving power for red is only about one-third of that for white, and for blue it is only about one-fifth of that for white[2].

On the basis of these arguments, it would seem that green and white are likely to be the most legible colors for self-luminous displays such as teletext, and that red and blue should be avoided[4,5]. It must also be remembered that red and blue have the lowest luminance of the seven teletext colors.

3.4.3 Chromatic aberration. Yet another significant factor is the phenomenon of chromatic aberration. Different wave lengths are refracted by different amounts as they pass through the eye. This means that only one color at a time can be in focus on the retina. If yellow/green or white are in focus, then blue will be focused in front of the retina and red behind it. This not only results in blurred images for the out-of-focus colors, but it also causes differently colored images to appear to be in different planes. This effect can be seen very clearly when red and blue are used in close proximity on a teletext page, and it is visually disturbing. The same phenomenon also causes the red and blue components of magenta to appear to separate. Magenta, therefore, is not a good color for substantial amounts of data.

3.4.4 Color discrimination. If color is to be used in a meaningful way on teletext displays, it is essential that users should be able to discriminate between and identify each of the seven colors without difficulty. The colors presently in use should cause few problems in this respect, though high levels of ambient illumination may sometimes result in confusion occurring between white and cyan, and yellow and green.

3.4.5 Choice of colors for optimum legibility. The available evidence suggests, therefore, that for large quantities of information displayed on a dark screen, green is likely to be one of the most legible colors. This is because it is produced by a single electron gun and the image is sharp, it has adequate luminance, and it is one of the colors to which the eye is most sensitive and for which acuity is greatest. White, yellow, and cyan are also likely to be highly legible, provided that the color registration on the receiver is properly adjusted. Magenta is not recommended because of the tendency of its red and blue components to separate out visually. Red and blue are unsuitable because they have low luminance values, the eye is relatively insensitive to them, and the effects of chromatic aberration will result in blurred images.

Where background color is used, it is those combinations of color giving the strongest brightness contrast which are likely to be most legible, for example, red and white, blue and white, and blue and yellow. Pairs of colors which are close together in the luminance hierarchy, even if they are markedly different in hue, will give an illegible result. On the blue background of the page heading in Figure 21.4, for example, standard alphanumerics in white are clearly legible, but the title in red is much less so (obvious even in a black and white print). Background color is probably best avoided altogether for continuous text, but it can be acceptable with less densely packed information, and it is often very useful for headings. Labels on diagrams too will often appear against a background color.

4. Designing Teletext Pages

4.1 Conveying the Structure of the Information

Given the visual characteristics of the teletext system, how does one go about designing teletext pages? If the information is to be easily understood, its visual appearance must clearly reflect its logical structure and must take into account the ways in which it will be used.

In order to represent the structure of the information accurately, it is necessary to be able to visually emphasize, relate, and divide items within the display. Visual emphasis can be used to indicate the relative importance of items, and often several levels of emphasis will be needed as in the case of systems of headings and subheadings, paragraphs and subparagraphs. Visual ways of dividing and relating information can be used to indicate whether items of information are similar or different in kind, and whether or not they are functionally related to one another. These methods of "coding" the information will help the user to appreciate the logical structure of the display, to find relevant items of information quickly, and to see how they are related to one another.

163	CEEFAX 163 Thu 21 May		11.27/21

MEAT PRICES w/e May 16

	AVERAGE PRICE PER LB		
	This Week	Change	Range
BEEF			
Topside/Silverside	188	n/c	176-198
Sirloin Boneless	221	+ 1	190-254
Rump Steak	258	+ 1	228-286
Chuck/Blade	143	+ 1	128-156
Stewing Steak	123	+ 1	109-138
Best Mince	96	+ 1	82-110
LAMB			
Fillet end leg	165	+ 3	136-188
Loin chops	172	+ 2	140-199
Shoulder	110	+ 2	88-132
NZ leg	125	+ 2	110-139
PORK			
Fillet end leg	103	n/c	86-124
Loin chops	117	n/c	106-126
Hand and spring	63	+ 1	46- 78

Figure 21.4. The use of background color. For standard alphanumerics, it is important to use colors which contrast strongly in brightness. White on blue is legible, but red (e.g., the title "Meat Prices") is barely so. With page headings, however, the larger area occupied by the lettering helps to compensate for poor contrast (the page heading here is in red).

4.2 Typographic and Spatial Coding in Printed Materials

In printed materials, these visual distinctions would normally be made by means of typographic variations and spatial "coding."

Typographic variations would include devices such as changes in type size, style, or weight and the use of italics and possibly capitals. They would be used mostly for creating hierarchical systems of headings, the most visually dominant variations (such as large sizes and bold) being used for the most important headings. Typographic changes would also be used to emphasize or distinguish individual words or phrases in continuous text.

Hierarchies of emphasis can also be created by means of spatial coding, as in the case of headings and subheadings which are distinguished from one another by the amount of space above and below them, and paragraphs and subparagraphs which are distinguished by different levels of indentation. This form of coding is also frequently used to indicate similarities or differences in kind and the extent to which items are functionally related. Similar or related items can be grouped together and dissimilar or unrelated items separated by space. Rules can also be used to relate or divide information.

4.3 Typographic and Spatial Coding on Teletext Displays

The possibilities for typographic coding on teletext displays are very limited, as we have seen. Graphics fonts can be used for main headings, but these will occupy a considerable proportion of the information area. Double-height characters might be used instead, but apart from these, capitals are the only other alternative. However, capitals are not recommended for long headings or for emphasis in continuous text.

The possibilities for spatial coding are restricted, too, because of the inflexible character grid and the limited number of character positions on each frame. If space is used too generously, the information will be fragmented over an undesirably large number of frames. On the other hand, if the information is densely packed in order to use fewer frames and to give the user a better overview of the content, then the result may be daunting in appearance and difficult to understand. A suitable balance must be found.

4.4 Color Coding on Teletext Displays

These limitations of the teletext system are compensated for to some extent by the availability of color, which can be used in conjunction with spatial coding to emphasize, relate, and divide items of information.

It was argued in Section 3.4.5 that only four of the available seven colors are suitable for use in continuous text or other large blocks of data. These are white, yellow, cyan, and green. Magenta, red, and blue, if they are used at all, should be reserved for non-essential information and for decorative purposes where this is appropriate.

The number of colors used on any one frame should be kept to a minimum. Three is a realistic number, since this allows two colors for the information itself and a third color for a heading. Research has shown that if three or four colors are used in a target detection task on a CRT, items of the same color tend to form a gestalt and are easily distinguished from the rest of the display. If more colors are used, the information becomes too fragmented and the gestalt is lost[6].

The distribution of colors on each frame should be related to the structure of the information. Careless use of color can cause confusion, because the different luminances of the colors will make some items of information appear to be more important than others. Thus, a hierarchical relationship may be implied where none exists, or one which does exist may be misrepresented or not represented at all. Similarly, an illogical use of color can suggest a relationship or a similarity in kind between items which are not in fact related or similar.

Color can be used for emphasis in the same way that typographic variations would be used in print. Different levels of importance can be indicated by choosing a hierarchy of colors, just as one might use bold for main headings, italics for subheadings, and so on. Assuming that the brightest colors are visually the most dominant, then the order of importance would be white first, then yellow, cyan, and green, in that order. Thus, white or yellow might be used for headings, and cyan or green for text.

Color can also be used to distinguish between different kinds of information. If these do not differ in importance, then it is best to choose colors which are close together in the dominance hierarchy, for example, white and yellow or cyan and green.

The functional relationship between items of information can also be indicated by means of color in certain circumstances. In using tables, for example, it may be used to guide the eye horizontally from column to column.

5. Dealing with Different Kinds of Information

5.1 Text

It is important that each page of text should be self-contained. Although it is possible to present the user with a series of frames under one page number, the length of time for which each frame appears on the screen will not necessarily suit everyone's reading speed. Concentration will be broken, and this will be very disruptive unless the frame break corresponds with a logical break in the information.

For most purposes, a single column layout will be preferable for continuous text. The maximum line length of 40 characters is already shorter than the 50 or 60 characters which research has suggested is optimum for printed text[7]. Lines of fewer than 20 characters would result in a large number of word breaks and a considerable wastage of space.

It is not advisable to fill every frame to full capacity. It has been shown that printed text with a generous amount of space within it is rated as "easier" and more interesting than text which has a more solid appearance[8]. There is rarely any justification for omitting the conventional character space after punctuation marks in order to pack the information more densely. This is aesthetically displeasing, and can suggest non-existent relationships between adjacent words. Hyphenation should be kept to a minimum, and non-standard word breaks should certainly be avoided.

The evidence discussed in Section 4.4 suggests that cyan or green will be the most suitable colors for text, with white and yellow reserved for headings. If it is desirable to distinguish certain words within the text, in the same way as italics might be used in print, it is best to use a color as close as possible to the text color in the hierarchy. Too great a contrast may attract too much attention and interfere with the normal reading process. Thus, yellow might be used for emphasis in cyan text and cyan in green text. It is doubtful, however, whether this kind of cueing has any real value in terms of improved comprehension and memory[9], and using color in this way may make it difficult to limit the total number of colors on the page to three.

Ideally, paragraphs should be between three and six lines in length and should be separated by a line space (see Figure 21.5). This will prevent the text from forming a daunting, solid block. Indentation of the first line of each paragraph will be unnecessary if a line space is used. Similarly, there will be no need for a change of color simply to indicate that a new paragraph has begun. This may cause the user to look for significance in the change of color where there is none.

In some cases, it may be necessary to indicate a change of subject by placing headings between paragraphs. The most satisfactory solution is likely to be a heading in upper and lower case which is distinguished from the rest of the text by its color. The selected color should be more dominant than the text color but less dominant than the main heading. Ideally, each heading should be preceded by a line space.

Headings should be ranged left. The eye naturally swings back to the beginning of each line, and centered headings will disrupt the normal pattern of reading.

5.2 Tables

As a general rule, tables on teletext should be kept as simple as possible and only essential information should be given. It is important, however, that the information which is given should be as explicit as possible. Abbreviations are best used sparingly, and if a key is required, it must always be given on the same page as the abbreviated information.

The possibilities for the layout of tables are somewhat limited by the rigidity of the grid. Where users need to read across

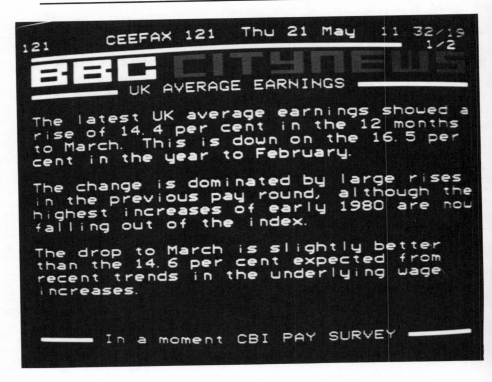

Figure 21.5. Short paragraphs separated by a line space are best for text.

between columns of information, the space between the columns should be just sufficient to separate them but no more. Unnecessary rules between columns will be distracting, tending to draw the eye down the columns instead of across them.

Color can be helpful in tables, but it should be used with great care. The choice of a different color for each column of information is not necessarily an advantage, since once again it will tend to draw the eye downwards instead of across. Where there is likely to be difficulty in reading across between columns, the use of two colors on alternate lines can sometimes be helpful in guiding the eye across the page. The two colors should be of similar luminance to avoid any suggestion of dominance.

5.3 Indexes and Lists

It is obviously important that the information available from the teletext system should be clearly indexed. Both Ceefax and Oracle have adopted a two-column layout for their main index pages, in order to fit in as much information as possible and thereby to give the user an overview of what is available (see, for example, Figure 21.6). Both have felt it necessary to resort to the use of leader dots to guide the eye to the correct page number. A possible alternative would be to place the page numbers to the left of the items. From research on printed information, there is no reason to think that placing the numbers first should cause any difficulty[10]. Alternatively, the page numbers might be given immediately after the items rather than ranged right. There is no virtue in placing the page numbers in a column, since the user is unlikely to want to compare the page numbers with one another. The use of a different color for the page number would be sufficient to distinguish it clearly from the text of the item itself. The problem of reading across to the correct page number is accentuated where the index occupies the whole width of the frame, as in Figure 21.7. This index would undoubtedly be easier to use if the page numbers were placed to the left of the item descriptions or if they followed immediately after them.

5.4 Graphics

5.4.1 Page headings. Information carried in the page heading will often be partially redundant, because the user has deliberately accessed the page and needs only a confirmation of its identity. On a tightly packed page, headings in space-consuming graphics fonts might be better replaced by double height characters, or even standard alphanumerics with background color. Where space permits, however, a bold, colorful heading can add interest to the page. If such headings are used, the lettering should ideally be professionally designed. It is all too easy to produce headings which are amateurish in appearance (Figure 21.7).

Figure 21.6. The Oracle "Front Page," or main index page.

5.4.2 *Logos and decorative devices.* As with page headings, these can add interest to the page, but they do need to be well designed. The Oracle logo in Figure 21.6 is a colorful and attractive logo. Care must be exercised in the positioning of logos. Decorations should never be allowed to occupy space which could otherwise be used to achieve a clearer display of the information itself.

5.4.3 *Graphs and charts.* Graphs and charts on teletext need to be kept very simple. Line graphs are difficult to produce satisfactorily because of the coarseness of the graphics matrix and

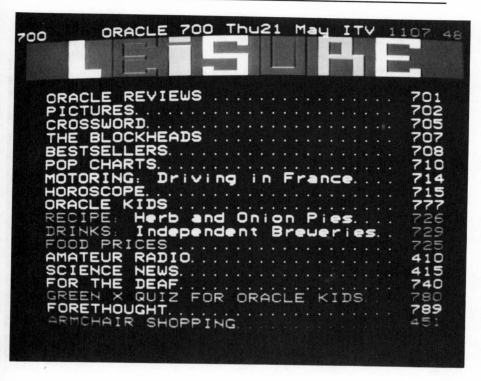

Figure 21.7. This index would be easier to use if the page numbers were placed to the right of the item descriptions or immediately following them. There is no apparent logic behind the use of color here (the latter nine entries are randomly in three different colors). The heading appears amateurish.

the unequal sizes of the cells. Color coding can be used to good effect if more than one line is necessary on a graph, but cross-over points are difficult to represent satisfactorily. Bar graphs, however, can be produced quite successfully (see Figure 21.8). Where the bars in a chart are made up of several variables, these can be color coded.

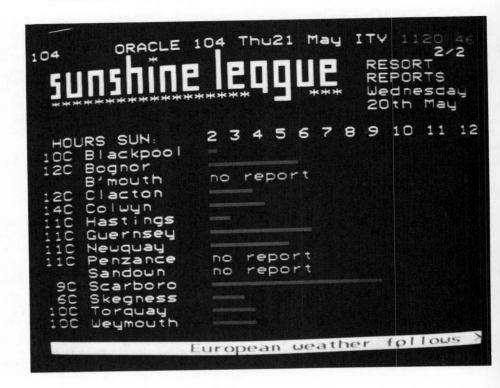

Figure 21.8. Simple bar graphs can be drawn quite successfully on teletext.

5.4.4 Diagrams. Satisfactory diagrams are difficult to achieve on teletext displays because of the problem of drawing diagonals and curves. Simple maps lend themselves reasonably well to the medium, however, because of their irregular outlines (see Figure 21.9).

6. Conclusions

The key to success in producing attractive and easily under-

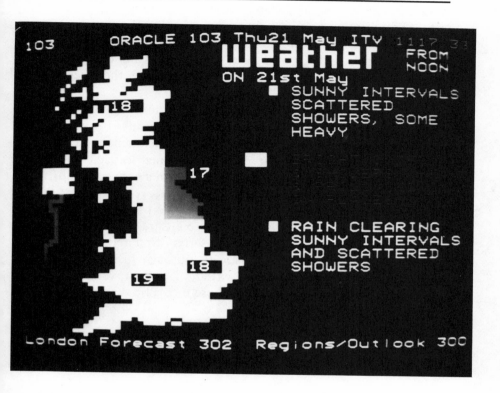

Figure 21.9. Simple maps are also possible. Care must be taken to insure that that the color of captions relates correctly to colored areas within the diagram.

standable teletext pages would seem to be the realization that this medium is very different from the printed word. It is necessary to approach the task of page design with an open mind in order to find ways of overcoming the limitations of the medium and at the same time making the best use of its potential. The problems are similar to those encountered in designing printed information in the sense that there is a need to find ways of relating, dividing, and emphasizing items of information, but the available means of doing this are somewhat different. Good page design requires skill and sensitivity, and it should rightly be in the hands of a professional designer. Unfortunately, it is sometimes the case—and this is particularly true of Prestel—that pages are designed by editorial or computer staff, who may not have the necessary degree of visual awareness.

There is no doubt, however, that the editor must work with the designer in order to produce a satisfactory result. Information cannot be transferred direct from a printed document to teletext or viewdata without extensive editing. The small capacity of the screen means that only essential information in a very simple form can be given, and sometimes it will be necessary to modify the content slightly in order to achieve a sensible page design. Much editorial work is also required in order to ensure that each page is complete in itself, even if it is part of a series of related frames.

The plea, then, is for a professional approach to the design of information for display on all teletext and viewdata systems. Only in this way can the full potential of these media be realized.

Notes

1. Tinker, M.A. *Legibility of print.* Ames: Iowa State University Press, 1963.
2. Graham, C.H. Discriminations that depend on wave lengths. In C.H. Graham (Ed.), *Vision and visual perception.* New York: John Wiley, 1965.
3. Ton, W.H. Optimal visual characteristics for large screen displays. *Information Display*, 1969, *6*(4), 48-52.
4. Barmack, J.E., & Sinaiko, H.W. *Human factors problems in computer generated graphic displays.* Arlington, VA: Institute for Defense Analysis, 1966.
5. Vanderkolk, R.J., & Herman, J.H. *Dot matrix display symbology study.* TRC Report T76-2172, July 1975.
6. Cahill, M.C., & Carter, R.C. Color code size for searching displays of different density. *Human Factors*, 1976, *18*(3), 273-280.
7. Spencer, H. *The visible word: Problems of legibility.* London: Lund Humphries, 1969.

8. Smith, J.M., & McCombs, M.E. The graphics of prose. *Journalism Quarterly,* 1971, *48,* 134-136.
9. Coles, P., & Foster, J. Typographic coding as an aid to learning from typewritten text. *Programmed Learning and Educational Technology,* 1975, *12,* 102-108.
10. Wright, P., & Fox, K. Presenting information in tables. *Applied Ergonomics,* 1970, *1,* 234-242.

Section Four:

Individual Differences
and Learning from Text

22.

Individual Differences
and Learning from Text

David H. Jonassen

1.0. Introduction

What makes an individual a good or poor reader—capable or incapable of comprehending the meaning of expository prose—is a function of general comprehension strategies and rapid, context-free word recognition (Stanovich, 1980). During reading, individuals decode words, assign meaning to them, and combine those meanings according to prior conceptions and relations. These processes are represented by a complex interaction of sub-processes, including feature extraction, orthographic (spelling), lexical (vocabulary), and syntactic knowledge, and semantic memory. The purpose of this chapter is to explore which of these processes produce individual differences in reading. Why are some individuals more capable of discourse comprehension than others? This last chapter is not meant as a comprehensive review of the research in each area (such an endeavor would require several volumes); rather, it is an overview (with exemplary research) of sources of individual differences in discourse comprehension. As an organizer, a flowchart illustrating the organization of the chapter is presented in Figure 22.1.

Comprehension of discourse involves the organization of meaning elements (propositions) derived from word combinations into coherent wholes and the ability to abstract the overall meaning of the text into gist (Kintsch & van Dijk, 1978). It is this abstraction of text that represents one's understanding of its meaning and allows one to recreate the discourse from memory. Gist is dependent upon the interpretation of the semantic

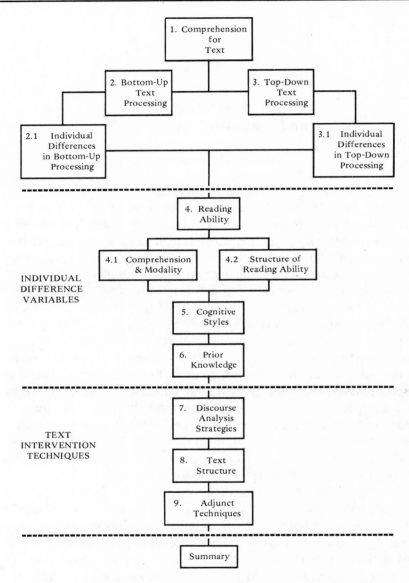

Figure 22.1. Flowchart illustrating chapter organization.

structure of a text passage. Individual differences in the sensitivity to the thematic or information structure of a passage and to sentence structure may be bases for differences in comprehension (Perfetti & Lesgold, 1977). Conflicting views regarding the source of individual differences focus on the relative roles of bottom-up versus top-down processing in comprehension.

2. Bottom-Up Processing

Bottom-up models of information processing suggest that meaning is constructed from the successive perception and encoding of lower level elements in discourse—such as words—and the subsequent combination of these smaller units into larger wholes. The most prominent of the bottom-up reading models is that of LaBerge and Samuels (1974). These models concentrate on the serial stages of the encoding process leading up to higher level processes. Their weakness is that they do not account for the empirical data that exist, because they contain no mechanism for allowing higher level processes to affect lower level processes (Stanovich, 1980).

2.1 Individual Differences in Bottom-Up Processing

Bottom-up models concentrate on the contributory role of the initial encoding process. The two major sources of individual differences involve short-term memory capacity and the speed of verbal coding (Perfetti & Lesgold, 1977). Verbal coding, the rapid recognition and assignment of meaning to words encountered in text (an essential process in discourse processing), is characteristic of better readers. As words are coded, they are transferred to the short-term memory buffer, where they are briefly retained. Short-term memory usually contains the contents of a short or moderate length sentence or phrase. As new words enter this buffer, prior words are lost unless they have somehow been recoded into long-term memory (Goldman, Hogaboam, Bell, & Perfetti, 1980). The amount of information that can be held in short-term (working) memory is a source of individual differences (Daneman & Carpenter, 1980; Kintsch & van Dijk, 1978), which in turn is a function of the efficiency of the verbal coding process

(Goldman *et al.*, 1980; Perfetti & Lesgold, 1977). The latter authors suggest overlearning (drill and practice) to overcome the deficits in word recognition that can overtax the limited short-term memory capacity of poor readers.

3. Top-Down Processing

Top-down models are dependent on higher level, semantic processing controlling the flow of information through lower level processes. According to these models, reading is seen as a process of hypothesis testing, not serial encoding. Readers begin with a belief or hypothesis and access text in order to verify that belief. The process is controlled by what Kintsch & van Dijk (1978) call macro-operators, which transform text-based propositions (meaning elements encountered in text) into sets of macro-propositions that represent the gist of the text (meaning elements in memory) by deleting or generalizing propositions irrelevant to their hypothesis and by inferring propositions when gaps exist in the text base.

Top-down models assume that the comprehension process is controlled by specific schemata and the meaning of the text, which is constructed as successive hypotheses are verified. This constructed meaning then aids in the identification of lower-order units, such as words. Top-down models contend that the reader's understanding of a passage is interpreted in terms of the structure of the passage as constructed from some combination of the reader's personal schemata and that provided by the author. Bottom-up readers are controlled by the individual units of the passage. It is a matter of *controlling the text presented* or of *being controlled by it.*

3.1 Individual Differences in Top-Down Processing

The most significant sources of individual differences in comprehension are those that show the effect of experience or background, *viz.*, prior knowledge (Perfetti & Lesgold, 1977). What one knows already will determine the relative difficulty of all lower level processes, such as verbal coding and working memory storage. Prior knowledge systems, as represented by an individual's personal schemata or knowledge structure, provide a framework of anchoring points for interpreting information presented in text (Anderson, Reynolds, Schallert, & Goetz, 1977). Individuals differ in knowledge as a function of age and social, cultural, and educational backgrounds. This variable will be considered in detail in a later section. Another possible variable affecting top-down processes is the ability and/or tendency to use the author's content structure. This issue will be more extensively addressed later.

3.2 Summary and Introduction to Difference Variables

As an alternative to either a strict bottom-up or top-down view of text comprehension, reading comprehension can be viewed as an interaction of top-down processing (those related to the overall thematic structure of text) and bottom-up processing (decoding, sentence comprehension, etc.). Individual differences can occur in any one of these processes. Poor readers tend to over-rely on either top-down or bottom-up processing, usually the latter (Spiro, 1979). This may result from the unavailability of appropriate knowledge schemata for interpreting text or from a number of skill related deficiencies. It is generally assumed that better discourse processors can switch. Given a deficit in one process, they can rely more on other knowledge sources or processes (Spiro, 1979; Stanovich, 1980). Rummelhart (1977) argues for the constant interaction of bottom-up and top-down processes based upon the simultaneous generation of hypotheses about both, related to difficulty of the text, prior knowledge structures in the reader, and so on.

The following review of these knowledge and skill components will include reading ability, cognitive styles and comprehension, and prior knowledge and comprehension as individual differences variables. The effects of intervention techniques, including the use of reading strategies, explicit text structuring, and text design on various types of readers, will be considered. The literature base in this area is surprisingly limited. Inevitably, the base will expand as the popularity of individual-difference research increases.

4. Reading Ability

Individual differences in reading ability affect text processing.

Such a declaration, on the surface, appears self-evident, even axiomatic. Everyone knows intuitively that good readers read better than poor readers! The purpose of myriad tests of reading ability is to establish just that fact. A review of all of those validation studies would only serve to verify the obvious. Recent research, however, has sought to *clarify* the concept of reading ability in terms of the processes entailed and their interaction with components of the text.

4.1 Comprehension and Modality

Comprehension, as stated earlier, is a process of organizing and condensing elements of the text presentation. The process is conceived to be essentially the same for written text or oral text, assimilated by reading or by listening. Differences in how individuals process both modes of text support this view. In a study by Samuels & Horowitz (1980), sixth graders were classified as good or poor readers on the basis of observations and reading tests. Varying the readability of textual material and the mode of presentation, the researchers found that on easy texts good readers (as expected) performed better on the reading task, while poor readers performed better than good readers when they *listened* to text. This latter advantage was not repeated for the harder text, although poor readers performed as well. These results supported a previous study that assessed sentence recognition ability where impulsive (a cognitive style) responders (and poorer readers) perform better under an auditory condition (Gray, Snowman, & Deichman, 1977). In another similar study, listening to stories produced better recall for good and poor readers. The good readers, however, were more sensitive to gradations of importance in the information presented (Smiley, Oakley, Worthen, Campione, & Brown, 1977). It appears that the extent of comprehension that is dependent upon successful decoding separates good from poor readers. Deficit-type poor comprehenders lack necessary vocabulary and decoding skills, as evidenced by their poor oral reading ability (Golinkoff, 1976). Poor readers are frequently able to understand the concepts; they are just not able to decode them. These studies suggest that listening and reading comprehension depend on the same basic conceptual processes (Smiley *et al.*, 1977); poor readers' difficulties may result primarily from deficient decoding ability. Most of the available research employed children. We would expect the same results with adult poor readers, since conceptual ability is developmental, so no deficit could be predicted for older listeners.

4.2 Structure of Reading Ability

As indicated in the first section of this chapter, a prevalent issue in this area is whether individual differences result from a preference for bottom-up or top-down processing. Do readers impose their own knowledge structures on the text, or do they employ the author's structure to control their text comprehension processes? Conflicting evidence has been presented. Good comprehenders, concluded Golinkoff (1976), in a major review of the literature, "use. . .a scan-for-meaning pattern" of "reading as a process through which to gain information about events and relations in the world" (p. 654). This clearly suggests a top-down preference. High ninth grade comprehenders, as measured by the Stanford Achievement Test, used the author's schema for organizing their responses in a free recall situation, whereas low comprehenders did not (Meyer, 1975; Meyer, Brandt, & Bluth, 1978), also indicating top-down processing. A subsequent regression analysis indicated that use of the author's top level structure was the best predictor of recall, that is, those who use the author's schema recall more. Using similar passages and the same method for analyzing recall protocols, Dunn, Mathews, & Biegen (1979) found that better readers recalled more subordinate information from the passage. Information high in the content structure of a passage contains the macro-operators that control top-down processes. Superior readers were less sensitive to the author's schema than lower ability readers; however, no readers consistently represented the author's content structure in their own memory structures, as Meyer had found. Dunn concluded that the data suggested developmental differences in comprehension and semantic recall. Does this also indicate a developmental trend toward top-down preference? It is clear that additional research is needed to clarify this important issue.

4.3 Implications

Where reading ability is a problem and learning is critical, audiotape your texts and make the tapes readily available. More research on text-based structure needs to be done before definitive prescriptions can be made. Generally, the structure of a passage should be made as explicit as possible, especially for lower ability readers. There is some indication that it may help low comprehenders who normally do use an author's structure (Meyer, Brandt, & Bluth, 1978).

5. Cognitive Styles and Comprehension

The preeminence of mental ability as a predictor of learning has generated some useful prescriptions for instructional designers (Allen, 1975). Mental ability, however, can be a conceptually amorphous entity—the G factor—signaling its *generality* as a measure of ability or processing. Factor analytic studies (Guilford, 1967; Sternberg, 1977, 1978) have done much to isolate the components of intelligence, however. In order to understand more specifically how certain cognitive processes differ in learners as a function of the processing demands of the task, researchers have considered the roles of cognitive styles and cognitive controls in learning. Cognitive styles represent stable, perceptual traits that affect how perceivers differentiate stimuli in various tasks. Cognitive controls are grounded in the psychoanalytic control of various cognitive, perceptual, and psychomotor processing tasks. Three decades of research in cognitive styles/controls have identified numerous traits, the instructional design implications of which have only recently been considered. For a review of these styles and their implications, see Ausburn and Ausburn (1978) and Jonassen (1979).

5.1 Cognitive Styles and the Reading Process

Cognitive styles as indicators of individual differences in discourse comprehension are predicated on matching the processing requirements of the reading task with those measured by the cognitive style. If a cognitive task analysis of the style matches that of the reading (or any other) task, the style can be used as a valid predictor of reading performance or as a diagnostic tool for educators. Salomon (1972) suggests three major types of instructional matches—*remediation* of learner's deficiencies, *compensation* for deficiencies by modeling cognitive behavior, and *preference* or *capitalization* on learner strengths. The matching of instructional task requirements to specified individual differences has evolved into a model of instruction (Messick, 1976). This matching process can be applied to comprehension of text materials. Crandell (1979) identified five educational cognitive style types based on preference for discourse and pictures in a segmented or composite form. Text forms were designed to match these styles and teach a psychomotor skill. The hypothesis that performance would improve as a function of the closeness of the match was weakly supported. Other results with other media and tasks have tended to substantiate this finding, with stronger support for the principle of matching (Salomon, 1979).

5.1.1 Field Dependence/Independence. The most prominent and extensively researched cognitive style is field dependence/independence, the tendency of the perceiver to be influenced by a prevailing background or context in which information is embedded. Based on the work of Witkin (1949), the style identifies field dependents as learners who cannot separate information from its surrounding context, or internally organize or structure that information. They do not function well independently and generally lack initiative. Field independents, on the other hand, analyze and differentiate components of any stimulus array, organizing and structuring it according to the requirements of the task. They are more active in dealing with their environment, more organized, and more assertive. Differences between field dependents and independents have been established for problem solving and concept tasks, sociability, self-perception, career choices, and others (Witkin *et al.,* 1977). The test most frequently employed to measure an individual's degree of independence is the Embedded Figures Test (Jackson, Messick, & Meyers, 1964), which assesses a broader dimension of cognitive functioning—articulated (analytic)/global dimension—that is an accepted measure of field independence.

Field independence has been more frequently related to reading performance than any other cognitive style. Significant correlations between reading scores and field independence in younger children have been found (Cohn, 1968; Watson, 1969; Wineman, 1971). While these studies are only correlative, they do establish a link between field independence and reading ability (Blanton & Bullock, 1973). When IQ is controlled, this relationship dissolves (Daku, 1977). Using extreme groups, Daku concluded that the Embedded Figures Test is a better indicator of intelligence than reading ability. Other research corroborates this conclusion in younger children.

Studies with adult undergraduates tend to produce clearer results. Annis (1979) reasoned that if field independents are better able to analyze organized material and to structure unorganized material, they should be more likely to remember and pick out material of high structural importance from either a structured or unstructured passage (reading or taking notes). This is exactly what she found—independents actively abstracted general principles from the passage, regardless of learning conditions. Dunn (1980) found that as text organization increases, analytics (field independents) recalled more superordinate information. Field independents have also been hypothesized to impose their own memory structure on passage structure (Spiro & Tirre, 1979). In reading an ambiguous passage, field independents scored better on the interpretation that employed their own knowledge rather than that supplied by the text, while field dependents scored equally low on both interpretations. It appears that field independents actively construct their understanding of a passage by employing their own knowledge structures.

5.1.2 Impulsivity/Reflectivity. A person's cognitive tempo describes his or her ability to inhibit initial responses and reflect on their accuracy, rather than responding impulsively, especially when he or she is uncertain about the response. Impulsives' need for quick success usually results in a higher error rate, while reflectives commit fewer mistakes. This style is measured most frequently by scores on the Matching Familiar Figures Text (Kagen, 1965). Researchers, such as Kiraisic & Sigel (1975), have contended that cognitive tempo is based solely on visual processing. When a sentence recognition task was presented visually and auditorially, reflectives did perform better under the visual presentation (Gray, Showman, & Deichman, 1977). Reflectivity, it appears, tends to be a visually oriented style.

Impulsives would be expected to have problems with reading comprehension and possibly with decoding. As King (1972) found, impulsivity can be expected to exert more influence during initial stages of reading. Reflectives are more accurate in recognizing words (Kagen, 1965), in reading for detail (Smith, 1974), and in critical reading (Lesiak, 1970) than impulsives. All of these results occurred among elementary school children. A developmental trend toward reflectivity (Kagen, 1965) would make cognitive tempo a more inappropriate concern with adult learners. Discourse elements of text, such as adjunct questions, might be expected to overcome impulsivity/reflection by forcing; however, they do not interact with impulsivity/reflectivity (Keller, 1975). To summarize, in terms of the reading process, impulsives tend to be less flexible in their processing approach, spending less time analyzing and decoding information (Gray, Snowman, & Deichman, 1977).

5.1.3 Leveling/Sharpening. A variety of other styles/controls have been related to the reading process. The best known of these is leveling/sharpening, a cognitive control that relates to the discreteness of memory traces retained by individuals. Levelers tend to blur memories together, especially those with similar characteristics, while sharpeners maintain the discrete identity of separate traces. Gardner and Lohrenz (1960) found that in retelling a story, levelers lose more themes and overall structure as well as details, producing inferior recall to sharpeners. Leveling/sharpening should be more related to comprehension skills than to the decoding process, although no evidence is available to support this.

5.2 Summary

The research relating cognitive styles/controls to reading processes is inconclusive. The limited volume of research has not consistently accounted for large portions of the variance in reading or text related performance. The most conceptually and empirically congruous results relate to the effects of field dependence/independence on discourse comprehension in adults and reflectivity/impulsivity on decoding by children. Field independents tend to impose more structure on the text (reading as a schema-related process) than do field dependents. Reflective children possess better word attack skills, so they tend to commit fewer mistakes. Numerous other cognitive and personality styles, including extraversion, achievement motivation, social desirability, dogmatism, locus of control, and others, have failed to interact with various reading processes. As Farley and Truog (1970) have suggested, individual sources of variance and reading comprehension may be difficult to find. The most potentially fruitful source of individual differences, prior knowledge, is presented next.

6. Prior Knowledge and Comprehension

One of the most important foci of comprehension research is on the interaction of the reader's prior knowledge with the content presented in the passage. Exemplary studies are presented below. The general belief is that prior knowledge is a principal determinant of what can be learned from text (Garner, 1979). Whether the prior knowledge is conceived of as top-down processing using personal schemata (Rummelhart & Ortony, 1977) or application of "world knowledge" (Bransford & Johnson, 1972), the importance of the role of the knowledge that the reader brings to the text cannot be denied. Each individual brings his or her own prior knowledge system to interact with the language cues in the text (Garner, 1979). This belief favors a top-down conception of text comprehension, employing personal knowledge structures, rather than the author's top-level structure. The traditional left-to-right, bottom-up (perception-to-comprehension) process of reading is not possible (Anderson, Reynolds, Schallert, & Goetz, 1977).

6.1 Research

"Every act of comprehension involves one's knowledge of the world" in addition, of course, to linguistic ability (Anderson *et al.*, 1977, p. 369). That knowledge provides the schemata which the reader uses to interpret text. The researchers hypothesized that individuals with different world knowledge will interpret text differently. Given two passages with intentionally ambiguous interpretations, physical education and music majors answered questions and recalled information in a manner consistent with their backgrounds. Each gave interpretations to the passages (disambiguation) related to his or her background. In fact, most of the students were totally unaware of any alternative interpretations. High level schemata cause people to "see" messages in certain ways, according to the authors.

In another study (Anderson, Spiro, & Anderson, 1978), the use of high level schemata for accommodating specific information in a passage was tested. The researchers reasoned that when a schema was present for fitting information into, retention would improve. Given passages containing the same information but in alternative settings (supermarket or restaurant), they hypothesized that since restaurant schemata are more consistent across readers, it would impose more structure on comprehension, resulting in greater recall and more consistent classification of items with those schemata. The stronger the schema available, the more items that were in fact recalled and correctly classified. The authors concluded that high level schemata provide "ideational scaffolding" (a term borrowed from Ausubel; see chapter on Advance Organizers) for textual information. High level schemata provide "slots" into which certain textual information fits.

6.2 Summary

"From the perspective of schema theory, the principal determinant of the knowledge a person can acquire from reading is the knowledge he or she already possesses. The schemata by which people attempt to assimilate text will surely vary according to age, subculture, experience, education, interests, and belief systems" (Anderson, Reynolds, Schallert, & Goetz, 1977, p. 378). The most replicable individual differences in comprehension of discourse are probably represented by prior knowledge systems.

6.3 Implications

Text writers and designers cannot assume that all readers will be able to make sense out of their discourse. It will depend largely upon available prior knowledge systems. Instructional designers in general need to be more sensitive to prior knowledge as a learner characteristic. Being aware of what schemata are available in the knowledge structures of the reader will help text writers use appropriate generalities and instances. This represents a very demanding order. Some possible solutions include incorporating pretests in a text to assess prior knowledge structures with subsequent branching to analogous information. The use of advance organizers or other "bridge builders" to help construct adequate prior knowledge structures is another idea. Designer, *know what your reader knows before writing. What you cannot assume the reader knows, you will have to provide.*

7. Individual Differences and Discourse Analysis Strategies

An important, but largely unplanned, outcome of schooling is learning to learn, that is, employing learned strategies in the solution of non-school learning problems. Knowledge that a procedure or set of procedures applies to some particular problem defines a strategy (Perfetti & Lesgold, 1977). Such strategies are normally automatically applied and can be substituted by new ones when taught. Strategies logically play an important role in learning from text, both in recall of text and in accessing information from text (see Waller's discussion of access structures). Commonly studied recall strategies include rehearsal (repetition requiring no understanding), categorization (using inherent organization), and elaboration (imposing individual interpretations), all of which can be trained (Brown, Campione, & Day, 1981). Although developmental differences were noted, little research relating individual differences and reading strategies is available. Levin (1971) recognized that we need to manipulate materials so they fit the strategies employed by certain types of readers (e.g., poor readers) or manipulate the strategies they employ to fit the materials. To date, we are convinced only that poor readers perform better when they listen and when the organization of textual materials is made more obvious (see previous sections). Since better readers are better informed, they are better able to relate new material to prior knowledge as well as select appropriate text processing strategies.

7.1 Mathemagenics

The mathemagenic literature (see Introduction to Explicit Techniques section) offers limited evidence of individual differences related to text processing strategies. Although poor readers benefit from listening, notetaking during listening becomes detrimental to their learning (Peters, 1972). Low ability learners (not necessarily poor readers) have benefited from notetaking where the learning task requires transfer skills (Peper & Mayer, 1978). However, no benefit seems to occur for simple recall tasks (Berliner, 1977). The mental demands of taking notes seem to detract attention from message decoding and semantic memory processes, unless the pace of presentation is very slow or time for notetaking is allowed.

The largest body of mathemagenic literature focuses on the effects of inserted questions in prose passages. It would seem reasonable to expect that such questions would benefit low ability learners, who generally possess inadequate reading and study skills. Rothkopf (1972) in fact found that low ability learners benefited more from inserted questions than other groups. Sanders (1973), on the other hand, found that lower ability learners did not benefit from inserted questions. A similar lack of aptitude by treatment interaction occurred when several cognitive styles were related to adjunct question inclusion (Hiller, 1974). It may depend on the type of questions and the mental activity stimulated by them. Low vocabulary learners did better without questions of any type. This type of reflective, integrative process is evidently one that lower ability readers do not normally conduct.

7.2 Summary

The literature on individual differences as they relate to processing strategies is inconclusive. It generally suggests that poorer readers need to invest a greater proportion of their attention to the comprehension of vocabulary and related syntactic processes, and that semantic processes are also easily distracted. Successful strategies or intervention techniques would break down the discourse into bite-sized chunks before requiring the poor reader to engage in additional processing, as confirmed by the programmed instruction literature. More research is needed to identify the parameters of these effects.

8. Text Structure and Individual Comprehension

The importance of the structure of content to the comprehension of a passage is undeniable. The issue, already explicated, is whether and when readers employ their own knowledge structures or use the author's textual schemata. Are readers merely verifying their own conceptual schemata in comprehending a passage (Rummelhart, 1977), or are they using the author's? Efforts at making the content structure more explicit suggest that individual differences are involved.

Content structures of discourse are conceived by most theorists to be hierarchical, consisting of a top level structure, macro-propositions (main ideas), and micro-propositions (specific ideas or facts) (Meyer, 1980). The top level structure includes rhetorical relationships that tie the propositions together hierarchically, i.e., interrelate sentences. Ideas located at the top levels of the content structure are generally recalled and retained better than ideas low in the structure, although this is affected by the type of relationships that occur (Meyer, 1975, 1977). Conflicting results (better readers recalling more at subordinate levels in the content structure) have been reported (Dunn, Mathews, & Beigen, 1979; Howell, 1980). Individual differences in age and verbal ability affect the ability of readers to use these relationships (Meyer, 1980). High verbal adults perform better on passages that contrast propositions rather than merely describing them. Low verbal, older adults have difficulty using all of these relationships but perform better on descriptive passages (listing attributes). It is generally believed that more capable comprehenders concentrate on the superordinate level of text, integrating that information into their own knowledge structures more readily.

Meyer (1975) developed the idea of *signaling* these rhetorical relationships. Signaling is non-content prose that explicitly points out the structure of content, i.e., the relationships between propositions presented in the prose. The effects of signaling on prose comprehension interact with individual differences. Low and average comprehenders benefited from the lack of signaling on the delayed retention test (Meyer, Brandt, & Bluth, 1978). The author's explicit statement of top level structure does not affect good comprehenders who are better able to abstract this information from text. While signaling produced superior immediate recall, the effect disappeared after a week. Meyer and her associates concluded that most learners do not use the author's textual schema. Those who do generally recall more, since the information is more consistent with the text structure.

9. Adjunct Techniques

The second section of this book explored explicit means of displaying text structure and meaning. These depended upon adjunct materials supplementing the discourse (e.g., diagrams, tables, flowcharts, etc.). Because most of these techniques are relatively new or even exploratory, little research on how they interact with individual differences is available. A few findings are presented below:

Adjunct Maps. The use of maps as visual advance organizers was investigated by Dean & Kulhavy (1979). When forced to attend to a relevant map prior to reading a passage, low vocabulary readers improved their performance while high vocabulary subjects did not. Constructing a spatial representation directs attention to graphic schema and aids assimilation of unfamiliar material.

Diagrams. Low verbal learners, when presented with picture-word or block-word diagrams, retained more from the former. They have more difficulty learning from more verbally-dependent materials, such as the block-word diagram (Holliday, Brunner, & Donais, 1977).

Analogies. When studying technical information, the effects of adjunct verbal analogies was assessed. These were found to benefit high verbal, low quantitative learners while decreasing the performance of high quantitative, low verbal learners (Bell & Gagne, 1980). Research relating individual differences to adjunct techniques is isolated and inconsistent. Without additional research, it would be premature to draw any meaningful conclusions.

Chapter Summary

A major determinant of individual differences is the ability of readers to apply prior knowledge structures as a context for comprehending discourse. The application of top-down processes cannot occur without strengths in front-end linguistic processes. Extracting meaning from text begins with word recognition and parsing, using the syntactic structure of sentences as a context for relating the words in it. Successful comprehension depends on the interaction of the schematic and syntactic processes. In proposing an interactive compensatory model of discourse processing, Stanovich (1980) concludes that good readers use these structural processes to monitor comprehension. That is the major distinction between good and poor readers. Cognitive monitoring (Flavell, 1981)—individual awareness of our own cognitive processing capabilities, and the application of cognitive strategies using the former as feedback—is all part of a new and important area of research—"metacognition." It would probably be reasonable to hypothesize that individual differences in reading and metacognitive capabilities such as cognitive monitoring are highly related. Those who are very capable of comprehending discourse are probably better at monitoring their comprehension. Recent evidence suggests that older students show more evidence of monitoring than younger students (Pace, 1980); similar differences are likely to exist among better and poorer same-aged readers. Better methods of assessing such internal processes are needed in order to gain more understanding of the role of such abilities in comprehension.

References

Allen, W.H. Intellectual abilities and instructional media. *AV Communication Review*, 1975, *23*, 139-170.

Anderson, R.C., Reynolds, R.E., Schallert, D.C., & Goetz, E.T. Frameworks for comprehending discourse. *American Educational Research Journal*, 1977, *14*, 367-381.

Anderson, R.C., Spiro, R., & Anderson, M.C. Schemata as scaffolding for the representation of information in connected discourse. *American Educational Research Journal*, 1978, *15*, 433-440.

Annis, L. *The effect of cognitive style and learning passage organization of study technique effectiveness.* Paper presented at the Annual Meeting of the American Educational Research Association, San Francisco, April 8-12, 1979.

Ausburn, L.J., & Ausburn, F.B. Cognitive styles: Some information and implications for instructional design. *Educational Communications & Technology Journal,* 1978, *26,* 337-354.

Bell, M.S., & Gagne, E.D. Individual differences and the use of analogies in technical text. *Resources in Education,* 1980, *15*(7), p. 177 (ED 183 617).

Berliner, D.C. *The generalizability of aptitude-treatment interactions across subject matter.* Paper presented at the Annual Meeting of the American Educational Research Association, Chicago, April 1977.

Blanton, W.E., & Bullock, T. Cognitive style and reading behavior. *Reading World,* 1973, *12,* 276-287.

Brown, A.L., Campione, J.C., & Day, J.D. Learning to learn: On training students to learn from texts. *Educational Researcher,* 1981, (2), 14-21.

Bransford, J.D., & Johnson, M.K. Contextual prerequisites for understanding: Some investigations on comprehension and recall. *Journal of Verbal Learning & Verbal Behavior,* 1972, *11,* 717-726.

Cohn, M.L. Field dependence-independence and reading comprehension. Unpublished doctoral dissertation, New York University, 1968.

Crandell, T.L. The effects of educational cognitive style and media format on reading procedural instructions in picture-text analgrams (unpublished doctoral dissertation, Cornell University). *Dissertation Abstracts International,* 1979, *40A,* 3195.

Daku, J.J. The relationship between field dependence/field independence and reading achievement at the sixth grade. Unpublished master's thesis, Rutgers University, 1977 (ED 149 288).

Daneman, M., & Carpenter, P.A. Individual differences in working memory and reading. *Journal of Verbal Learning and Verbal Behavior,* 1980, *19,* 450-466.

Dean, R.S., & Kulhavy, R.W. *The influences of spatial organization in prose learning.* Paper presented at the Annual Meeting of the American Educational Research Association, San Francisco, April 8-12, 1979.

Dunn, B.R. *Individual differences in semantic recall from text.* Paper presented at the Annual Meeting of the American Educational Research Association, Boston, April 7-11, 1980 (ED 189 133).

Dunn, B.R., Mathews, S., & Beigen, G. Individual differences in the recall of lower level textual information (Tech. Report No. 150). Urbana, IL: University of Illinois, Center for the Study of Reading, 1979 (ED 181 448).

Farley, F.H., & Truog, A.L. Individual differences in reading comprehension. *Journal of Reading Behavior,* 1970, *3*(1), 29-35.

Flavell, J.H. Cognitive monitoring. In W.P. Dickson (Ed.), *Children's oral communication skills.* New York: Academic Press, 1981.

Gardner, R.W., & Lohrenz, L.J. Leveling-sharpening and serial reproduction of a story. *Meninger Clinic Bulletin,* 1960, 23-4, 295-304.

Garner, R. *The importance of cognitive styles research for understanding the reading process.* Paper presented at the Annual Meeting of the American Educational Research Association, San Francisco, April 8-12, 1979 (ED 172 148).

Goldman, S.R., Hogaboam, T.W., Bell, L.C., & Perfetti, C.A. Short-term retention of discourse during reading. *Journal of Educational Psychology,* 1980, *72,* 647-655.

Golinkoff, R.M. A comparison of reading comprehension processes in good and poor readers. *Reading Research Quarterly,* 1976, *11,* 623-659.

Gray, L.R., Snowman, J., & Deichman, J. *The effect of stimulus presentation mode and cognitive style on sentence recognition memory.* Paper presented at the Annual Meeting of the American Educational Research Association, New York, April 1977 (ED 142 966).

Guilford, J.P. *The nature of human intelligence.* New York: McGraw-Hill, 1967.

Hiller, J.H. Learning from prose text: Effects of readability level, inserted question difficulty, and individual differences. *Journal of Educational Psychology,* 1974, *66,* 202-241.

Holliday, W.G., Brunner, L.C., & Donais, E.L. Differential cognitive and affective responses to flow diagrams. *Journal of Research in Science Teaching,* 1977, *14,* 129-138.

Howell, W.L. Expository prose recall by young hospitalized schizophrenics. Unpublished doctoral dissertation, Florida State University, 1980.

Jackson, D.N., Messick, S., & Meyers, C.T. Evaluation of group and individual forms of embedded figures, measures of field-dependence. *Educational and Psychological Measurement,* 1964, *24,* 177-192.

Jonassen, D.H. Cognitive styles/controls and media. *Educational Technology,* 1979, *19*(6), 28-32.

Kagen, J. Reflection-impulsivity and reacting ability in primary grade children. *Child Development,* 1965, *35,* 609-678.

Kagen, J. Developmental studies. In A. Kidd & J. Rivoire (Eds.), *Perceptual and conceptual development in children.* New York: International Universities Press, 1966.

Keller, D.F. The effect of individual differences among elementary age children upon learning from text with interspersed questions (unpublished doctoral dissertation, Indiana University). *Dissertation Abstracts International,* 1975, *35*(A), 5926.

King, I.B. An experimental investigation of the potential of reflection-impulsivity as a determinant of success in early reading achievement. Unpublished doctoral dissertation, Boston College, 1972.

Kintsch, W., & van Dijk, T.A. Toward a model of text comprehension and production. *Psychological Review,* 1978, *85,* 363-394.

Kiraisic, K.C., & Sigel, A.W. Recognition memory for pictures: Evidence for a feature-analytic basis of cognitive styles. *Bulletin of the Psychonomic Science,* 1975, *6,* 453-456.

LaBerge, D., & Samuels, S.J. Toward a theory of automatic information processing in reading. *Cognitive Psychology*, 1974, *6*, 293-323.

Lesiak, J.F. The relationship of the reflection-impulsivity dimension and the reading ability of elementary school children at two grade levels. Unpublished doctoral dissertation, Ohio State University, 1970.

Levin, J.R. Some thoughts about cognitive strategies and reading comprehension (Theoretical Paper No. 30). Madison: University of Wisconsin, Research and Development Center for Cognitive Learning, 1971 (ED 064 692).

Messick, S. Personal styles and educational options. In S. Messick & Associates (Eds.), *Individuality in learning*. San Francisco, CA: Jossey-Bass, 1976.

Meyer, B.J.F. The structure of prose: Effects on learning and memory and implications for educational practice. In R.C. Anderson, R.J. Spiro, & W.E. Montague (Eds.), *Schooling and the acquisition of knowledge*. Hillsdale, NJ: Erlbaum Associates, 1977.

Meyer, B.J.F. *Text structure and its use in the study of reading comprehension across the adult life span.* Paper presented at the Annual Meeting of the American Educational Research Association, Boston, April 7-11, 1980 (ED 184 110).

Meyer, B.J.F., Brandt, D.M., & Bluth, G.J. *Use of authors' textual schema: Key for ninth graders' comprehension.* Paper presented at the Annual Meeting of the American Educational Research Association, Toronto, Canada, March 1978 (ED 151 771).

Pace, A.J. *The ability of young children to correct comprehension errors: An aspect of comprehension monitoring.* Paper presented at the Annual Meeting of the American Educational Research Association, Boston, MA, April 1980.

Peper, R.J., & Mayer, R.E. Notetaking as a generative activity. *Journal of Educational Psychology*, 1978, *70*, 514-522.

Perfetti, C.A., & Lesgold, A.M. Discourse comprehension and sources of individual differences. In M. Just & P. Carpenter (Eds.), *Cognitive processes in comprehension*. Hillsdale, NJ: Erlbaum Associates, 1977.

Peters, P.L. Effects of note-taking and rate of presentation on short-term objective test performance. *Journal of Educational Psychology*, 1972, *63*, 276-280.

Rothkopf, E.Z. Variable adjunct question schedules, interpersonal interaction, and incidental learning from written material. *Journal of Educational Psychology*, 1972, *63*, 87-92.

Rummelhart, D.E. Toward an interactive model of reading. In S. Dornic (Ed.), *Attention and performance* (Vol. VI). Hillsdale, NJ: Erlbaum Associates, 1977.

Rummelhart, D.E., & Ortony, A. The representation of knowledge in memory. In R.C. Anderson, R.J. Spiro, & W.E. Montague (Eds.),

Schooling and the acquisition of knowledge. Hillsdale, NJ: Erlbaum Associates, 1977.

Salomon, G. Heuristic models for the generation of aptitude-treatment interaction hypotheses. *Review of Educational Research,* 1972, *42,* 327-343.

Salomon, G. *Interaction of media, cognition, and learning.* San Francisco, CA: Jossey-Bass, 1979.

Samuels, S.J., & Horowitz, R. *Good and poor reader recall of oral and written expository discourse at two levels of difficulty.* Paper presented at the Annual Meeting of the American Educational Research Association, Boston, MA, April 8, 1980 (ED 188 138).

Sanders, J.R. Retention effects of adjunct questions in written and aural discourse. *Journal of Educational Psychology,* 1973, *65,* 181-186.

Shavelson, R.J., Berliner, D.C., Ravitch, M.M., & Leoding, D. Effects of position and type of questions on learning from prose material. Interaction of treatments with individual differences. *Journal of Educational Psychology,* 1974, *66,* 40-48.

Smiley, S.S., Oakley, D.D., Worthen, D., Canpione, J.C., & Brown, A.C. Recall of thematically relevant material by adolescent good and poor readers as a function of written versus oral presentation. *Journal of Educational Psychology,* 1977, *69,* 381-387.

Smith, K.M. The influence of cognitive style and intelligence variables in aided reading comprehension (unpublished doctoral dissertation, University of Wisconsin). *Dissertation Abstracts International,* 1974, *34*(A), 6466.

Spiro, R.J. Etiology of reading comprehension style (Technical Report No. 124). Urbana: University of Illinois, Center for the Study of Reading, 1979 (ED 170 734).

Spiro, R.J., & Tirre, W.C. Individual differences in schema utilization during discourse processing (Tech. Rep. No. 111). Urbana, IL: University of Illinois, Center for the Study of Reading, 1979 (ED 166 651).

Stanovich, K.E. Toward an interactive-compensatory model of individual differences on the development of reading fluency. *Reading Research Quarterly,* 1980, 32-71.

Sternberg, R.J. *Intelligence, information processing, and analogical reasoning.* Hillsdale, NJ: Lawrence Erlbaum Associates, 1977.

Sternberg, R.J. *Toward a unified componential theory of human reasoning,* Tech. Rep. No. 4. New Haven, CT: Department of Psychology, Yale University, 1978 (ED 154 421).

Watson, B.L. Field dependence and early reading achievement. Unpublished doctoral dissertation, University of California, Los Angeles, 1969.

Wineman, J.H. Cognitive style and reading ability. *California Journal of Educational Research,* 1971, *22,* 74-79.

Witkin, H.A. Perception of body position and of the position of the visual field. *Psychological Monographs,* 1949, *63*(1), Whole No. 302.

Witkin, H.A., Moore, C.A., Goodenough, D.R., & Cox, P.W. Field-dependent and field-independent cognitive styles and their educational implications. *Review of Educational Research*, 1977, *47*, 1-64.

Index

Access function, 162, 183, 350-351
(*see also* access structures)
Access structures, 134, 144-150, 180
Access to detail—structured writing, 351
Accessing text, 133
Active structural network, 6
Adjunct maps, 457
Adjunct questions, 130, 178, 455
(*see also* mathemagenic behaviors)
    related to cognitive styles, 455
Adjunct techniques—comprehension, 457
Advance organizers, 132, 183, 253-275
    assimilation theory, 265
    characteristics, 258
    classes of, 259-260
    conclusions from research, 263
    criticisms, 264
    definition, 258
    examples, 260
    formats of, 273
    forms of, 272
    functions of, 258
    non-examples, 261
    original research, 262
    research results, 262-264
    transfer of learning, 265
    utilization of, 268

    writing of, 268-273
        defining types, 268
        procedure for writing comparative organizers, 270-271
        procedure for writing expository organizers, 269-270
        suggestions, 272
Aesthetic evaluations of text—computer systems, 394
Algorithms, 11, 47, 132, 345
    compared with heuristics, 233
    defined, 233
Alternate structure—variant (*see* case structure)
Analogies, 73-74, 80, 457
Anchoring points, 259
Animation, 403
Assimilation encoding theory
    defined, 265
    research conclusion, 265-267
Author—relationship to reader, 32

Behavioral psychology
    feedback or knowledge of results, 216
    law of effect, 215
    law of use and disuse, 215
    overt response, 216
Binary decisions, 329
Blank space, 402
Blocking, 343